D1478965

WORKS ISSUED BY
THE HAKLUYT SOCIETY

THE THREE VOYAGES OF EDMOND HALLEY
IN THE *PARAMORE*

SECOND SERIES
NO. 156

HAKLUYT SOCIETY

COUNCIL AND OFFICERS, 1980–81

Figure 1. Edmond Halley (1656–1742). From an oil painting by Sir Godfrey Kneller *c.* 1710. Greenwich Observatory, National Maritime Museum Collections.
Reproduced with permission

THE THREE VOYAGES OF
EDMOND HALLEY
IN THE *PARAMORE*
1698–1701

EDITED BY

NORMAN J. W. THROWER

THE HAKLUYT SOCIETY
LONDON
1981

ISBN 0 904180 02 6

Printed in Great Britain
by Robert MacLehose and Company Limited
Printers to the University of Glasgow

Published by the Hakluyt Society
c/o The Map Library,
The British Library, Reference Division
London WC1B 3DG

To my wife Elizabeth
whose shared enthusiasm for Halley
as a sailor, a scientist, and a man
made this task a pleasure

CONTENTS

VOLUME I

VOLUME 2

MAPS IN PORTFOLIO FORMING VOL. 157

ILLUSTRATIONS

MAPS IN PORTFOLIO (Volume 2)

PREFACE

In a sense this book had its origins when, as a schoolboy in England, I first learned of Edmond Halley and of the comet which bears his name. Much of the inspiration came from my sea-faring ancestors especially my grandfather Captain Joseph Bayley, the first commander of the exploring vessel *Windward* on the Jackson–Harmsworth Expedition to Franz Josef Land. It was this ship which returned Nansen to Norway after his dramatic meeting with Jackson on the ice on 17 June 1896 and which was subsequently presented by A. C. W. Harmsworth (later Lord Northcliffe) to Peary and used by him in the Arctic – two notable examples of international co-operation in exploration.

More directly the book began some twenty years ago when as a student of geography and the history of science, I became interested in the beginnings of isometric cartography. Such investigations lead inevitably and inexorably to Edmond Halley, several of whose maps are reproduced in this volume; these maps resulted from Halley's voyages undertaken between 1698 and 1701. Thus my study of Halley's travels developed naturally from earlier work, which was facilitated by a sabbatical leave from the University of California, Los Angeles (UCLA), spent in England in 1961.

Specific research on Halley's sea journeys began in 1964 when I received a John Simon Guggenheim Memorial Foundation Fellowship which enabled me to visit the main centres containing materials relating to Halley including The British Library (formerly the library departments of the British Museum), The Royal Society, The Public Record Office, The Royal Geographical Society, The National Maritime Museum, Greenwich and The Bodleian Library. Officials at all of these institutions were most helpful and courteous in dealing with my many requests. Pre-eminent among those who encouraged me at this stage was the late Dr R. A. Skelton, then Superintendent of the Map Room at the British Museum and Joint Honorary Secretary of the Hakluyt Society, who made his vast knowledge of the pertinent sources available to me with characteristic generosity.

Work continued in California on the Halley materials until 1970, when I was again granted sabbatical leave. An award from the Penrose Fund of the American Philosophical Society made another visit to Britain possible. At this time archives previously visited were rechecked and new sources of information examined. Professor Eila M. J. Campbell of Birkbeck College, London University, Joint Honorary Secretary of the Hakluyt Society, gave unstintingly of her time in answering many questions having to do with form and fact, over a period of several years in Britain and Canada and by mail. Dr Helen Wallis, Map Librarian, British Library (formerly known as Superintendent of the Map Room of the British Museum), on a number of different occasions and in several different places from London to Los Angeles, extended a helping hand. Likewise, Brigadier Richard A. Gardiner, Keeper of the Map Room at the Royal Geographical Society, rendered invaluable assistance, particularly in arranging for the maps that illustrate this volume to be reproduced. The National Maritime Museum made its files on Halley available.

It is a pleasure to acknowledge help afforded by Mr Colin A. Ronan of Cambridge, an authority on Halley, and Dalrymple specialists Dr Howard T. Fry, now of Queensland, Australia, and Dr David A. Lanegran of Minnesota. Professor Stephen B. Baxter of the Department of History, University of North Carolina, kindly read the Introduction. Commander D. W. Waters, Commander D. Howse, Miss K. Lindsay-MacDougall and Mr A. H. W. Pearsall of the National Maritime Museum, Mr R. A. Penfold of the Public Record Office, Mr H. M. T. Cobbe of the British Library and Mr N. H. Robinson, Librarian of the Royal Society, all made specific contributions to this study.

Most of the writing and compilation was accomplished during the academic year of 1972–73, when I was the William Andrews Clark Memorial Library Professor at UCLA. The Clark Library, specializing as it does in aspects of English culture in the seventeenth and eighteenth centuries, was a most congenial and appropriate place to complete my work on Halley. It would have taken much longer to have brought this study to publication form without the facilities of the Clark Library and its generous staff: Robert Vosper, Director; William E. Conway, Librarian; Edna C. Davis, Associate Librarian; and others. By happy circumstance the period especially emphasized in the Clark Library collections, 1640–1750, includes Halley's dates (1656–1742). The Clark Library endowment also made possible a visit to Britain in the summer of 1973 for final checking of sources.

Support by grants from the UCLA Committee on Research over a number of years is gratefully acknowledged. Similarly assistance from the

UCLA Department of Geography is greatly appreciated, especially the services of the office staff including Pearl Segel, Carol LeBoy, Cheryl Finger, Judith Atwood, and Jean Schilling. My thanks go to graduate students Anna Lang, Louise Wilhelm and Magdalen Woo who spent many hours in proof reading and collating; also to Noel Diaz, Staff Cartographer at UCLA, who executed the final maps and line drawings. The index is by Alison Quinn. Finally it is with gratitude that I acknowledge the support of my family in England and the United States.

NORMAN J. W. THROWER

Pacific Palisades, California
October 1974

INTRODUCTION

Samuel Pepys wrote of Edmond Halley, 'Mr Hawley – May he not be said to have the most, if not to be the first Englishman (and possibly any other) that had so much, or (it may be) any competent degree (meeting in them) of the science and practice (both) of navigation?'[1] In this comment Pepys indicates the dual character of Halley's contribution to seamanship, an approach at once theoretical and practical.

England had already produced men such as Richard Hakluyt and John Dee who had provided a philosophical and theoretical framework for her expanding geographical horizons. Among mathematical practitioners and seamen who had contributed to improvements in navigation were Sir Francis Drake and Edward Wright.[2] As Pepys indicated, Halley combined to a degree not evident before his time a wide range of talents both in the field of science and of practical navigation. Although his contemporary William Dampier and his successor Captain Cook achieved more in geographical discovery, Dampier himself paid tribute to Halley's gifts of innovation, and Cook was to benefit from Halley's scientific inventions. Halley's grasp of scientific theory and practice far surpassed that of other British seamen of his day, and even surpassed (as Pepys suggests) the achievements of leading men in other countries who were active in this field. Halley was the first to commission and command a naval vessel for

[1] J. R. Tanner (ed.), *Samuel Pepys's naval minutes* (London, 1926), p. 420. Pepys's rendering of the name 'Hawley' is one of several spellings for his surname in Naval and other official documents. However, 'Edmond Halley' is the form in which it was entered on his marriage certificate, *Notes and Queries*, ser. 11, vol. 4 (1911), 85, 198, and on his will, *Notes and Queries*, ser. 13, vol. 155 (1928) 24–5, and in the journal of the Third Voyage, the only one with his full signature (Figure 12). Frequently, 'Edmund' has been used by others for his Christian name which he usually abbreviated to Edm., and his surname has been spelled (and pronounced) in various ways – Hailey, Hayley, Haley, Haly, Hally. This last is the form commonly used by Halley's contemporary Robert Hooke in his Diary (see pp. 20–1).

[2] E. Wright, *Certaine errors in navigation* (London, 1599). See also E. G. R. Taylor, *Late Tudor and early Stuart geography, 1583–1650* (London, 1934) for background information on English navigational practices before Halley's time, on which subject also see D. W. Waters, *The art of navigation in England in Elizabethan and early Stuart times* (London, 1958). E. G. R. Taylor, *The mathematical practitioners of Tudor and Stuart England* (Cambridge, 1954), extends beyond the period of Halley's voyages and refers to several of his writings on navigational science. More general works which also cover Halley's period include E. G. R. Taylor, *The haven-finding art: A history of navigation from Odysseus to Captain Cook* (London, 1956) and J. B. Hewson, *A history of the practice of navigation* (Glasgow, 1951).

the purpose of scientific exploration.[1] He was the initiator, and commander of the three voyages in the *Paramore*, 1698 to 1701.

Edmond Halley[2] was born on 29 October 1656 (8 November, New Style[3]) at his father's country house at Haggerston in the parish of Saint

[1] S. Chapman, 'Edmond Halley as physical geographer, and the story of his charts', *Occasional Notes No. 9*, *Royal Astronomical Society* (1941), p. 5. In this article Professor Chapman makes the bold claim that Halley's voyage was 'the first sea journey undertaken for a purely scientific object'. In the sense that an already well-known scientist planned and captained an extended voyage to test his own theories without any idea on his part of commercial advantage (see Documents 1 (pp. 250–1), 33 (pp. 268–70), 78 (pp. 301–2)), this is true. By his contemporaries and for a long time after his death Halley was considered '. . . the second [after Newton] most illustrious of the Anglo-Saxon Philosophers', *Nature*, 21 (1880), p. 303.

[2] Recently two short, book-length biographies of Halley have appeared: A. Armitage, *Edmond Halley* (London, 1966), in the series, 'British men of science', general ed. Sir G. de Beer, pp. xi and 220, and C. A. Ronan, *Edmond Halley: Genius in eclipse* (London & New York, 1969), pp. x and 252. Prior to the publication of these two books the lack of general biographical studies on this scientist was noted by a number of writers on Halley. Miss A. M. Clerke, author of the article on Halley in the *Dictionary of national biography*, 14 (1890), pp. 104–9, reprinted with corrections, 8 (1909), 988–94 pointed out that several abortive attempts were made to write a full-scale Halley biography. A memoir on Halley, thought to have been written by Martin Folkes P.R.S., around 1742, appears to have been the basis of the 'Éloge' of Halley by M. Mairan (see below) but the original MS is not extant. Another article appears in *Biographia Britannica*, 4 (1757), 2494–520; information for this study was provided, in part, by Halley's son-in-law Henry Price who was not always accurate in the information he furnished. The Rev. Israel Lyons (1739–75) collected material for a Halley biography, but death prevented completion of the work, as it did in the case of the next serious Halley biographer, Professor Stephen P. Rigaud (1774–1839). The Rigaud Collection was presented to the Savile Library which was incorporated in the Bodleian Library, Oxford, in 1884. Yet another attempt to write a Halley biography was made about 1880 by Professor Charles Pritchard but the project was abandoned. Miss Clerke considered writing a book on the subject but confined her work on Halley to the article in the *Dictionary of national biography*, mentioned previously. All Halley scholars in this century have been indebted to Eugene Fairfield MacPike of Chicago, who compiled a number of short studies on Halley which were consulted but are not cited here because information they contain is either included or summarized in larger works referenced below. MacPike also prepared a MS memoir on Halley, with a bibliography by Alexander J. Rudolph, Assistant Librarian of the Newberry Library, Chicago, where these unpublished items are now deposited. E. F. MacPike, *Correspondence and papers of Edmond Halley*, History of Science Society Publications, new series 2 (Oxford, 1932), pp. xiv and 300, includes the 'Éloge de M. Halley' (in French) by Jean Jacques D' Orteous de Mairan (mentioned above), pp. 15–27, and biographical excerpts from other authors, especially in Appendix xviii, 'Halley's character and personality', pp. 261–71. See also E. F. MacPike, *Hevelius, Flamsteed and Halley: three contemporary astronomers and their mutual relations* (London, 1937), pp. ix and 140, and A. J. Rudolph with notes by E. F. MacPike, 'Material for a bibliography of Dr. Edmond Halley', *Bulletin of Bibliography*, 4 (1904), pp. 54–7, and E. F. MacPike, *Dr. Edmond Halley: a bibliographic guide to his life and work arranged chronologically* (London, 1939), pp. 1–54. However, those who have most seriously studied the life and work of Halley, including Armitage and Ronan, agree that the definitive biography of this great scientist has yet to be written.

[3] Unless otherwise indicated all dates pertaining to Halley's voyages refer to the Julian Calendar (Old Style) which was in use in England long after the completion of Halley's three voyages in the *Paramore*, and indeed for a decade after his death. For amplification see C. R. Cheney (ed.), *Handbook of dates for students of English history* (London, 1945), pp. xvii and 164.

Leonard, Shoreditch.[1] He was the first of three children – a sister Katherine apparently died in infancy and a brother Humphrey survived into his twenties. Halley's father, also Edmond Halley, was a successful business man who carried on the trade of soap boiler and purveyor of salt as well as looking after his estate of a thousand pounds a year in rental property.[2] Much of his property was destroyed in the Great Fire of London (1666), which marks the beginning of some decline in the fortunes of Halley senior. Nevertheless his business was still prosperous after this disaster. One of his apprentices taught the young Edmond writing and arithmetic before he was sent to St Paul's School. Although when Halley entered St Paul's is unknown, it is believed to be during the last years of the High Mastership of Samuel Cromleholme.[3] According to some authorities Halley became the Captain of St Paul's in 1671 at the age of fifteen,[4] but it is with Thomas Gale (1635?–1702), who was appointed as High Master in August 1672, that Halley's name is particularly associated. Gale, who came to St Paul's from Cambridge University where he had been Regius Professor of Greek for some six years, was a notable classical scholar. In addition, he appreciated scientific learning and probably Halley was influenced by the new High Master in both the arts and the sciences.

Halley developed his intellectual abilities at St Paul's, where he made his first recorded scientific observation. In 1672 he measured the variation (declination) of the magnetic compass, a schoolboy observation which, along with others, he subsequently published.[5] While still at St Paul's Halley also familiarized himself with the use of the celestial sphere so that Joseph Moxon the mathematician and hydrographer observed, '. . . that if a star were misplaced in the globe he [Halley] would presently find it.'[6] Halley also made astronomical observations and acquired from his father 'a curious apparatus of instruments',[7] which he took with him to Oxford when he entered Queen's College as a commoner in the summer of 1673.[8]

[1] This area, about three miles northeast of Saint Paul's Cathedral, is now in the Borough of Hackney.

[2] Ronan, 1969, p. 1, n. deals with this matter.

[3] Died, 21 July 1672.

[4] *Biographia Britannica*, 4 (1757), p. 2494. It is doubted by some that Halley would have attained this position at such an early age. See Ronan, 1969, p. 6, n.

[5] 'A theory of the variation of the magnetical compass', *Philosophical Transactions*, 13 (1683), 210. See p. 22, n. 2 for Halley's definition of 'variation'.

[6] J. Aubrey, *Brief Lives*, ed. A. Clark (Oxford, 1898), p. 282.

[7] *Biographia Britannica*, 4 (1757), p. 2494.

[8] Writing about this period of his life some years later Halley observed: 'From my tender years I showed a marked bent towards mathematics; and when, about six years ago [1672], I first devoted myself wholly to astronomy, I derived so much pleasure and delight from its study as anyone inexperienced therein could scarcely believe.' Armitage, 1966 p. 25.

In 1676, while an undergraduate, Halley published his first scientific paper in the *Philosophical Transactions*.[1] It was a brilliant geometrical explication and extension of the Keplerian hypothesis of the elliptical orbits of planets.

About this time Halley approached Henry Oldenburg, the editor of the *Philosophical Transactions* and also the Secretary of the Royal Society, about a proposal to observe the constellations in the southern hemisphere (not visible from the latitudes of Europe). He had in mind a star catalogue similar to that for the northern hemisphere which was based on the observations of Hevelius in Danzig, Cassini in Paris, and Flamsteed in England. Halley was already acquainted with the Reverend John Flamsteed who in the previous year (1675) had been appointed by King Charles II as 'Astronomical Observator' (first Astronomer Royal).[2] In the future there was to be much acrimony on the part of Flamsteed toward Halley. However, in the summer of 1675 the senior astronomer acknowledged the assistance of 'the ingenious youth, Edmond Halley, an Oxonian' in observing two lunar eclipses, valuable for determining longitudinal position on land, and praised his independent observations.[3] Apparently Halley discussed with Flamsteed and others the best site for his projected southern hemisphere observations. The Cape of Good Hope (then a Dutch settlement) and Rio de Janeiro (a Portuguese settlement) were considered, but it was decided that St Helena would be most satisfactory. The South Atlantic island of St Helena was then under East India Company jurisdiction.

At Oxford Halley studied under the Reverend John Wallis (1616–1703), Savilian Professor of Geometry, and under his student Edward Bernard (1638–96), who had succeeded Sir Christopher Wren as Savilian Professor of Astronomy in 1673. All of these men were able mathematicians and Wallis, sometime Fellow of Queen's College was (like Wren) an original Fellow of the Royal Society. In 1676 Halley felt ready to make his own contribution to science and left Oxford prematurely, probably because his request for support for the southern hemisphere project had been successful. The Secretary of State for the Northern Department, Sir Joseph Williamson (1633–1701), student, Fellow, and benefactor of Queen's College and later one of the two Presidents of the Royal Society,

[1] 'Methodus directa & geometrica, cujus ope investigantur aphelia . . .', *Philosophical Transactions*, 11 (1676), 683–6. Halley published in all eighty contributions in the *Philosophical Transactions*.

[2] E. W. Maunder, *The Royal Observatory, Greenwich* (London, 1900), p. 40.

[3] Armitage, 1966, p. 18.

1677–80, approved the proposal. It was brought to the notice of King Charles II by Sir Jonas Moore (1617–79), Surveyor of Ordnance, who, as a mathematician and Fellow of the Royal Society, had been one of those who had promoted the foundation of Greenwich Observatory. The King endorsed Halley's project and commended it to the Directors of the East India Company, who agreed to allow Halley and a friend, James Clark,[1] passage on the first ship leaving for St Helena. Halley's father generously provided his son with an annual allowance of three hundred pounds to defray expenses including board, but accommodation was to be made available in the Governor's house or other suitable residence.

Halley and Clark, who was to serve as his assistant, left London in the *Unity* in November 1676 and arrived at St Helena in February of the next year. Here they soon set up an observatory near the highest point of the island, Mount Actaeon (*c.* 800 metres).[2] Observations were begun using a large sextant, with telescope attached, a smaller quadrant, a pendulum clock, several telescopes including one twenty-four feet long, and two micrometers.[3]

St Helena, lying in a prevailingly low pressure area with much overcast weather, proved to be a poorer station for astronomical observations than had been reported. In spite of this and the lack of co-operation on the part of the Governor, Gregory Field, Halley determined the places of 341 stars, most of which are not seen from any part of Europe. He also observed eclipses of the Sun and the Moon, and the transit of Mercury across the Sun. Halley also found that the length of the pendulum of his clock had to be shortened in relation to its length in England in order to provide accurate time (as previously observed by Jean Richer in Cayenne, c. 1672, and published in 1679). This had important implications for the determination of the shape of the Earth by Newton. About a decade after his return to England, Halley, in recalling his stay in St Helena, wrote that he had been engaged, 'in an employment that obliged me to regard more than ordinary the Weather.'[4] Halley's meteorological observations

[1] Not much is known of Clark, whose name is also spelled Clerk.

[2] I. Gill, *Six months in Ascension* (London, 1878), p. 33. Mrs. Gill, who was visiting St Helena about 200 years after Halley's stay, seems to have found the site of his observatory on the mountain overlooking the first burial place of Napoleon I, who died in confinement in St Helena in 1821.

[3] MacPike, 1932, p. 2.

[4] 'An historical account of the trade winds, and monsoons, observable in the seas between and near the tropicks . . .', *Philosophical Transactions*, 16 (1686), 155.

in the Atlantic were published in the *Philosophical Transactions*.[1] Halley and Clark left St Helena in March 1678 in the *Golden Fleece* and reached England before the end of May. In the course of the voyages to and from St Helena Halley also took magnetic observations.[2]

Upon his return to England Halley set about preparing his astronomical observations for publication and in a few months had produced a catalogue which was to be the first printed volume containing telescopically determined star positions.[3] The book includes an appendix with Halley's observations of the transit of Mercury, and is accompanied by a large, folding star chart or celestial planisphere.[4] In honour of the reigning monarch Halley named a constellation *Robur Carolinum* (an allusion to the escape of Charles II by concealment in an oak tree after the Battle of Worcester). A copy of the work was presented to King Charles who, at the instance of Sir Joseph Williamson, wrote to the Vice Chancellor of Oxford University on 18 November recommending Halley 'for the degree of M.A. without any condition of performing any previous or subsequent exercises for the same'.[5] The degree was granted on 3 December 1678. Meanwhile Halley received further recognition for his work in mathematics and astronomy by being elected a Fellow of the Royal Society on 30 November of the same year, Sir Jonas Moore being his sponsor.

It was not long before Halley was to travel abroad again, this time to represent the Royal Society in an attempt to resolve a dispute between English and continental astronomers regarding the relative merits of instruments with telescopic and open sights. In the tradition of Tycho Brahe, Johannes Hevelius (1611–87), an astronomer and merchant of Danzig, was an advocate of instruments with open sights and therefore naked eye observation for most astronomical purposes. Although he used telescopes for his important lunar observations, Hevelius believed that large instruments with open sights were superior for measuring stellar angles and suggested this in correspondence with astronomers at the Royal Society, of which he was a Fellow. The English scientists, notably

[1] *Ibid.*, pp. 153–68.

[2] *Philosophical Transactions*, 13 (1683), 219. Halley specifically calls attention to his own observations on magnetic variation in the Atlantic during his first visit to St Helena.

[3] E. Halley, *Catalogus stellarum Australium, sive supplementum catalogi Tychonici . . .* (London, 1679).

[4] Sir E. Bullard, 'Edmond Halley (1656–1741),' *Endeavour*, 15 (1956), 189–99, contains a good reproduction of Sir Edward's own copy of Halley's star chart which has never been folded.

[5] Ronan, 1969, p. 42. Charles II appears to have received a prepublication copy.

Robert Hooke (1635–1703) and Flamsteed believed that, properly used, telescopic sights were preferable and stated this in such a manner that a heated controversy ensued. The purpose of Halley's visit to Danzig was to enable him to see Hevelius at work and perhaps to mollify the older scientist who was much respected in England. Halley had employed an instrument with telescopic sights on St Helena and was in agreement with his fellow-countrymen on the matter. Nevertheless, he patiently went through the operation of making direct observations with Hevelius and was tactful enough not to disclose to the older astronomer his true feelings on this subject. Halley remained on good terms with Hevelius while in Danzig, and after his return to England the two corresponded in a friendly manner for several years; but Halley's attitude towards Hevelius changed after the latter published his *Annus Climactericus* in 1685. In the preface to this work there are several incorrect statements concerning Halley who refrained from making public his opposition to them.[1]

Following his return from Danzig, Halley lived in London and Oxford and among other activities made plans for a grand tour of France and Italy. His companion on this tour was Robert Nelson (1656–1715) who, like Halley, was a Fellow of the Royal Society and the son of a wealthy merchant.[2] In November 1680, just before the tour began, Halley saw a great comet which he and Nelson observed again early the next month on their journey to Paris. Once there Halley sought out Jean Dominique Cassini (1625–1712), who had become director of the Paris Observatory in 1671. Cassini's researches included studies of the motions of planets, especially Mars and Jupiter; and following the suggestion of Galileo he prepared tables of the revolutions of the satellites of Jupiter, so that they could be used for determination of geographical longitude.[3] Cassini welcomed Halley, who made observations of the comet in Paris. After travelling through France, Halley and Nelson arrived in Rome, from which centre they toured widely in the Italian countryside. Halley left Italy in the middle of November 1681 and returned to England alone by way of Genoa, Paris and Holland, taking more than two months on the journey.

Three months after Halley returned to England, he was married to

[1] MacPike, 1937, pp. 95–6.

[2] Later Nelson became a well-known writer on religious topics.

[3] J. D. Cassini, *Éclipses du premier satellite de Jupiter pendant l'année* (Paris, 1692). The method (which Halley employed on his voyages) involves observing with a telescope the occultations of the satellites at a certain place and comparing the time of the events with the time at another distant point as predicted and recorded in tables. The time difference between the two can be converted into degrees of longitude.

Mary Tooke, daughter of an officer at the Exchequer.[1] The wedding was solemnized at St James's, Duke's Place (near his father's City premises), on 20 April 1682. Halley and his bride, with whom he was to live happily for more than fifty years, moved to Islington. Here, presumably supported by subvention from either his or his wife's family or both, Halley pursued his astronomical observations, setting up a small observatory, without the necessity of having regular remunerative employment.

He also took an increasingly important role in the affairs of the Royal Society and in 1683 published two papers in the *Philosophical Transactions*. The first was concerned with Saturn and its satellites, but the second, 'A Theory of the Variation of the Magnetical Compass'[2], is of greater significance in the present study. In this work he included a table of 55 observations of magnetic variation (declination) from forty-seven places. The five readings for London (including his own of 1672) covered more than a century. Using these data he challenged the suggestions of William Gilbert and Henry Bond, and also of Descartes, concerning local or even continental-sized land masses for explaining the global features of Earth magnetism. He also attempted to formulate a general magnetic theory by postulating four magnetic poles to account for variation and for its temporal change over the Earth (secular variation). This last characteristic, discovered in 1634 by Henry Gellibrand[3] and reported in the following year, is discussed by Halley in his articles. He was also aware of the contributions to the study of Earth magnetism made by Athanasius Kircher (1624–80), whom he mentions by name. In the concluding passage of his article Halley wrote: 'But to calculate exactly what it [magnetic variation, i.e. declination at a point] is, in any place assigned, is what I dare not yet pretend to; tho I could wish it were my happiness to oblige the world with so useful a piece of knowledge.'[4]

[1] It has often been stated that Mary Tooke was the daughter of the Auditor of the Exchequer, but Sir Robert Howard was Auditor in Receipt of the Exchequer from 1673 to 1698, and neither his predecessors, to 1660, nor his successors were named Tooke (Tuke, etc.) according to J. Haydn, *The book of dignities*, 3rd ed. (London, 1894), pp. 166–7.

[2] *Philosophical Transactions*, 13 (1683), 208–21, 'The Variation of the Compass (by which I mean the deflection of the Magnetical Needle from the true Meridian),' is the way Halley defined the term, p. 208. The word used generally today is 'declination' by surveyors but still, usually, 'variation' by sailors.

[3] H. Gellibrand, *A discourse mathematical of the variation of the magneticall needle together with its admirable diminution lately discovered* (London, 1635). In this work Gellibrand stated that 'the variation is accompanied with a variation' by which he meant that, in addition to declination or variation, as defined by Halley (n. 2 above), there is also secular change or variation, a phenomenon also discovered independently on the Continent at about this time.

[4] *Philosophical Transactions*, 13 (1683), 220.

Halley's next paper in the *Philosophical Transactions*, 'A theory of the tides at the bar of Tunking',[1] was appended to a communication by a Mr Francis Davenport on the anomalies of the tides at Batsha in the Gulf of Tonkin, off the south coast of China. Davenport tabulated the height of the tides according to the phase in the lunar month, described the nature of the sand bar at the entrance to the port and gave instructions concerning the best time to navigate across it. He could not satisfactorily explain the consistent irregularity of the ebb and flow at Batsha where there was only one high tide a day, except every fortnight when there was no tide at all. This was followed by tides increasing to a maximum reached in seven days after which they again declined. Halley attempted to place these observations into a framework related to lunar position but wrote, '. . . to *philosophize* thereon, and to attempt to assign a reason, why the *Moon* should in so particular a manner influence the *waters* in this one place, is a task too hard for my undertaking, especially when I consider how little we have been able to establish a Genuine and satisfactory *Theory* of the *Tides*, found upon our own *Coasts*, of which we have had so long Experience.'[2] Halley's discussion on the tides, like his earlier observations on the length of the pendulum, was to have importance in Newton's research.

In August 1684 Halley first visited Isaac Newton (1642–1727) in Cambridge to discuss celestial motion. Halley had previously come to the conclusion, depending on Kepler's laws, that the ratio between the time a planet takes to travel round the Sun and the average distance of the planet from the Sun could be explained by the inverse square law, i.e. that the Sun attracts each planet with a force that depends upon the inverse square of the distance between the Sun and that planet. Hooke also affirmed this principle but neither he nor Halley could furnish the necessary mathematical proof; Newton had already accomplished this and, at the urging of Halley, agreed to prepare his findings for publication, with the Royal Society bearing the expense.[3]

It is possible that, as originally conceived, Newton's work had been thought of as an article for the *Philosophical Transactions* but it grew into a substantial volume. Meanwhile Hooke was claiming primacy for

[1] *Philosophical Transactions*, 14 (1684), 685–8. [2] *Ibid.*, 687.

[3] I. B. Cohen, *Introduction to Newton's 'Principia'* (Cambridge, 1971), pp. xxvi and 380, includes the most recently published authoritative account of the relationship between Halley and Newton and his *Principia*, which is '. . . one of the glories of the human intellect, a founding document of our modern exact science' (p. 3). Halley lauded the *Principia* as 'a divine Treatise'.

fundamental ideas in Newton's work, particularly for originating the inverse square law. In the face of this Newton was ready to abandon a large section of the work which became the *Principia*, calling natural philosophy an 'impertinently litigious Lady'.[1] Newton was only dissuaded from this course by another meeting with Halley, and a letter in which Halley wrote: 'I hope you will see cause to alter your former Resolution of suppressing your third Book.'[2] The manuscript was ready in the summer of 1686, but the Royal Society was unable to meet publication costs. Halley therefore not only edited Newton's *Principia* and saw it through the press, as agreed, but also paid for the publication himself.[3] Commenting upon the *Principia*, Augustus De Morgan wrote: 'But for him [Halley], in all human probability, the work would not have been thought of, nor when thought of written, nor when written printed.'[4] Grant wrote of Halley that '. . . among all of those who have thus contributed indirectly to the progress of knowledge, there is none who exhibits such a bright example of disinterestedness and self-sacrificing zeal as the illustrious superintendent of the first edition of the Principia.'[5] Halley prefixed hexameters laudatory of Newton in the first edition, 1687, and wrote an explanatory letter, including a discussion of the tides, to accompany a copy which was presented to King James II.[6]

In 1685 Halley had accepted the position of Clerk to the two Secretaries of the Royal Society, Sir John Hoskins (1634–1705) and his old High Master, Thomas Gale.[7] Why Halley took this post which required him to resign his Fellowship in the Royal Society is not clear. Perhaps he wished to involve himself more deeply in the affairs of the Society, or, he now needed the admittedly modest salary. However, subsequent events suggest that Halley was far from impoverished and, in any case, his stipend was paid with great irregularity. Halley's duties included handling the Society's correspondence and the editing of the *Philosophical Transactions*.

[1] Sir Isaac Newton, *The correspondence of Isaac Newton*, vol. 2, ed. H. W. Turnbull (Cambridge, 1960), p. 437; and Robert Grant, *History of physical astronomy* (London, 1852), pp. 15–40.

[2] Newton, vol. 2, p. 441.

[3] Ronan, 1969, p. 81. Newton in his preface affirmed Halley's role in the publication of the *Principia*.

[4] Quoted in Ronan, 1969, p. 88.

[5] Grant, 1852, p. 31.

[6] MacPike, 1932, pp. 207–8, Appendix VI, is an English translation of these verses. Halley's letter, which begins 'To the King's Most Excellent Majesty', was printed in the *Philosophical Transactions* in 1697, with some minor changes.

[7] Sir H. Lyons, *The Royal Society, 1660–1940: a history of its administration under its charters* (Cambridge, 1944), p. 75.

In addition to preparing the *Principia* for the press and to discharging his other editorial and secretarial duties, Halley found time to engage in diverse research activities of his own. He published in the *Philosophical Transactions* papers on gravity, eclipses, the hydrological cycle, and prevailing winds. The last, 'An historical account of the trade winds, and monsoons, observable in the seas between and near the tropicks, with an attempt to assign the phisical cause of the said winds' was illustrated by an untitled chart, which has since been called 'Halley's Chart of the Trade Winds'.[1] It shows the global arrangement of the surface winds in the lower latitudes (approximately 33° N to 33° S) and has been called 'the first meteorological chart'.[2] Halley tells us a good deal about the way he compiled the wind chart. He used previous writers' descriptions of winds, the observations of sailors and his own experience on St Helena, and his journeys to and from that island. Halley's thermal explanation of the causes of the tropical winds is now only partly accepted. The map, however, became immediately influential and was used by, among others, William Dampier (1652–1715), who extended the delineation of the trade winds to the Pacific after his voyages in that area. Halley had not visited the Pacific but in spite of inadequate information he had correctly postulated that the general pattern of the prevailing surface winds in the lower latitudes would be similar all over the earth, a fact borne out by Dampier's observations.

In the year 1688 the Halleys became the parents of two girls (Margaret and Katherine or Catherine) and were later to have a son, Edmond, born in 1698, the year Halley embarked on his First Voyage.

Most years between this time and Halley's appointment to command the *Paramore* saw at least one and often several of his papers published in the *Philosophical Transactions*.[3] He became interested in geo-chronology, using the increasing degree of salinity of ocean water as a measure of time. His investigations on this subject extended the age of the Earth well beyond contemporary estimates. He experimented with magnetic compasses, thermometers and barometers – instruments he was later to use every day on shipboard. Other work included studies in hydrology

[1] *Philosophical Transactions*, 16 (1686), 153–68. See also N. J. W. Thrower, 'Edmond Halley and thematic geo-cartography', in *The terraqueous globe* (Los Angeles, 1969), pp. 3–43; and 'Edmond Halley as a thematic geo-cartographer', *Annals of the Association of American Geographers*, 59 (1969), 652–76.

[2] Chapman, 1941, caption under his Figure 1.

[3] MacPike, 1932, pp. 272–8, Appendix 14, contains a reasonably complete list of Halley's published work.

and, more specifically, on the silting of ports.[1] He pursued his investigations on atoms, optics, conic sections and also discussed historical subjects, such as the time and place of the invasion of Britain by Julius Caesar.

The practical side of Halley's interests is evidenced by his concern between 1689 and 1691 with deep sea diving. It was about these activities of Halley's that Flamsteed wrote, 'If he wants employment for his time he may go on with his sea projects.'[2] These experiments required the use of a frigate lent for the purpose by the Admiralty. Halley designed a satisfactory diving bell which was lowered to ten fathoms and enabled divers to work with freedom and comfort for nearly two hours at a time. Halley himself made a descent in the bell and later invented a diving suit fitted with pipes, for air and respiration, and a lantern. During these experiments Halley made studies on the behaviour of sound and light below water; the latter was used by Newton in his *Opticks*, completed in the early years of the eighteenth century.

Halley also continued his astronomical studies. He proposed the idea of measuring the distance from Earth to Sun by observing the transits of the planet Venus, which comes much closer to the Earth than other planets. Transits of Venus occur in pairs separated by about eight years with intervals of more than one hundred years between the pairs. By observing a closer celestial body from two or more stations widely separated geographically, parallactic measurement is greatly facilitated and, in turn, measurement to a body more distant from the Earth is simplified. These ideas are the essence of Halley's paper of 1691 where he also has a table of previous and future occurrences of the transit of Venus. Halley was to return, in a paper dated 1716, to a discussion of this phenomenon, which he called '. . . by far the noblest [sight] astronomy affords . . .'[3] and affirmed,' I strongly urge diligent searchers of the heavens (for whom, when I shall have ended my days, these sights are being kept in store) to bear in mind this injunction of mine and to apply themselves actively and with all their might to making the necessary observations'.[4] Halley, in partial dependence on Kepler and noting the 1639 observation of Jeremiah Horrocks (for whom Halley had the greatest admiration),

[1] A. K. Biswas, 'Edmond Halley F.R.S.: hydrologist extraordinary,' Royal Society of London, *Notes and Records*, 25 (1970), 47–57.

[2] Francis Baily, *An account of the Rev. John Flamsteed* (London, 1835), pp. 132–3.

[3] Ronan, 1969, p. 108.

[4] Armitage, 1966, p. 104. The pertinent original Latin text from Halley's paper, *Methodus singularis quâ Solis Parallaxis sive distantia à Terra, ope Veneris intra solem conspiciendae, tuto determinari poterit, Philosophical Transactions*, 29 (1714–6), 460, is reprinted in J. C. Beaglehole, *The Life of Captain James Cook* (London, 1974), p. 101 n. 1.

correctly predicted the next transits of Venus to take place in 1761 and 1769 which were occasions for considerable interest in this phenomenon in the scientific world. The latter prediction was recalled when the Royal Society set up on 19 November 1767 a 'committee for the transit' to make recommendations on the matter.[1] In 1768 James Cook was commissioned a lieutenant in the Royal Navy to lead an expedition to the South Pacific Ocean with the primary objective to observe the transit of Venus.

In 1692 Halley published 'An account of the cause of the change of the variation of the magnetical needle; with an hypothesis of the structure of the internal parts of the Earth'.[2] Here he elaborated his previous idea of an Earth with four magnetic poles. To explain geomagnetism and, in particular, secular variation he now suggested that the Earth is composed of an outer shell and an inner globe (or nucleus) separated from each other by a fluid medium. He postulated that each of these parts of the Earth possesses two poles making a total of four poles, and that the outer shell rotates at a slightly greater rate than the nucleus. Halley suggested that if later observations should show this explanation to be inadequate then more than two concentric spheres, each with its own magnetic field and speed of rotation, might be needed. Even today there is still no adequate explanation of, or general agreement on, the causes of Earth magnetism; but Halley's ideas are '... astonishingly close to modern theory, considering that he could have no knowledge of electromagne ism'.[3] Halley was aware of the possible deficiencies of his theory, for he offered it only as a 'Hypothesis which after Ages may examine, amend or refute'.[4]

[1] J. Cook, *The journals of Captain James Cook on his voyages of discovery*, ed. J. C. Beaglehole. Hakluyt Society, extra series, no. 34 (Cambridge, 1955), vol. 1 pp. 511–19, Appendix II. In this monumental work the late Professor Beaglehole reviews events, with documentation, leading up to the first voyage of Captain Cook and refers to Halley's variation charts in later volumes. Earlier writers on Cook's voyages have emphasized Halley's predictions of the transit of Venus, e.g. A. H. Carrington, *Life of Captain Cook* (London, 1939), pp. 49–52. Negative factors appear to have contributed to the appointment of Cook in preference to the civilian Alexander Dalrymple, the Royal Society's choice, i.e. stories of 'mutiny' on Halley's voyage circulating among Navy officials; see A. Kitson, *Captain James Cook, R.N., F.R.S.* (London, 1907), p. 187. Howard T. Fry, *Alexander Dalrymple and the expansion of British trade*, The Royal Commonwealth Society, Imperial Studies, 29 (London, 1970), pp. xxvii and 330, deals, with reasons for the selection of Cook rather than Dalrymple, especially on pp. 267–79.

[2] *Philosophical Transactions*, 17 (1692), 563–78.

[3] F. F. Evison, 'Geophysics and the world of Edmund Halley,' Inaugural Address, The Victoria University of Wellington, 1968, pp. 1–24; Professor Evison, pp. 11–12, paraphrases Sir Edward Bullard (1956), thus: '... by reading Halley's two papers on the Earth's magnetic field one can learn more about the origin of the field and its secular variation than will be found in all that was written in the succeeding 250 years.' See also Sir Edward Bullard, 'Edmond Halley: the first geophysicist,' *Nature*, 178 (1956), 891–2; and Ronan, 1968, 241–8.

[4] *Philosophical Transactions*, 17 (1692), 578.

In 1691 Edward Bernard resigned his position as Savilian Professor of Astronomy at Oxford and Halley applied for the vacant chair. He was investigated concerning charges of unorthodoxy by clerics who regarded him as 'a skeptick, and a banterer of religion',[1] a view fostered by Flamsteed who was jealous of Halley's growing reputation. Halley's writings suggest that although he believed that the Earth was considerably older than the contemporary estimates, he did not, presumably, agree with the theory of an eternal world. Affirmation of belief in such a theory would, according to the then current theology, presuppose that he did not believe in Creation and was therefore an atheist. Halley invoked the Deity in his will and on several occasions in his journals and certainly was not, as he had been branded, 'an avowed and shameless infidel'.[2] The Royal Society supported Halley's candidacy for the Oxford professorship with a testimonial prepared by Thomas Gale (soon to become Dean of York). Even with this strong support Halley did not receive the desired post.

Halley resigned his editorship of the *Philosophical Transactions* in 1692 but continued as Clerk to the two Secretaries of the Royal Society. In the middle of the decade he began his serious studies of comets (related particularly to the comet of 1682) which were not to be published until some years after his return from his voyages and which have now, rather than any other of his contributions, perpetuated his name.[3]

In 1696 Halley left London to become Deputy Comptroller of the Mint at Chester, an appointment which was influenced by Newton, then Warden and later Master of the Mint. Halley did not enjoy the routine administrative work at the Chester Mint or the corruption, real and potential, associated with the recoinage. In his spare time he took the opportunity afforded in a new locale of making observations and reporting these to the Royal Society of which he was still Clerk to the Secretaries.[4] He wrote letters on eclipses and meteorological phenomena at Chester and one 'Concerning the Torricellian Experiment tryed on the top of Snowdon-hill and the success of it'.[5] Halley's remarkably accurate measurement of the elevation of the highest peak in Wales was

[1] MacPike, 1932 p. 264 and following, discusses different opinions on Halley's religious views in some detail.

[2] *Ibid.* p. 267.

[3] 'Astronomiae cometicea synopsis', *Philosophical Transactions*, 24 (1704–5), 1882–99. Ronan (1969, p. 219) points out that there was no mention of the prediction of the return of comet in the obituary notices which appeared after Halley's death.

[4] Halley was much taken with the Roman remains at Chester and wrote a letter to the Royal Society on an ancient altar he found there, with a transcription on its text.

[5] *Philosophical Transactions*, 19 (1697), 582–4.

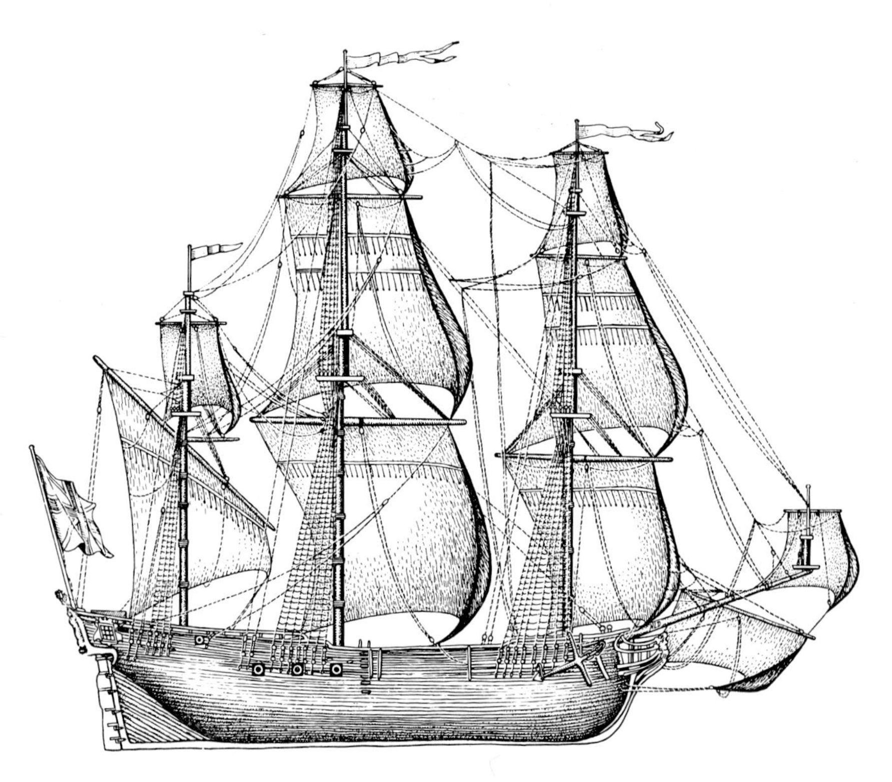

Figure 2. Drawing reconstructing His Majesty's Ship *Paramore* from Documents 6 and 9 and other sources.

accomplished with the use of a barometer during a holiday in 1697. In addition to these letters the *Philosophical Transactions* also printed Halley's explanatory letter on the tides which had accompanied the copy of the *Principia* which was presented to King James II.[1]

While Halley was at Chester, Czar Peter (later called the Great) began his tour of western Europe for the purpose of learning shipbuilding, and for several months he was engaged in this occupation in Holland. However, England had become a leading shipbuilding nation by this time and Peter accepted an invitation from William III to work at the Deptford yards, east of London.[2] This was early in 1698, just before Halley returned to London, when the work at Chester was completed and the Mint there was closed. Halley was now free to do as he wished, having previously declined other appointments offered him by Newton. Accordingly, when Peter requested that he should be instructed in the 'New Science', Halley was apparently happy to teach the Czar, who had taken up residence in John Evelyn's house at Deptford. It was to this abode that Peter invited Halley, '. . . and found him equal to the great character he had heard of him. He [Peter] asked him many questions concerning the fleet which he intended to build, the sciences and arts which he wished to introduce into his dominions, and a thousand other subjects which his unbounded curiosity suggested; he was so well satisfied with Mr Halley's answers, and so pleased with his conversation, that he admitted him familiarly to his table, and ranked him among the number of his friends.'[3]

HALLEY'S VOYAGES: PREPARATIONS

The earliest plans for the first two voyages undertaken by Edmond Halley 'to improve the knowledge of the Longitude and variations of the Compasse'[4] were made some years before the journey actually began.

[1] Ibid., pp. 445–57, 'The true theory of the tides, extracted from that admired treatise of Mr. Isaac Newton, intituled *Philosophiae naturalis principia mathematica*; being a discourse presented with that book to the late King James.'

[2] K. Waliszewski, *Peter the Great*, trans. by Lady Mary Loyd (London, 1897), pp. 93–6. Ian Gray, 'Peter the Great in England,' *History Today*, 6 (1956), 225–34, and Bernard Pool, 'Peter the Great on the Thames,' *The Mariner's Mirror*, 59 (1973), 9–12.

[3] *Biographia Britannica*, 4 (1757), p. 2517.

[4] Document 33, pp. 268–70. Instructions for the First and Second voyages are quite similar, as comparison of the above cited document and Document 78, pp. 301–2, will reveal. John Aubrey in his *Brief lives* (p. 283) states: 'I have often heard him [Halley] say that if his majestie would be but only at the charge of sending out a ship he would take the longitude

In Robert Hooke's Diary, 11 January 1693, there is a cryptic entry: '... RS met Little said. nonsense about infinites. Hally SRS ... Hally of going in Middletō[n's] ship to Dis[cover] ...'[1] This was followed in March of the same year by a formal 'Proposal of Mr. Middleton and Mr. Haley to compasse the Globe for Improvement of Navigation' presented to the Royal Society.[2] In this document the Royal Society was asked to help obtain a small vessel specifically to study the variations of the compass in the Pacific Ocean and to investigate methods of discovering longitude at sea. The proposed journey was to be from east to west around the Earth.

Little is known of Middleton, but he is believed to be the same Benjamin Middleton who was elected Fellow of the Royal Society in 1687.[3] As originally conceived, Middleton was to underwrite the cost of the voyage, and the observations were to be made by Halley, 'whose Capacity for Such Purposes is Supposed to be Sufficiently knowne ...'.[4] The Royal Society agreed to support the proposal;[5] and on the day of the meeting at which it was discussed, 12 April 1693, Hooke made the following entry in his Diary: 'RS met ... Hally & Middleton made proposals of going into ye South Seas & Round the World. bouyed up by Herbert. Hill. &c.'[6] The Lords of the Treasury reported favourably on the proposal

and latitude right ascensions and declinations, of ... southern fixed starres'. Halley probably made such statements soon after his return from St Helena in 1678 and obviously before 1696, the year of the last entry by Aubrey. However, this allusion is not as direct as the quotation from Hooke in the text above (see note 6).

[1] Extract from the unpublished MS Diary of Robert Hooke, British Library Sloane MS 4024, reprinted in MacPike, 1932, p. 186. Unfortunately, the last statement appears incomplete in the MS. MacPike extracted references to Halley in Hooke's Diary and reprinted these. The last reference to Halley in this source is 24 July 1693, p. 186. MacPike took 'Hally SRS' to mean that his Clerkship had terminated and that he was reinstated as a Fellow; however, Halley was not replaced as Clerk until 8 March 1699 (Documents 47, p. 278; 48, p. 278–9). The abbreviation might suggest *Societatis Regalis socius*. He was re-elected Fellow on his return from his Atlantic voyages and elected to the Council, 20 November 1703. *The Record of the Royal Society*, 4th ed. (London, 1940), pp. 157, 342, 344.

[2] Document 1, pp. 250–1. A later allusion to circumnavigation appears in a letter dated 19 May 1699 from James Gregory to Colin Campbell: 'Mr Hally has gott a ship from the government, in which he has sett sail to goe round the globe on new discoverys, and the rectifying of geography,' Newton, vol. 4 (1709), p. 311.

[3] *Record of the Royal Society* (1940), p. 385. A Benjamin Middleton (son of Colonel Thomas Middleton, Commissioner of the Navy at Chatham and Surveyor, died 1672) was a member of Grays Inn (1670) and Fellow of Emanuel College, Cambridge (1688).

[4] Document 1, p. 251.

[5] Document 2, p. 251.

[6] Hooke's Diary, reprinted in MacPike, 1932, p. 186. The two supporters of the project are presumably John Herbert (Ronan, 1969, p. 161), elected F.R.S. in 1677 (rather than Lord Charles Herbert or Thomas Herbert, Earl of Pembroke, both members of the Society at this time), and Abraham Hill (1635–1721), one of the original members of the Royal Society who was elected 22 April 1663, *Record of the Royal Society* (1940), p. 375.

and Queen Mary II gave encouragement, as indicated in Admiralty Orders to the Navy Board, 12 July.[1] By this order a vessel of 'about Eighty Tuns Burthen' was to be specially built at the royal shipyard at Deptford.[2] This was a somewhat larger ship than the one which had been requested. It was to be maintained at their Majesties' expense, with Middleton responsible for the provisioning and wages. An Admiralty Order of 1 April 1694 speaks of 'the New Pink ordered to be built at Deptford for Colonel Middleton' and to be named 'the Paramour'.[3] Pink is the generic name for a type of ship (which originated in the Netherlands) with three masts, flat bottom, and bulging sides above the water line. Being of narrow stern above deck they were difficult to board and were used particularly for carrying stores. Among the attributes of the pink was its ability to make its way readily in shallow water. The pink was built by Fisher Harding, the master shipwright of Deptford, and was ready for launching 1 April 1694. Her dimensions as given by Harding in a letter to the Surveyor 14 May 1694 were: length 52 feet; breadth (beam) 18 feet; and depth (draught) 9 feet 7 inches, 89 Tuns.[4]

An unexplained delay of two years followed the launching, but in early 1696 activity concerning the project resumed. In an undated letter to Newton, thought to have been written in the spring of 1696, Halley states, 'I had waited on you on Saturday, but I was obliged to go on board my frigatt,' and adds 'I will waite on you at your lodgings to-morrow morning to discourse the other matter of serving you as your Deputy'.[5]

[1] Document 4, pp. 252–3.

[2] Document 4, p. 252.

[3] Document 8, pp 255–6. The reference to Colonel Middleton lends support to the notion that it was his son Benjamin who was promoting the project. 'Pink' is derived from the Middle Dutch 'pincke', 'pinke' (Ronan, 1969, p. 162), forms sometimes used in the Documents, as well as the French 'pinque', etc. 'Paramour' is one of several spellings of the vessel commanded by Halley. 'Paramore' is the spelling of the ship's name preferred by Halley as indicated by the titles of all three journals which form the bulk of this study, and was the form most frequently used by him in correspondence. Of course, the original spelling (whatever it might be) is used in the documents. It is also rendered 'Parrimore', a spelling used in a number of official documents as well as 'Parramore', etc. MacPike and Armitage use 'Paramour' and Ronan 'Paramore'; Halley's ship has also been called the *Pink Paramour!* In J. J. Colledge, *Ships of the Royal Navy*, 1 (1969), p. 408, she is listed as 'PARAMOUR Pink 6, 89 bm, 64 × 18 ft. Deptford 4. 1694 Sold 22.8.1706'. In the *Mariner's Mirror*, 52, 1966, p. 202 and p. 394, there is an exchange of information on Halley's ship and the answer corroborates the above, as follows: 'Naval Pink. *Paramour* pink. Built at Deptford 1694 (Harding). L. (gundeck) 64 ft, (keel), 54 ft. B. 18 ft; D. 9 ft 7 in. 89 tons, 10 guns? 6 guns 50 men. 1702: Unton Deering; bomb ketch in Rooke's squadron, 1703; Robert Stevens. Mediterranean. sold 1706.'

[4] Document 9, p. 256.

[5] MacPike, 1932, pp. 96–7. The reference to 'Deputy' alludes to Halley's impending service at the Mint at Chester. Also see Newton, vol. 4 (1967), pp. 190–1.

On 4 June 1696 Halley received a Commission to be Master and Commander of his Majestie's Pink;[1] warrants were granted for a boatswain, gunner and carpenter on the same day.[2] Apparently at Halley's request the Admiralty directed that for the better maintenance of discipline the men should be borne in the normal way but that Halley would give security for the repayment of wages at the end of the voyage, which was considered 'a private Affaire'.[3] However, since only a ten or twelve month absence was now envisaged, the original ambitious plans for the voyage had obviously been modified.[4] Sir John Hoskins, the fourth President of the Royal Society, and formerly one of the Secretaries to whom Halley was responsible in his position of Clerk, provided the necessary bond of £600 to cover the estimated cost of the voyage.[5] It was anticipated that £340.17.4 of this amount would be paid in wages. In a letter received by the Navy Board on 19 June 1696, Halley had drawn up a list of the proposed ship's company which consisted of fifteen men and two boys 'Which with myself, Mr Middleton and his servant will be in all twenty persons'.[6] This seems to be the last reference to Middleton and, on 15 August 1696, the Admiralty ordered that the pink be laid up in wet dock until further orders.[7]

This rather surprising action, after preparations were so far advanced, can be explained by Halley's appointment to the Mint at Chester. From a letter he wrote to Dr Hans Sloane we know that Halley was already there by at least 12 October 1696.[8] Only after his work at the Mint was completed could he reside again in London. However, we may conclude that he had returned to the capital by early 1698. Having refused more than

[1] Document 11, p. 257. The singular form is used because Queen Mary II died on 28 December 1694, after which King William III reigned as sole monarch until his death on 8 March 1702.

[2] Document 12, p. 258.

[3] Document 14, p. 259.

[4] Documents 15, pp. 260–1, 22, p. 264. Among earlier English shipmasters, Drake took nearly three years, and Cavendish well over two years (in a remarkably speedy passage) to sail around the world. Dampier, engaging in piracy along the way, took twelve years to circumnavigate (1679–91) and Anson took nearly four years (1740–4).

[5] Document 15, p. 260. Sir John Hoskins, Baronet (1634–1705), elected Fellow of the Royal Society, 20 May 1663, Secretary (with Thomas Gale), 16 December 1685 to 30 November 1687, had been President from 30 November 1682 to 30 November 1683. *Record of the Royal Society* (1940), p. 335.

[6] Document 15, p. 260.

[7] Document 16, p. 261.

[8] MacPike, 1932, p. 97. Halley wrote a letter with this date from Chester Castle to Dr Hans Sloane (1660–1753). Sloane was elected Fellow of the Royal Society in 1684, was Secretary from 30 November 1693 to 30 November 1710 and President, 1727–41 (*Record of the Royal Society* (1940), p. 336).

one offer of employment from Newton, Halley was now ready to turn his attention again to the matter which had been so long in his mind – a scientific voyage. A further delay of a crucial month or so was occasioned by the Czar requesting that the *Paramore* be rigged and brought afloat so that he could conduct sailing experiments with her.[1] Although William III had already presented a yacht, the *Royal Transport*, to the Czar (who had also been aboard various naval vessels) all desires of the royal visitor were gratified, including apparently his wish to use the *Paramore*. Peter left England on 25 April 1698, to the great relief of his hosts.

By early July Halley received from the Secretary of the Admiralty, Josiah Burchett, a directive concerning an appointment to speak with the Lords of the Admiralty.[2] Toward the end of the same month the Navy Board was directed to improve the sailing qualities of the pink by girdling (sheathing) her with planks. She was now going on a 'Particular Service', which suggests that the Navy had taken over full responsibility for the voyage.[3] This order was followed on 9 August 1698 by another which stated, 'Whereas his Majesty has been pleased to lend his Pink the Paramour to Mr. Hawley for a Voyage to the East Indies or South Seas, Wee do hereby desire and direct you, to cause her to be forthwith Sheathed and Fitted for such a Voyage and that shee be furnished with Twelve Monthes Stores proper for her.'[4] Two days later Halley was summoned by the Lords of the Admiralty, and about a week after this meeting another commission was issued to him.[5] This second commission, essentially the same as the earlier one, was dated 19 August 1698, the same day Halley's name was entered in the Wages Book. Meanwhile,

[1] Document 17, p. 262. The important letter containing this information seems to have been overlooked by all writers on Halley and Peter the Great. It is interesting that the first 'captain' of the *Paramore* was the Czar, who observed, 'that he would far rather be an admiral in England than Tsar in Russia.' See Gray, 1956, p. 233. If Peter was as rough in his treatment of the little ship as he apparently was of Sayes Court, the county home of John Evelyn at Deptford where he stayed, the vessel would have needed refitting before Halley could use her on an extended voyage!

[2] Document 19, pp. 262–3. Josiah Burchett (1666?–1746) was body servant and clerk of Secretary of the Admiralty Samuel Pepys, from 1680 to 1687 when he quarelled with his master, but pleaded to be taken back. After the Revolution and the imprisonment of Pepys, Burchett became first Joint Secretary (1693–4) and then Secretary of the Admiralty, 1698–1742).

[3] Documents 20, p. 263; 21, p. 263. In spite of this decision, as late as 5 November 1698 the voyage of the *Paramore* is still referred to as a 'Private Service'; see Document 38, p. 273.

[4] Document 22, p. 264. The sheathing in this case was wood; metal, especially lead, was also used at this time. See Sir W. L. Clowes, *The Royal Navy: a history*, 2 (London, 1898), p. 4 and p. 240; allusions to 'girdling' and 'doubling' in the correspondence and journals refer to this additional 'skin' of planks on the bottom of the ship.

[5] Documents 23, p. 264; 24, p. 265.

on 15 August, a boatswain/gunner, John Dodson, had been appointed and rigging begun on the pink.[1] Over the next two months the crew was entered, among these being Surgeon George Alfrey (Alfry) apparently the only individual especially requested by Halley.[2] Alfrey was entered 22 September to be followed on 10 October by the Mate, Lieutenant Edward Harrison.[3]

In total thirty-three names were entered in the wages book; but thirteen men were discharged or released before the vessel sailed, leaving a full complement of twenty. A last minute petition for five more men was not granted, but apparently Halley's request for two azimuth compasses, a yawl, and some fishing gear met with approval. Unfortunately, however, no inventory of the scientific instruments used on shipboard exists.[4] He was also provided with £100 for contingencies.[5] After the guns had been mounted, six three-pounders and two smaller guns in swivels, the pink was ready to set sail.[6] Orders and Instructions based largely on Halley's own recommendations were issued on 15 October; these called for an extensive voyage in the Atlantic, but not to the Pacific or Indian Oceans. Halley, in addition to observing variations of the compass and the situation, including longitude and latitude of ports

[1] Document 61, pp. 289–91.

[2] Document 26, p. 265.

[3] Document 61, p. 290. There was no provision in the original plan for a second officer (Document 15, pp. 260–1). It was Halley who requested a commissioned officer as he acknowledged retrospectively in a letter to Burchett dated 23 June 1699, 'Your Honour knows that my dislike of my Warrant Officers made me Petition their Lopps that my Mate might have the Commission of Lieutenant, therby the better to keep them in obedience' (Document 50, pp. 281–2). Edward Harrison was an officer with about eight years' service when he was commissioned Lieutenant of the *Paramore*, 4 October 1698 (Document 32, p. 268). In 1694, Harrison had proposed to the Royal Society various methods of finding longitude at sea, in a paper which Halley read to the Council; the paper offered no new ideas and it was largely ignored. However, this did not discourage Harrison from publishing his 'solution' to the problem in a book, *Idea longitudinis: being a brief definition of the best known axioms for finding the longitude* (London, 1696). Harrison advocated the use of magnetic variation for finding longitude at sea and reemphasized the value of using eclipses for the same purpose. Ironically Harrison begins the Dedication of his volume as follows: 'It is a saying in the *Navy*, He that knows not how to obey *Command*, is not worthy to bear command ...' and continues, 'As it is the Duty of a Subject to be True and Loyal to his Prince, so it is the Duty of Servants, to be Faithful, Humble and Submissive to their Masters.' Later he states '...if I know more than others it is by Divine Authority' and adds 'My Knowledge of Mathematics is little'.

[4] Ronan, 1969, pp. 176–7. We can only make inferences from the journals on this subject See also *Edmond Halley, 1656–1742: a conversazione to celebrate the tercentenary of his birth*, British Astronomical Association, London, 1956. This catalogue describes certain of Halley's instruments exhibited at the Society, but none known to have been taken by him on his voyages.

[5] Documents 34, p. 270; 25, p. 265; 26, p. 265; 29, pp. 266–7.

[6] Documents 27, pp. 265–6; 31, pp. 267–8.

he called at, was to go far enough south to discover 'Terra Incognita' which it was thought might be in the South Atlantic.[1]

THE FIRST VOYAGE

When the *Paramore* weighed anchor at Deptford on Thursday 20 October 1698, she carried twenty persons which was the number she was allowed for the Atlantic journey. The regular complement consisted of Edmond Halley, commander of the Pink; Edward Harrison, lieutenant and mate; George Alfrey, surgeon; John Dunbar, midshipman; John Dodson, boatswain and gunner; Thomas Price, carpenter; seven able seamen – Peter Ingoldsby, John Thompson, James Glenn, David Wishard, Samuel Withers, Thomas Daviss, and John Vinicot; Matthew Butts, gunner's mate; William Dowty, carpenter's mate; Caleb Harmon, captain's clerk; Richard Pinfold, captain's servant; John Hodges, boatswain's servant; Robert Dampster, carpenter's servant; and Thomas Burton, servant.[2]

At the outset of the voyage the weather was stormy and the *Paramore* took refuge in Portland Road. Here Halley wrote a letter to Burchett, dated 1 November, in which he asked for the ship's ballast to be changed from sand to shingle, and for additional caulking.[3] Even during the brief stay in Portland Road, and under difficult circumstances, Halley began his observations of magnetic variation, finding the area then $6\frac{1}{2}°$ west of true (geographical or astronomical) north. With an azimuth compass Halley could determine magnetic variation at a place by one or, more accurately, by two observations. Presumably at Weymouth he used a single measurement of the magnetic amplitude at sunset (making allowance for refraction on the horizon) and then compared this figure with the Sun's computed azimuth from geographical north.[4] The other method

[1] Document 33, pp. 268–70. 'Terra Incognita' can be taken to be the great southern continent equivalent to land masses in the mid-latitudes of the northern hemisphere whose existence had been postulated in antiquity, i.e. *Terra Australis*.

[2] Document 61, pp. 289–91.

[3] Document 36, pp. 271–2.

[4] W. Falconer, *A new universal dictionary of the marine*, modernized and enlarged by Dr William Burney (London, 1815), p. 10, defines magnetical amplitude: 'an arch of the horizon, contained between the sun or a star, at the time of its rising or setting, and the magnetic east or west point of the horizon pointed out by the compass; the difference between this and the true amplitude is the variation of the compass, the true amplitude

which he employed, where conditions allowed, consisted of taking two measurements of the Sun's magnetic amplitude, i.e. at sunset and sunrise, half the difference between these two amplitudes being the variation, which was applied to the ship's position at midnight. Obviously the second method is normally the more reliable of the two. The magnetic variation recorded in Portland Road was the first of a great number of such observations he was to make on his voyages.

However, the more immediate problem of the condition of the ship now concerned Halley and he decided to backtrack to Portsmouth for the necessary overhaul. When approaching Portsmouth, Halley met the squadron of Admiral Benbow, which the *Paramore* saluted with five guns; the Admiral returned the same number of guns as a tribute to Halley who, as a Captain, would not normally have merited treatment equal to that of Benbow.[1] At Portsmouth the work on the ship was considered so vital that it was approved by the Commissioner[2] even before the Admiralty orders arrived. The need for re-caulking arose because the nails used to attach the wooden sheathing had split the planks, and shingle was wanted for ballast, because the water-logged sand choked the hand pumps. The *Paramore* was ready to sail on 15 November but bad weather again delayed her.

The crew were apprehensive of going alone so Halley sent Lieutenant Harrison to Benbow, who was soon to leave for the West Indies, to ask for protection. The Admiral agreed to escort the little ship past the African coast, with its dangers from pirates. Halley, nevertheless, wished to make this official and wrote on the matter to Burchett who replied affirmatively.[3] Burchett also wrote to Benbow that he should protect the *Paramore* in so far as he could, but not to go out of his way in doing so.[4] Storms continued and Halley lost his small boat, which was

being an arch of the horizon included between the east or west point of the center of the sun or star, at its rising or setting.

'If the magnetical amplitude be found to be 61°55 at the time when it is computed as above to be 39°25 then the difference is the variation westward, 22°30.'

[1] John Benbow (born 1653) at this time was Rear Admiral, having recently (9 March 1697–8) been appointed Commander in Chief of the King's Ships in the West Indies. In 1701 he was Vice Admiral of the Blue (under Sir George Rooke) and became a national hero when in the summer of 1702 he engaged a superior French force in the Atlantic and continued to fight after most of his captains had deserted him. The offending officers were court martialled; Benbow died 4 November 1702 of wounds received in the action. See J. Burney, *A chronological history of the discoveries in the South Sea . . .*, 4 (London, 1816), p. 384. Burney devotes pp. 384–7 to Halley's two Atlantic Voyages.

[2] The Commissioner at Portsmouth at this time was Henry Greenhill, who was appointed in April 1695 and transferred in August 1702.

[3] Documents 42, pp. 274–5; 44, p. 276;

[4] Document 43, pp. 275–6.

replaced by the Commissioner. The ships left port on 29 November and, after an uneventful voyage, reached Madeira in mid December. Here Benbow and his squadron parted from the *Paramore*. Halley went ashore to obtain wine on 19 December, and wrote a short but informative letter to Burchett.[1] Two days later the *Paramore* left Madeira to continue the journey southward along the coast of Africa.

The instructions concerning the journal were faithfully carried out each day. Besides recording compass variation, wind, course, miles sailed in the twenty-four hour period, and latitude and longitude from London, remarkable occurrences were reported. Biological phenomena were recorded as when the *Paramore* ran into a colony of what appear to be jellyfish, while sailing to St Iago in the Cape Verde Islands. Here, as Halley reported in a letter written several months later, the *Paramore* was fired on by two ships which turned out to be English merchantmen, one under the command of Mr John Way.[2] The masters of these vessels had mistaken the *Paramore* for a pirate ship in spite of her Union flag, which they believed might be false colours and not to be trusted. No damage was done and, after admonishing them, Halley proceeded to obtain water and wood from St Iago for his run across the Atlantic to the island of Trinidada (Trinidade, off the coast of Brazil) his next objective. The ship left St Iago on 6 January and, as the journal reveals, soon got into the Doldrums where little progress could be made. Halley rationed the water supply and by 8 February had decided, rather than try for Trinidada, about 20° South latitude, to sail for Fernando Loronho (Fernando de Noronha), about 4° South.

As they drew near to this island Halley began to have serious trouble with his crew. Boatswain Dodson was on watch when Halley discovered him early in the morning attempting to sail past Fernando Loronho, contrary to orders, rather than for the island. The *Paramore* anchored off the island, of which a profile drawing and sketch map were made.[3] Observations ashore revealed that little of value to a crew in need of refreshment was available and, particularly disappointing, no fresh water.

After refurbishing as best he could, Halley sailed on 23 February for the coast of Brazil where, a few days later, he noted that his charts were inaccurate.[4] The Paraiba River south of the 'nose' of Brazil (about 7°

[1] Document 45, p. 277 [2] Document 49, pp. 279–80.

[3] Journal of the First Voyage, pp. 99–100.

[4] He does not specify which charts these are, but presumably he had Dutch 'waggoners' aboard as well as John Narborough's map; we do not know for certain, and thus a comparison of Halley's determinations with those represented on maps which could have been available to

South latitude) was reached on 26 February. Here the Portuguese were hospitable and Halley entertained an interpreter and a detachment of soldiers on his ship, apparently the first English vessel to visit the area in thirty years. Halley was invited to visit the Governor, Dom Manuel Soarez Albergaria, at the town of Paraiba, which he did two days later.[1] The Governor allowed Halley to replenish his water supply and to obtain enough sugar and tobacco for the continuation of the voyage but not for trading purposes. Later Halley wisely refused to engage in illicit trade in dyewood, whose export from Brazil was absolutely prohibited. Relations were sensitive, as indicated by Surgeon Alfrey being kept hostage ashore while a Portuguese pilot was aboard the *Paramore*, but Halley handled the situation with characteristic tact and diplomacy. He also attempted to make what observations he could under the circumstances, including eclipses of the first satellite of Jupiter, which would give an accurate determination of longitude; but he was frustrated in this effort because of the height of the planet and the lack of a support for his telescope.[2] Similar observations on the eclipse of the Moon were more successful and longitude was determined by this means. Although he was not permitted to sound the river, Halley made what observations he could on tides in addition to magnetic variation and other phenomena called for in his instructions. A Samuel Robinson joined the ship, 8 March.

Winter in the Southern hemisphere was now approaching but Halley decided against staying in Brazil and continuing his journey southward later on; rather he elected to go northward to Barbados where he hoped he might exchange those crew members who were recalcitrant. In the West Indies he hoped to find a flag officer, possibly Benbow, who could approve such a change. The *Paramore* had difficulty sailing in the face of the north-easterly trade winds, but on 1 April the vessel was in sight of Barbados. Here Harrison, who was on watch, flagrantly disobeyed Halley, and was insolent as well. For his insubordination the Lieutenant was confined to his cabin for the night. Faced with this, Halley now resolved to take charge of the navigation himself.[3] The *Paramore* anchored in

him is not possible. In "Some remarks on the variation of the magnetical compass," *Philosophical Transactions*, 29(1714), 165–68, Halley refers to observations on longitude made at the Strait of Magellan by John Wood during Narborough's voyage of 1670 and also to observations made in the same area by Captain John Strong in 1690.

[1] Now João Pessoa; see Appendix A, pp. 349–53, for place names, etc., for the First Voyage.

[2] Perhaps Halley had with him the twenty-four foot telescope which he had used on St Helena but, as indicated previously, we are not informed on this point. See Journal of the First Voyage, p. 102, and n. 1.

[3] Document 50, pp. 281–2.

Carlisle Bay, Barbados, where Halley again determined longitude (by eclipses of the satellites of Jupiter), and observed magnetic variation and tidal ranges. At Barbados Robinson, whose rank is not given, was discharged, 3 April.[1]

On 19 April the *Paramore* left Barbados and sailed past Martinique, Desseada (Désirade) and arrived on Antigua on the 24th. He prepared his ship for a speedy return to England, a course he had now definitely decided upon. After Halley replenished his water supply at St Christopher (St Kitts), he sailed for Anguilla where further supplies were put aboard. The *Paramore* set sail for England on 9 May and, passing close to Bermuda (which was not seen), reached the Scilly Isles 20 June.

Two days later Halley anchored at Plymouth, from which port on 23 June he sent a letter to Burchett.[2] In this he gave details of his journey from the West Indies, called attention to the success of the voyage in the face of difficulties and expressed the hope that he would be permitted to sail again (this time earlier in the season) to complete the work. Halley also discussed the problems he encountered with Harrison and Dodson and asked that others be appointed in their places. The Secretary replied on 29 June that orders had been sent to Sir Clowdisley Shovell to try Harrison at a Court Martial.[3] On the same day the ship was ordered to sail to Deptford to be laid up and paid off.[4] The Court Martial, which was held on 3 July, only reprimanded Harrison to Halley's dissatisfaction.[5]

Halley's wish to sail again was soon granted and before the ship was laid up and paid off on 20 July 1699, he seems to have been making plans for a Second Voyage. Although Halley's request that he be sent out on a Second Voyage was granted by the Lords of the Admiralty, his petition

[1] Document 61, p. 290.

[2] Document 50, pp. 281–2.

[3] Document 51, p. 283. Sir Clowdisley [Cloudisley, Cloudesly, etc.] Shovell (1650–1707) had been promoted in October 1696 Admiral of the Blue after a Navy career of over thirty years. At the time of Halley's return from his First Voyage, Shovell was commanding a squadron which was guarding the Channel. He was appointed Admiral of the White on the Accession of Queen Anne (8 March 1701/2) and Commander in Chief of the Fleet on 1 May 1705. Shovell died after his flagship the *Association*, and two other ships of a fleet returning from the Mediterranean, struck the Bishop and Clerk rocks off the Scilly Isles, 22 October 1707. The great loss of life on this occasion was to spur the awarding of a government prize for 'the discovery of the longitude'.

[4] Documents 51, p. 283; 52, pp. 283–4.

[5] The punishment which Shovell meted out to Harrison was all that was legally allowed because 'the only charge Halley could bring was one of insolence' (Ronan, 1969, p. 169). After this Harrison resigned his commission and entered the merchant service. See Document 57. p. 287.

for a different vessel was denied, and after the *Paramore* had been refitted, she was furnished with guns and ready for sea duty by mid September.[1]

The Council Minutes of the Royal Society contain several references to Halley during the period of his absence. These have to do mainly with his Clerkship, and on 8 March 1699 a satisfactory successor, Israel Jones, had been appointed.[2] Once back in London, Halley was soon attending the regular meetings of the Society and reporting on phenomena he had witnessed on his voyage. On 19 July, two weeks after Harrison's Court Martial, Halley presented the Society with a branch of a Barbados Fig (i.e. Banyan) tree.[3] At the next weekly meetings of the Society, he showed the Fellows part of a mangrove plant, and two weeks later another botanical specimen.[4] On 16 August, he presented a sea chart on which he had plotted his observations of magnetic variation, and also illustrated that Brazil was incorrectly shown on current maps.[5]

THE SECOND VOYAGE[6]

An interval of only a little over a month, from 20 July to 24 August 1699, separated the discharge of the crew from Halley's First Voyage and the beginning of rigging for the Second.[7] On the latter date the first names

[1] Documents 64, pp.292–3; 65, pp. 293–4; 72, p. 297.

[2] Documents 46, pp. 277–8; 47, p. 278; 48, pp. 278–9.

[3] Document 60, p. 289. The tree is *Ficus Bengalensis*, from the beard-like aerial roots of which the Portuguese *las barbadoes*, 'the Barbadoes' is thought to be derived.

[4] Documents 63, p. 292; 68, p. 295.

[5] Document 69, p. 295.

[6] Halley's First and Second Voyages in the *Paramore* have sometimes been thought of as being two parts of the same expedition. It is true that similar general objectives were in view and in this sense the Second Voyage could be considered as a continuation or completion of the First. From Chapman, 1941, pp. 4–5, who wrote perceptively on the wind and magnetic charts of Halley, we might infer that he was commander of only one voyage of the *Paramore*. However, the fact that the ship was laid up after the first journey, that Halley received a new commission, and that another set of instructions was issued make it quite clear that these were two separate voyages. This view is supported by Alexander Dalrymple, who printed Halley's Atlantic voyages in 1773 under the title, *Two voyages made in 1698, 1699 and 1700, by Dr. Edmund Halley*. Dalrymple published Halley's voyages. along with others, in 1775, in *A collection of voyages chiefly in the Southern Atlantic Ocean*. Halley requested that the second set of instructions not only contain directions for him to discover land between South America and Africa but that he reach specific latitudes in the southern hemisphere, i.e. between 50° and 55° south in the Atlantic. This is the most significant difference between the Orders and Instructions for Halley's First and Second Voyages and was to have very important implications for the later expedition. Compare Documents 33, pp. 268–70 and 78, pp. 301–2. See R. P. Stearns, 'The course of Capt. Edmond Halley in the year 1700', *Annals of Science*, 1, (1936), 294–301, for another short account of Halley's Second Voyage, especially, and its results.

[7] Documents 61, pp. 289–91; 91, pp. 312–4.

were entered in the Wages Book for the Second Voyage. Eventually nine crew from the First Voyage were entered, but of these two did not sail from Deptford. Thirty-two men and one boy were originally entered in the Wages Book, some merely for rigging. Of this number ten were dismissed and one added before the ship left England. Of the first eight individuals to sign on, seven had been on the First Voyage, the exception being William Brewer who was appointed Boatswain in place of Dodson. As Halley pointed out in a letter to Burchett dated 4 September, Brewer had only one arm and since Halley thought this to be a handicap in case of emergency, three or four extra hands were requested.[1] Thus, although the complement for the Second Voyage was originally the same as for the First, i.e. twenty individuals, twenty-four were eventually allowed.[2] They were Edmond Halley, commander; George Alfrey, surgeon; Thomas Greenhaugh, midshipman; Edward St Claire, mate; William Brewer, boatswain; Thomas Price, carpenter; six able seamen, Thomas Daviss, John Mackintosh, Robert Leonard, William Small, Peter Abber and James Glenn; two ordinary seamen, Edward Jackson and Henry Humphrys; Nicholas Whitbread, gunner's mate; Peter Ingoldsby and John Small, both listed as carpenter's mate; George Brock, quartermaster; William Curtiss, captain's clerk; Richard Pinfold, captain's servant; William Lang, surgeon's servant; Thomas Fenn, carpenter's servant; Dennis Clossier, boatswain's servant; and Manly White, a boy entered as a captain's servant. Thus in place of the lieutenant, one able bodied seaman, and one servant on the First Voyage, there was a mate, a quartermaster, an extra carpenter's mate, two ordinary seamen, a surgeon's servant and an extra captain's servant, on the Second.

The *Paramore* weighed anchor on 16 September; five days later Halley reported to Burchett that the ship sailed much better than previously, as the result of the refitting.[3] When they reached the east coast of Kent, Halley wrote letters to Burchett on successive days, 26 and 27 September, informing him that the *Falconbird*,[4] a well-armed ship belonging to the Royal African Company,[5] had agreed to accompany the *Paramore* along the African coast. In the second of these letters Halley intimated that he

[1] Document 72, p. 297. [2] Document 91, pp. 312–4. [3] Document 80, pp. 302–3.

[4] This merchant ship also known as *Falcon bird*, *Faulconbird* and *Falconbridg* was a "Guiney man of 30 Gunns." See pp. 123–9 and Documents 81, p. 303; 82, p. 304.

[5] The Royal African Company, which received its charter from King Charles II in 1672, carried on the 'triangular' trade with West Africa (Guinea Coast) and the West Indies and England. See Daniel Defoe, *An essay upon the trade to Africa* . . . (London, 1711); and also Documents 81, p. 303 and 82, p. 304.

was confident that those who might have been less than satisfied with his performance on the First Voyage would be happy with the result of the expedition he was now undertaking. He began observations in the Channel on variation and, a new feature, on temperature and pressure.[1] During a delay, Halley seems to have exchanged one of his two ordinary seamen, Edward Jackson, for an able bodied seaman, Joseph Phillips. The *Paramore* cleared the coast of England on 28 September and sailed down the Channel, encountering first a fleet of Danish ships who reported a privateer (which turned out to be an English merchantman) and then a flying Dutchman with false colours. Halley must have been glad to be in the company of the *Falconbird*, even though the dangers proved to bc unreal.

The merchant ship parted from the *Paramore* as the two ships neared Madeira.[2] As the *Paramore* approached the island the sea was so rough that it was decided not to go ashore for wine as planned, and an accident occurred which was to leave its scar on Halley for the rest of his life. On the 13 October the boy Manly White fell overboard and, although valiant efforts were made to save him, these proved fruitless in the raging seas.[3]

[1] Unfortunately no details are given about the instruments used for these observations or the scales employed. In the case of the thermometer it would seem from the data collected that it had a scale with greater amplitude than the Fahrenheit. The range of Halley's observations on temperature is between 101 degrees at 7°.40′ N. latitude to – 3 degrees at 52°.06′ S. latitude. We are not told where and under what conditions the observations were made, presumably on deck; but Halley does mention the temperature in his cabin on several occasions, which suggests that he had a thermometer there. Ronan, 1969, p. 171 n., makes the suggestion that the scale might be arbitrary and adds the puzzling statement that 'both the Fahrenheit scale and that of Réaumur (0° = freezing to 80° = boiling point of liquid in thermometer [and gradually taken as boiling point of water]) were in use'. Actually G. D. Fahrenheit (1686–1736) invented his thermometer *c.* 1714, and R. A. F. de Réaumur (1683–1759) reported his *c.* 1730. Absolute figures for the barometeric readings (Halley's high 30.01 and low 27.40) are not as important as relative ones. Of course, Halley well understood the general relationship between weather and pressure (i.e. the increasing possibility of overcast and rainy weather with decreasing pressure, and the clearing tendency associated with increasing pressure) as indicated by his statements on this subject in the journal. He also makes note of 'sensible' temperature varying with humidity. Further, we know from the Royal Society records that Halley was interested in, and tested, barometers and thermometers both before and after his Atlantic voyages (see Document 95, p. 316).

[2] See Appendix B, Selected Place Names: Halley's Second Voyage, pp. 355–61, for various spellings and other facts relating to places, especially foreign ones, mentioned in the text.

[3] The 'Memoir' reprinted in MacPike, 1932, p. 8, states that although Halley had '. . . 4 times crosst the Line, and went directly from thence into the cold Climates of the South, he lost not one Man, but brought home every Soul with him he Carryed out, in good health'. To explain this enigmatic statement MacPike speculated that the boy Manly (or Manley) White might have been picked up at some island, while admitting that there is no evidence for this, and (p. 247, n. 1) went so far as to suggest St Helena, visited '*circa* 30 March 1700', as the island. Since St Helena was not reached until long after the tragedy, MacPike's chronology is

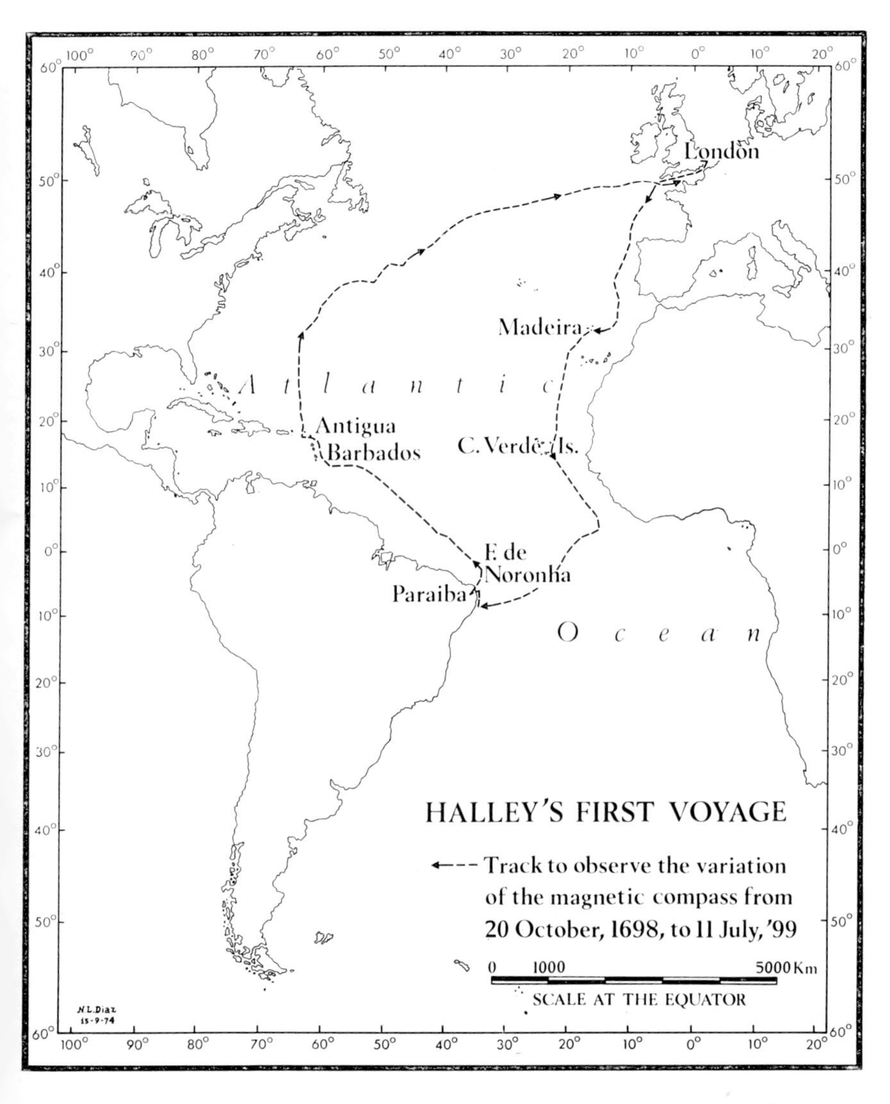

Figure 3. Track of Halley's First Voyage in the *Paramore* as reported in his Journals.

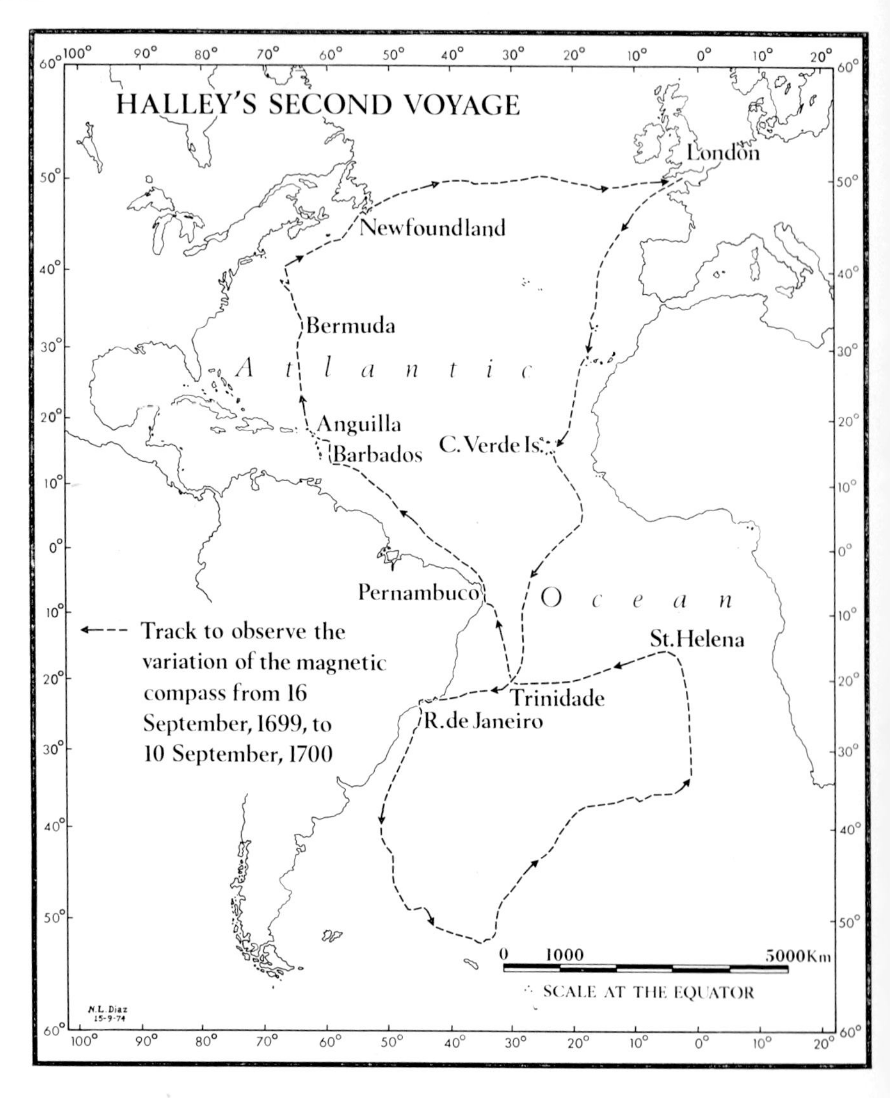

Figure 4. Track of Halley's Second Voyage in the *Paramore* as reported in his Journals.

On the following day William Gothern, an able seaman, was entered in the roster.[1]

The ship continued its journey southward, following approximately the course she travelled on the First Voyage, the island of Sal in the Cape Verdes being reached 22 October. Here a Portuguese permitted the English sailors to hunt wild animals for food, but salt which was provided proved dirty. Observations continued to be made when at all possible. The ship sailed to the larger island of St Iago, where Halley met an English merchant ship whose master, John Taylor, came aboard the *Paramore*. Local water was obtained but not much else because of the high price charged by the Portuguese Governor and the generally unco-operative attitude of the officials.

Halley's letter to Burchett of 28 October indicated that, in spite of these difficulties, he was pleased with the ship's company and with the progress that had been made.[2] He looked forward to reaching his farthest south before the New Year and, toward this end, he made his way across the Atlantic for the coast of Brazil. In this passage he carefully reported the variable weather conditions but, at first, did not report the magnetic variation (Figure 5).[3] The ship crossed the Equator 16 November and by 14 December had reached Rio de Janeiro. Here Halley wrote another letter to Burchett, which apparently is not extant and, in fact, may never have reached England. In spite of the lack of this document and a hiatus in the journal from 15 to 28 December we may infer from other documents that Halley replenished his stores in Rio, and we know for certain

obviously incorrect in this instance. MacPike further speculated that the term 'man' might exclude a boy, but certainly 'Soul' does not! From an entry in *Biographia Britannica*, 4, p. 2502, n. [o] we learn that Halley did not, 'lose a single man of his company by sickness,' but that through the misfortune of losing the boy '. . . who by some unlucky accident was thrown over board and drowned, the captain [Halley] was so deeply affected with the loss, that during his whole life afterwards he never mentioned it without tears.' As we know from Document 91, p. 313, Manly White signed on in England 17 September 1699; and we could add that Halley's record of losing only one crew member in all of his extensive voyaging is remarkable at this period by any standards. See also Journal of the Second Voyage, p. 130.

[1] Document 91, p. 313. We are not informed how the addition was made to the crew on this date when the *Paramore* appears not to have docked at Madeira. Perhaps Gothern was a supernumerary aboard the *Paramore* (although he is not listed in the Wages Book as having entered in England) and with the loss of Manly White, could be carried on the payroll, or he may have been picked up from a passing ship, but this is not explained.

[2] Document 83, p. 305.

[3] Halley obtained data, which could be used with adjustment, from this area on his First Voyage and may not have thought that it was necessary to make observations again. Ronan, 1969, p. 171, suggests that Halley may have collected data which he did not report. An appealing idea, quite unsubstantiated, is that he might have entered the observations directly on to what became the manuscript of the Atlantic Chart of magnetic variation, which is now lost, and did not repeat it in the journal.

that he obtained rum in place of the wine not taken aboard at Madeira.[1] Peter Abber appears to have left the *Paramore* at Rio.

On 29 December, the ship left Rio for the journey southward to reach the latitudes that Halley had himself recommended in the Instructions. On this run the journal is full of recordings of observations on a variety of phenomena which must have occupied much of Halley's time. In addition to the data specifically called for in his Instructions, he recorded weather conditions and fauna encountered. Samples of seaweed were taken up when it seemed interesting to Halley and other members of the crew. The weather became progressively colder as they sailed into the 'roaring forties'. Various birds including penguins of two kinds were seen, and what might, from the description, have been small whales. Freezing conditions set in when the little ship reached the fifties, even though it was now late January and the height of summer in the southern hemisphere. Great cliffed features came in view, which were thought at first to be landforms but closer examination from a small boat showed them to be solid ice. On 1 February 1700 Halley reported his farthest south, 52° 24′. He had great trouble extricating the ship from iceberg infested waters because of foggy weather, contrary winds, and a 'leewardly' ship. By a combination of expert navigation and good fortune incredible dangers were passed by 5 February, when latitude 49° 55′ was attained and temperatures increased slightly. However, this was accompanied by unpleasantly humid conditions which prevailed for some time.

Halley continued to make daily meteorological observations and shows his great ability as a generalizer in his remarks on prevailing temperature differences on the western and eastern parts of the South Atlantic in the mid-latitudes.[2] Tristan da Cunha was seen on 17 February; but Halley elected not to land there but to seek refreshment at the Cape of Good Hope. The *Paramore*, however, was driven north of the Cape in such heavy seas that Halley decided to steer for St Helena. The flooding of the ship by high waves had caused considerable loss of provisions and supplies of fresh water were running low. For reasons not explained, Thomas Greenhaugh ceased to be midshipman on 4 March; James Glenn was appointed to this position the next day.[3] There must have been much relief when ,on 11 March, St Helena was sighted.

[1] Document 84, pp. 306–7.

[2] The worldwide pattern of circulation and temperature differences of the surface currents of the oceans was not understood until over a century later through the researches of Alexander von Humboldt, Matthew Fontaine Maury, and others.

[3] Document 91, pp. 312–3.

Here the ship anchored, her supplies were replenished, and Halley took the opportunity of writing to Burchett.[1] In his letter Halley recounted the voyage up to this point, emphasizing the great dangers he has passed through in the high latitudes of the southern hemisphere. Halley was of the impression that the icebergs he had seen were islands of ice; it seemed inconceivable that these features which rose 200 feet above sea level could be afloat because, as he suggested, seven times this mass would be below water. Perhaps it was the desire to have discovered land, even apparently useless ice covered islands, that influenced the usually rational Halley in this instance. But he is confident that their Lordships at the Admiralty will be satisfied with his rich harvest of observations. On 13 March, William Burch was entered in the Wages Book as a boatswain's servant.[2] By 30 March all was ready and the ship left St Helena.

Halley now wished to visit the Island of Trinidada (Trinadade) which he had hoped to reach on his earlier voyage. First he sailed across the Atlantic and then, when he attained the latitude of the Island, steered westward (i.e. parallel sailing). The weather was generally good and the rocks of Martin Vaz were sighted and sketched on 14 March. The next day Trinidada was 'discovered'. Fresh water was needed and, after anchoring off the rocky shore on the 17th, the big job of exchanging brackish water, taken on at a rainy St Helena, was begun with the aid of a long boat. A pair of Guiney (Guinea) hens and breeding stocks of goats and hogs were put ashore, which survived and produced feral descendants.[3] Halley landed and rowed round the island in his pinnace to make the most detailed map of any feature seen on the voyage.[4] The English needed a station for further explorations in this area and, in the uninhabited island of Trinidada with its good water supply, Halley may have thought he had found it.[5] At all events he took possession of the island in the name of the King and left the Union flag flying.[6]

[1] Document 84, pp. 306–7. [2] Document 91, p. 313.

[3] Apparently as recently as the early part of this century descendants of stock left by Halley still survived on South Trinidade from the observations of a traveller that 'Wild goats and wild hogs liberated on the island in 1700 by the astronomer Halley still roamed the ridges.' *Notes and Queries*, 154 (1928), 152–3. Presumably Halley left the animals for the use of future voyagers.

[4] The Journal of the Second Voyage, p. 186.

[5] The Falkland Isles, sighted by John Davis in 1592 and visited by Captain John Strong in 1690, came to serve this function after 1765, when they were formally claimed by the British crown.

[6] The Union Flag consisting at this time of St George's cross, red with white fimbriation on St Andrew's flag – the white saltire with blue ground. This had been used, with interruptions, since the Union of the Crowns of England and Scotland, 1603. Its use, particularly

Much work was still to be done, so on 20 April they set sail for the coast of Brazil. In a little over a week of northwesterly sailing Pernambuco (Recife) was reached. After some delay occasioned by a severed anchor cable, the services of a local pilot were obtained to take the *Paramore* to shore. Halley was hospitably received by the Portuguese Governor who allowed him to reprovision his ship. Upon enquiring, Halley learned that Europe was at peace, on which point he had not had information for eight months;[1] this was important since Halley intended to complete his mission by way of the West Indies.

The helpfulness of the Portuguese contrasted with the treatment Halley received from a Mr Hardwick (Hardwyck) who represented himself as the English Consul but in reality seems to have been the servant of the Royal African Company. Halley was made a prisoner in Hardwick's house while the 'Consul' inspected the ship, assuming her to be a privateer. The unprecedented nature of the voyage was such that this mistake is somewhat understandable, but when Halley showed Hardwick his commissions, this should have been enough. Eventually all was resolved, the self-styled consul released Halley with apologies, and the *Paramore* left Pernambuco 4 May, sailing northward towards the Caribbean Islands. Observations on various natural phenomena were made with the same thoroughness as previously; and on 21 May, Barbados was reached and William Burch discharged the next day.[2]

Halley went ashore to see Governor Ralph Grey, as on his previous visit, but he was advised not to stay because of disease on the island. Some water was procured but the men were not allowed shore leave at Bridgetown. As a result of his brief exposure, Halley became so sick that his skin peeled and he was forced to stay in his cabin.[3] The mate, Edward St Claire, navigated the ship out of Barbados where an anchor was lost on a coral reef. In spite of precautions, some of the crew also contracted the disease but Surgeon Alfrey proved more than equal to the heavy call that was put on his services.[4]

at sea, was the subject of a proclamation by Charles II, 18 September 1674 (printed in *The London Gazette*, 924, p. 28, September 1674), apparently written by Pepys. See Samuel Pepys, *Naval Minutes*, ed. J. R. Tanner, Navy Records Society, 60 (London, 1926), p. 77.

[1] Following the Treaty of Ryswick, October 1697, and before the War of the Spanish Succession, in which the English became involved in 1702, there was a brief period of peace in Europe.

[2] Document 91, p. 313.

[3] Enquiries made in the course of the present study from several physicians specializing in tropical diseases elicited these opinions: an African gastro-intestinal disease imported with the slaves; yellow fever, endemic in the Caribbean; typhoid fever, because of the peeling of the skin. However, it was stressed that these are conjectures, not diagnoses.

[4] Document 85, p. 308.

Passing Antigua, the ship next called at St Kitts, where a stay of about a week was made. This afforded an opportunity for needed repairs to be made and for the rigging to be overhauled under the direction of Boatswain Brewer. The crew was supplemented by the addition of an ordinary seaman, William French, who signed on the day the *Paramore* reached St Kitts.[1] This island, though a good watering place, had few of the other commodities that were needed and, in addition, the pinnace was damaged so that other stops would have to be made before the return voyage across the Atlantic could be undertaken. On 5 June the *Paramore* left for Anguilla which was reached in one day. Here dry wood was put aboard, the ship was reprovisioned in so far as possible and the crew given shore leave. It was clear that another stop should be made, so on 10 June the ship steered for Bermuda which was sighted after ten days of pleasant sailing in fair weather.

From the journal and accounts which he subsequently rendered it is clear that Halley decided to have everything necessary done to the ship at Bermuda.[2] The *Paramore* was careened and cleaned, while Carpenter Price with the help of three local men caulked her. A fresh coat of paint was applied where necessary and a new 315 lb anchor purchased from Samuel Day, the Governor of Bermuda.[3] Because of an offer of employment which seemed attractive to him the Mate, Edward St Claire, requested his discharge and it was given to him on 11 July; his place was taken by a Mr St George Tucker, an experienced master who wished to go to England.[4]

The crew being complete and healthy and the ship in good condition, Halley secured the services of a pilot, Zachary Briggs, to see him out of the harbour and shaped his course for Cape Cod. Just before he left Bermuda, Halley wrote a letter to Burchett summarizing the voyage since his last letter from St Helena.[5] As they sailed northward, the weather deteriorated but observations continued to be made. Halley had intended to touch shore in New England, but bad weather prevented him and he decided to sail directly to Newfoundland, off the coast of which he met some French fishermen who appear to have been helpful in preventing the *Paramore* from running aground on hidden rocks along a misty

[1] Document 91, p. 313.

[2] Document 133, p. 341.

[3] Document 133, p. 341. Samuel Day was lieutenant governor from 20 October 1698 to 18 December 1700. He was the fifth of the chief administrators of the Islands under the English Crown following the dissolution of the Bermuda Company in 1683.

[4] Document 91, p. 313.

[5] Document 85, pp. 307–8.

coast.[1] This helpfulness contrasted with the reaction of the English fishermen encountered further along the coast, who avoided the *Paramore*, believing her to be a pirate ship. One of the English fishing crews, bolder than the rest, fired on the *Paramore*. Halley sent out his boat to fetch the offending skipper, Humphrey Bryant of Bideford, Devon; and he was brought aboard the *Paramore* and questioned about his action.[2] The man's explanation satisfied Halley, especially when he learned that the Newfoundland coast had recently been visited by pirates.

At Toad's (Tors) Cove on the Newfoundland Coast, the *Paramore* took on fresh water, which was abundant, as was birch wood (a point appreciated by Halley, who seems to have had a high regard for the resources of these northern colonies at a time when they were much neglected in favour of the West Indies by major European powers).

On 6 August, Halley bore away from Newfoundland for his return, and by parallel sailing reached the Scilly Isles in some twenty days. The *Paramore* anchored at Plymouth on 27 August and, on the same day, Halley wrote Burchett announcing his arrival.[3] Owing to contrary winds and the leeward tendency of the *Paramore*, progress up the Channel was slow. At the Downs on 2 September, Halley wrote again to Burchett as he did five days later when at Long Reach.[4] Secretary Burchett responded to these letters on 19 September when he informed Halley that he might come to the Admiralty, but to be sure to have all his accounts in order when he appeared.[5] The crew had been paid off on 18 September and the ship was laid up.[6]

Halley now had an opportunity to renew his old association with members of the Royal Society. He wrote to Dr Hans Sloane on the 26 October about some social matters,[7] and four days later attended the weekly meeting of the Royal Society.[8] On this occasion he showed the Fellows what may have been the manuscript of his Atlantic Chart of Magnetic

[1] Both the French and the English fished the Grand Banks, generally in different areas. Halley might have expected from the French the treatment he received a little later from his compatriots. But the French were helpful rather than hostile and, in general, Halley seems to have received better treatment from foreigners on his Atlantic voyages than he did from the Englishmen whom he encountered.

[2] Armitage (p. 145) suggests, in spite of the preceding reference to 'English Fishboats', that the home port Humphrey Bryant was Biddeford, Maine, rather than Bideford, Devon. However, according to Mr Albert Pearce of the McArthur Public Library in Biddeford, Maine, '. . . the name Biddeford was not adopted for this area until 1718, when it replaced the designated Saco.' Letter dated 1 February 1973 to the present editor.

[3] Document 88, pp. 309–10.

[4] Documents 89, p. 310; 90, p. 311.

[5] Document 92, p. 314.

[6] Document 91, pp. 312–4.

[7] Document 93, p. 315.

[8] Document 94, p. 315.

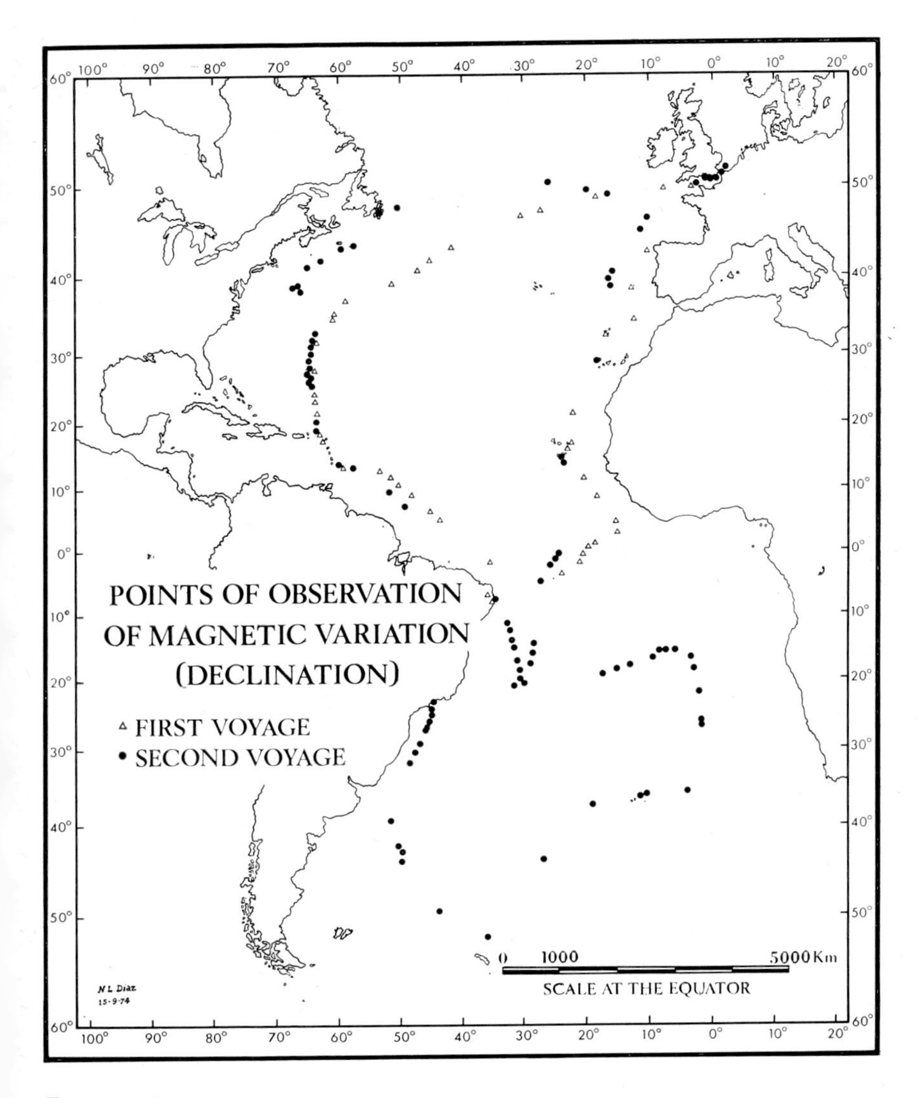

Figure 5. The points of observation of magnetic variation (declination) made by Halley on his First and Second Voyages and used in the construction of the Atlantic Chart, 1701.

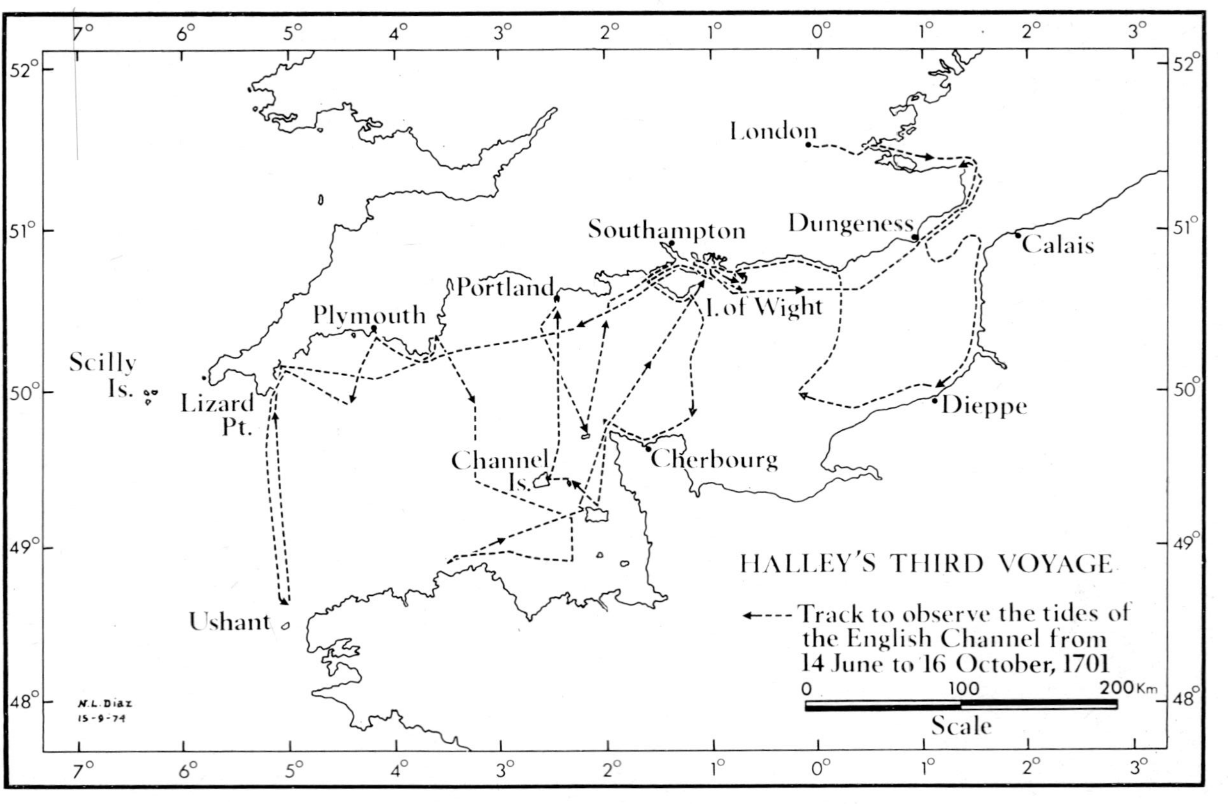

Figure 6. Track of Halley's Third Voyage in the *Paramore* as reported in his Journals.

Variation. Since this was so soon after his return, Halley may have begun the draft on board ship.

To add to the approximately fifty observations on magnetic variation from the First Voyage, Halley now had about double that number from the Second. Some were of places he had visited earlier; in a number of cases he does not seem to have made a second observation and for others he did not complete the computation in the journal after taking the evening and morning amplitude, but this could easily have been done later on. The number of observations available from other sources is not known, but Halley certainly had enough point values for the construction of an isogonic map of a large oceanic area.

Before the assembled Fellows, Halley also related his encounter with the icebergs and reiterated his belief that they were fixed;[1] he stated that he failed to get a sounding (which, in fact, might argue against this notion). On 27 November, Halley reported on new barometers and thermometers and on 30 November was re-elected a Fellow of the Society.[2]

Early in the new year, 5 February 1701, Halley showed the Society a map on which his route in the Atlantic had been plotted, with magnetic variations indicated, as well as improved locations of many geographical features delineated. It is impossible to tell from the evidence whether this was a manuscript or an engraved map but since he did not present the copy to the Society it is quite likely that it was a finished draft, soon to be engraved. He reported on the long-necked creatures he had seen off the southeastern coast of South America and called them 'a kind of Tortoises'.[3] Presumably these are the same as pictured and described in the Atlantic Chart as being 'of a Middle Species between a Bird and a Fish, having necks like Swans and swimming with their whole Bodyes always under water'.[4] Their identification remains a matter of conjecture.[5]

Publication of the highly original isogonic chart of the Atlantic Ocean is a fitting end to Halley's two great ocean journeys. The Second Voyage was such an eminently satisfactory venture that it must have fulfilled every expectation of its promoters. In addition Halley had brought back a crew presumably of good morale and a ship in excellent condition.

[1] Document 94, p. 315.

[2] Documents 95, p. 316; 96, p. 316.

[3] Document 97, pp. 316–7.

[4] See Atlantic Chart in portfolio.

[5] Document 97, pp. 316–7, the Atlantic Chart, and the Journal of the Second Voyage, p. 160, and n. 1 should be consulted on this matter.

THE THIRD VOYAGE

Halley was not yet ready to give up his command, for he had further scientific voyaging in mind. On 23 April 1701 he wrote to Burchett requesting that he be provided with a small vessel so that he could examine the tides of the English Channel.[1] Halley wished to conduct his experiments in the coming summer, so, if the project were to be undertaken then, a quick response to his request was necessary. No time was lost, and on 26 April the following official actions were taken: a letter was written from the Admiralty Office to the Navy Board approving the project;[2] Halley's commission was issued;[3] rigging was begun on the *Paramore*, which was to be provided with special equipment requested by Halley – two small boats, two extra cables and an extra anchor;[4] and guns for the ship were ordered from the Tower of London.[5] Halley could hardly have expected a more expeditious response to his requests; for example, his commission was dated the same day as asked for, perhaps anticipating Halley's letter on this subject.[6] At all events it appears that the Lords of the Admiralty were ready and willing to support Halley in his endeavours, indicating that any misgivings that they might have had after the First Voyage were now dispelled by his excellent performance on the Second.

Although rigging began 26 April and the *Paramore* was in good condition, it was some weeks before she could begin sea duty. The problem was that Halley had greater difficulty assembling a crew for Channel duty than he had for his more extended voyages.[7] Part of the reason was that the wages paid by the Navy were not competitive with those which could be obtained in the merchant service, which does not appear to have been such a great problem for the earlier voyages. Halley first complained about the difficulty of recruiting in a letter to Burchett dated 29 April.[8] He noted that, although the ship was ready to sail, men were not volunteering to serve aboard her. On 30 April only Halley and the boatswain, Richard Price, had been entered in the Wages Book, and during the month of May less than half of the complement allowed for

[1] Document 98, p. 317
[2] Document 100, pp. 318–9.
[3] Document 102, p. 319.
[4] Documents 99, p. 318; 103, p.320
[5] Document 101, p. 319.
[6] Document 99, p. 318.
[7] Document 129, pp. 336–7.
[8] Document 104, p. 320.

this voyage was entered.[1] On 31 May Halley wrote again to Burchett asking assistance in obtaining men, even if it required taking them out of warships.[2] He promised to return the men should war break out and his project thus be terminated. This letter brought action from the Admiralty Office, but although Halley was allowed three impressed men the problem was by no means fully solved. Again on 4 June Halley wrote to Burchett about personnel, asking that he be allowed any men willing to serve him from warships.[3]

In early May while Halley was waiting for his crew to be assembled, he received a reward which can be taken as an indication of royal approval. A letter dated 6 May from the Lords of the Admiralty to the Navy Board indicated that King William ordered Halley to be paid two hundred pounds, 'in consideration of his great Paines and care in the late Voyage he made for the discovering the Variation of the Needle.'[4]

He also continued to attend the Royal Society meetings. On 7 May Halley demonstrated the manner in which he measured variation at sea, using two compasses for a comparison of results.[5] A week later he was again at the Royal Society making observations on the dip of the magnetic needle.[6] On 4 June he presented the Royal Society with a map based on observations collected on his earlier voyages.[7] Presumably this was a printed copy of the newly engraved Atlantic Chart which, a week later, he displayed and explained at a meeting of the Royal Society.[8]

On 9 June Halley received from Burchett authorization to hire a pilot when such was required for the Channel survey.[9] Although only fifteen names had been entered in the Wages Book before 12 June, on this date Orders and Instructions for the Third Voyage were issued.[10] As before, these were basically of Halley's composition and in them he was charged particularly to observe the course of the tides, high and low water, the set and strength of the flood and tides, including especially irregular and half tides. He was also to survey the French and English coasts and engage in other work to improve navigation in the Channel for the benefit of sailors of all nations. Reporting and publication of appropriate data were called for at the conclusion of the voyage, when Halley was to return the *Paramore* to the Thames.

Sea duty began on 14 June although Halley was still short of the full

[1] Document 129, p. 336.
[2] Document 110, p. 323.
[3] Document 115, pp. 325–6.
[4] Documents 105, p. 321; 107, p. 322.
[5] Document 106, p. 321.
[6] Document 109, p. 322.
[7] Document 114, p. 325
[8] Document 118, p. 328.
[9] Document 116, p. 326.
[10] Document 119, pp. 328–9.

complement allowed for the voyage, but he seems to have been promised more men on the way.[1] On 16 June he anchored at the Downs; here he procured four more men from Rear Admiral John Munden (Mundon) to bring the total up to twenty-three after they entered, 19 June.[2] Only later when a pilot was taken on was the full complement of twenty-four (according to the Wages Book) aboard, and at no time were the twenty-five men (permitted by the Lords letter of 26 April) on the ship.[3] When the *Paramore* weighed anchor off the Downs on 19 June, only Halley and Richard Pinfold, who had been captain's servant on both the First and Second Voyages, had entered for all three of these scientific expeditions.[4] The regular complement for the Third Voyage was as follows: Edmond Halley, commander; William Erles, surgeon; Job Fake, midshipman; Richard Davis, mate; Richard Price, boatswain; Richard Cole, carpenter; five able seamen, Samuel Pitts, Richard Stephens, Peter Drane, Alexander Jones, and John Onyon; two ordinary seamen, William Tayler and John Rawlins; Mark Taylor, boatswain's mate; Henry Bayly, carpenter's mate; John Bradbury, quartermaster; Richard Pinfold, captain's clerk; Thomas Cook, cook; James Calverly and John Davis, commander's (i.e. captain's) servants; Moses Cathness, surgeon's servant; William Wright, carpenter's servant and Charles Lucas, boatswain's servant. The position of cook was a new appointment not appearing on the previous lists for the *Paramore*. Richard Pinfold was promoted from captain's servant to captain's clerk and, as before, the only appointment specifically requested by Halley was that of surgeon, in this case William Erles.[5]

Although Halley's Third Voyage in the *Paramore* lacked the adventurous qualities of the First and especially the Second Voyage, it was to produce results of great practical utility to the navigators of the Channel. The objectives of the voyage were outlined by the Vice President of the Royal Society, Sir John Hoskins, for the benefit of the Fellows a few days after Halley had left on the voyage.[6] At this meeting, Sir Robert

[1] Document 129, pp. 336–7.

[2] John Munden had been promoted Rear Admiral, 14 April 1701, after a distinguished naval career of some twenty-five years. He was knighted on 30 June 1701 and the next year (28 January 1702) was appointed Rear Admiral of the Red. Later in 1702 he was court-martialled for allowing a squadron of French ships to slip past him in the Bay of Biscay, but although he was acquitted (13 July 1702) he was 'discharged from his post and command in the Royal Navy.' He died on 13 March 1719.

[3] Documents 100, p. 318; 129, p. 336.

[4] Documents 61, p. 290; 91, p. 312; 129, p. 336.

[5] Document 108, p. 322.

[6] Document 121, p. 330; Sir John Hoskins, Baronet, was serving as Vice President having previously been Joint Secretary, and President. He was a lawyer and Master in Chancery who had taken a great interest in Halley's career and put up a bond for £600 for the First Voyage.

Southwell, original Fellow and former President of the Royal Society, appears to have advocated a practical approach to Channel navigation in his response to the Vice President's statements.[1]

The details of the Third Voyage can best be read in the journal. Halley noted that on 2 July he saw Sir Clowdisley Shovell's flagship at Spithead. A few days later he was on the French side of the Channel where he obtained a pilot, Peter St Croix, from the Deputy Governor of Jersey.[2] In a letter to Burchett, Halley summarized his accomplishments in the forty days intervening between his departure from the Downs and his return to Spithead, 29 July.[3] He had anchored all over the eastern part of the Channel and felt that, although the tidal situation was complicated, he was now in a position to describe it. Poor weather had driven him into port where he heard rumours of wars. He hoped that neither this contingency nor bad weather would prevent him from completing his survey before the end of the summer.

Halley was soon back at sea again, this time to survey the western part of the Channel. On 6 August, he landed at the then new Eddystone Lighthouse[4] and later, off Torbay, met the fleet of Admiral Sir George Rooke, which had taken refuge from bad weather.[5] For the same reason, the *Paramore* put into Dartmouth, where Halley made interesting observations on shifts in wind direction. Here Halley wrote a letter to Burchett in which he pointed out the difficulties of his work occasioned by the poor weather he had encountered and the small numbers of men he

[1] Document 121, p. 330. Sir Robert Southwell, President of the Royal Society (1 December 1690 to 30 November 1695), had been envoy extraordinary to Portugal and, while serving as P.R.S., Secretary of State for Ireland.

[2] Document 133, p. 341. Peter St Croix was to be aboard for fifty-eight days, until 7 September.

[3] Document 122, p. 331.

[4] The Eddystone Lighthouse which Halley saw was a stone structure with a wooden lantern, the so-called Winstanley Tower, named after Henry Winstanley, who began to build in 1695 and completed it in 1698. In the following year it was strengthened, and heightened to 120 feet above the rock. The first building was destroyed in a great storm 26 November 1703 and the lighthouse has been replaced several times since that date.

[5] Admiral of the Fleet Sir George Rooke (1650–1709), was one of the most famous British sailors of this period. At the time Halley encountered his fleet, Rooke had recently returned from Sweden where he was commander-in-chief of a powerful force of English and Dutch ships sent to support Charles XII against the Danes. Rooke had had a distinguished career of over thirty years and, as a captain, had raised the siege of Londonderry (1688). He was knighted in 1693 for his part as Vice Admiral (under Russell) at Barfleur and La Hague or Hogue (1692), where he greatly distinguished himself. In 1691 Rooke had been appointed as Extra Commissioner of the Navy, Admiral of the White in 1695, and Admiral of the Fleet, 1696. With Admiral Sir Clowdisley Shovell, Rooke took part in the capture of Gibraltar in the summer of 1704.

had to handle the anchors.[1] However, the survey soon continued on both sides of the coast and by early September, Halley was back at the Channel Islands. At St Hilary (St Hilier), Jersey, the *Paramore* was cleaned; before she left 8 September, the Jersey pilot, Peter St Croix, was discharged. Spithead was reached again 11 September, and Halley applied to Commissioner Henry Greenhill for provisions for one month.

On 13 September, Halley wrote to Burchett summarizing his expedition from the time of the last letter.[2] He was confident that the Lords of the Admiralty would be satisfied with his survey of the coasts and his observations on tidal phenomena in the Channel of which, he believed, he had discovered some general principles. With a month's provision now aboard he hoped to return to the Thames before the winter set in to report personally on his accomplishments. He continued his survey of the approaches to Portsmouth, including profile sketches of part of the Isle of Wight.[3] At the suggestion of Commissioner Greenhill, Halley sounded part of Southampton Water, which delayed his getting into the Channel until 27 September.

Having completed his survey he now made his way quickly toward Long Reach where, 2 October, he anchored and wrote again to Burchett.[4] In his letter Halley asked permission to come to London to report on the work he had been engaged on during the summer. The *Paramore* was ordered to be laid up and the guns taken off; the crew were discharged 16 October, when the journal also ends.[5]

Halley received only a token salary at payoff; he was reimbursed later. The total paid in wages over a period of a little more than four years was slightly over one thousand pounds to three crews involving, altogether, for shorter or greater periods of time, some one hundred persons. This does not include the gratuities which Halley received and which are noted separately.

[1] Document 124, pp. 332–3.

[2] Document 125, p. 333.

[3] Journal of the Third Voyage, p. 246.

[4] Document 126, p. 334.

[5] Documents 127, pp. 334–5; 128, p. 335. The *Paramore* was laid up following Halley's Third Voyage. Then she was refitted, more heavily armed and used as a bomb ketch in Sir George Rooke's squadron in 1702 in the war against France. Unton Deering was Captain, 6 March to 13 October 1702, and from 16 October Captain Josiah Mighells was her commander. The next year under Captain Robert Stevens she went to the Mediterranean; Stevens was captain of the *Paramour* from 29 March to 24 October 1703, after which she was used by the Muster Master of the fleet for a few years. In 1706 the Master Shipwright at Deptford reported that she was in need of repair and the Navy Board could see no further use for the vessel. Accordingly, the *Paramore* was ordered to be sold by inch of candle and was bought by Captain John Constable for £122 on 22 August 1706.

Halley now resumed his civilian life, but official or unofficial exchanges having to do with the voyages took place in the ensuing months. For example, on 27 January 1702, Halley wrote a long and informative letter to Sir Robert Southwell, on his method of surveying coasts by triangulation.[1] On February 17, Halley wrote to Burchett asking for permission to speak with him, presumably on matters having to do with the financing of the voyages.[2] The next day, he presented an account of the amount expended from the £100 imprest money he had received.[3] He had spent £47.18.10., leaving a rather greater amount unused, and he asked that he might be allowed to keep the balance. The matter of the payment of Halley's wages was raised on 20 February in a letter from the Lord High Admiral to the Navy Board.[4] A series of letters on the general subject of payments followed during the next two months. King William III died 8 March 1702 and was succeeded by his sister-in-law, Queen Anne, who ordered the last official action concerning Halley's voyages. A letter dated 20 April 1702, states: 'It being her Mats Royl Will and pleasure that the Summ of two hundred pounds shall be payd to Captain Edmd Halley (over and above his Pay as Captain of her Pink the Paramour) as a reward to him for his Extraordinary pains and care he lately tooke, in observing and setting down the Ebbing and Flowing, and setting of the Tydes in the Channell as also and bearing of the heads-lands on the Coasts of England and France.'[5] With this royal and official approbation Halley returned to his more sedentary pursuits.

CARTOGRAPHIC RESULTS OF HALLEY'S VOYAGES

The tangible results of Halley's voyages are three journals and a number of published maps. With the present volume, the journal of Halley's Third Voyage is published for the first time.[6] Versions of the journals of the

[1] Document 131, pp. 338–40, and n. 1, p. 338.

[2] Document 132, p. 340.

[3] Document 133, pp. 341–2.

[4] Document 134, p. 342.

[5] Document 139, p. 345.

[6] Halley was named in a proposal for publishing a collection of voyages in four volumes, in 1702. This was to include translations of voyages by foreigners, as well as those of the English. It was to contain 240 maps and give an account of the advances in navigation from the first use of the magnetical needle, and directions for future travellers. Halley was to provide an annotated list of books, the preface was apparently to be written by John Locke, and A. and J. Churchill of Paternoster Row were to be the publishers (E. Arber, ed., *The term catalogues*, 3 (June 1701, p. 265). Awnshaw and John Churchill did publish, beginning in

First and Second Voyages were first published some thirty years after Halley's death by Dalrymple.[1] The more immediate influence of Halley's voyages relates to the cartographic record. Apart from a profile sketch and a sketch map of the Island of Fernando Loronho (Fernando de Noronha) in the manuscript of Halley's First Voyage, which were not reproduced in Dalrymple's publication, there is no direct cartographic evidence of this expedition. It is hard to say how much of the data gathered in the First Voyage could have been used for his Atlantic Chart, because many of the areas observed in that enterprise were visited again on the Second Voyage and better data were obtained.[2] However, presumably the Atlantic Chart, which was published soon after the Second Voyage, relies on observations made on both of Halley's expeditions, and on those of other seamen.[3] The Atlantic map is titled, A New and Correct Chart *Shewing the* Variations *of the Compass* in the Western & Southern Oceans *as observed in ye* year 1700 *by his Maties Command* by Edm. Halley (Figure 7 and the Atlantic Chart in portfolio). The date usually ascribed to the map is 1701;[4] it was published after Halley's return from the Second Voyage on 18 September 1700, and presumably before 8 March 1702, since it is dedicated to King William III who died on this date.[5] From references in the Journal Book of the Royal Society it is

1704, four volumes of voyages which went through several editions, with additional volumes. Professor Quinn has written: 'This was first advertised as being by Edmond Halley though afterwards it was "supposed to be written by the celebrated Mr Locke." The attribution to Locke is false; that to Halley very doubtful, and the author was probably a Churchillian hack.' David B. Quinn, *The Hakluyt handbook*, Hakluyt Society (Cambridge, 1974), p. 141.

[1] Dalrymple, 1773 and 1775.

[2] Perhaps Halley's statement in his 'Description' to accompany the Atlantic Chart (Appendix D, p. 365) that the '*Curve-Lines* . . . are design'd according to what I my self found in the *Western* and *Southern* Oceans, in a Voyage I purposely made at the Publick Charge in the Year of our Lord 1700', suggests that the idea of the isogonic lines came to him on the Second Voyage and not on the First. He says nothing about the 1698–9 venture in the 'Description' or in the title of the map.

[3] We know that Halley consulted the writings of earlier voyagers. For example, he noted that the unpublished journal of Captain John Strong, who visited the Falkland Islands in 1690 was 'very well kept' (H. M. Wallis, 'English enterprise in the region of the Strait of Magellan,' in J. Parker (ed.), *Merchants and scholars* (Minneapolis, 1965), p. 212).

[4] Because of Halley's statements to the effect that his Atlantic Chart was based on observations made in 1700 – both on the map itself and in the 'Description' to accompany this work (Appendix D, p. 365) – it might be natural to assume that the map was published in that year, but this is almost certainly not the case.

[5] To complicate this chronology, in the Map Room of the Royal Geographical Society there is a proof copy which lacks the dedication and which is used for the facsimile in the portfolio of this volume because it is a very early pull from the plate and superior to any other copy seen by the present writer. Compare this with Figure 7, which is a small reproduction of the map with the dedication, and consult Appendix E, pp. 368–9.

THE

Description

AND

USES

Of a New and Correct

SEA-CHART

Of the Western and Southern

OCEAN,

Shewing the Variations of the *COMPASS.*

THE Projection of this *Chart* is what is commonly called *Mercator's*; but from its particular Use in *Navigation*, ought rather to be named the *Nautical*; as being the only true and sufficient *CHART* for the *Sea*. It is supposed, that all such as take Charge of Ships in long Voyages, are so far acquainted with its Use, as not to need any Directions here. I shall only take the Liberty to assure the Reader, that having taken all possible Care, as well from Astronomical Observations, as Journals, to ascertain the Scituation and Form of this *Chart*, as to its principal Parts, and the Dimensions of the several Oceans; he is not to expect that we should descend to all the Particularities necessary for the Coaster, our Scale not permitting it. What is here properly New, is the *Curve-Lines* drawn over the several Seas, to shew the Degrees of the *Variation* of the *Magnetical Needle*, or *Sea Compass*: which are design'd according to what I my self found in the *Western* and *Southern* Oceans, in a Voyage I purposely made at the Publick Charge in the Year of our Lord 1700.

That this may be the better understood, the curious Mariner is desired to observe, that in this *Chart* the Double Line passing near *Bermudas*, the Cape *Verde Isles*, and Saint *Helena* every where divides the *East* and *West Variation* in this *Ocean*, and that on the whole Coast of *Europe* and *Africa* the *Variation* is Westerly, as on the more Northerly Coasts of *America*, but on the more Southerly Parts of *America* 'tis Easterly. The Degrees of *Variation*, or how much the Compass declines from the true North on either Side is reckoned by the Number of the Lines on each side the double Curve, which I call the *Line* of *No Variation*; on each fifth and tenth is distinguished in its Stroak, and numbered accordingly, so that in what Place soever your Ship is, you find the *Variation* by Inspection.

That this may be the fuller understood, take these Examples. At *Madera* the *Variation* is 3 and ½d. West; at *Barbadoes* 5½d. East; at *Annabon* 7d. West; at Cape *Race* in *Newfoundland* 14d. West; at the Mouth of *Ric de Plata* 18d. East, &c. And this may suffice by way of Description.

As to the Uses of this *Chart*, they will easily be understood, especially by such as are acquainted with the Azimuth Compass, to be, to correct the Course of Ships at Sea: For if the Variation of the Compass be not allowed, all Reckonings must be so far erroneous: And in continued Cloudy Weather, or where the Mariner is not provided to observe this Variation duly, the *Chart* will readily shew him what Allowances

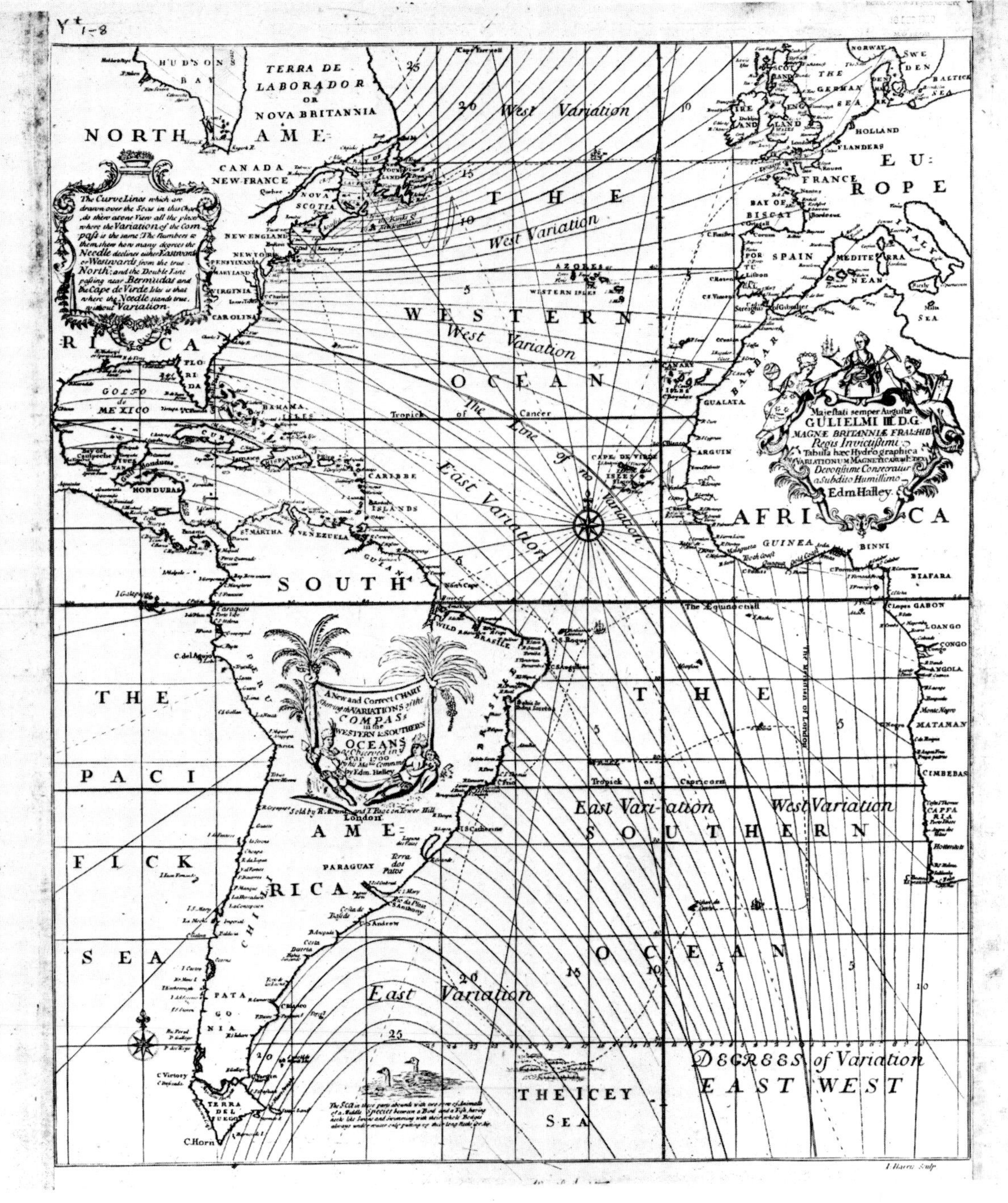

he must make for this Default of his Compass, and thereby rectify his Journal.

But this Correction of the Course is in no case so necessary as in running down on a Parallel *East* or *West* to hit a *Port*: For if being in your Latitude at the Distance of 70 or 80 Leagues, you allow not the Variation, but steer East or West by Compass, you shall fall to the Northwards or Southwards of your Port on each 19 Leagues of Distance, one Mile for each Degree of Variation, which may produce very dangerous Errors, where the Variation is considerable; for Instance, having a good Observation in Latitude 49d. 40m. about 80 Leag. without *Scilly*, and not considering that there is 8 Degrees West Variation, I steer away *East* by Compass for the Channel; but making my way truly *E.* 8d. *N.* when I come up with *Scilly*, instead of being 3 or 4 Leagues to the South thereof, I shall find my self as much to the Northward: And this Evil will be more or less according to the Distance you sail in the Parallel. The Rule to apply it is, That to keep your Parallel truly, you go so many Degrees to the Southward of the *East*, and Northward of the *West*, as in the *West Variation*; but contrariwise, so many Degrees to the Northwards of the *East*, and Southwards of the *West*, as there is East *Variation*.

A further Use is in many Cases to estimate the Longitude at Sea thereby; for where the *Curves* run nearly *North* and *South*, and are thick together, as about Cape *Bona Esperance*, it gives a very good Indication of the Distance of the Land to Ships come from far; for there the Variation alters a Degree to each two Degrees of Longitude nearly; as may be seen in the *Chart*. But in this Western *Ocean*, between *Europe* and the *North America*, the Curves lying nearly East and West, cannot be Serviceable for this Purpose.

This Chart, as I said, was made by Observation of the Year 1700, but it must be noted, that there is a perpetual tho' slow Change in the *Variation* almost every where, which will make it necessary in time to alter the whole System: at present it may suffice to advertise that about *C. Bona Esperance*, the West Variation encreases at the Rate of about a Degree in 9 Years. In our Channel it encreases a Degree in seven Years, but slower the nearer the Equinoctial Line; as on the *Guinea* Coast a Degree in 11 or 12 Years. On the *American side* the *West Variation* alters but little; and the *East Variation* on the *Southern America* decreases, the more Southerly the faster; the *Line of No Variation* moving gradually towards it.

I shall need to say no more about it, but let it commend it self, and all knowing Mariners are desired to lend their Assistance and Informations, towards the perfecting of this useful Work. And if by undoubted Observations it be found in any Part defective, the Notes of it will be received with all grateful Acknowledgement, and the Chart corrected accordingly.

E. HALLEY.

This CHART is to be sold by *William Mount*, and *Thomas Page* on *Tower-Hill*.

Figure 7. Halley's Atlantic Chart, 1701, showing magnetic variation and with the (later) description pasted on the sides. See portfolio for a facsimile of an earlier print of this map.

Reproduced by permission of the Royal Geographical Society, London

possible to make more precise inferences about the date. Since Halley presented a copy to the Royal Society on 4 June 1701, it is likely that it was published shortly before this time.[1] Soon after his return from the Atlantic, 30 October 1700, he had shown the assembled Fellows what appears to be a manuscript of the Atlantic Chart; on 5 February 1701 there is another reference to a map which fits the description of the Atlantic Chart.[2] It is impossible to say whether this was the engraved map or another manuscript version; but if it had been published, it is likely that Halley would have presented a copy on this occasion, unless it was the engraved copy which still lacked the dedication (see copy in portfolio). From this we might infer that the Atlantic Chart was published between 5 February and 4 June 1701, possibly closer to the latter date.

Halley's Atlantic Chart is presumably the first published isogonic (magnetic declination) chart and, apparently, the earliest printed isoline map.[3] We know from the writings of Athanasius Kircher that a (manuscript) isogonic chart of a limited area was drawn in 1630 by a Jesuit Father of Milan, Christoforo Borri, based on his own observations and on those of others.[4] Apparently Borri, in the expectation that the isogones would be useful for navigation, represented them as parallel lines. Kircher was aware that such a simplification was incorrect and seems to have worked on isogonic maps himself which were never completed, although he hoped to include such with his great study on magnetism. Halley did indeed refer to Kircher in his writings[5] but gave no indication that he

[1] Document 114, p. 325. The Royal Society no longer possesses a copy of this map.

[2] Documents 94, p. 315; 97, p. 316.

[3] An isoline map or chart is one in which a series of lines connects points of equal value. By this definition a map of coastlines would not be an isoline chart, although one which shows high- and low-tide lines could be so classified. In fact, the first known isoline map is a very simple manuscript chart with lines passing through points having equal depth of water (isobaths) drawn in 1584 by Peter Bruinss. Another manuscript map of this type appeared in 1697 by Pierre Ancelin. Commenting upon this, the late Dr R. A. Skelton wrote to the present writer, 'It is hard to believe that no cartographer between these two dates thought of joining up points of equal depth but these are the only ones to come to light' (16 August 1968). It is not likely that Halley would have known of these two specific maps (both are of limited areas of rivers in the Low Countries), or of the isoline concept applied to depth values generally. The terms isarithm and isometric line are synonymous, meaning a line representing a constant value obtained from measurement at a series of points, while an isopleth is a line connecting points assumed to have equal value; isagram and isoline are more general terms embracing both of the above concepts. Like other elegant ideas, once developed, the isoline concept now seems simple enough but centuries of map-making passed before it was conceived.

[4] A. Kircher, *Magnes: sive de arte magnetica opus tripartitum*, 2nd ed. (Cologne, 1643).

[5] *Philosophical Transactions*, 13 (1683), p. 215. Halley argues against Kircher's hypothesis of 'Magnetical Fibres' for explaining Earth magnetism.

derived the idea of isogonic lines from him or from any other source. Halley, in the 'Description' which he prepared later to accompany the Atlantic Chart, claimed that the technique was new and of his own invention. He states, 'What is here properly New, is the *Curve-Lines* drawn over the several Seas, to shew the Degrees of the *Variation* of the *Magnetical Needle*, or *Sea Compass*: which are design'd according to what I my self found in the *Western* and *Southern* Oceans, in a Voyage I purposely made at the Publick Charge in the Year of our Lord 1700' (Appendix D, p. 365). Halley's claim can be accepted. The isogones, rather than any other characteristic, set Halley's cartographic work apart from all earlier extant charts and make it one of the most important maps in the history of cartography.[1] Halley called the isogones 'curve lines' but for many years they were known as Halleyan or Halleian lines, until they took their present designation from Hansteen.[2]

Unlike Halley's earlier folded Chart of the Trade Winds, which accompanied his article on this subject in the *Philosophical Transactions* (1686), the Atlantic Chart appeared as a large separate flat sheet map published by Richard Mount and Thomas Page, Tower Hill, London. The engraving was the work of John Harris. Originally there was no accompanying explanatory text, but evidently it was later felt that to make the map more useful to navigators a 'Description' was desirable, which Halley prepared. This was printed separately in two sheets to be pasted on to the sides of the map (Appendix D, p. 365–7). The map employs the Mercator (or, as Halley preferred to call it, the Nautical) Projection. Two of the several states of the map are reproduced in this

[1] It is remarkable how little notice has been taken of Halley's Atlantic Chart, or indeed any of his considerable cartographic achievements, in the general literature of the history of cartography. In the periodical literature there are a number of articles on different aspects of Halley's work, some of which deal with his mapping endeavours. The Atlantic Chart was lost to cartobibliographers for a very long period until it was re-discovered by the American geophysicist, L. A. Bauer, who published a small reproduction of it in his article 'Halley's earliest equal variation chart', *Terrestrial Magnetism*, Baltimore, 1 (1896), 28–31 (Bauer founded this periodical, now the *Journal of Geophysics*). In addition to articles by Chapman (1941) and by Thrower (1969) involving Halley's isogonic maps, three small pieces on these maps have appeared in the *Geographical Journal* as follows: E. A. Reeves, 'Halley's magnetic variation charts,' 51 (1918), 237–40; A. R. Hinks, 'Edmond Halley as physical geographer' (Review article of Chapman's larger study), 98 (1941), 293–6; and R. A. Gardiner, 'Edmond Halley's isogonic charts,' 137 (1971), 419–20. See also N. J. W. Thrower, *Maps and man: an examination of cartography in relation to culture and civilization* (Englewood Cliffs, New Jersey, 1972), pp. 62–71 and 164–5. In general, scientists, especially great scientists such as Humboldt, Hansteen and Airy, rather than historians of cartography (or science) have shown the greatest appreciation of Halley's cartographic work.

[2] Christopher Hansteen (1784–1873), Norwegian astronomer, who wrote widely on Earth magnetism and coined the term 'isogone' *c.* 1820.

volume: the large map folded in a portfolio accompanying this work is a facsimile of what must have been one of the first pulls from the plate. It is probably a proof, for it lacks the dedication which appears on subsequent states (Figure 7).

In addition to the isogones, the chart contains the track of Halley's Second Voyage (but not of the First) and two compass roses, one near the centre with radiating lines. These rhumb lines which, portolan style, might have been thought of use in navigation, were not of much value for this purpose on a chart of such a large area and were not drawn on the later World Chart. Other features include three decorative cartouches framing verbal information; a ten degree graticule of latitude (60° N to 60° S) and longitude (20° E to 100° W); and the delineation of the coasts of the lands bordering the North Atlantic (The Western Ocean) and the South Atlantic (The Southern Ocean). Among the place names are a number which appear in the journal (see Appendices A, pp. 349–53, and B, pp. 355–61), and a good many which do not. These last include Pepys Island, off the coast of Patagonia at 47° S and 67° E. Halley's Islands of Ice, marking his farthest penetration southward, are shown in The Icey Sea (Antarctic Ocean), and between these features and Tierra del Fuego the unidentified creatures with swan-like necks are pictured and described.[1]

Halley by his detailed delineation of the isogones hoped to help solve the longitude problem. In his journal of the Second Voyage, on 22 November 1699, Halley wrote, 'My Variation observed last night and this Morning was much about 3°. Easterly whence I cannot be farr from the Coast of Brasile.' Furthermore, in his 'Description' of the Atlantic Chart he suggests that this map can be used for an estimation of longitude where the isogones are closely and evenly spaced and oriented in a north-south direction as off the coast of the Cape of Good Hope, but not if they are irregularly and widely spaced and run in an east-west direction as in the North Atlantic at that time. The agonic line which he called 'the line of no variation' is clearly marked on the map as are areas designated as having east or west variation, in one degree increments, with five degree and ten degree levels in different, heavier, lines. Halley was well aware of secular changes in magnetic declination and in the 'Description' gives the

[1] Chapman, 1941, p. 6, suggests that the creatures referred to were reported by travellers and beyond Halley's immediate experience. However, we know from his journal of the Second Voyage, p. 160, and also from his report to the Royal Society (Document 97, pp. 316–7) that Halley had seen such creatures himself. Ronan, 1969, p. 179, discusses this puzzling matter at some length.

approximate rate of increase or decrease at various places; he noted that the entire work would have to be revised from time to time.[1]

Interestingly, it was not Halley's first isogonic chart but a work largely derived from it which became influential and was widely used at sea. This was his 'A New and Correct *Sea Chart* of the Whole World *Shewing the* Variations of the *Compass as they were found* in the year *M.D.C.C.*,' dedicated to Prince George of Denmark, Lord High Admiral of England (Figure 8 and Appendix E).[2] The World Chart appeared in several states, editions (including foreign ones), and revisions until the end of the eighteenth century. In his World Chart Halley extended the isogones to areas he had not visited but for which he had good information, particularly the Indian Ocean.[3] The eastern part of the agonic line runs through east Asia and central Australia; the seventy degrees of longitude embracing these areas is repeated on some versions. However, he had no reliable data on the Pacific and thus the isogones were interrupted across this ocean. Halley noted on the map, 'I durst not presume to describe the like Curves in the South Sea wanting accounts thereof.'

Although the representation of the Atlantic Ocean was basically the same as on the earlier map, even this part of the World Chart was altered. The wind roses, rhumb lines, as well as the unidentified sea creatures and their description and Halley's Islands of Ice were all omitted. A significant addition was the delineation of the Falkland Islands. Because of their portrayal on Halley's influential map, with the name which Captain John Strong gave to the sound which separates them (in 1690), they became established as the Falkland Islands.[4] From Strong's journal Halley had taken data which showed Cape Horn to be 10° too far to the west.

Among other interesting features were the then recently discovered 'Dampeirs Streights' (Dampier's Passage) between New Guinea and New Britain explored by William Dampier in the *Roebuck* in late 1699 and early 1700. California is represented as an island, as it appeared on maps

[1] The World Chart was revised later as indicated in Appendix E.

[2] Prince George of Denmark was the consort of Queen Anne from 1683 until his death in 1708. On 17 April 1702 he became Generalissimo of all Her Majestie's Forces and on 21 May, Lord High Admiral of England. Thus the World Chart cannot have been published before that date, but probably later in the same year. Like the Atlantic Chart the World Chart became difficult to find, as Chapman, 1941, p. 11, reported.

[3] In his 'Description' to accompany the World Chart Halley referred to his own observations in the Atlantic in 1700, and that he had adapted for the same year data of '. . . several Journals of Voyages lately made in the *India-Seas*'.

[4] Wallis, 1965, p. 213, from British Library Sloane MS. 3295, f. 24.

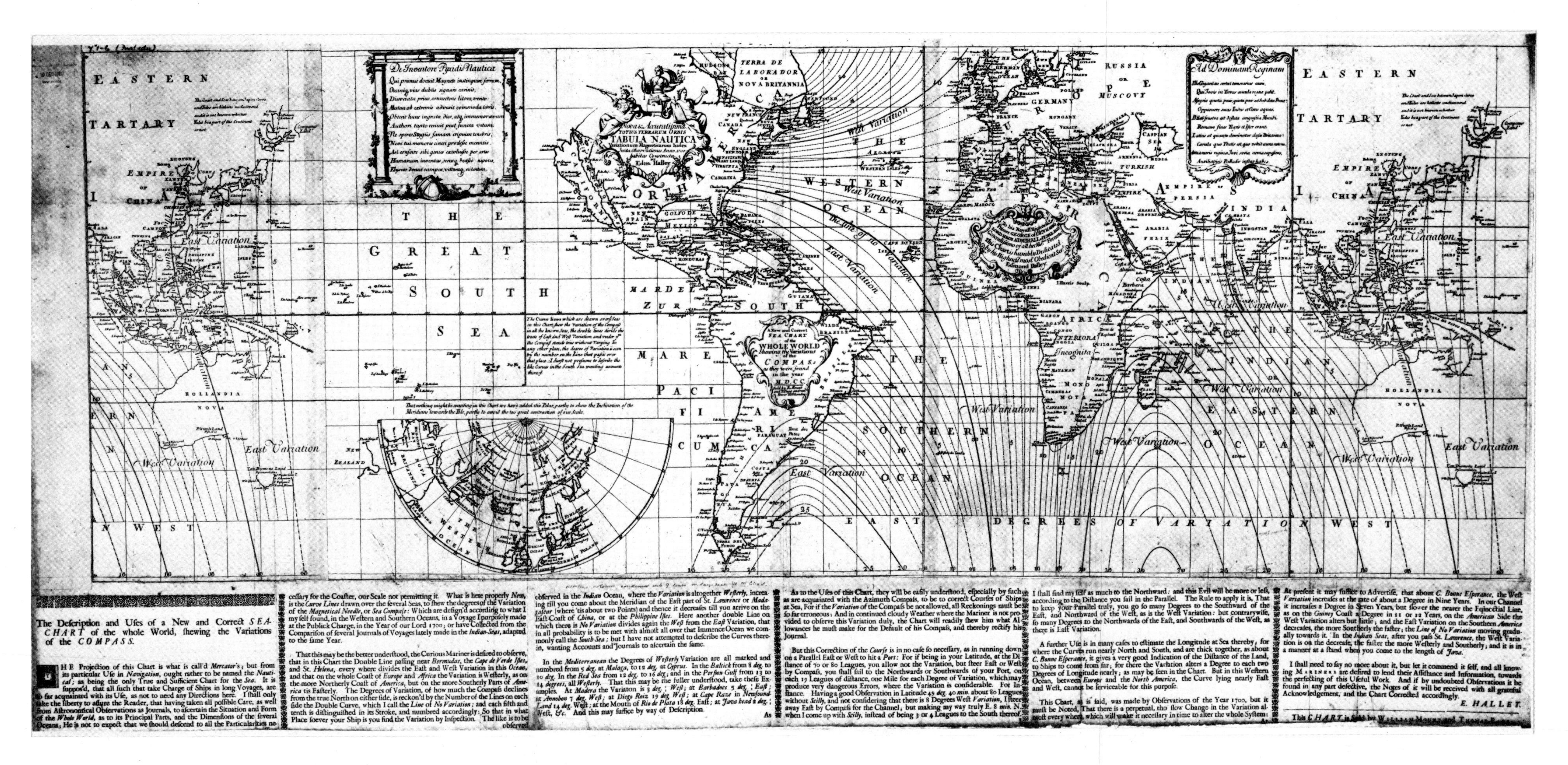

The Description and Uses of a New and Correct *SEA-CHART* of the whole World, shewing the Variations of the *COMPASS*.

THE Projection of this Chart is what is call'd *Mercator*'s; but from its particular Use in *Navigation*, ought rather to be named the *Nautical*; as being the only True and Sufficient Chart for the *Sea*. It is suppos'd, that all such that take Charge of Ships in long Voyages, are so far acquainted with its Use, as not to need any Directions here. I shall only take the liberty to assure the Reader, that having taken all possible Care, as well from Astronomical Observations as Journals, to ascertain the Situation and Form of the *Whole World*, as to its Principal Parts, and the Dimensions of the several Oceans, He is not to expect that we should descend to all the Particularities necessary for the Coaster, our Scale not permitting it. What is here properly *New*, is the *Curve Lines* drawn over the several Seas, to shew the degrees of the Variation of the *Magnetical Needle*, or *Sea Compass*: Which are design'd according to what I my self found, in the Western and Southern Oceans, in a Voyage I purposely made at the Publick Charge, in the Year of our Lord 1700; or have Collected from the Comparison of several Journals of Voyages lately made in the *Indian-Seas*, adapted to the same Year.

That this may be the better understood, the Curious Mariner is desired to observe, that in this Chart the Double Line passing near *Bermudas*, the *Cape de Verde Isles*, and St. *Helena*, every where divides the East and West Variation in this *Ocean*, and that on the whole Coast of *Europe* and *Africa* the Variation is Westerly, as on the more Northerly Coast of *America*, but on the more Southerly Parts of *America* tis Easterly. The Degrees of Variation, of how much the Compass declines from the true North on either side, is reckon'd by the Number of the Lines on each side the Double Curve, which I call the *Line of No Variation*; and each fifth and tenth is distinguished in its Stroke, and numbred accordingly: So that in what Place soever your Ship is you find the Variation by Inspection. The like is to be observed in the *Indian* Ocean, where the *Variation* is altogether *Westerly*, increasing till you come about the Meridian of the East part of St. *Lawrence* or *Madagascar* (where 'tis about two Points) and thence it decreases till you arrive on the East Coast of *China*, or at the *Philippine Isles*. Here another double Line on which there is *No Variation* divides again the *West* from the *East* Variation, that in all probability is to be met with almost all over that Immence Ocean we commonly call the *South Sea*; but I have not attempted to describe the Curves therein, wanting Accounts and Journals to ascertain the same.

In the *Mediterranean* the Degrees of *Westerly* Variation are all marked and numbred from 5 *deg.* at *Malaga*, to 12 *deg.* at *Cyprus*. In the *Baltick* from 8 *deg.* to 10 *deg.* In the *Red Sea* from 12 *deg.* to 16 *deg.*; and in the *Persian Gulf* from 13 to 14 *degrees*, all *Westerly*. That this may be the fuller understood, take these Examples. At *Madera* the Variaton is 3 *deg.*; *West*; at *Barbadoes* 5 *deg.*; *East*; at *Annobon* 7 *deg.* *West*; at *Diego Roiz* 19 *deg.* *West*; at *Cape Raze* in *Newfoundland* 14 *deg.* West; at the Mouth of *Rio de Plata* 18 *deg.* East; at *Java head* 2 *deg.*; *West*, &c. And this may suffice by way of Description.

As to the Uses of this Chart, they will be easily understood, especially by such as are acquainted with the Azimuth Compass, to be to correct Courses of Ships at Sea, For if the *Variation* of the Compass be not allowed, all Reckonings must be so far erroneous: And in continued cloudy Weather where the Mariner is not provided to observe this Variation duly, the Chart will readily shew him what Allowances he must make for the Default of his Compass, and thereby rectify his Journal.

But this Correction of the *Course* is in no case so necessary, as in running down on a Parallel East or West to hit a *Port*: For if being in your Latitude, at the Distance of 70 or 80 Leagues, you allow not the Variation, but steer East or West by Compass, you shall fail to the Northwards or Southwards of your Port, on each 19 Leagues of distance, one Mile for each Degree of Variation, which may produce very dangerous Errors, where the Variation is considerable. For Instance. Having a good Observation in Latitude 49 *deg.* 40 *min.* about 80 Leagues without *Scilly*, and not considering that there is 8 Degrees West *Variation*, I steer away East by Compass for the Channel; but making my way truly E. 8 *min.* N. when I come up with *Scilly*, instead of being 3 or 4 Leagues to the South thereof, I shall find my self as much to the Northward: and this Evil will be more or less, according to the Distance you sail in the Parallel. The Rule to apply it is, That to keep your Parallel truly, you go so many Degrees to the Southward of the East, and Northward of the West, as is the West Variation: but contrarywise, so many Degrees to the Northwards of the East, and Southwards of the West, as there is East Variation.

A further Use is in many cases to estimate the Longitude at Sea thereby; for where the Curves run nearly North and South, and are thick together, as about *C. Bonne Esperance*, it gives a very good Indication of the Distance of the Land, to Ships to come from far; for there the Variation alters a Degree to each two Degrees of Longitude nearly; as may be seen in the Chart. But in this Western Ocean, between *Europe* and the *North America*, the Curve lying nearly East and West, cannot be serviceable for this purpose.

This Chart, as is said, was made by Observations of the Year 1700, but it must be Noted, That there is a perpetual, tho' slow Change in the Variation almost every where, which will make it necessary in time to alter the whole System: At present it may suffice to Advertise, that about *C. Bonne Esperance*, the West *Variation* increases at the rate of about a Degree in Nine Years. In our Channel it increases a Degree in Seven Years, but slower the nearer the Eqinoctial Line, as on the *Guiney* Coast a Degree in 11 or 12 Years, on the *American* Side the West Variation alters but little; and the East Variation on the Southern *America* decreases, the more Southerly the faster; the *Line of No Variation* moving gradually towards it. In the *Indian Seas*, after you pass St. *Lawrence*, the West Variation is on the decrease, the faster the more Westerly and Southerly; and it is in a manner at a stand when you come to the length of *Java*.

I shall need to say no more about it, but let it commend it self, and all knowing MARINERS are desired to lend their Assistance and Information, towards the perfecting of this Useful Work. And if by undoubted Observations it be found in any part defective, the Notes of it will be received with all grateful Acknowledgement, and the Chart Corrected accordingly.

E. HALLEY.

This *CHART* is Sold by WILLIAM MOUNT and THOMAS PAGE

Figure 8. Halley's World Chart, 1702, showing magnetic variation and with the Description pasted on the bottom.

for about one hundred and fifty years.[1] Understandably, coastal delineations reflect the current knowledge of the world's shores; in areas not visited by Halley he was wholly dependent on others.

As before, the main map employs the Mercator Projection with a ten degree graticule of latitude and longitude. There is an inset of half of the North Polar region an an azimuthal projection and also five decorative cartouches. Two of the cartouches contain the title of the map, one with an English and one with a Latin text. Two contain poems – one lauding the unknown inventor of the magnetic compass, and the other Queen Anne as the patroness of Britain's expanding maritime interests.[2] One contains the dedication to Prince George.

Together the Atlantic and World Charts represent a remarkable cartographic compilation based on observations, many by Halley himself, over an extensive area of the ocean surface. They well merit the praise of Hellmann, who described Halley's magnetic charts as 'a masterpiece of practical navigation, of the utmost value also for theoretical study, and based on a new method of graphical representation which was of the greatest importance to all branches of physical [he could have added 'and cultural'] geography'.[3]

Chapman refers to the availability of Halley's magnetic charts in these terms:[4]

> Gradually the copies of Halley's charts became quite out of date, and most of them were worn out with use, until few remained; of these a small number found their way into great libraries, and perhaps some still lie forgotten and undiscovered in public or private hands. In 1870 Sir George Airy (1801–1892), another famous Astronomer Royal at Greenwich, who shared the geomagnetic interests of his predecessor Halley, remarked that reference was often made to Halley's Magnetic Chart, but that he 'had not ascertained that any writer had ever seen it.' 'As I was desirous' (he wrote) 'of making myself acquainted with a document so important in the history of magnetic science, I made enquiries in nearly every Academy in Europe, but could not find anywhere a copy of this Chart.' This widespread search ended, somewhat strangely, in his finding a copy almost on his own doorstep, namely in the British Museum, London, where he reported 'one copy of the original edition'; he caused photolithographic reproductions of this copy to be made and distributed, one set almost full scale (114 × 48 cm.), and another set on a smaller scale ($66\frac{1}{2} \times 27\frac{3}{4}$). The chart which

[1] R. V. Tooley, *California as an island*, Map Collector's Series, No. 8 (London, 1964), pp. 1–28.

[2] Chapman, 1941, p. 9, printed a translation of these poems by his wife.

[3] G. Hellmann, *Neudrucke von Schriften und Karten über Meteorologie und Erdmagnetismus*, no. 8, Berlin, 1897, p. 10, translated and quoted by Chapman, 1941, p. 5.

[4] Chapman, 1941, p. 11.

he thus republished was the World Chart . . .; Airy apparently never realized the existence of the Atlantic Chart (this was perhaps a remarkable case of 'Eyes and no eyes,' for a framed copy of this chart has hung for many years on the walls of the Royal Astronomical Society, and the unregarding eyes, probably of Airy, and certainly of many other astronomers, have often fallen upon it).

Actually, Halley's magnetic charts were not nearly so rare as Airy and, perhaps, Chapman believed, and a number have come to light in recent years (Appendix E).

The other cartographic contributions of Halley's Atlantic Voyages in the *Paramore* include the before-mentioned profile and sketch map of Fernando Loronho from the First Voyage, published for the first time in the present volume. In the journal of the Second Voyage there are profiles of the Islands of Ice, the Rocks of Martin Vaz, and the Island of Trinidada as well as a sketch map of the last feature. All of these sketches from the Second Voyage were re-drawn and engraved on a single plate in Dalrymple's versions of Halley's journals of his first two voyages in the *Paramore*.[1]

Halley's survey of the English Channel in the *Paramore* also had important cartographic expression. The map produced as the result of the Third Voyage is titled, 'A New and Correct *Chart of the Channel between* England & France *with considerable Improvements not extant in any Draughts hitherto Publish'd; shewing the Sands, shoals, depths of Water and Anchorage, with ye flowing of the Tydes, and Setting of the Current; as observ'd by the Learned* Dr. Halley' (see Figure 9 and the Channel Chart, in portfolio).[2] This undated chart, probably issued in 1702, is in two large sheets, one showing the eastern and one the western part of the Channel. Again the publisher was Mount and Page, but no individual engraver's

[1] Dalrymple, 1773 and 1775. Plate H. Vid: p. 34.

[2] Both MacPike, 1932, and Chapman, 1941, overlooked this important chart (as have others using these sources alone) as pointed out by Hinks, 1941, pp. 295–6, who briefly describes it. A slightly more extended treatment of it is found in J. Proudman, 'Halley's tidal chart,' *Geographical Journal*, 100 (1942), 174–6. MacPike, 1932, failed to enter the Channel Chart in his 'List of Halley's Published Writings, Arranged Chronologically', pp. 272–8, although he did include the Atlantic and World Charts. There is a reference to the Channel Chart in the 'Memoir of Dr. Edmond Halley' reprinted by MacPike, 1932, p. 9. See also D. Howse and M. Sanderson, *The sea chart* (Newton Abbot, 1973), pp. 80–1; Armitage, 1966,pp.148–53 (portion of Channel Chart reproduced opposite p. 149); and Thrower, 1968 and 1969, with illustrations of all and part of the Channel Chart. Halley's earlier coastal surveys were reported in the *Journal Book of the Royal Society* as follows: July 3, 1689, 'Halley produced his Seadraught of the Mouth of the River of Thames, wherein he saith, that he hath corrected severall very great, and considerable faults in all our Sea-Carts hitherto published'; and for November 15, 1693: 'Halley produced his draught of the West Coast of Sussex between Selsey and Arundell with the line form and situation of the dangerous sholes called the Owers' (reprinted in MacPike, 1932, p. 215 and p. 233).

name appears on the map. There seem to be other issues, and it was re-engraved for the 1723 edition of *Great Britain's Coasting Pilot* and used in that work for several decades afterwards.[1]

Some features of the chart employed techniques which were cartographic conventions by Halley's time and which he had used before. Thus there is a very liberal scattering of depth values in fathoms.[2] The map is criss-crossed with rhumb lines emanating from two main centres (one on each sheet) and over a score of subsidiary points; these directional indicators give the map the appearance of a portolan chart.[3] Latitude is expressed with one degree, ten minute, and one minute divisions, with considerable variation among them, on the right margin and left margin of the map considered as a whole. Longitude is not indicated except by some irregularly spaced meridians the values of which are not stated. Analysis of the projection indicates no increase of the spacing of parallels in higher latitudes, but rather the reverse, over the limited area shown. Therefore, Mercator's projection was not used for this chart and in fact it is difficult to discern what projection was intended. The coastlines are well drawn with shoals and other features shown.

In a letter to Sir Robert Southwell, Halley described his method of marine surveying in some detail;[4] he indicated his preference for taking angles by the Sun rather than the compass and explained his resection method of coastal survey which can be accomplished on a ship under sail. On the tidal charts two insets are included, one of Plymouth, with some written instructions to navigators, and one of the Isle of Wight and adjacent parts of the English coast. There is a graphical scale with twenty divisions of English and French leagues for the general chart; the representative fraction is about 1:1,150,000.

The main theme of the map which sets it apart from all previous charts is the indication of the tides. Halley explained his symbolism in these terms on the map itself:[5]

[1] A. H. W. Robinson, *Marine cartography in Britain* (Leicester, 1962), pp. 42–3, n. 53. This chart appeared with or without attribution in various pilot books from 1703 until the end of the eighteenth century.

[2] Interestingly, Halley did not use isobaths, which might have been expected in the light of n. 3 p. 57 above. The first known published isobathic chart was that of Nicholas Samuel Cruquires (Cruquius) of the Merwede River, dated 1729; and for the whole of the Channel the earliest was that of Philippe Buache, 1737.

[3] See Waters, 1958, pp. 62–4 and plates XXI–XXIII, on this subject.

[4] Document 131, pp. 338–40. This letter, written at the behest of the addressee a few months after Halley's return from the Channel voyage, throws much light on his method of coastal surveying and should be read in conjunction with this discussion.

[5] See Channel Chart in portfolio.

The Litteral or Roman Figures shew ye Hour of High-Water, or rather ye End of the Stream that setts to ye Eastward, on ye Day of ye New & Full Moon. Add therefore ye time of the Moons Southing or Northing to ye Number found near ye place where yor. Ship is, and ye Sum shall show you how long ye Tide will run to ye Eastward. But if it be more than 12 subtract 12 therefrom. The Direction of ye Darts shew upon what Point of ye Compass ye Strength of ye Tide sets.

This formula, which is still applicable, well illustrates Halley's great ability to reduce complex phenomena to a general rule.

More than thirty arrows showing direction and over fifty Roman numerals indicating time were distributed over the Channel from the coast of Kent to Cornwall. Halley's information is in approximate agreement with present day measurements of tidal phenomenon in this area. To make such measurements it is necessary to anchor; we know from his letters that Halley did so many times.[1] He implied that the end of the tidal flood (stream) is coincident with high water which modern hydrographers do not accept; also Halley's note on the map between Winchelsea and Barque (Berck), 'Here the two Tides meet', locates this variable phenomenon too precisely.[2] Nevertheless, Halley's tidal chart is a cartographic achievement of great originality and utility.

Halley appears to have written a short piece on navigation in the English Channel published as a broadside (1701), probably based on his recent experience.[3]

For several Years last past it has been Observed, that many Ships bound up the Channel, have by mistake fallen to the Northward of *Scilly*, and run up the *Bristol Channel* or *Severn Sea*, not without great Danger, and the Loss of many of them. The Reason of it is, without dispute, from the Change of the Variation of the Compass, and the Latitude of the *Lizard* and *Scilly*, laid down too far Northerly by near 5 leagues. For from undoubted Observation the *Lizard* lies in 49° 55′, the middle of *Scilly* due West therefrom, and the South part thereof nearest 49° 50′, whereas in most Charts and Books of Navigation they are laid down to the Northward of 50°: and in some full 50° 10′. Nor was this without a good Effect as long as the Variation continued Easterly, as it was when the

[1] Document 124, pp. 332–3.

[2] Proudman, 1942, p. 176.

[3] Ronan, 1969, plate 13 reproduces this broadside, 'An Advertisement Necessary to be Observed in the Navigation Up and Down the Channel of England.' This short essay 'communicated by a Fellow of the Royal Society' and dated 1701 is attributed to Halley. Since it deals with matters that he was investigating at this time, i.e. geographical position, magnetic variation and its change, and navigational practices, it is most probably by him. At the bottom of the broadside is the imprint 'LONDON: Printed for *Sam. Smith* and *Benj, Walford*, Printers of the Royal Society, at the *Prince's Arms* in St. *Paul's* Church-Yard, 1701.'

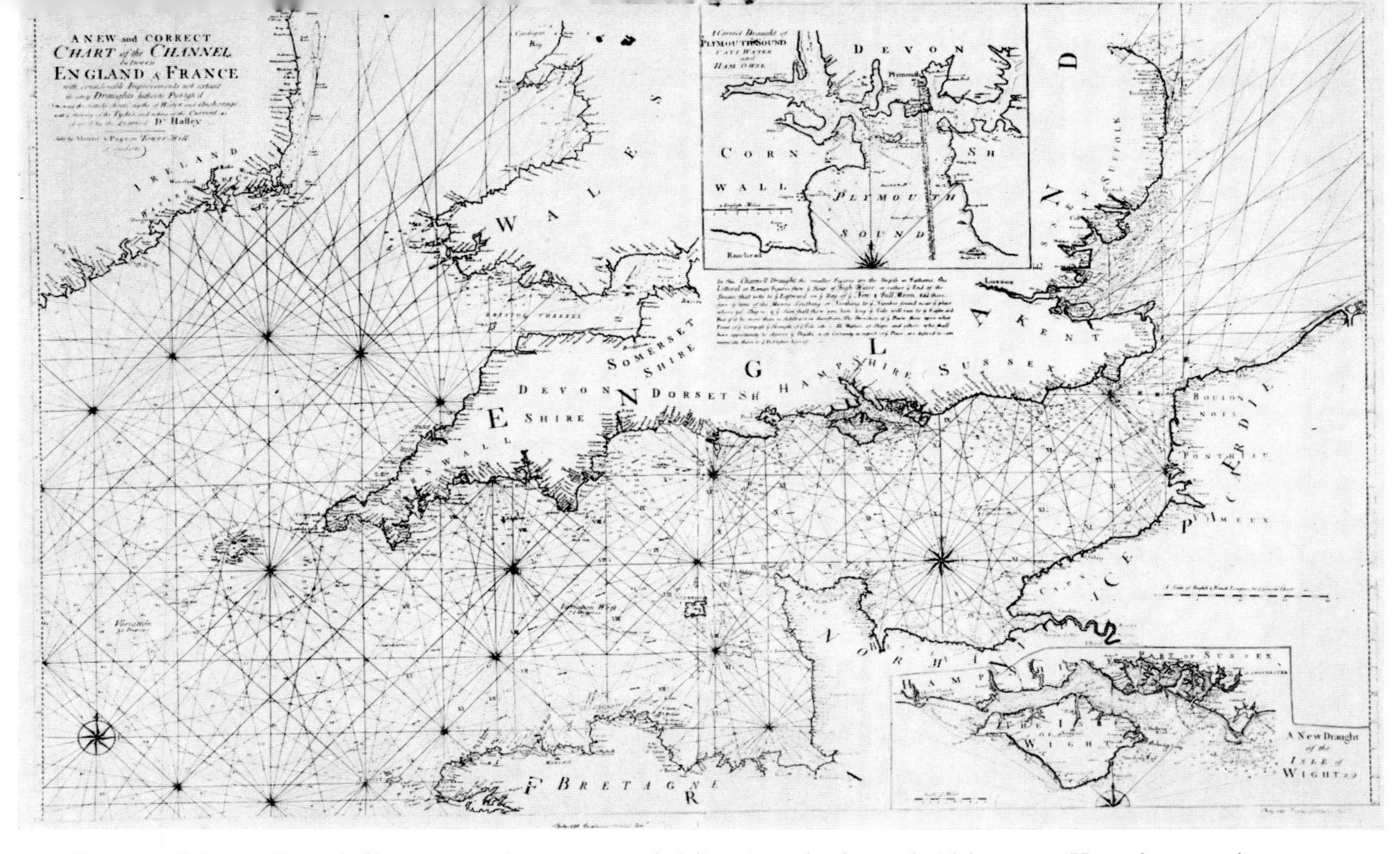

Figure 9. Halley's Channel Chart, 1702, showing coastal delineation, depths, and tidal ranges. Here the two sheets are together; see portfolio for separate two-sheet facsimile. *Reproduced by permission of the Royal Geographical Society, London*

tto be 50°.28′ by a good observation, whence Dunnose lies in 50.30 at
sunn sett the Variation was 7°.40′, Arundell bearing due North and
Dunnose W½N.

♂ 27. Next Morning being Just a breast with Beachy head, the Sun being
5 degrees high, was found 26′ to the Northwards of the East, whence ye
Variation 7°.17′. all the morning long it proved little wind, so that wee
were forced to drop our Anchor in about 15 Fath water, to the Eastward
of Beachy head. about Noon there sprung up a Gale of Wind at SW.
with which, about midnight we arrived in the Downes: being mid-
way between Dengyness and Dover I observed the Variation 7°.20′ West.

☿ 28 I found Sr Cloudsley Shovell Admirall of the Blew riding in the Downs
I waited on him for Ordrs but found none, so I obtained his leave to come up to Lond.

♃ 29 I went post from Deale to London.

♀ 30. By Mr Secretary Burchetts order I returned for Deale, and Satturday July
1st I gott betimes thither, where Sr Clously Shovell enquired into the reason
of my returne, and appointed Munday Morning for a Court Martiall to try
my Leiut: I gott one Tonn of Bear out of the Rochester by the Admiralls
Orders.

July.

☽ 3 At a Court Martiall my Leiutenant received a Reprimand for his
undecent Carriage towards me, and I received Orders from the Flagg
to Saile for the River, Wind E b N.

♂ 4 It blew so hard at North, that the Pilote would not weigh this day. Wind

☿ 5 at ENE we weighed and gott into Ramsgate road, and rode in 8.
Fathom Water.

♃ 6 Wind at ENE and NEbE, we turned through the Braker Channell
and haveing Weatherd the Foreland came at high water to an Anchor
in West gate Bay.

♀ 7 Wind as before, we gott over the Flatts and into the River, about
midnight the Wind came up at SW and SSW, so that we could gett
no higher than the Hope.

♄ 8 With the Day Flood, we turned up the river into Long reach.

☽ 10 We gave notice at the Tower and at Woolwich that they might
fetch our Gunns and Gunners Stores

♂ 11 The Gunns and Gunners Stores were delivered to the Tower
Officers and that Same Evening we moord our Shipp
at Deptford —

Edm: Halley

Figure 10. The last page (f. 8v.) of the MS of Halley's First Voyage, in another hand, but signed by Halley.

Reproduced by permission of the British Library, London

A Journal of a Voyage in his Maties Pink ye Paramore intended for the Discovery of ye Variation of the Compass kept by Edmund Halley Commander anno 1699 & 1700.

♄ Septemb^r 16. I order'd the Pink to fall down from Deptford to Gallio[n] to see if all our men were on board, and to be assured of them which was accordingly done that afternoon Wind at WSW.

☽ 18. I came on board my selfe at Gallion, and that same evening we Anchored in Gravesend reach a little below the Town Wind at SW.

♂ 19. I waited at Gravesend for my Slops and my Pilote to carry me into the downs who came on board about noon.

☿ 20. It blew so Fresh at W and WSW that we could not weigh our Anchors till Flood, when haveing got them up, we had such a Gale that we came against the Flood into Margate road that evening.

♃ 21 about 11 of the clock we came to an Anchor in the Downs the Middle of the Town bearing about West from us, the wind being about WSW obliged us to make severall boards before we got to our Anchoring place.

♄ ☉ 22. 23. 24. The wind continued blowing hard at W and WSW so that no ships could Stirr out of the Downs.

☽ 25 The wind came up at NW whereupon all the small Craft weighed and stood to the Southward, and in the afternoon they were followed by the Winchester and another man of Warr bound to Cadiz. the Falconbird bound to Guiney haveing promised to keep me Company, and not thinking fitt to weigh with so bare a wind I stirred not and before night the Wind returned to the WNW and afterwards to West.

♂ 26. The Wind was at SSW a gentle Gale and by Night it came by the South to the SE Small Wind with thick Foggy Rain This day it was low water at Deale carefully observ'd at 5¾:15 past M and the Streame ran to the Southwards from abo^t two till past 8.

☽ South at 10^h 15' high water at Deale SE moon

☿ 27. About Sunn Rise we had a very fine Sky and a Curious Gale at ESE to Isleford the Amplitude at rising 10½ and ...

Variation in the Downs this Morning 7° 52'

Figure 11. The first page (f. 10) of the MS of Halley's Second Voyage, in another hand, and not signed by Halley.

Reproduced by permission of the British Library, London

A Journall of a Voiage in his Ma:ties Pink The Paramore: for discovery of the Course of the Tides in the Channell of England.
By Edmond Halley Commandr. Anno. 1701.

38

1701

♄ June 14. I fell down from Deptford with the afternoon Ebb and at night came to an Anker off of Gravesend, wind at WSW a steady gale

☉. 15. about noon with the same wind we weighed and sailed down the river and about 8h. P.M. we ankered in the first Hopes between the Redsand and Spanyard.

☽. 16 Wind between W and SW. we past the Flatts, and about four P.M. came to an anker in the Downs, where the wind being westerly I continued the 17th and 18th and procured four men from Rear Admirall Mundon then in the Downs, in the Plymouth. Whilest I was here I observed the Course of the tide in the Downs. viz that a SbE and NbW Moon makes high water by the shore but the stream setts to the Northward till a SSW moon or somewhat later.

♃. 19 I weighed out of the Downs this Evening with a small gale of SW wind at 9½h. the tide then turning to the Southward and drove all night with the Tide

♀ 20 a little before Sunrise I ankered under the pitch of ye South foreland, about a mile from shore, the middle between the two Light houses bearing NNW. here I saw the turn of the Tide both ways, and observed that it ran to the Westward till a SE moon, and to the Eastward which is commonly call'd the Flood till a SW or IIIh Moon. but that it was high Water by the Shore with a S½E ☽ or XI½. the set of the Flood between ENE and NEbE. The tide being done about 11h, I weighed with an easy gale at NEbN and at 5h I came to an anker off of Dungeness a small mile from the Beach the Light house bearing NbE. Here I rode till the next day morning when I found it was

♄ 21 high water by the Shore a little before eight that is with

Figure 12. First page (f. 38) of Halley's Third Voyage, autograph.
Reproduced by permission of the British Library, London

Two Voyages made in 1698, 1699 and 1700,

By

Dr. EDMUND HALLEY,

Publiſhed from the Original Manuſcript

In Poſſeſſion of

THE BOARD OF LONGITUDE.

LONDON:

Printed in the Year MDCCLXXIII.

Figure 13. Title Page of Dalrymple's version of Halley's first two Voyages, 1773.

Reproduced by permission of the Royal Geographical Society, London

A D V E R T I S E M E N T.

THE Voyages of the celebrated Dr. Halley are now publiſhed for the firſt time; the Board of Longitude, in whoſe poſſeſſion the Original MSS. are, having been ſo obliging as to communicate them to me for this purpoſe.

The name of Dr. Halley will probably raiſe expectations in the Publick which his Journals will be far from ſatisfying; this has induced me to give the Journals *verbatim*, that the reader may be ſatisfied there is no ground to complain of the *Editor's omiſſions:* although, I think, had the *ſecond* voyage been reduced to *tables* it would have been more diſtinct.

The Journal of Dr. Halley's *firſt* Voyage is written on ſundry *ſcraps* of paper, and ſome parts repeated in different places, and ſo blended that it was a very difficult matter to make it out intelligibly; I find no account at all of his departure from Barbadoes, ſo that there is a deficiency of a few days in this part of the voyage; and the concluſion is alſo wanting.

The MS. obſerves * *before* the Variation ſignifies it was obſerved in the Morning, * *after* it, in the Evening.

Soho-Square,
24th July, 1773.

ALEXANDER DALRYMPLE.

Figure 14. Advertisement from Dalrymple's printed version of Halley's first two voyages, 1773.

Reproduced by permission of the Royal Geographical Society, London

A

Collection of Voyages

Chiefly in

The Southern Atlantick Ocean.

Publiſhed from Original M.S.S.

By

ALEXANDER DALRYMPLE.

LONDON:

Printed for the Author, 1775.

Sold by *J. Nourſe*, Bookſeller in Ordinary to His Majeſty; *P. Elmſly*, Strand; *Brotherton* and *Sewell*, Cornhill; *Jefferys* and *Faden*, St. Martin's-Lane; and, *A. Dury*, Duke's-Court.

Figure 15. Title page of Dalrymple's published version of Halley's first two voyages, 1775.
Reproduced by permission of the British Library, London

Charts were made. But since it is become considerably Westerly, (as it has been ever since the Year 1657.) and is at present about 7 1/2 Degrees; all Ships standing in, out of the Ocean, East by Compass, go two Thirds of a Point to the Northward of their true Course; and in every eighty Miles they Sail, alter their Latitude about 10 Minutes; so that if they miss an Observation for two or three Days, and do not allow for this Variation, they fail not to fall to the Northward of their Expectation, especially if they reckon *Scilly* in above 50 Degrees. This has been by some attributed to the Indraught of St. *George's* Channel, the Tide of Flood being supposed to set more to the Northward, than is compensated by the Ebb setting out. But the Variation being allowed, it hath been found that the said Indraught is not sensible, and that Ships steering two Watches *EbS* for one *East*, do exactly keep their Parallel. This practice is therefore recommended to all Masters of Ships, who are unacquainted with the Allowances to be made for Variation; as also that they come in, out of the Sea, on a Parallel not more Northerly than 49° 40′, which will bring them fair by the *Lizard*.

Nor is this the only Danger to which Ships are exposed in the *Channel*, on account of this Change of the Variation; for this last Winter has given us more than one Instance of Shipwreck upon the *French* coast and the *Casketts* of Ships newly departed from the *Downs*. And though perhaps this were not the only Cause of those Losses, yet it cannot be doubted but it concurred thereto: For by the late curious Survey of the Coast of *France*;[1] compared with what has been done for our own (though perhaps not altogether so exactly) it appears that the true Course from the Land of *Beachy* or *Dungyness* to the *Caskett*-Rocks, is but West 26 Degrees Southerly; which in former Times, when the Variation was as much Easterly, as now 'tis Westerly, was about *SWbW* by Compass, and then a *WSW* Course, then called *Channel-Course*, was very proper for all ships bound into the Ocean: But at present whoso steers a *WSW* Course in the *Channel*, though never so near to the Shore of *Beachy*, will not fail to fall in with the *Casketts*, or rather to the Eastwards thereof: It follows therefore, That as the Compass now Varies, the West by South Course be accounted the *Channel*-Course, instead of *WSW*; which Course from a reasonable Offing from *Beachy-head* will carry a Ship fair without the *Isle of Wight*, and about mid-way between *Portland-Bill* and the *Caskett* Rocks; which are scarce 14 Leagues asunder, and nearly in a Meridian. If this Notice be thought needless by those, whose Knowledge and Experience makes them want no Assistance; yet if it may contribute to the saving of any one Ship, the Author thereof is more than recompenced for the little pains he has taken to communicate it.

Although Halley gave up his active naval command after the Channel survey at the age of forty-six, he continued to interest himself in cartography and navigation to the end of his long life. The three major maps, the Atlantic and World isogonic charts and the Channel tidal chart,

[1] See p. 233, n. 2.

which resulted from the *Paramore* voyages were of immediate practical value in navigation as well as forming the basis for further scientific investigations.[1]

THE JOURNALS OF THE *PARAMORE*

Halley's cartographic work was both the most immediately useful and enduringly influential result of his three voyages in the *Paramore*. But these expeditions also produced journals which, at least in the case of the First and the Second Voyages, by his instructions he was required to keep.[2] Happily, manuscript versions of the journals of all three voyages survive.[3] Versions of the journals of the first two voyages were published by Alexander Dalrymple some thirty years after Halley's death, and thus an opportunity is afforded to collate and compare the manuscript versions and the printed account in each of these two cases. No such opportunity is available for the journal of the Third Voyage which is here published for the first time. This is the only journal entirely in Halley's hand and thus, fortunately (for we have no other source with which to compare it), is the most reliable.

Manuscripts of the three journals are now in the British Library, and it is these which are transcribed and printed in the present volume.[4] The original materials are bound together as Additional Manuscript 30368, Parts 1 and 2. Part 1 consists of the following: Journals of two voyages in the Atlantic in H.M. Pink *Paramore*, for the discovery of the variation of the compass by Edmond Halley, Commander, 20 October 1698 to

[1] Chapman, 1941, pp. 12–15, discussed some of these possibilities with respect to magnetic charts, while Proudman, 1942, pp. 174–6, did the same for tidal charts. In modern plate tectonics and other geophysical investigations, earlier magnetic information is of great value. An obvious use would be to show the manner in which the Earth's magnetic field changes through time.

[2] Documents 33, p. 269; 78, p. 301. There is only the implication that a journal would be required in the case of the Third Voyage, Document 119, pp. 328–9.

[3] In a letter dated 1 April 1969 the late Dr R. A. Skelton wrote to the author: 'Add. MS 30368 is the document nearest to Halley's own composition and you could hardly have a better authenticated non-holograph copy of the journals since this MS has his signature and corrections. It should certainly be collated with the text printed by Dalrymple and where they differ I think you should follow the manuscript.'

[4] Dalrymple used manuscripts other than those now in the British Library in his publication of the journals of Halley's First and Second Voyages. Ronan, 1969, p. 164 and n., alludes to and consults the manuscript journals in the British Library; but other students of Halley, including MacPike, Chapman, Armitage, etc., seem unaware of the existence of these important documents.

11 July 1699, and 16 September 1699 to 10 September 1700. The first journal, folios 1 to 9, is signed on folio 8v (Figure 10); the second journal, unsigned, folios 10 (Figure 11) to 36 has additions probably by Halley (on several folios). Both journals are royal folio and neither is autograph. In contrast with the above, the journal of Halley's Third Voyage is entirely autograph and small folio. Part 2 consists of the following: A journal of a voyage in H.M. Pink *Paramore* for the discovery of the course of the tides in the English Channel by Edmond Halley, Commander, 1701, holograph, folios 37 to 47 (Figure 12).[1] These manuscripts were acquired by the British Museum in 1877 when they were bought at Sotheby's, presumably from the estate of Sir Henry Weysford Charles Plantagenet Rawdon-Hastings, 5th Earl of Moira and 4th Marquess of Hastings, who died 12 November 1868, when these titles became extinct.[2] The manuscripts were transferred to the British Library in 1973.

We can now turn to Dalrymple's printed and published version of the journals of Halley's First and Second Voyages.[3] If copies of the charts resulting from Halley's *Paramore* expeditions are not especially plentiful, then this is also true of Dalrymple's published version of the voyages.[4] One copy used in the present study is contained in the Library of the Royal Geographical Society, London, where it is catalogued as *Two voyages made in 1698, 1699 and 1700, by Dr. Edmund Halley, published from the original manuscript in possession of the Board of Longitude* (by

[1] British Museum, *Catalogue of additions to the manuscripts in the British Museum in the years 1876–1881* (London, 1882), p. 72, and a letter from the Department of Manuscripts, British Museum, 26 November 1968; *Sotheby's sale catalogues: Catalogue of valuable manuscripts and autograph letters*, Entry for Tuesday, 5 June 1877, p. 5: '15 Astronomy. Halley's Journal of Voyages in his Majesty's Pink, the Paramore intended for the discovery of the Variation of the Magneticall Compass, 1698, 1699, and Journal of a Voiage for discovery of the course of the Tides, 1701, together 3 parts, 2 in 1 vol. royal folio, calf, and the third small folio, sd.' Royal folio is 20 × 35 inches folded once in the longer dimension to make leaves 20 inches tall by 17½ inches wide; small folio is, of course, of lesser size in both dimensions.

[2] This information was ascertained from a crest pasted on the inside (back and front) of the new binding, cut from an earlier binding, gold on leather. This crest was compared with a bookplate in another known Rawdon item in the British Library, MS 36537, and data from Sir J. B. Burke, *A genealogical history of the dormant, abeyant, forfeited and extinct peerages of the British Empire* (London, 1883). It is not known when or how the Rawdon-Hastings family came into possession of these manuscripts.

[3] Two scholars who have worked in detail on Dalrymple in recent years are Dr Howard T. Fry, formerly at Cambridge University and now of the Department of History, James Cook University of North Queensland, Australia; and Professor David A. Lanegran, formerly at the University of Minnesota and now of Macalester College, Saint Paul, Minnesota (see Bibliography).

[4] Dalrymple's earlier *An account of the discoveries made in the South Pacifick Ocean, previous to 1764* (London, 1767), is, however, more available and much better known than his volumes dealing with the Atlantic voyages.

Alexander Dalrymple) (London 1773).[1] This gathering has a title page and an Advertisement on the verso as shown in Figure 13 and Figure 14, respectively. It contains no material on voyages other than Halley's except two illustrations: 'Track of M. Louzier Bouvet in sight of Cape Circumcision,' Published by Act of Parliament by A. Dalrymple, 25 March 1775 and 'Plan of Camarones Bay in Lat. 44.50 S on the East Coast of Patagonia M.S. 1770,' Published by Act of Parliament by A. Dalrymple, 30 March 1775. Apparently Dalrymple did not put the work on the market until 1775 when it appeared as, *A collection of voyages chiefly in the southern Atlantick Ocean, published from original M.S.S.* by Alexander Dalrymple, London: Printed for the Author, 1775 (Figure 15). This more comprehensive work contains everything in the earlier one and much more besides, including the original Advertisement and title page from the 1773 gathering. However, in the 1775 version, these two elements are placed *between* the First and Second Voyage, whereas in the Royal Geographical Society's version they are in the expected position at the beginning of the work. In this version there is no division between the two voyages and the Second simply follows the abstract of the First. The materials which are common to the Royal Geographical Society's version and other gatherings seem to be identical. Scrutiny of the Advertisement (Figure 14) will indicate that none of the statements made in the third sentence/paragraph is true of the British Library manuscript of the First Voyage which is signed by Halley (see Journal of Halley's First Voyage, following).

[1] This version is not listed in the *National Union Catalog* (United States, Library of Congress, pre-1956 imprints) nor, apparently, in the catalogues of the following libraries, each of which has at least one copy of the 1775 version: The British Library (four copies); Naval Library, Ministry of Defence (Great Britain); The Library of Congress (United States); United States, Department of Defense Library; New York Public Library; Yale University Library; John Carter Brown Library; and the Mitchell Library, Sydney, New South Wales. The British Library lists under Dalrymple, *A Catalogue of the extensive and valuable library of books . . . late the property of Alex. Dalrymple . . . which will be sold at auction . . . on Monday, May 29, 1809* (November 6, 1809; February 15, 1810) etc., 3 parts, J. Barker (London, 1809, 1810), R. Watt *Bibliotheca Britannica, or a general index to British and foreign literature*, 4 vols. (Edinburgh, 1824), vol. 1, p. 281, lists: Dalrymple, Alexander: *Proposition for Printing by Subscription the MS Voyages and Travels in the British Museum* (London, 1773). However, since the manuscripts of Halley's voyages did not reach the Museum until 1877, the proposal could not have included these. Ronan, 1969, p. 164 n., refers to a version of the Dalrymple work being published in 1773. In the same footnote referred to above, Ronan says of the manuscript which Dalrymple borrowed from the Board of Longitude, 'The log [journal] was never returned, and when Dalrymple's house was burned it was assumed that the log perished. Sometime about 1877 the log was sold privately and purchased by the British Museum.' The above suggests that the Board's manuscript copy of Halley's journal, used by Dalrymple, somehow survived and was the same one which was

It is clear from the above together with even a cursory examination of the British Library manuscript that different materials are involved. For example, the British Library manuscript of Halley's First Voyage contains information which Dalrymple complained was lacking in sources available to him.[1] On the other hand, the Journal of the Second Voyage in Dalrymple is in some particulars more complete. Thus the collation and filling out of the manuscript by footnotes is perhaps the most valuable part of the present study.

Halley's Voyages should have become well-known through the publication of Dalrymple's *Collection of Voyages*. Such does not appear to have been the case, because by the time they were available in print news of Cook's Voyages (First, 1768–71, Second, 1772–4, and Third, 1776–9) was breaking upon a public which could not be expected to be enthusiastic about expeditions which had been undertaken decades earlier by a long deceased scientist. A great deal of the impact of Halley's Voyages was lost through their tardy publication.

HALLEY'S VOYAGES IN RELATION TO OTHER OFFICIAL ENGLISH VOYAGES OF EXPLORATION IN THE SEVENTEENTH AND EARLY EIGHTEENTH CENTURIES

Alexander von Humboldt referred to Halley's voyages in these terms: 'Never before, I believe, had any government fitted a naval expedition for an object whose attainment promised such advantages to practical navigation, while at the same time, it deserved to be regarded as peculiarly scientific and physico-mathematical,'[2] and Captain S. P. Oliver stated, 'We do not often think of him as a sailor; and yet, previous to Cook, Captain E. Halley was our first scientific voyager,'[3] while Professor S. Chapman asserted that Halley's Atlantic Voyage(s) was '. . . the first sea journey undertaken for a purely scientific object.'[4] We may recall that long before his *Paramore* voyages Halley had formulated

sold in 1877 to the British Museum. However, comparison of Dalrymple's rendition and the British Library MS indicates that quite different copies are involved.

[1] See appropriate entries in the Journal of Halley's First Voyage, following, and especially ns. 3, p. 88; 2 p. 92, and 1, p. 111 pertaining to that Voyage.

[2] A. von Humboldt, *Cosmos: a sketch of a physical description of the universe* (London, 1849), p. 336.

[3] S. P. Oliver, 'Proposed monument to Halley,' *The Observatory*, 35 (1880), 349.

[4] Chapman (1941), p. 5.

hypotheses which he wished to test through observation; his resulting maps are eminently quantitative. Halley's special talent as a scientist was his ability to collect and organize a mass of data and reduce it to order.[1] The instructions which he composed for his Atlantic Voyages are quite free from suggestions concerning commercial or strategic advantage. Others may have had such ideas and used them to promote the voyages but Halley was concerned with, as he put it, 'the Discovery of Nature.'[2] Thus, in these terms and bearing in mind the fact that Halley (an already famous scientist) was the leader of these expeditions and not merely attached to them, the statements of Humboldt, Oliver, and Chapman seem to have a great deal of veracity.

Halley's voyages invite comparison with some earlier English voyages of exploration. A document in the Public Record Office, 'Ships Employed on Scientific Missions between 1669 and 1860', lists such voyages.[3] There are four before Halley's (or three if we regard two of them as belonging to the same expedition), namely: Captain John Narborough in the *Sweepstakes* (1669–71); Captain William Flawes in *Prosperous* (1676); Captain John Wood in the *Speedwell* (1676); and Captain John Strong in the *Welfare* (1689–91). Actually Wood and Flawes travelled in convoy and only Flawes' ship returned, with both crews.

The voyage of Narborough in the *Sweepstakes* to Valdivia, Chile, was undertaken with prospects of trade with South America. The Strait of Magellan was navigated both ways.[4] Some surveying was accomplished and a chart of the Strait produced.[5] Motives of trade as well as exploration inspired the promotors of this expedition. As Anson observed, Narborough's voyage was 'rather an encouragement to future trials of this kind, than any objection against them.'[6]

The voyages of Captains Wood and Flawes in 1676 to Novaya

[1] Bullard, *Endeavour* (1956), 199.

[2] Document 1, p. 250.

[3] P.R.O. Adm. R. 3/34, 'Ships Employed on Scientific Missions between 1669 and 1860,' compiled by B. Poulter and after his death, in 1929, bound and placed on the search room shelves. A few corrections have subsequently been made on the document.

[4] *An account of several late voyages and discoveries to the South Seas, 1. Sir John Narbrough's Voyage* (London, 1694), pp. 1–128, with map of Patagonia and inset of Magellan Streights; and James Burney, *A chronological history of the discoveries in the South Sea or Pacific Ocean*, 3 (London, 1813), pp. 316–82. The name Narborough is usually rendered thus in modern usage, but often Narbrough in earlier works.

[5] Greenville (Grenville) Collins, later a distinguished hydrographer, served under Narborough on this voyage (Burney, 3 (1813), 319). Narborough's Chart of the Strait of Magellan, first published in 1673 and again in 1694, was used by later English explorers (Wallis, 1965, p. 211).

[6] Richard Walter, ed., *Anson's voyage around the world* (1748 Revised ed. (London 1928), p. 89.

Zemlya actually discouraged further British exploration in that direction for many years.[1] Thus we can turn directly to the voyage of Captain John Strong in the *Welfare*.[2] This was a commercial enterprise in which Dr John Radcliffe had a big financial interest and from which he was looking for a large monetary return on his investment. In January 1690 Strong reached the 'Southern Islands' of John Davis and discovered and sailed through a strait which he called Falkland Sound.[3] This appellation appeared on Halley's World Chart of 1702 for the islands as well as the sound which separated them, and thus, by usage, the Falkland Islands received their present designation.[4] Strong sailed on through the Strait of Magellan and by October 1690 had reached Juan Fernandez. From this island Strong rescued buccaneers left there some years earlier; he returned by way of the coast of Chile, the Strait of Magellan, and the West Indies to England. Although two prizes were taken by the *Welfare* on the way home, the promoters of the project lost some £12,000. Thus, the voyage was unsuccessful in its main objectives but it is remembered for Strong's discovery of Falkland Sound. None of these ventures can be described as scientific voyages.

An expedition much more like those of Halley in many respects was that of William Dampier in the *Roebuck* (1699–1701). This voyage which properly appears after Halley's, chronologically, was described by a distant relative of the explorer, W. C. D. Dampier-Whetham, as 'the first attempt at a voyage planned for the deliberate purpose of scientific navigation.'[5] For some years before this appointment William Dampier had been a buccaneer and under difficult circumstances had kept a careful journal. Through the publication of his *A new voyage round the world* (1697),[6] Dampier came to the notice of influential persons including Charles Montagu (later Earl of Halifax), President of the Royal Society,

[1] James Burney, *A chronological history of north-eastern voyages of discovery* (London, 1819), pp. 77–83, contains a summary of these voyages. L. P. Kirwan, *The white road* (London, 1959), p. 38, describes the undertaking as '. . . a futile and farcical expedition led by two drunken Englishmen Wood and Flawes' which 'served only to discourage further effort.' Wood had sailed as Master's Mate under Narborough on his 1669–71 voyage to South America.

[2] Burney, 4 (1816), pp. 329–37, summarized Strong's Voyage, as he did Halley's two Atlantic Voyages, pp. 384–7.

[3] Named for Anthony Cary, 1st Viscount Falkland, Commissioner and later (15 April 1693 to 2 May 1694) First Lord of the Admiralty.

[4] Wallis, 1965, p. 213.

[5] W. C. D. Dampier-Whetham, 'William Dampier, geographer' (a review of Clennell Wilkinson's *William Dampier*), *Geographical Journal*, 74 (1929), 478–80.

[6] This went through four editions in the first two years to be published later as Volume I of the four parts of *Dampier's Voyages* (1711).

1695–8, who received the dedication. Montagu introduced Dampier to Edward Russell, First Lord of the Admiralty (1694–9), the newly-created Earl of Orford. Dampier, who was involved in discussions with the Council of Trade, was given a commission in the Royal Navy with directions to lay plans for a voyage of geographical discovery; motives of trade as well as strategy were involved in this projected journey to the East Indies. The *Roebuck* (290 tons) was selected for the expedition and a crew of fifty signed on. Like Halley, Dampier had under him a regular Navy lieutenant who resented serving under a Captain not brought up in the Navy. After many vicissitudes, in March 1700, Dampier was beyond any land marked on the charts he possessed and made his most important discovery, that New Guinea and New Britain were separate islands divided by a strait. This was soon to be known by the name of its discoverer, 'Dampeirs Streights' as it appears on Halley's World Chart, 1702, or Dampiers Passage. On the return journey to England the *Roebuck* sprung a leak off Ascension Island and the crew were fortunate to reach shore by raft. A passing English convoy brought them back to England some months after Halley had concluded his two Atlantic voyages.

During those parts of his voyage when he was in areas not frequented by English ships, especially, Dampier kept a careful journal as he had on earlier voyages. He was an astute observer, especially of flora and fauna, but not a theorist.[1] Dampier himself testifies to this in a passage relevant to the present study because it involves Halley and his magnetic charts.

Another thing that stumbled me here was the *Variation,* which, at this time, by the last Amplitude I had I found to be but 7 deg. 58 min. W. whereas the Variation at the *Cape* (from which I found my self not 30 Leagues distant) was then computed, and truly, about 11 Deg. or more: And yet a while after this, when I was got 10 Leagues to the Eastward of the *Cape*, I found the Variation but 10 Deg. 40 Min. W. whereas it should have been rather more than at the *Cape.* These Things, I confess did puzzle me: neither was I fully satisfied as to the Exactness of the taking the Variation at Sea: For in a great Sea, which we often meet with, the Compass will traverse with the motion of the Ship; besides the Ship may and will deviate somewhat in steering, even by the best Helmsmen: And then when you come to take an *Azimuth,* there is often some difference between him that looks at the Compass, and the Man that takes the Altitude heighth of the Sun; and a small Error in each, if the Error of both should be

[1] Joseph Shipman in his *William Dampier: seaman-scientist* (Lawrence, Kansas, 1962), p. 60, reminds us that John Masefield, in his edition of *Dampier's Voyages* (London, 1906), did not accept that the 'faithful chronicling of minute natural detail', which was so typical of Dampier's work, 'is the work of a great intellect'.

one way, will make it wide of any great Exactness. But what was most shocking to me, I found that the Variation did not always increase or decrease in Proportion to the Degrees of Longitude East or West; as I had a Notion they might do to a certain Number of Degrees of Variation East or West, at such or such particular Meridians. But finding in this Voyage that the Difference of Variation did not bear a regular Proportion to the Difference of Longitude, I was much pleas'd to see it thus Observ'd in a Scheme shewn me after my Return home, wherein are represented the several Variations in the *Atlantick* Sea, on both sides the Equator; and there, the Line of no Variation in that Sea is not a Meridian Line, but goes very oblique, as do those also which shew the Increase of Variation on each side of it. In that Draught there is so large an Advance made as well towards the Accounting for those seemingly Irregular Increases and Decreases of Variation towards the S.E. Coast of *America*, as towards the fixing a general Scheme or System of the Variation every where, which would be of such great Use in Navigation, that I cannot but hope that the Ingenious Author, Capt. Halley, who to his profound Skill in all Theories of these kinds, hath added and is adding continually Personal Experiments, will e'er long oblige the World with a fuller Discovery of the Course of the Variation, which hath hitherto been a Secret. For my part I profess my self unqualified for offering at any thing of a General Scheme; but since Matter of Fact, and whatever increases the History of the Variation, may be of use towards the setling or confirming the Theory of it, I shall here once for all insert a *Table* of all the *Variations* I observed beyond the *Equator* in this Voyage, both in going out, and returning back; and what Errors there may be in it, I shall leave to be corrected by the Observations of Others.[1]

In this passage Dampier displays several characteristics which mark his work generally: objectivity in his accounts of a wide range of natural phenomenon; description; a fine graphic style of writing; and modesty to which John Evelyn referred when he wrote that Dampier was '. . . a more modest man, than one would imagine, by the relation of the Crue he had sorted with.'[2] This reference is to Dampier's piratical ventures in which, as on the *Roebuck*, he was more modest in his writing than in his actions. Objectivity, description, and perhaps modesty are ideally a part of science. But there is more than these attributes to scientific activity which involves, in addition, hypothesis, theory, experimentation and prediction. These last qualities, in addition to the others, are evident in the work of Halley to a high degree. They are not especially a feature of the writings of Dampier who for a virtually self-taught observer was remarkable; but by his own testimony he was not a scientist.

[1] William Dampier, *A voyage to New Holland, &c in the year, 1699* (London, 1703), pp. 99–102.

[2] William Bray, ed., *Memoirs, illustrative of the life and writings of John Evelyn, Esq. F.R.S.*, 2 (London, 1818), 61.

AFTER THE VOYAGES, HALLEY'S LIFE AND WORK, 1702 TO 1742

Halley's interests during the years 1702 to 1742, the second half of his professional career, focussed particularly on pure mathematics and astronomy, although he continued to concern himself with the application of these studies to navigation and cartography until his death. Between the end of 1702 and late in 1703 Halley made visits to Vienna and Istria as an emissary of Queen Anne. He served as an adviser on the fortifications of the Istrian ports of Trieste and Boccari (Buccari, Bakar – southeast of Fiume), evaluating the suitability of these ports for English warships.[1] He was received by the Emperor Leopold, who showed his esteem for the scientist by giving him a diamond ring from his own hand. Halley met Prince Eugene, Marlborough's great ally of the War of the Spanish Succession; the work in Istria was a contribution to the allied victory in this conflict. On his journey through Hanover, Halley also met and dined with the future King George I of England.

Once his service on the Continent was over, Halley returned to England, where he became a candidate for the Savilian Professorship of Geometry at Oxford. This position had fallen vacant on the death of his old mentor Dr John Wallis, 28 October 1703. In his candidature Halley was again opposed by Flamsteed who wrote, 'Dr. Wallis is dead. Mr. Halley expects his place. He now talks, swears, and drinks brandy like a sea captain, so that I much fear his own ill-behaviour will deprive him of the vacancy.'[2] However, neither Flamsteed's invective nor any reservations remaining on the part of churchmen could this time prevent Halley from receiving an Oxford professorship. Significantly, before this appointment, Halley had already been elected to the Council of the Royal Society on 30 November 1703.[3]

On the occasion of his inaugural address at Oxford, 24 May 1704, Halley gave an account of the origins and progress of geometry from antiquity to his own time. At Oxford he undertook to translate and edit a number of early mathematical works. This not only involved his con-

[1] MacPike, 1932, especially 'Appendix XIII, Halley's two missions to Vienna (1702–3),' pp. 248–50.

[2] MacPike, 1937, p. 98, quotes a passage in a letter from Flamsteed to his former assistant Abraham Sharp, 18 December, 1703.

[3] *Record of the Royal Society*, 1940, p. 336.

siderable knowledge of classical languages but also Arabic, which he learned in order to effect the translation into Latin of texts not surviving in the original Greek. This was also the period of Halley's great publication on comets, 'Astronomiae cometicae synopsis'[1] In this brilliant paper Halley applied the Newtonian planetary physics to cometary science. The spectacular return of the comet which Halley had seen in 1682, 'about the year 1758' as he had predicted, and its periodic return every seventy-six years since, have overshadowed all of Halley's other accomplishments. In the popular mind this is Halley's sole claim to distinction, which is unfortunate in view of his contributions to many fields of knowledge, including mathematics. His work in this latter field particularly was given formal recognition when, in 1710, he was created D. C. L. at Oxford.

At this time Halley was embroiled in a dispute with Flamsteed, owing to Flamsteed's failure to publish his observations made at Greenwich which had practical value in navigation. As a public servant, albeit an inadequately paid one, Flamsteed was required to publish his observations, which he was reluctant to do except on his own terms. Newton, who needed the observations to demonstrate his own theories, supported Halley and a committee was formed to which Flamsteed reluctantly gave up his manuscripts. With financial support from the Royal purse, publication began and was completed, with additions by Halley, as *Historiae coelestis* (1712). Flamsteed was infuriated by these additions, and burnt those parts of the book which were not entirely his own work in all copies he could find – this in spite of the fact that Halley had earlier sent Flamsteed page proofs, which he had had an opportunity to correct.[2]

Although Halley was now resident in Oxford where he had a small observatory constructed on the roof of his house,[3] he visited London frequently. His own research at this time included methods of precise determination of longitude on land by use of lunar eclipses, the relationship between the aurora borealis and Earth magnetism, and on the extraordinary meteor of 1719.

In 1713 Halley became Secretary of the Royal Society in succession to Sir Hans Sloane, and in the spring of 1715 he made preparations for viewing a total eclipse of the Sun at the Society's premises (then at Crane Court, Fleet Street). Before this event took place Halley published a

[1] *Philosophical Transactions*, 24 (1704–5), 1882–99.

[2] Ronan, 1969, pp. 190–3.

[3] This observatory, which is pictured in MacPike, 1932, facing p. 124, still exists, although it no longer serves its original purpose.

broadside, 'A Description of the Passage of the Shadow of the Moon, over England, In the Total Eclipse of the Sun, on the 22nd Day of April 1715 in the Morning.' This contains another of Halley's original contributions to cartography – a map, drawn before the event, showing the track of the shadow of the eclipse over England together with the time in seconds it would take to pass across the country. He published this, as he said, so that the phenomenon 'may give no surprize to the People, who would, if unadvertized, be apt to look upon it as Ominous'.[1] The eclipse, confirmed Halley's predictions and opened up other useful lines of astronomical investigation.

On the last day of the year 1719 Flamsteed died, and Halley, who was the logical successor, was appointed 9 February 1720 as Astronomer Royal. In the following year Halley gave up his Secretaryship of the Royal Society to concentrate on his new work. It will be recalled that a fundamental reason for the establishment of the Greenwich Observatory was for the improvement of navigation. As an astronomer with great practical knowledge of seamanship, Halley was now in a peculiarly strong position to further this objective. In fact the instructions from King George I called for Halley 'to apply himself to the correction of lunar tables and star places "in order to find out the so much desired Longitude at Sea, for the perfecting of the Art of Navigation".'[2] His first duty, however, was the refitting of the Observatory which had been stripped of all instruments and furniture by Flamsteed's widow. In this, apparently, she had been within her rights, for Flamsteed had paid for the equipment out of his meagre salary. Halley obtained a grant of £500 from the government to re-equip the Observatory with a transit instrument, a mural quadrant (both made by England's greatest horologist, George Graham), clocks and other necessary and basic apparatus.[3] With this equipment Halley, in 1722, began a long term project of observing the Moon during the 18 year period of the saros.[4] Since he was now sixty-five years of age this was indeed an ambitious programme but he lived long enough to complete the work.

In 1728 the clockmaker John Harrison (1693–1776) visited Halley at

[1] Armitage, 1966, p. 174 quotes the entire legend; and Ronan, 1969, plate 16, illustrates a later state of the map showing the actual track of the 1715 and other eclipses. The earlier map is reproduced in Bullard, *Endeavour*, 1956, 198, and Thrower, *Annals*, 1969, 674.

[2] Armitage, 1966, p. 209.

[3] Ronan, 1969, p. 203.

[4] A regular cycle in the sarotic period of 223 lunations (18 years 11 days) after which the Moon returns to approximately its initial position relative to the Sun, to its node in the ecliptic and to its apogee.

Greenwich. Harrison, a largely self-educated man, had already invented a gridiron pendulum fitted with alternate strips of metal with different expansion rates to minimize temperature change on the pendulum clock. He had also invented a practically frictionless 'grasshopper' escapement which, in conjunction with his gridiron pendulum, gave remarkable accuracy to his clocks. He showed Halley drawings of a marine clock which he proposed to build. Halley advised him not to communicate at once with the Board of Longitude (which was more interested in results than proposals) but to consult George Graham. Graham lent money to Harrison who proceeded to build a timepiece which was controlled by two balances rather than a pendulum. This large instrument was tested successfully on a sea journey of limited extent. At a meeting of the Board attended by Halley in 1737 it was vo ted to encourage Harrison with the first of several awards he was to receive over the years. Harrison continued to improve his clocks until he had made a small accurate timepiece, the ancestor of the modern chronometer. When Harrison was in his eighties, in 1776, more than three decades after Halley's death, he finally won the prize for the solution of the problem of longitude.[1] A later Astronomer Royal, Nevile Maskelyne (1738–1821), who compiled the *Nautical Almanac*, attempted to prevent Harrison from receiving the whole award. This was in contrast with the generous attitude of Halley who, years earlier, had given encouragement and excellent advice to Harrison.

One of the most touching events of Halley's life occurred in 1729 when Queen Caroline of Ansbach, the virtuous, tactful, and clever consort of King George II, visited the Royal Observatory. She learned that Halley had been a Navy captain and obtained for him, through the King, a grant of half pay as post captain which he received until the end of his life.[2] This was in addition to his salaries as Astronomer Royal and Savilian Professor at Oxford so that, with his investments and what remained of his inheritance, Halley could not be described as a poor man.[3] The

[1] H. Quill, *John Harrison: the man who found longitude* (London, 1966), pp. 34–6.

[2] Ronan, 1969, p. 211, suggests that 'Halley had held his commission from 1698 to 1701, a period of rather more than three years, and technically he therefore qualified for the rank and pay of "post captain" for which a period of not less than three years service was the official requirement.' The actual date of Halley's second commission was 19 August 1698 and the Third Voyage ended 16 October 1701 – less than two months over the official perio d This was Halley's term of continuous active Naval service, which does not date from his first commission, 4 June 1696.

[3] Among the MacPike manuscripts in the Newberry Library, Chicago, there is a reference from an uncited source to the effect that the Queen offered to raise the salary of the Astronomer Royal from £100 (which it had been from the time of Flamsteed's initial appointment

Queen's action may have been more to honour Halley for his services than to improve his financial situation.

Because of the time-consuming nature of his duties at Greenwich and his advancing age, Halley's publications in this period of his life were understandably less frequent than previously. Newton was now dead and Halley, as the greatest living English scientist, was asked to endorse various projects. In this spirit he wrote a foreword for the *Atlas maritimus & commercialis*, 1728, containing recommendations on the use of the projections included in the volume for great circle sailing.[1] Halley's testimonial is printed on Henry Popple's map of North America, which is described as the most accurate map of the area at the time. Significantly his last publications in the *Philosophical Transactions* concerned observations on magnetic variation and longitude at sea (1732) and a brief note on a lunar eclipse (1737–8).[2]

Mary Halley, the astronomer's wife for more than fifty-five years, died 30 January 1736, and was buried in the churchyard of St Margaret at Lee, a short distance from the Observatory. Some time after his wife's death Halley suffered a partial paralysis of his right hand, apparently the result of a minor stroke, but he was able to continue his observations with the help of an assistant. In June 1736 Halley made his will, in which he stated ,'And as to my Body, my Will and Desire is that it may be Interred in the same grave with that of my Dear Wife lately deceased, in the Churchyard of Lee in Kent.'[3] To his son Edmond, a surgeon in the Navy, Halley had already made over the greater part of his landed estate. Most of the remainder of his effects were to be equally divided between his daughters, Margaret (who was never married), and Catherine, wife of

over fifty years earlier) to which Halley replied: 'Pray, your Majesty do no such thing, for if the salary should be increased it might become an object of emolument to place there some unqualified needy dependent, to ruin the institution.'

[1] *Atlas maritimus & commercialis; or, a general view of the world* (London, 1728). This large volume, the geographic descriptions in which are the work of Daniel Defoe, contains Halley's foreword twice – once at the beginning of the complete work and once before the pilotage section which was often used separately. Halley reiterated what he had said in his Descriptions accompanying the Atlantic and World Magnetic Charts, namely that the Mercator Projection 'ought really to be called the Nautical'. In making this suggestion, Halley may have had in mind that although Mercator, the Fleming, developed this best known of map projections in 1569, it was Edward Wright, the English mathematician, who first published tables for its construction in his *Certaine errors in navigation* (London, 1599).

[2] 'Observations of latitude and variation taken on board the Hartford, in her passage from Java Head to St. Hellena, Anno Dom. 1731/2,' *Philosophical Transactions*, 37 (1731–2), 331–6; and 'Observations made on the eclipse of the Moon, on March 15, 1735/6', *Philosophical Transactions*, 40 (1737–8), 14.

[3] MacPike, 1932, pp. 255–7, contains 'Appendix XVI: Halley's will with comments'.

Henry Price. Halley's son died February 1741, about a year before his father.

In the last years of his life Halley weakened gradually but his mind remained clear to the end, which came 14 January 1742, in his 85th year, while he was sitting peacefully in a chair. He was buried, as requested, in the same grave as his wife, over which his daughters erected a tomb. This tomb fell into disrepair but, because of his captaincy in the Navy, it was restored by the Admiralty in 1845 and the original stone let into the wall of the old Observatory at Greenwich in an upright position. The inscription can be translated (in part) as follows:

Under this marble peacefully rests, with his beloved wife, Edmond Halley, LL.D., unquestionably the greatest astronomer of his age. But to conceive an adequate knowledge of the excellencies of this great man, the reader must have recourse to his writings, in which all the sciences are in the most beautiful and perspicacious manner illustrated and improved. As when living he was so highly esteemed by his Countrymen, gratitude requires that his memory should be respected by posterity. To the memory of the best of parents their affectionate daughters have erected this monument in the year 1742.[1]

Later Halley's two daughters and his son-in-law were buried in the grave at Lee and inscriptions recording these facts were added to the tombstone. The church of St Margaret is now in ruin and Halley's tomb is again in a state of disrepair and even difficult to find.[2]

Appropriately, Halley, like other famous scientists, is honoured by having a lunar crater named for him.[3] In 1957 the Royal Society called its permanent scientific base in Antarctica, Halley Bay, in recognition of Halley's role as a founder of modern geophysics.[4]

But it has often been remarked that no public memorial in England adequately represents the estimation in which Halley is held. This unfortunate omission can perhaps best be explained by a document in the archives of the Royal Society.[5] This document, which honours

[1] Ibid., pp. 258–60, contains 'Appendix XVII: Inscriptions on Halley's tomb at Lee'. Halley's elder daughter Margaret, 'Who died on the 13th Octob. 1743. In the 55th year of her age,' is interred in the same grave and later Catherine (Price), the younger daughter, 'Who died Novr the 10th 1765 aged 77 Ys,' and her husband, Henry.

[2] In MacPike, 1932, opp. p. 260, the tomb (visited by the present writer in September 1973) is pictured. Airy suggested the restoration of Halley's tomb, in which Airy's immediate predecessor as Astronomer Royal, John Pond, d. 1836, is also buried.

[3] The crater, Halley, is at 8° S and 6° E.

[4] Halley Bay is at 75° 30′ S and 26° 42′ W. On the frieze in the Lecture Theatre at the Royal Geographical Society's House, Halley's name is enrolled with those of other great British explorers and travellers.

[5] Royal Society, *Collectanea Newtoniana*, compiled by Charles Turnor, 1837, 4, 25–7, folios 28–42.

Newton, was written long after his death and contains essays on his associates. The piece on Halley begins, 'In that bright constellation of learned men by whom Newton was surrounded, his friend and admirer Edmond Halley shines forth conspicuously; remarkable alike for the brilliance of his genius and for the vast extent of scientific research on which that genius was brought successfully to bear.' It then goes on to discuss the high points of Halley's life and concludes:

Thus was this friend, Countryman, and disciple of Newton esteemed throughout his long and useful life during which he flourished under six crowned heads and received favors from each of them which were the pure effects of his singular merit, and this merit being as well known abroad, as at home, it is not surprising that foreigners should in viewing the Tombs in Westminster Abbey, after admiring the monument of Sir Isaac Newton, sometimes ask for that of his friend Halley. The reason of its not being there, is probably one deeply to be deplored, namely, that being an infidel in religious matters, he was (notwithstanding his splendid philosophical attainments) scarcely worthy to be enrolled amongst those illustrious dead who repose in peace around the Christian Newton.[1]

For his anticlerical attitude if not for his liberal views on religion Edmond Halley 'a truly great man of prodigious versatility and most attractive personality'[2] seems to have been denied specific official recognition in the past. Let us therefore now pay tribute to Halley who, among his many other accomplishments, was the first to captain a Navy vessel[3] on a series of extended and purely scientific voyages, sponsored by an academy.

[1] Unlike his usual straightforwardness, on religious subjects Halley was often equivocal but on at least one occasion he stated that he was a Christian. In an interview in 1691 when questioned by Edward Stillingfleet, then Bishop of Worcester (1689–99) and previously Dean of St Paul's (1677–89), Halley replied 'My Lord, that is not the business I came about. I declare myself a Christian and hope to be treated as such' (Ronan, 1969, p. 119). Perhaps it is not too late to correct the injustice against the memory of Halley.

[2] Bullard, *Endeavour*, 1956, 189.

[3] In the long run, the most important contribution of the Royal Navy to humanity at large, might be support given to peaceful operations such as the explorations of Halley, Cook, and Darwin.

THE JOURNALS

THE JOURNALS

Notes on Transcription

The manuscripts which are transcribed below are now in the British Library, Reference Division. In the texts which follow, the journals are presented in chronological order. In the case of the First and Second Voyages many of the footnotes are concerned with variations between the British Library manuscripts and the Dalrymple 1773 and 1775 versions. The Journal of Halley's Third Voyage is here published for the first time.

In making the transcriptions the following procedures were followed: 1. photographic copies of the three journals were obtained from the British Library; 2. a typescript was made from each of the journals; 3. the typescripts were taken to the Manuscript Department of the British Library and compared by the present editor word for word with originals, and corrections made on the spot; 4. a paleographer rechecked the corrected transcriptions with the originals. Later the corrected typescripts of the First and Second Voyages were compared with Dalrymple's versions. The footnoting of all three journals was the last operation.

In the footnotes the abbreviation MS refers to the appropriate British Library manuscript of Halley's voyages and D to Dalrymple's 1773 printed version (in the case of the First and Second Voyages). When a word, number or short passage is footnoted, the source abbreviation is given first followed by a comma, then the quoted word, etc., with a full stop at the end of the quotations. When longer passages are quoted these follow a colon, and are set up as close to the original as feasible. The colon is also used for entries where the source abbreviation is not directly in juxtaposition with the reference and the quotation is normally terminated with a full stop. The above procedures minimize the use of inverted commas – quotation marks – which are used only to avoid ambiguity.

Catchwords are included only when they are in line with a regular line of the text in the MS. If a date, e.g. March, is repeated as at the heading of a page in the MS where the entry continues, it is also omitted. Below is a list of standardized symbols and abbreviations used in the journals, D, and documents; variations follow the standard in parentheses. They are arranged in general categories.

SYMBOLS USED IN THE JOURNALS

ASTRONOMICAL SYMBOLS

Halley's symbols and variations	*Meaning*	*Printer's type equivalents*
☉ (☉)	Sunday; sun	☉
☽	Monday; moon	☽
♂	Tuesday	♂
☿	Wednesday	☿
♃ (♃♄)	Thursday	♃
♀ ♀♄	Friday	♀
♄	Saturday	♄
♎	Libra	♎
♐	Sagittarius	♐

COMMON SYMBOLS

h	hour	6*h*
* (*)	If before a number, variation taken in the morning; if after a number, variation taken in the evening; if before and after a number, variation taken at both times	*

Halley's symbols and variations	*Meaning*	*Printer's type equivalents*
o	degree	$6^\circ\frac{1}{2}$ West
′	minute	49°.50′
″	second	10*h*.11′.44″
⊃	*-nce*	(none)
=	hyphen; word division or sentence continuation	(not used)
^	circumflex	^
&c	*et cetera*	&c
o̲	th	o̲
φ	; *-tude*	(none)
£ (£	pound sterling	£
⌗	fact unknown	(none)
~	[insignificant]	(not used)

ABBREVIATIONS, SUFFIXES, ELISIONS, ETC.

S (S)	*-der*; *-uire*; *-r*; *-er*	r
S̶	*-ber*; *-ry*; *-ary*; *-or*; *-er*	r
θ (o e)	*-the*; *-th*; *-don*; *-on*; *-unt*; *-nd*; *-itto*; *-any*; *-ion*; *-able*; *-tion*	Lond$^{\theta}$

Halley's symbols and variations	*Meaning*	*Printer's type equivalents*
	pound (weight)	(none)
	-ant; *-ent*	t
	-ber; *-er*; *-or*; *-our*; *-ry*; *-ary*	r
	-itude; *-ude*; *-tion*	(none)
	-ude; *-nces*; *-ances*; *-tion*	(none)
	-ude; *-don*; *-able*; *-nce*; *i*; *ti*; also, word elision, or two of same letter	(none)
	-tion; *-tude*; *-er*	(none)
	-de; *-rd*; *-aid*; *-nd*; *-out*	d
	-rd; *-ed*	d
	-ut; *-t*; *-rd*; *-ught*; *-tude*; *-unt*; *-r*	t
ll	*-all*	ll
tt	*-ll*; *-onel*	(none)
	ye; rd; nd	d
	-ur; *-er*; *-ir*; *-re*; *-r*	r
	-ing	g
t (t t)	*-unt*	(none)
	-randum; when above a 'c', means '*ti*'	(none)

Halley's symbols and variations	*Meaning*	*Printer's type equivalents*
ꝑ	per	p
ℒ	per (alternate form)	p
a'	*-itude from* [probably, from Latin *ab*, meaning 'away from']	a′
[illegible]	*-itude*	(none)
ꞃ (n)	*-on*; *-ain*; *-in*	n
t	at	t
[illegible]	*-any*	(none)
~ (~ ≈)	sentence continued below	~
e	*-re*; *-r* (i.e., p^{e}sent=present)	p^{e}sent
‖	:	‖
Cwt	a hundred weight	Cwt
ti (t)	pound sterling (alternative form)	ŧi (t) (L)
ꝺ	*-ur-*	ꝺ

Not included on the above lists are various decorations and some unique symbols.

[THE FIRST VOYAGE AND ABSTRACT] Oct. 1698

(f.1) A Journall of a Voyage in his Majes:^{ties} Pink the Paramore entended for the Discovery of the Variation of the Magneticall Compass by Edmund Halley Comand.^{r}[1]

♃ 20. Octob:[2] Wind WSW a Small Gale I sailed from Deptford about Noon, and that next day we Anchored in Gravesend reach about halfe a Mile below the Town, I return'd to London to settle my accounts with the Victualing Office.—[3]

♂ 25.—I return'd on board and that day we fell down over against Hole haven Wind at West

☿ 26. Wind at SW we went through the new Channel and about 4 in the evening came to an Anchor near the Bouy of the Red sand

[1] Dalrymple titles this simply: Dr. HALLEY's FIRST VOYAGE. For a discussion of Dalrymple's published version of Halley's First and Second Voyages, see Introduction: The Journals of the *Paramore*, pp. 66–9.

[2] Although the Journal starts officially on 20 October 1698, rigging had begun some nine weeks earlier on 15 August. See Document 61, p. 290.

[3] The first entry well illustrates differences in form between the MS journal and D, in which it is rendered: October, 1698. Th. 20. WIND W S W a small gale, I sailed from Deptford about noon, and the next day we anchored in Gravesend Reach, about half a mile below the Town, I returned to London to settle my accounts with the Victualling Office.

As can be seen, differences here have to do mainly with abbreviation, capitalization, contraction, punctuation and spelling. In the MS proper names are sometimes rendered in lower case, e.g. portland; and especially parts of proper names where more than one word is involved are often uncapitalized, e.g. MS, Gravesend reach; D, Gravesend Reach. The MS also makes greater use of symbols, as for days of the week. Occasionally a different word is used which does not alter the sense of the passage, e.g. MS, that; D, the. There is internal variation in spelling in the MS and in D, and between them, e.g. MS, Victualing; D. Victualling. Hereafter attention will be drawn by footnote mainly to differences between D and the MS only if they are judged to be significant, where the sense of the text is improved, where there are important deletions or additions, etc. See Appendix A, pp. 349–53, for spelling, etc., of selected place names for the First Voyage.

♃ 27. It proved calm all day, the little wind that was at SSW. Variation obser'd 7°W.[1]

♀ 28. Little wind at SW and SSW, we weighed to go over the flatts, but made little of it till after noon, when there sprung up a Stout Gale of NE Wind, with which we past the Narrows and Anchored in Margate Road

♄ 29. Wind at East and ENE we weighed at peep of day and turned it through the Gull stream where to my great satisfaction[2] I found the weakness of my Crew and that our Vessell was very Leewardly for all the Shipps out turned us and went away before us.

☉ 30. The Wind blew so hard at North that we were forced to hand our Top sailes, about 2. the Isle of Wight bore from us NNW the body of it, but it being cover'd with Snow, Some that ought to have known it better, tooke it for portland. In this bad Weather we found our Shipp Leaky and our pumps brought up abundance of our Sand ballast at night we tryed under a main saile and drove to the Southward —

☽ 31.—in the Morning we were out of Sight of Land, so we halld[3] in for the Shore Wind at NE and made the high Land of St Albans all covered with Snow: but being gotten the Length of Portland, the wind took us Short at West, and forced us into portland road, and I got an opportunity to informe the Admiralty of our being so Leaky, and that we thought it

[1] D sets this last statement off separately as though it might apply both to 27 and 28 October.

[2] D renders this 'dissatisfaction'. At first reading this seems more reasonable; however Halley might well have meant satisfaction in the sense that he was happy to have discovered these deficiencies early enough so that something could be done about them, as indeed it was in the case of the vessel. See Documents 36 to 41, pp. 271–4.

[3] D, hauled. Where there is consistent variation in spelling, if noted at all, it is usually only indicated at the first occurrence.

proper to have her Searcht, and our Ballast Shifted for Shingle, for that we — found the Sand to Stoke and Gall our pumps. —

♂ 1. Novemb[r]: I Dispatcht my Letter to the Lords out of portland road[1] it being Calm, designing either for portsmouth or plymouth, as the Wind should present that next blew, haveing prayed Orders, to both places to refitt us. In portland road I observed the Variation 6°½ West.

☿ 2. in the Morning the Wind came up at SW a fresh Gale and we weighd and Stood into the Needles, but the Tide of Ebb running Strong out we could Scarce Stem it and made it night before we gott to an Anchor which we did a little to the Westward of Yarmouth in the Isle of Wight

♃ 3.—Wind at SW we weighed and came about one to an Anchor at Spitt head where we found Capt Fowles Commodore in the abscence of Admirall Benbow —[2]

(f.1v.) ♀ 4.—Novemb[r]: We fired 5 Gunns and hung out all Colours for the Kings day[3] the Wind blew so hard Westerly that we could not go into the Harbour.

♄ 5. We fired 5 Gunns for Powder Treason;[4] in The night it blew so hard that most of the Shipps drove and we lett go our Sheat[5] Anchor to hold us. — A French Merchant man being a

[1] Document 36, pp. 271-2. For the action taken on this request see Document 38, p. 273. In both the First and Second Voyages D usually sets new months off, e.g. November 1698, and represents this as a page heading until it changes.

[2] D, Bembow. John Benbow (1653–1702) at this time was Rear Admiral.

[3] The birthday of William III, born at The Hague (1650) With his consort, Mary, he accepted the English crown on 13 February 1689 and they reigned jointly as King William III and Queen Mary II until her death, 28 December 1694, after which William ruled alone. Thus at the time of Halley's Voyages, William was the sole monarch, which he remained until his death, 8 March 1702.

[4] Guy Fawkes Day commemorating the foiling of the Gunpowder Conspiracy, – the attempt to blow up Parliament, 5 November 1605.

[5] D, sheet.

little to[1] near the Spitt had like to have beene lost on it having Struck severall times. —

☉ 6.—Fine weather and Southerly Winds, we got into the Harbour where we found order to Search us and shift our Ballast. The Commissioner and Officers[2] shewed great readiness to dispatch us.

☽ ♂ ☿
7. 8. 9. They gott all things out of us, and on Thursday 10$^{\theta}$, We gott into the Dock. The Variation in portsmouth Harbour 7°West

♂ 15. She came out of the Dock, having been throughly searcht, and a new coat given her, twas the opinion that her leaks proceeded from the Spikes that brought on her dubling; and Splitt the Planks —

☿ 16. We gott in our Shingle Ballast, and by the 18th all things were putt on board again and Stowed, but the wind continued bloweing so hard at West and WSW, that there was no stirring till

♂ 22. This day having a moderate gale at NW, we went out of portsmouth harbour, and Joyned Admirall Benbow at St Hellens, Saluting him with 5 peices and he returned me as many.[3] I sent my Lieuten^{t} with my respects to him and to entreat him to take care of us.[4]

☿ 23. This morning it blew extream hard at W and WbS, we lost our small boat being ill belayed from our Stern, and it being a great Sea and the night dark soe could not recover her.

[1] D, too.

[2] The Dockyard Commissioner at Portsmouth at this time, Henry Greenhill, and his staff. See p. 243 n. 1. and Document 37, p. 272.

[3] At this time the exact number of rounds for particular occasions was not prescribed although, as now, on joyous occasions an odd number was usually fired. Halley as a Captain would, of course, not normally have merited the same number of guns as Benbow but it has been said that 'the Admiral to mark his respect for Dr. Halley returned the salute with the same number of guns'. Burney, 1816, p. 384.

[4] See Documents 42 to 44, pp. 274–6.

♃ ♀ ♄ 24.25.26. It continued to blow extream hard about the West, so that I could not go on shore to gett another boat without which I cannot proceed

☉ 27. The Gale moderating I waited on the Commissioner who readily granted me another boate

☽ 28. The boat was delivered me and that night carried on board

♂ 29. Early in the Morning the Wind came up to NE and after to NNE and flew[1] a fine gale, and Admirall Benbow gave the Signall for Sailing; so we gott up our Anchors and by two of the Clock we were all under Saile.

☿ 30. We Steard down the Channell WSW, Wind NNE at Noon the Start bore NbE from us 6 or 7 Leagues So I Judg my Self in Latitude 49°.50′ and Longitude to the West from London 4°.00′ hence I take my Departure.

(f.2)

Decemr:	Day	Wind	True Course	Miles	Lattitude correct	West Longi-tude from Lon ⊖	⊖ Variati	Remarkable Occurrances[2]
♃	1	NNESbW	W10S	77	49.37	5.57		about Noon all at once the Wind veared from the
♀	2	NNW	S31W	156	47.23	8.00		S b W with a Stout gale, both Ways which the
♄	3	NNE	S37W	79	46.20	9.10		Admirall told me when I waited on him was a thing
☉	4	NE	SSW	96	44.51	10.3		a man might use the Sea
☽	5	ENE	S2W	133	42.38	10.9	*5.30	all his Lifetime & not se the Like—
♂	6	SE	S29W	89	41.20	11.7		3 in the Afternoon I

[1] D, blew.

[2] In D headings for the tables are substantially the same as in the MS, except that the day of the week and date of the month are included in the same column in D under the first heading, which also indicates the year, e.g. Dec. 1698, and below this, Th. 1, etc. Also in D there is no heading, 'Remarkable Occurrances', although information in this category from the MS is sometimes given either within or below the table. In other tables in D other headings may be missing as indicated in various footnotes below.

☿	7	EbStoS	S26W	75	40.12	11.50		waited on Admirall Bembo on Board his Shipp ——[1]
♃	8	SbWtoE	S31 ½W	52	39.28	12.25		
♀	9	EtoSSE	S18W	66	38.25	12.51	*5.0	
♄	10	ENE	S17E	145	36.6	11.57		Squalley Weather[2]
☉	11	EtoSE	S9W	97	34.30	12.15	*4.20*	
☽	12	East	S	72	33.18	12.15		
♂	13	SSE	W29S	110	32.25	14.9		Fine Moderate Weather[3]
☿	14	SSEtoSW	W	45	32.25	15.3		A * before the Variation Shews it was observed in the Morning; when after it, in the Evening.[5]
♃	15	SEtoEbS	W10S[4]	55	32.15	16.7		

This day about 11.[6] the Southern of the two Ilhas Desiertas[7] was seen the South part bareing West by North about 5 Leagues off about 4 We came up with it and then hall'd in for the Island of Madera NWbW we lay by till the Moon rose and then the Admirall made a Trip to Windward the better to recover the Road of Fonchiall.[8] By Noon Decem^{r} 16. we were got close in with the Town but the Admirall Stood off and on and would not Anchor, So I went on Shore in order to gett my Wine and that night the Admirall left us on account of Holy Dayes[9] and the great Suff[10] of the Sea I could not get my Wines

[1] D renders this passage: '1. About noon all at once the wind veered from the SbW to the N N W with a stout gale both ways, which the Admiral told me when I waited on him was a thing a man might use the sea all his life-time and not see the like. 3. In the afternoon waited on Admiral Benbow on board his ship.' Of course, in both D and the MS the numbers, when used in this manner, indicate the date to which the entry refers.

[2] D omits.

[3] D omits.

[4] D, *W 10 S. The asterisk refers to a footnote which reads: '*One MS. says W 10 ½ S.' In the MS, the asterisk is used as in the statement in the bottom right of the table (see n. 5 below), not for footnotes.

[5] D omits this important statement here but in his Advertisement which precedes the 1773 published journal he notes: The MS observes * *before* the Variation signifies it was observed in the Morning, **after* it, in the Evening. See Figure 14.

[6] D, 11^{h}. In the MS the abbreviation h is sometimes used for hour, or a phrase (e.g. by the clock) is employed. There is often, as here, no specific indication what a number means in the MS, although it is usually evident from the context.

[7] D often uses italics for place names, as here, or for other purposes, e.g. for foreign words or for emphasis.

[8] Following Fonchiall, as elsewhere, when a new day's entry begins, D usually starts a new paragraph with the date indicated. See n. 1 p. 94.

[9] D, the Holidays.

[10] The inrush (of the sea) towards the shore. Document 45, p. 277, gives an account of events described in the passage.

off till Tuseday the 20th in the Evening. I observed the Town of Fonchiall to lie Duely in 32°. 30′ And by my reckoning the Longitude thereof is 16°.45′ or 1h.7′ West from London the Variation observed on Shore was just 4° to the Westward Wensday the 21 in the Morning we stood out of Fonchiall road, and I directed my course for the Island of Sall which is about 5°½ more Westerly than Madera[1]

	Day	Wind	Course	Miles	Latt correct	West Longit from Lon	Variat	Remarkable Occurances
☿	21	ENE	SWbS	15	32:20	16.55		At Noon Fonchiall bore
♃	22	ENE–NE	S41½W	134	30.40	18.39		N E b N 5 Leagues Distant[2]
♀	23	NE.ENE	SW[3]	110	29.19	20.5		Constant Settled fair
♄	24	NE.NNE	SbW	76½	28.4	20.22		Weather with a Fresh Gale of Wind[4]
☉	25	NNE.NbE	SbW	77½	26.48	20.39		

(f.2v.)

Decembr	Day	Wind	Course	Miles	Latt correct	West Longit from Lon	Variat	Remarkable Occurances
☽	26	NE–NEbE	SbW	117	24:53	21.4		A Fresh Steady Gale of Trade Wind ——[5]
♂	27	NNE	Ditto[6]	114	23.1	21.28		
☿	28	NNE.NE	D°	111	21.12	21.51	*2.0*	
♃	29	NNE.E	S—	89	19.43	21.51		at Six this Morning ye Island of Sall was seen Distant about 6 Leags the Land appearing in 4 hills from the SW b W to W b S. ——[8]
♀	30	E.ENE	S—	103	18.0	21.51		
♄	31	E.NE	S.WSW[7]	71	16.50	22.0	———	

[1] D renders this passage: W. 21. Early in the Morning we weighed and stood out of *Fonchiall Road*, and at Noon the *Town* bore NEbE about 5 leagues; we being bound for the *Cape de Verde Islands*, I directed my Course for the *Island of Sall* which is about 5°.½ more westerly than *Madeira*.

[2] D omits this note in his table, but includes the information in the statement in n. 1 above.

[3] D, *S W. The asterisk refers to a footnote which reads: *One MS. in pencil says S 42 ½ W.

[4] D omits.

[5] D omits.

[6] D, S b W. D does not use Ditto (or, as in MS immediately below, an abbreviation for this word) in the tables.

[7] D, ‡ S. W S W. The double dagger refers to a footnote which reads: ‡ One MS. says S 7 W 71 miles.

[8] D omits, but renders this information in the text following the table as follows: This

The Lattitude of the Middle of the high Land of Sall is justly 16°.40′ and it's Longitude 22° from London Close under the Lee of this Iseland the Variation was but halfe a degree Westerly.[1] I could not go on Shore here by reason of the great Suff of the Sea, so at Evening I bore away for St Iago SSW to avoid a Sunke Rock that lies in the fair way between Bonavista and St Iago. The Next Day at 10 in the fore-noon I past through a Streak of Water in appearance turbid, but when in it, We took up some Water, and it was full of Small transparent globules, but less than white peas intersperst with very small blackish Specks These globules were so numerous as to make the Sea of a yelow muddy Colour There Substance appear'd like that of our Squidds or Urtica Marina and there were two or three Sorts of them our people Tooke them for Spawn of Fish, but I believe them a Smaller sort of Squidds.[2] — At 6 the North point of St Iago was seen bearing South, so I went a way South by E, and by three in the Morning under the high Land of St Iago it fell Calme for 6 hours, by noon the East point of the Island of St Iago bore S and the body of the Isle of May

Morning we lay by for *Sall*, and as soon as it was day the *Island* appeared in *four hills*, bearing from SWbW to SWbS about six leagues off.

Again the bearing differs from the MS.

[1] D renders this passage: January, 1698–1699. The Latitude of the *middle* of *High Land of Sall* is justly 16°. 40′ N, and its longitude 22°. W. from London. – Close under the lee of *this Island*, the Variation was but *half a degree* Westerly.

[2] D renders this interesting passage as follows: M. 2. The next day at 10 in the Forenoon we passed thro' a streak of Water in appearance turbid, but when in it we took up some of the Water and it was full of small *transparent globules* somewhat less than white peas, their substance appeared like that of our *Squids* or *Urtica Marina*, but interspersed with very small blackish specks, these globules were so numerous as to discolour the Sea, and there were two or three sorts of them: Our People took them for *Spawn of Fish*, but I believe them to be a small sort of *Squids*.

It has been suggested from this description that they had run into a colony of jellyfish (Armitage, 1966, p. 141).

ENE,[1] and a fresh Gale ariseing at NE we came that Evening into the Bay of praya on the South side of the Island Latt 14°50′ Long 22°. 30′ West the Isle of May and Sall are due North and South from each other[2]

January	1	ENE	SWbS	65	15:56	22.37		We had here a Gentle Gale amongst ye Islands —[3]
☽	2	Ditto	S15½E	54	15.4	22.22		

January the 6th in the Morning haveing fill'd all our Casks and gotton Wood of the Governour at a very extravagant price, Wee Stood off to Sea; for the Island of Trinadada, to refresh there: the Suns amplitude this Morning was 22°. 20′ and the Moons then setting 16°.40′.[4]

♀	6	NNE[5]	SEbS	12	14.39[6]	22.25		At Noon the port of praya bore N E b N 4 Leagues Distã [7]
♄	7	NEbN	D°	171	12.16	20.48		
☉	8	NEbE	D°	142	10.18	19.27		A Stout Gale of the Trade Wind —[8]
☽	9	D°	D°	132	8.28	18.12	1°W*	
♂	10	NE ENE	S40E	128	6.50	16.50		

[1] D has an asterisk here which refers to a footnote as follows:
*[Another Paper says]

Jan. 1698–9	True Course	Miles	Lat.	Long.
Su. 1.	S W b S	65	15°.56′	22°.37′
M. 2.	S 15½ E	54	15. 4	22. 22

At Noon the *East Point* of the Island St Jago bore S°. and the body of the *Isle of May* E b N ½ N. and that same Evening we came to an anchor in *Praya Bay*.
Compare this with the text and table in the Journal of the First Voyage pertaining to these dates. The square brackets are Dalrymple's.

[2] D, Lat. 14°. 50′ N.° Long. by reckoning, 22°. 30′ W. D begins a new paragraph: The *Isle of May and Sall* are justly due N°. and S°. from each other.

[3] D omits this table except as a footnote; see n. 1 above where D begins the dating practice, 1698–9 (Old and New Style) which he uses in this journal until 1 April 1699, and so on. Note also the omission of the wind category in the D footnote table, n. 1 above.

[4] D adds after this sentence the words, 'At Noon'. Then follows the table beginning 6 January to 18 February after which the text begins again.

[5] D includes no entries under Wind, until 1 February.

[6] D, 14°. 39′ N. Symbols are sometimes added for the first entry on a page in D.

[7] D omits.

[8] D omits.

(f.3)

January	Day	Wind	Course	Miles	Latt Corect	West Long a London	Varia	Remarkable Occura
☿	11	NEbE	E38½S	87	5.56	15.42		The Aire grew so thick
♃	12	ENE.E	S26½E	62½	5.00	15.14		and hazey that we could not See the Sunn rise
♀	13	ENE Calm	S29E[2]	12½	4.49	15.8		or Sett under 5 degrees of
♄	14	Calm EbN	S18½E	9½	4.40	15.5	0.00[3]	Atitude[1]
☉	15	Calme	——[4]	——	4.41	15.5		No Variation
☽	16	North	S—	38	4.3	15.5		We were plagued with a Sort of Musquito's wch
♂	17	N.NNW	S—	63	3.0	15.5		we Suppose came from
☿	18	Calme	W37S	5	2.57	15.9		Guiney —[5]
♃	19	N.SE calm	S2½W	22	2.35	15.10		Violent Rains
♀	20	S.SbN	E25½S[6]	23	2.25	14.49		at 8 in the Morning we
♄	21	N. Calm	S17E	10½	2.15	14.46		lost our fore Top-Mast
☉	22	WtoS	NNW	37	2.49	15.00	o o	No Variation[7]
☽	23	SbW.SSW	WbN	41	2.57	15.40		at 6 this Morning —
♂	24	South	W14S	53½	2.44[8]	16.32		We saw a Saile standing to the Eastward who
☿	25	SbE	W20S	65	2.22	17.33		shew'd us portuguise Colurs —
♃	26	SbW	S24¼E[9]	12	2.11	17.28		Gentle Gales next to
♀	27	SE	W4½N	13	2.12	17.41		Calme: we find a Current Setting us to the
♄	28	SE	SWbS	14½	2.00	17.49		Nothwards —
☉	29	SSE	WbS	29	1.54	18.17		The Calms continuing I
☽	30	SbEtoSbN	SW	14	1.44	18.27		put the Ships Company to 3 pints p Day of Water[10]
♂	31	SW.SSE	South	10	1.34	18.27		We gott a Dolphin of abot. 20 weight[11]
Februa	1	SSWtoSEbE	S15W	24	1.11	18.33	1°E—*[12]	
♃	2	SE	S35½W	34	0.43	18.53		Little Wind but
♀	3	SEbS	W30½S	34	0.26	19.22	*1⅓E*	Sometimes Squalls with Rain[13]

[1] Probably 'Altitude' is meant, D omits. [2] D, S 29½ E.
[3] D, *No Variation*. This is expressed verbally here and elsewhere.
[4] D, Calm. [5] D omits.
[6] D, W 25½ S. This is more likely than E as stated in the MS.
[7] D enters *No Variation* in the Variation column for 23 January, and above this includes the note: A great set to the Northward. Thereafter there are no notes in D until 28/29 January – see n. 10, below.
[8] D, 2°.44′ N. The symbol is for the first entry on a new page in D. [9] D, S 24½ E.
[10] D omits. For 28/29 January D includes a note: Great riplings as of overfalls of a current.
[11] D omits. [12] D, 1. E*. Slight differences in the form of such entries occur occasionally.
[13] D omits.

♄	4	S.SSE	W16S	32	0.17	19.53		
☉	5	SbEtoSSW	S27E	11	0.12	19.43		I find my Selfe Sett by a Strong Stream to the Northward
☽	6	SEbS.toSWbS	N7W	8	0.20	19.44		
♂	7	SEbE	SWbS	29	o South 4[1]	20.00		
☿	8	ESE	SSW	32	0 34	20.12	*1½E	I resolved to goe to Fernando Loronho in Search of Water[2]
♃	9	SEbE	S27W	20	0 52	20.21		
♀	10	EbS	S9½W	18	1 10	20.24		This Morning we lay by to Scrubb our Shipp —

(f.3v.)

♀ Februa	Day	Wind	Course	Miles	Lattitud correct	West Longit from Lon	Varia-tion	Remarkable Occurances
♄	11	SE.EbS	S16½W	39	1.47	20.35		
☉	12	SbE.SEbS	W20S	23½	1.55	20.57	*2½E*	The Calms still Continue wth Some Squalls of Raine[3]
☽	13	SEtoNW	S16W	26	2.20	21.4		
♂	14	W.WNW	S	53	3.13	21.4		Rain all Day
☿	15	NNE.ESE	S21.W	14	3.26	21.9		This morning I observed the ☽ apply to a Starr in *fasciâ* ♐ ii *boreali* and conclude my Selfe 50 Leags to the East of Fornando Loranho[5]
♃	16	ESE	W2½S[4]	60	3.48	22.5		
♀	17	ESE	W2½S	72	3.51	23.17		

This Morning between two and three looking out I found that my Boatswain who had the Watch, Steard a way NW instead of W (we now baring down W. for the Iseland of Fernando Loronho) I conclude with a designe to miss the Iseland, and frustrate my Voyage, though they pretended the Candle was

[1] D, 0.4S. D omits the line above this entry.
[2] D omits.
[3] D omits.
[4] D, W 21½ S.
[5] D renders this passage: This morning I observed the ☽ apply to a Star *in fascia* ♐ ii and concluded myself 160 leagues more westerly than our account, and but 50 leagues to the East of *Fernando Loronha*.

If Halley was capable of such a mistake, it is certainly understandable how less skilful navigators made great errors in this period when longitudinal position was a major problem at sea. This error may be partly explained by the malfunctioning of the log-line of which Halley complains later and, perhaps, by events which took place aboard the ship at about this time. An appropriate correction was not made in the journal immediately. D has an entry in the table (not in MS) under the appropriate headings as follows:

S. 18	W 14½	24	3.57	23.40

out in the Bittacle, and they could not light it. about 3. in the afternoone we we[1] made the Iseland about 6 Leagues off us; bearing SWbW: The next day we came to an Anchor under the Lee of the Island, haveing narrowly escaped a Sunk Rock; that lies off the SW point of the Island. I went on Shore to see what the Iseland might afford us, but found nothing but Small Turtle Doves and Land Crabbs in abundance, neither Goats nor hogs nor any people; we saw many green Turtle in the Sea and in Someplaces their Tracks on the Sand, but could Catch none, by reason of the great Suff of the Sea; we searcht the whole Lee Side of the Iseland but found no fresh water; we lookt not on the windward side because we found such a Suff on the Lee side: here we againe scrubb'd our Shipp and gott some Wood and Sett up all our Shrouds and brought our Masts more aft. we found a four Clock Moon to make high Water, and it flows about 6 Foot on a Spring. The Variation observed on Shore was not full 3 degrees East.[2] The Island is but Small, about 7 Miles Long and very Narrow. The Middle thereof is in Latt 3°57′ South, and Longit by reckoning from London 23°.40′ West.[3] The Appearance thereof when the high pico like a Steeple bears SWbW at 5 Leagues distance is thus ———[4]

[1] The word 'we' is not repeated in D.

[2] D here omits this and the preceding sentence but imparts this information later. See n. 4 below. These events which occurred 19 February are set off in separate paragraphs in D.

[3] This figure is corrected to 34.00 in the table at the end of the MS, p. 117 but D repeats the figures as given in the journal in his text, and Abstract for 19 February, p. 119.

[4] D does not include the profile sketch below and has an asterisk at the end of this sentence which referst o a footnote which reads: *This view is not amongst Dr. Halley's Papers.

D then adds a paragraph: 'At this island a four o'clock Moon makes *high water* and it rises about six foot on a Spring. The variation observed on Shore was not fully 3°. E.' See n. 2 above.

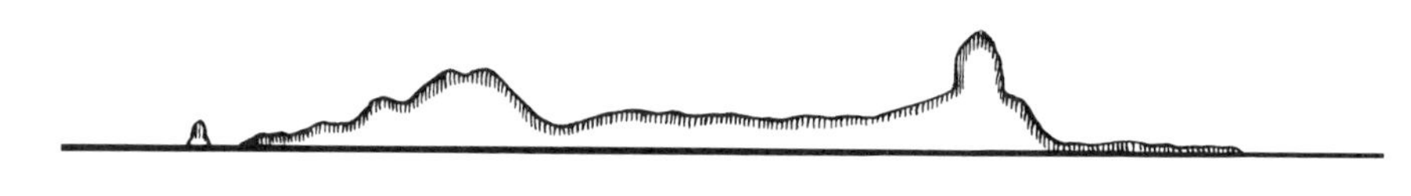

(f.4)

The plan of the Island

Fernando Loronho —[1]

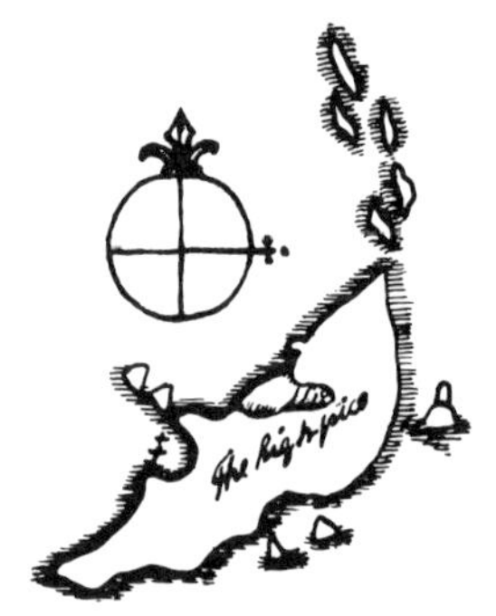

A Sunk Rock
Six foot Water

Wanting Water I resolved to goe directly for Pernambuco and Accordingly[2] Thursday the 23^{d} in the Morning I weighed and Shaped my Course SSW and by Noon the Island bore NEbN. at about 7 Leagues distance

[1] D omits this plan as well as the profile which precedes it, see p. 99 n. 4.

[2] D omits the remainder of the sentence but adds instead, after 'accordingly' (without punctuation): I ordered our Course, supposing I might confide in the Charts for so small a distance, Five several Draughts making the Westing to be from 210 to 240 miles, and the difference of Latitude being 4°. I steared away S S W and having made but 102 milles Meridian Distance we fell in with the Coast of *Brasile* in the Night, in the Latitude of 7°.6′S. to my great surprize, the whole distance sailed being but 222 miles.

See entry in MS for 26 February following the table.

February	Day	Wind	Course	Miles	Lattitu	West[1] Long Lon	Variat	Remarkable Occurances
♃	23	ESE	SWbS.	21	4.14[2]	23.50		A fine Steady Gale[3]
♀	24	ESE	S25 ½W	61	5.9	24.16		
♄	25	SEbE	S21 ½W	92	6.35	24.50		
☉	26	SEbE & EbS	S44W	43	7.6	25.20		This day we find our Selves Sett above 20 Miles to the Nortward of our reckong

This 26th of February in the Morning we fell in with the Coast of Brasile about 3 of the Clock, and came to an Anchor til Day, fearing foul ground, it being Moderate Weather. Cape Blancho bore SSE, and Cabo Dello NbW both at about 2 or three Leagues distance from us, in 5 fathom Water Sandy — ground:[4] we had not yet made halfe our Westing, as the Charts have it. five Severall of my own, made it from 210 or 240 Miles, but we found it but 100 Miles, which all people Bound to that way ought to observe. nor can currents be the whole Cause thereof, for we were but 60 houres in our passage and observ'd no Current where we rode at Anchor.[5] about 9^h a portuguise boat came close under our Stern to see what we

[1] In the heading of this table D omits West (above Long.) and London (below). Hence 23°.50′ W, is D's first entry in this column; all of these entries are short by about ten degrees of longitude. D also omits the heading Variation altogether, presumably because there are no observations of this phenomenon to record in this short table.

[2] D 4.°14′S. Again this is the first entry of a table with no directional indication in the heading, also missing in MS heading in this case.

[3] D omits this note and the following one in this column but adds in the space beginning at the top of the column: At Noon *the Island* Fernando Loronho bore N E b N about 7 leagues distant.

[4] D begins the paragraph thus: We fell in with the *Coast of Brasile* this 26th February, in the Morning about three of the Clock and came to an anchor, fearing foul ground, it being moderate weather; when it was day *Cape Blanco* bore S S E about seven miles off*, and *Cabo Dello* N b W about the same distance from us, in five fathom water, sandy ground.—

The asterisk refers to a footnote in D, *Another Paper says two or three leagues.

[5] D omits the passage which begins here and continues to Stowed (p. 102, n. 1). The Governor was Dom Manuel Soarez Albergaria. See Document 49, p. 280.

were, but would not come on board, so we sent our boat after them to see where we might get Water and two of our hands offering to Stay on Shore two portuguises came off in the Boat who told us that in the River of Paraiba there was very good water easy to come at, and that it was but 3 Leagues thither, just behind Capo Dello. In the afternoon the Governour of Pariaba Sent down the Serg^{t} Major and an interpreter to invite me on Shore and to perswade me to Water in his River promising to Send me a Pilote the next Morning which I (f.4v.) agreed to, and accordingly on Monday we came into the Mouth of the River and I entertain'd the Serg^{t} Major and Some of the portuguise Officers on board The next day I went up to the Town of Paraiba to pay my respects to the Governour, who gave us leave to take what Water we had need off, and tould us we should have Sugar and Tobacco for our own use but not in any quantity to trade with, which he said he could not answer so I return'd on board That Night, and the next day I order'd some of our Cask to be put on Shore: the Watering place was no other than a pitt in the Sand, into which the Water Soakt but Slowly — but it was-not Sensibly Brackish, and kept very well at Sea Our Cask proveing leaky and wanting an expert Cooper lost us some time in the filling them so it was the tenth day of March before we had gott all filled and Stowed I[1] hoped to have observed the Eclipse of the first Satellite of Jupiter, on March the 7th in the Morning· but the great hight of the Planet, and want of a convenient support of my — long Telescope made it impracticable, so I was forced to be satisfied

[1] D begins a new paragraph: March 1698–9. I hoped to have observed the Eclipse of the First Satellite of Jupiter on March the —— in the Morning; etc.

with the observation of the End of the Eclipse of the Moon March 5th in the evening — which as well as I could discern it, through the Clouds ended at $6^h.17'$; and the Moon appearing clear at $6^h.22'\frac{1}{2}$ was in penumbra so thick that I could not judge the Eclipse ended above 5 or 6 Minutes. And the night we fell in with the Coast viz Februr 25th I observ'd the Moon to apply to the Bulls Eye and that the Starr was in a right line with the Moons horns when it was $10^\circ.26'$ high in the West, or at $10^h. 11'. 44''$ from both which observations I conclude the Longitude of this Coast full 36° to the Westward of London[1]

I observed the Variation on board and on Shore $3^\circ.30'$[2] East with all the Curiosity I could. This River of paraiba is one of the finest in Brasile, being broad and deep and a Tide runs far up into the Country. It flows as near as I could Judg East and West, and rises eight or nine foot on a spring Tide. Our pilote — Scrupuling to go out with us, I was forced to leave my Chirurgeon hostage on shore by the Governours order, which detained us till Sunday Morning March 12th when we turned it over the Barr which goes out NEbN or thereabouts from the Rivers mouth. and there is four or five fathom over it at Low Water it is prohibited to Sound their ports otherwise I would have more curiously described this River, where they (f.5) told us no English ship had been for 30. years last past. This

[1] A much better figure than previously but actually $34^\circ 53'$ W. D, after London, adds: 'wherefore we have been set by the *Currents* to the Westwards, during the long calms, *not less than* 200 *leagues*.' D then omits all of the paragraph down to the table but adds in its place two short paragraphs:

The Variation accurately observed on shoar was $2^\circ.44'$.

On Sunday, March 12th, we left the *Coast of Brasile* and stood to the Northward, upon a wind to get an offing, and by Noon *Cape Dello* bore S W of us about 4 leagues distant, and by observation.

[2] The Variation observations hereabout in the MS and D do not agree with each other, or with the Atlantic and World Charts, which appear to rely chiefly on observations made by Halley on his Second Voyage.

River lies exactly in 7 degrees South Latitude and at Noon March 12th Cape Dello bore SW 4 Leagues off

March	Day	Wind	Coarse	Miles	Latt: Cor	Long West ⊖ from Lon	East[1] ⊖ Variat	Remarkable Occurrances[2]
☉	12	SE.SEbE	NE	12	6.48[3]	35.50[4]		
☽	13	D⊖	E35N	49	6.20	35.10		Rainy Weather wth Squalls
♂	14	D⊖	NNE	65	5.20	34.45		This Morning we againe brought our fore top Mast by the board
☿	15	ESE.SEbE	NEbN	48	4.40	34.18		
♃	16	SE.SEbE	NNE.	65	3.40	33.53		

[5]Thus far we kept as near the Wind as we could, to gain an offing from the Coast of Brasile; but finding my self set 68 Miles to the Northward in these four days, beyond our Logg, and the Winter Season in the Southern Climates advancing apace, I conclude the Northerly Currents already made and that as we are foul and but ill by a wind we should[6] not be able to weather Cape St Augustine at least without great loss of time, which will oblige us to Winter in Brasile; and my Officers shewing themselves uneasy and refractory I this day chose to bear away from Barbadoes in order to exchange them if I found a Flagg there[7] so at 6 in the Morning I bore away North and at two afternoon North West

[1] D omits this heading and column, probably because no entry is made.

[2] D omits this heading and column and the two notes below.

[3] D, 6°.48′ S. This is the first entry in the column with no directional indication in the heading.

[4] D, 35°.50′ W. D has only 'Long. Correct.' as the heading above this first entry in the column. The correction for longitudinal position has been made following the observation of 26 February. See p. 101, n, 1 above, and the entry following this in the journal.

[5] D precedes this paragraph with 'March 1698–9'.

[6] D, shall.

[7] D, 'if I could find a flag there'.
Halley means a flagship with an officer of flag rank aboard. Perhaps he hoped to enlist the aid of Benbow who reached Barbados in February 1699 and proceeded to hunt down pirates along the Spanish Main, returning to England by way of Newfoundland in the summer of 1700.

♀	17	SE	N40½W	85	2.35	34.48		
♄	18	NNE.NEbE	N37W	55	1.51	35.12	3.0°*[1]	here the North Easterly Trade Wind Sett in and held without any Variation
☉	19	NE	W43N	58	1.21	36.3		
☽	20	NE	NW	93	0.7S	37.9		
♂	21	D⊖[2]	W43N	120	1.15N	38.37		Much Rain with Gloomy Cloudy Weather to the 23d
☿	22	D⊖	NW	98	2.24	39.47		
♃	23	NEbN	W13N	106	2.48	41.30		by a good observation I find my Selfe Set to the Southard During these Rains[3]
♀	24	NE	NW	114	4.10	42.50	* 4.0*	
♄	25	D⊖[4]	D⊖	123	5.37	44.17	4½*	
☉	26	D⊖	W38N	115	6.48	45.48		A Constant Steady Gale & fair Weather, for all the way to Barbadoes[5]
☽	27	D⊖	W42N	124	8.10	47.20	*5 0*	
♂	28	D⊖	W39N	119	9.25	48.53		
☿	29	NEtoENE	W40N	106	10.33	50.14	*5¼*	
♃	30	ENE	W37N	99	11.32	51.33	*5¼—	
♀	31	E.EbN	W35N	121	12.42	53.12	5*	

(f.5v.)

Aprill	Day	Wind	Coarse	Miles	Lattit	Long	Varia	Remark: Occurrances
♄	1	NEbE	W15N	125	13.14	55.16	[6]	Barbadoes Seene —
☉	2	NEbE	WbS	55	13.3	56.11		

Aprill 1st[7] about 6 in the Evening, the Sunn then Ready to Sett, we discover'd the Topps of the Island of Barbadoes, at such a distance as it was Scarse possible to see it farther; it bearing West and WbS by Compass, about 8 Leagues off as we judged.[8] We went away SW till 10h and then lay by till day, with our head to

[1] D, 3°.–'E. D omits all variation entries below this in the table down to 31 March except for 28 March, 5.¼. This may be misplaced from 29 March.

[2] D, N E. D also uses the same notation in the succeeding entry in this column. As mentioned previously, D does not use the word Ditto or an abbreviation for this in such cases.

[3] D omits all entries in this column above and including this line but adds for 25 March: By Morning and Evening observation compared just 4°. — E.

[4] D has no more entries, only a series of straight lines, in this column to 1 April, when his table ends. See ns. 5, 6 below.

[5] D omits this note but adds here to the entry for 27 March: Carefully observed full 5°; and for 30 March: Much about ½ a point E.

[6] D includes '4.45' here but omits the note following, and all of the next line, i.e. all of the entries for 2 April.

[7] D, April, 1699. Below this he begins a new paragraph: S. 1. This day about . . .

[8] D adds: So that by reckoning there is but 20°. of Longitude between *Cape Dello in Brasile*

the Southward, and by Morning[1] Aprill 2$^{\theta}$. we were so farr to the Southward, that we could Scarce see the Island bareing NNW. my Lieuten^{t}. then haveing the Watch clapt upon a wind, pretending that we ought to goe to Windward of the Island, and about the North end of it, whereas the Road is at the most Southerly part almost. he persisted in this Course, which was Contrary to my orders given overnight, and to all sence and reason, till I came upon Deck; when he was so farr from excusing it, that he pretended to justifie it; not without reflecting Language; about 6 I commanded to bear away NW and NWbN and before 11 we came to an Anchor in Carlisle bay. I was Sollicitous to gett the true Longitude of this Island, which from the Accounts I had had from others I knew to be about 59° to the Westward of London The Emersions of Jupiters Satellites were very proper for my purpose, but having been by Clouds defeated of those on the 6th. and 13th. of Aprill in the Morning; I resolved to attend the next, which was to fall out the 14th day a little before midnight, I gott all things ready and found that at 11^{h}. 50′[2] after noon, the Satellite was very small as beginning to disappear; when the wind shakeing my Tube, I was willing to gett a more coverd place to observe in, that I might be more Certain, but when I again gott sight of the Planett the Satellite appeared no more vizt after 11^{h}. 5′½ If this have been observed in Europe the Longitude of

and *the Barbadoes*; but by Celestial Observation *the Barbadoes* is 59°. more Westerly than London, so that we have been set 60 leagues to the Westward.

[1] D ends the sentence here, without punctuation, and begins a new paragraph: 'Su. 2. We . . .' Here, as elsewhere, D uses a new paragraph to set off events of a new day, or a new thought, etc.

[2] D, 11^{h}. 50^{m}.. This symbol for minute is not the one D normally uses.

Barbadoes will be sufficiently determin'd thereby, but supposing — Mr Cassinis Tables[1] true, and the Immersion at 11^{h}. 51′, which it was very nearly, the Longitude of the Island of Barbadoes from London will be 59°. 5′. so that I have been sett about 3 degrees to the Westwards in this runn from Brasile to Barbadoes beyond my reckoning[2] The Variation here by many (f.6) Trialls both on Shore and on board was found to be butt 5° to the Eastwards of the N. A Six a clock Moon makes high Water in Carlisle Bay and it flows ordinarily on a Spring tide about 4 foot. The Governour Ralph Gray Esqr desired me to Convey a Letter for him to Coll^{o} Collingwood at the Leeward — Islands, which I received not before the eighteenth Instant. The next Morning Aprill ye 19th I weighed Anchor out of Carlisle Bay, and at noon the North part of the Island bore East about 4 Leagues distant[3]

Aprill[4]	Day	Wind	Course	Miles	Lattit	Longit	Varia	Remarkable Occur
☿	19	NEbN	NWbN	18	13.20	59.30		
♃	20	NE.ENE	N21W	90	14.44	60.3		Cape Torment in Marti nicha bore West about 5 Leagues distant (22°)
♀	21	EbN & E	N2E	55	15.39	60.1		
♄	22	East	N23W	72	16.45	60.30		At Noon ye East part of Desseada bore South distant 22 Miles (23°)
☉	23	D^{o}	W23½N	62½	17.10	61.30		We this Morning againe brought our fore Top mast by the Board

[1] Giovanni Domenico Cassini (1625–1712). The reference to Halley's tube or telescope in this passage is tantalizingly brief, as are other references to instruments used on his Atlantic Voyages.

[2] Halley wrote a letter from Barbados to Burchett explaining events since he left Madeira. See Document 49, p. 279–80.

[3] D omits this passage (at the beginning of f. 6) which begins, The Variation . . . and adds instead: Variation several times observed both on board and ashore was as near as might be full 5.°E. Below this he adds: [Here some part of the Journal is wanting.] Square brackets are Dalrymple's.

[4] D omits this table entirely; see footnote 3 above.

In this Course we Saw on Thursday morning the Isle of Martinica which is much bigger than Barbadoes, reaching in Lattitude from 14°. 20′ to at least 14°.50′. and there is a high flatt hill very remarkable in Lat 14°.30′, and Longit 60°.30′. Satturday the 22^{d}. at Noon, wee made Desseada as far of as we could well discern it, it being some what Hazey and Latitude — thereof is 16°.23′. and before Sun sett haveing Steard away WbN about 10 Leagues we made the Island of Antegoa the highest Land bearing about WNW. Sunday 23^{d}. about 11^{h} we came to an Anchor in 7 Fath on the out side of the shole, which lies to the Westwards of Antegoa abo^{t}: a League from shore and the same Morning we brought our fore Topp mast by the board a third time haveing already fisht it twice,[1] we were obliged to use our spare topmast which we now fitted for a fore topmast The next day[2] I deliver'd the Governour of Barbadoes his letter to Coll^{o} Collingwood and after we had gott up our fore topmast, I ordered the Boats to gett what wood they could haveing found it a very Scarce commodity at Barbadoes and here by reason of the great Suff of the Sea we found it some what difficult to gett it off I attended the Immersions of the first Satellite of Jupiter which happened the 29th in the Morning about halfe an hour past three, but though the night were generally clear yett all the time[3] was intercepted by a Cloud and the opportunity lost.

(f.6v.)

Here I often observ'd the Variation to be very near five degrees Easterly, as at Barbadoes. The high land of S^{t}. Christophers

[1] D, having abroad fisht him twice. (That is, to fasten a piece of wood, technically called a fish, on a mast, etc. to strengthen it.)

[2] D inserts, [Monday 24th]. Square brackets are Dalrymple's.

[3] D inserts, Jupiter.

bore nearest WNW. Mevis[1] WbN, Redondo WSW,[2] and Monteserrat SWbS. p Correct Compass. and sometimes part of Guadalupe appear'd in the SbE, but at a greate distance. I was unwilling to wait here any longer, finding it absolutely necessary to change some of my officers, which I found I could not do, without returning into England, so I resolved to fill all my Cask with Water at St Christophers, where[3] is the best in all the Islands, and easyest to come by; and accordingly Aprill 29th afternoon we weighed and haveing Anchored in foul ground, our Anchor brought up a rock of a vast bigness, so that we could Scarce purchass it with our Windlass, and whose weight rais'd our Sterne about 8 Inches; It gave us some trouble to clear it, but by Sun Sett we gott it off the Fluke of the Anchor, and made Saile:[4] the next Morning Aprill the 30th. we were gotten close under Nevis the high land of which took a way our Wind, so that we were becalmed till near noon, when a Gale Springing upp at ENE we Stood over for St Christophers; at noon we were in the Latitude of 17°. 19′ Long 62.16. The North part of Nevis and South end of St Christophers being then just in one & bareing due East.[5] about 9h we were again becalmed for Severall hours off of palmito point, the high land[6] takeing away our Wind: Butt a little before Sun Sett we had a fine Gale off Shore with which we turned into the old Road: here the Water

1 D, Nevis. Nevis is used elsewhere in the MS.

2 D has an asterisk here which refers to a footnote: *Another Paper says, *Redondo* 17°.00′. 61°.5′.

3 D, which.

4 D, sail. D then starts a new paragraph beginning: Su. 30. The...

5 D, ... Long. 62°. 16′, the *No. Point* of *Nevis* and the *So. End* of *St. Christopher's* being then just shut in one and bearing due *East*.

6 D, *Palmito Point* the *high Land*...

(f.7) proveing excellent good, I order'd our empty Cisterns to be fill'd with it, and all the Cask, and to Stow away all things as coveniently as might be,[1] for a Long runn: We found all sorts of provisions dear and Scarce here, as at the other Islands; but at Anguilla we were informed they were more plentifull. I found the Variat$^{\theta}$ here to be 5°. 30′ Easterly, and the Latitude of the old Road 17°. 30′ Satturday May the 6th about Sunn sett we weighed out of St Christophers Road, and that night passed between St Eustachia and Saba;[2] the next morning by Day St Bartholomey bore East, being ragged Land appearing Rocks,[3] and the High Land of St Martins bore NE.

Sunday 7th at Noon Lat 18°. 10′ Long 62°.50′ The North Point of St Martins closed in with the South part of Anguilla then bore East due; that Evening I came to an Anchor in the Road of Anguilla, which is a white Sandy Bay to Leewards, about 4 Miles from the West point of the Island: here by severall observations I found the Variation 5° :15′ East.

The 8th. and 9th. I provided my Selfe with hens and other refreshments, — such as as the place afforded, and Tuesday afternoon set Saile for England I Steard away North between Dog Island and Turpentine Tree Island, and about 7 Dog Isle bore West about halfe a League off; I reckon my Selfe to depart from Latitude 18°.20′ Long 62°.50′ west from London.

[1] D omits the word, be.
[2] D, *Suba*. See Appendix A, p. 352.
[3] D, . . . appearing like *Rocks*, . . .

May—	Day	Wind	Course	Miles	Latt	Long	Varia[1] East	Remarkable Occurrances
☿	10	EbN	N6½W	86	19.45	63.00		
♃	11	EbN	N9W	119	21.42	63.20	4.15*[2]	A Steady Fresh Gale of Wind[4]
♀	12	D	NbW[3]	103	23.23	63.42	3.15*	
♄	13	D	N13W	58½	24.20	63.56	*2.30*	
☉	14	S. West[5]	N3E	63	25.23	63.53		This day the Trade Wind left us in Lat: 25°:00[6]
☽	15	S. WSW	N2½E	71	26.34	63.50		
♂	16	WbN. W	N4E	79	27.52	63.44	*1.–*[7]	Fine Moderate Weather
☿	17	W. WbN	N2E	94	29.26	63.40		
♃	18	WS. W.	N3½E	75	30.41	63.35		Near the Merridian of Bermudas I find Noe variation in Lat 31°00′
♀	19	W WNW	NbE[8]	65	31.45	63.27	0 0–[9]	

(f.7v.)

May	Day	Wind	Course	Miles	Latt	Long	West Varia	Remark Occurrances
♄	20	W.SW	N27E.	31½	32.13	63.10		We this Evening lookt out for Barmudas but Saw it not —[10]
☉	21	SSE.SEbE	NE	82	33.11	62.00		
☽	22	NW	NEbN	70	34.0[11]	61.00		
♂	23	N.toEbN	N7E	34	34.33	60.55	*3.0*[12]	This Evening I observed the Moon to apply to a Starr in the foot of Leo.[14]
☿	24	ENE —	N4E	23	34.56	60.57	*3.30*[13]	
♃	25	SbW.SW	N37E	49	35.35	60.20		

[1] As before, there are differences in some of the headings of this table between D and the MS. Most of these differences are not significant except in the variation column; D, Variat. (see footnote 2 below); and in 'Remarkable Occurrances' which heading is omitted altogether in D, as are most of the entries in this category, as indicated below.

[2] D, 4°.15′*E. This is the first entry in a column with no directional indication in the heading.

[3] D, N 6 W. This could also be so interpreted from the MS.

[4] D omits.

[5] D, S. W. In this and similar entries in this column in D, the wind directions are justified as close to the bounding lines as possible to avoid confusion. Thus, in this case, S. to W. is meant, not SW or Southwest.

[6] D omits.

[7] D, 1.0*. The note following this is omitted.

[8] D, N 6 E. See n. 3 above.

[9] D in place of this entry, and for the notes for this and the preceding day (which he omits), states, *No Variation.*

[10] D omits.

[11] D, 34.00.

[12] D, *3. 00*W. Because of the heading this designation is necessary. See footnotes 1 and 2 above. Some variation entries both in D and in the MS, as here, appear to be between days rather than for one or the other.

[13] D, *3. 30*W. Entry between lines; see concluding sentence in n. 12 above

[14] D omits.

	♀ 26	SW.NWbW	NE	116	36.57	58.40	*4 30–[1]	A Fresh Steady Gale of Wind
	♄ 27	NW	N42½E	118	38.24	57.00[2]		
	☉ 28	NW.NbW	E16½N	74	38.45	55.30		A hard Gale of Wind[3] these 3 dayes — (28–30 May)
	☽ 29	N.NbW	E3S	110	38.40	53.10		
	♂ 30	N.NNW	E2½S	69	38.37	51.42	*6.30*[4]	
	☿ 31	WSW.SbW	N27½E	82	39.50	50.53		A hard Storme of Southerly and Southwesterly Wind[5]
June —	1	S.WbN	E37N	100	40.50	49.9		
	♀ 2	WbN	E2S	95	40.47[6]	47.3	7–0*[7]	
	♄ 3	NNE to ESE	NEbN	42	41.22	46.33		
	☉ 4	SE.SSE	E24.N	70	41.50	45.7	9–20*[8]	Fine Moderate Weathr for Severall dayes
	☽ 5	WbS.SW	E31N	108	42.45	43.2		
	♂ 6	WNW.NNW	E31N	68	43.20	41.42	*10.20	Close Cloudy Weather with Rain and a continua Fogg[9] (6–8 June)
	☿ 7	EbN.SSW.	N30E	74	44.24	40.38		
	♃ 8	SW.SWbW	E30N	142[10]	45.35	37.44		
	♀ 9	SW	E21N	153	46.30	34.19		A Constant Fresh Gale of Wind for many dayes[11]
	♄ 10	WSW.WbS	E7N	165	46.50	30.20	*8–30[12]	
	☉ 11	WbS	E15N	137	47.25	27.5	*8–30	
	☽ 12	WbS.WNW	E15½N	131	48.00	23.56		The Collour of the Sea begun to Change the 12th. in the Morning the Moon apply'd to a Starr in Line piscium by which I find my Selfe 25 Leagues more Westerly than my Reckoning[13]
	♂ 13	NWbW	E14½N	162	48.40	20.00	*8.30*	
	☿ 14	WbN.SSW	E15½N	106	49.8	17.25		
	♃ 15	SSW.W	E4N	106	49.16	14.44		
	♀ 16	W.WNW	E4N	105	49.24	12.4		
	♄ 17	SEbS	E26N	32	49.38	11.20		

[1] This is the end of the page in D where the entry for this day in the preceding column and this one are rendered respectively: 58. 40W and *4. 30 W. The note which follows in the MS is omitted in D.

[2] Because this is the beginning of a new page in D, the entries for 27 May for course, latitude, and longitude are respectively: N 42°. ½ E, 38°. 24′ N, and 57°. 00′ W.

[3] D brackets the four days: 28, 29, 30, and 31 May, rather than the first three of these as in the MS, and the note following reads in D, Hard Gales of Wind.

[4] This entry which in the MS is between the lines for 30 and 31 May is opposite the latter date in D where it is rendered '*6°. 30′ *W' being the first such entry on the page.

[5] D omits.

[6] There is a correction on the MS and it appears to have read, 47. 47 before amendment. It might now be mistaken for '49. 47' on the MS but, obviously, by the course is 40. 47. It is so rendered in D.

[7] D, 7. 00*. [8] D, 9. 20*. The note following is omitted. [9] D omits.

[10] D, 112. The MS entry of 142 miles seems more reasonable when the positions on this and the following day are plotted on a modern chart. The *Paramore* is being driven by the mid-latitude westerlies and is making good time. See mileage for several succeeding days.

[11] D omits. [12] D omits. He includes this same figure below as in the MS.

[13] D omits this note but in its place beginning exactly in line with the entries for 12 June states: Colour of the Sea changed.

☉ 18	SEbStoNNW	East	137	49.37	7.48	6.25*	At Sunn Sett Struck ground at 80 Fath: at Sunn Sett had ground at 60 Fath Scilley Seene[1]
☽ 19	WbN.W	E1 ½S	107	49.34	5.2		
♂ 20	W.WbN	E21 ½N	62	49.57	3.32	*5.40	

About 9^{h}. of ye Clock this Morning, the North part of Scilley (f.8) was seen bareing East halfe South about 3. Leagues distant: at noon the s^{d}.[2] North part bore due East, Variation allowed; so haveing a very good observation I make the Lattitude thereof 49°.57′. We found a Strong Tide of Ebb setting us to the Southwards and Westwards, which held us till about halfe an hour past one or[3] a South SE Moon, when the Flood being made, we past to the Nortwards of the Islands, the Wind being SW. I find by my reckoning that I am 48 Leag^{s}. before the Shipp, which I attribute to the shortness of our Logg line, the halfe Minute glass being full Measure: and for the Same reason I have no where in my account allowed for the heaving home of the Logg, when we went before the Sea: By Sunn set we had past the Islands, and in the Night I stood away first SE, then ESE, and by Morning we were so farr to the Southwards that we could not see the Land, especially it being thick and hazey; we hall'd in NE and by Noon we made the Lizard bareing West and the Deadman NbE. I had then a good observation and make the Lattitude of the Lizard no more than 49°.54′; we endeavoured to gett this evening up with the Ram head, but the wind dying away, a thick fogg came on, and we

[1] D omits this note. At the bottom centre of the table, below the last line of entries, he adds the statement: [The rest wanting]. The square brackets are Dalrymple's. On a line below this but justified to the right hand margin of the page is the word, ABSTRACT (caps.). On the three following pages in D (20, 21, and 22) there is an abstract of the voyage, probably of Dalrymple's composition since the impersonal pronouns (their and his) are used, and from other internal evidence (see pp. 116–7). All the rest of the log of the First Voyage (i.e. MS f.8, f.8v, and f.9) is missing in D.

[2] said.

[3] The word 'or' is pencilled in.

were becalmed off of Low.[1] At Sun sett the Variation was 6°.40′ West The Rock of Low bearing NE halfe a League off

♃ 22. In the Morning a Small breise of wind at North sett us to the Eastw^rds^: and when the Fogg cleared up we found our Selves near the Ram head, but the wind being Easterly, a very small Gale, we could not fetch it, so came to an anchor in 15 Fathom about two Miles to the Westwards of it, in the afternoon it fell Calme, and with the Flood we towed with both our boats on head, and brought the East point of the Ram head to bear North, but could not gett into plymouth Sound.

♀ 23. Next day by noon we towed into the Sound, and came to an Anchor in very good ground: St Nicholas Isle bearing NbW, and the two Towers of the Cittadell in one, in a bout 6 Fath: water. I waited on the Commision^r^ but found no Ord^rs^: he granted me a supply of Butter and Cheese and I gave my people leave to divert themselves on Shore Satturday the 24th.[2]

☉ 25. I made Sayle early on Satturday morning haveing a fine Gale at SW for the Downes, at noon the Start bore EbN and the bolt head NbE: at Sunn Sett I observed the Variation to be 7°. 16′ West, being then about Mid way between portland and the Start.

☽ 26. at Noon the Needles bore N ½ E. and Dunnose EbN I found (f.8v.) the Latitude to be 50° 28′ by a good observation, whence Dunnose lies in 50°.30′ at Sunn sett the Variation was 7°.40′, Arundell bearing due North[3] and Dunnose W ½ N.

[1] Full stop pencilled in on MS, as are some of the other diacriticals in this part of the MS.

[2] Having arrived at Plymouth, Halley immediately wrote to Burchett summarizing his voyage from the West Indies. See Document 50, pp. 281-2.

[3] Originally, Nort on the MS; h added in pencil.

♂ 27. Next Morning being Just a breast with Beachy head, the Sun being 3 degrees high was found 26° to the Northwards of the East; whence ye Variation 7°17′. all the morning long it proved little wind, so that wee were forced to drop our Anchor in about 15 Fath water, to the Eastward of Beachy head. about Noon there Sprung up a Gale of Wind at SW. with which about midnight we arrived in the Downes: being midway between Dengyness and Dover I observed the Variation 7°.26′ West.

☿ 28. I found Sr Cloudsley Shovell Admirall of the Blew[1] riding in the Downs I waited on him for Ord^{rs}: but found none, so I obtained his leave to come up to Lon$^{\theta}$:

♃ 29. I went post from Deale to London[2]

♀ 30. By Mr Secretary Burchetts order I returned for Deale, and Satturday July 1st I gott betimes thither, where Sr Clously Shovell enquired into the reason of my returne, and appointed Munday Morning for a Court Martiall to trie my Leiut: I gott one Tonn of Bear[3] out of the Rochester by the Admiralls

July. Order.

☾ 3. At a Court Martiall my Leiutenent received a Reprimand for his undecent Carriage towards me,[4] and I received Orders from the Flagg to Saile for the River, Wind EbN.

♂ 4. It blew so hard at North, that the pilote would not weigh this

[1] Sir Clowdisley Shovell, Admiral of the Blue.

[2] See Document 51, p. 283, dated 29 June, but which is Burchett's reply to Halley's letter of 23 June 1699 from Plymouth referred to in n. 2 p. 114 above. Documents 53, p. 284 and 54, pp. 284–5 are also dated 29 June and refer to the impending payoff of the *Paramore* and removal of her guns.

[3] That is, a tun of beer from the *Rochester* (50 guns, 4th rate of 1693, broken up, 1748).

[4] In Document 57, p. 287, Halley expresses dissatisfaction with the outcome of the Court Martial.

day. Wind at ENE we weighed and gott into Ramsgate road,

☿ 5. and rode in 3. Fathom Water.

♃ 6. Wind at ENE and NEbE, we turned through the Braker Channell and haveing Weather'd the Foreland came at high Water to an Anch^r in Westgate Bay.

♀ 7. Wind as before, we gott over the Flatts and into the River, about midnight the Wind came up at SW and SSW, so that we could gett no higher than the hope.

♄ 8. With the Day Flood we turned up the river into Long reach:[1]

☽ 10. We gave notice at the Tower and at Woolwich that they might fetch our Gunns and Gunners Stores

♂ 11. The Gunns and Gunners Stores were delivered to the Tower Officers and that Same Evening we moord our Shipp at Deptford —

Edm: Halley[2]

(f.9) A Table of the true Latitudes & Longitudes of the Severall Islands and Ports mentioned to have been seen in this Voyage ——[3]

	Lat.	Long W: from Lond^θ
The Lizard — — — —— — — —— —	49°.54′	5°.30′
North part of Scilley — —— —— ——	49.57	7.10
Madera — — — — — —— ——	32.30	16.45
Isle of Sall — —— —— — —— —	16.10[4]	22.00
St. Iago ye North Cape —— —— —— —	15.18	22.40

[1] See Document 58, p. 288. [2] Autograph in different ink; see Figure 10.

[3] There are discrepancies between some of the entries in the table and in the text of the MS journal, and between these and the text and Abstract in D; some of these differences are minor and may relate to the particular point of observation recorded, while two are major as indicated below.

[4] 16°. 40′, in both the text of the MS journal and in D; see p. 95, n. 1 above.

Isle of May — — — — —	15.05	22.00
Porto praya South side of St. Iago — — —	14.50	22.30
Fernando Loronho — — — —	3.57S	34.00[1]
Cape Dello at the Mouth of ye River of paraiba in Brasill — — — —	7.00S	36.00
Barbadoes — — — — —	13.10	59.05
Martinica — — — — — —	14.35	60.20
Desseada — — — — —	16.23	60.30
Antegoa — — — — — —	17.10	61.27
Monte serrat North end — — — —	16.50	61.47
Redando — — — — — —	17.2	61.55
Nevis Road — — — — — —	17.15	62.10
Old Road of St Christophers — — —	17.30	62.25
Eustachia — — — — —	17.36	62.40
Saba — — — — — —	17.42	62.55
St Bartholomew — — — — —	17.55	62.35
St Martins — — — — — —	18.05	62.50
Anguilla — — — — — —	18.15	62.50

[1] 23°. 40′, in both the texts of the MS journal and D; this is the most serious discrepancy, which is discussed in p. 99, n. 3, and p. 101, n. 1. It has obviously been corrected in this table but not, interestingly, in the D Abstract, p. 119 (which see). None of the other co-ordinates appear to differ by more than 20′ of latitude or longitude with comparable entries in the MS or D.

ABSTRACT[1]

1698.

Oct. 20. SAILED from *Deptford*
21. Anchored in *Gravesend Reach*
28. Anchored in *Margate Road*
31. Anchored in *Portland Road*, the Vessel being *leaky*

Nov. 2. Went through the *Needles*, and anchored off the Isle of *Wight*
3. Anchored at *Spitthead*
6. Went into the *Harbour*
10. Got into the *Dock* — Variation in *Portsmouth Harbour* 7°. W.
15. Came out of the *Dock*
22. Went to *St. Helens* and joined Admiral Bembow[2]
23. Lost their *small boat* which broke adrift
28. Got another Boat
29. Sailed
30. Took a *departure* from the *Start*

Dec. 1. Remarkable change of Wind at once from S b W to N N W a stout gale both ways
15. Saw the *Desiertas*
16. Anchored at *Madeira*
20. Town of *Fonchiall* in 32°.30′N, Long. by reckoning 16°.45′W. Variation observed on Shoar just 4°. W.
21. Left *Madeira*
31. Saw *Sall.* Latitude of the *middle* of the *High Land* 16°.40′N. Long. 22°. W. Variation close under the lee of this Island but *half a degree* Westerly

1698–9.

Jan. 1. Could not go ashoar on account of the great Surf. Bore away for *St. Jago.*[3]

[1] This Abstract is found only in D who seems to have compiled it himself from the MS copies of Halley's journal available to him.

[2] Differences in spelling between D and the MS (e.g. St. Hellens, Benbow, etc.) have already been alluded to. See Appendix A, p. 349-53, for comparative place name spellings.

[3] It is possible to ascribe these events to this particular day from D or the MS, or to the preceding one, 31 December.

2. Passed through some *turbid* Water, supposed *Squids*
Got sight of *St. Jago* and Isle of *May*
In the Evening anchored in the *Bay* of *Praya* on the S°. *side* of the *Island* Lat. 14°.50′N. Long. by reckoning 22°.30′W.
Isle of *May* and *Sall* are due N°. and S°. from each other

6. Sailed for *Trinidada*

Feb. 18. Got sight of *Fernando Loronha*[1]

19. Anchored under the *lee* of the Island, having narrowly escaped a *sunk* rock that lies off the *S W Pt. of the Island.*
The Island has neither Goats nor Hogs, nor any People; found nothing but Turtle-doves and Land Crabs in abundance; saw many *green Turtle* in the *Sea* but could catch none by reason of the great Surf; found no fresh water on the *lee side* of the Island
The Island is about 7 miles long and very narrow; the middle of it is in 3°.57′S. Long. by reckoning 23°.40′W. 4 o'Clock Moon makes high water; it rises about 6 feet on a spring. Variation observed on shoar not fully 3°.

23. Left *Fernando Loronha*, wanting Water resolved to go for *Pernambuco*

26. Fell in with the Coast of *Brasile*, great error of Draughts.

Mar. 5. Observed the Eclipse of the Moon — conclude the Longitude full 36° W. — Set *not less than* 200 *leagus*[2] to the Westward. — Variation observed on shoar 2°.44′E.

12. Left Coast of *Brasile*

16. Finding a strong Current to Northward, and Winter setting in, afraid of being obliged to winter in *Brasile* Bore away for *Barbadoes* to change his Officers

April 1. Saw *Barbadoes* — 60 leagues to westward of account

2. Anchored in *Carlisle Bay*

14. Observed an Eclipse of Jupiter's Satellite Long.

[1] Actually the *Paramore* came within six leagues of the island that afternoon.
[2] D obviously means leagues in this passage, as elsewhere.

1699.

59°.5′W. Variation several times observed both aboard and on shoar full 5°E.

20. Saw *Martinica*, Lat. 14°.20′. to 14°.50′N.
High flat hill 14.30. Long. 60.30 W.

22. Saw *Desseada* Lat. 16.23.
Saw *Antegoa*

23. Anchored on the outside of the shoal which lies to the Westward of *Antegoa*

24. Great Surf. — Variation 5°E. — Bearings of other Islands from thence

Redondo 17°.00′N. 61°.5′W.

St. Christopher's best Water of all the Islands and easiest got

29. Weighed from *Antegoa*, brought up a vast rock with the anchor; its weight raised the Stern 8 inches

30. Saw *Nevis* and *St. Christopher's*. — N°. Pt. of *Nevis* and S°. Pt. of *St. Christopher's* bore *East* when Lat. was 17°.19′N. Long. 62°.16′W.

Anchored in the *Old Road* of *St. Christopher's*

Excellent Water at *St. Christopher's*, but all sorts of Provisions dear and scarce as at the other Islands. Variation 5°.30′E. Lat. of *Old Road* 17°.30′N.

1699.

May 6. Sailed from *St. Christopher's*, and that Night passed between *St. Eustachia* and *Suba*[1]

7. Saw *St. Bartholomy* and *St. Martin*

Noon Lat. 18°.10′N. Long. 62°.50′W. N°. part of *St. Martin's* closed in with S°. part of *Anguilla*, bore *East*

Anchored in the *Road* of *Anguilla*, which is a *white sandy bay*, about 4 miles from West point of the Island. — Variation 5°.15′E.

8.–9. Provided himself with such refreshments as place afforded and sailed for England
Lat. 18°.20′N. Long. 62°.50′W.

[1] MS, Saba. For information on place names for Halley's First Voyages used by D, including his Abstract, see Appendix A, pp. 349–53.

Passed between *Dog Island* and *Turpentine Tree Island*
June 12. Lat. 48°.00'N. Long. 23°.56'W. Colour of Sea changed[1]

[1] This information is added by D from the last table in his version of the journal of the First Voyage. This table ends on Tuesday 20 June after which there are no entries, and he concludes with the Abstract as printed above.

[THE SECOND VOYAGE AND ABSTRACT]

(f.10)

A Journal of a Voyage in his Ma:tis Pink
ye Paramore intended for the Discovery of
ye Variation of the Compass kept by
Edmund Halley Commander anno 1699 & 1700.—[1]

♄ Septembr 16.[2] I order'd the Pink to fall down from Deptford to Gallio[3] to see if all our men were on board and to be assured of them which was accordingly done that afternoon Wind at W S W.

☽ 18. I came on board my selfe at Gallions and that Same evening we Anchored in Gravesend reach a little below the Town Wind at S W —

♂ 19. I waited at Gravesend for my Slops[4] and my Pilote to carry me into the downs[5] who came on board about noon

☿ 20. It blew so Fresh at W and W S W that we could not weigh our Anchors till Flood, when haveing got them up, we had

[1] D renders the title thus: A Journal of a Voyage made for the Discovery of the Rule of the Variation of the Compass in his Majesty's Ship Paramore Pink, EDMUND HALLEY Commander, Anno 1699 and 1700.

Compare the above with the title of Halley's Second Voyage in the MS; see also Figure 11. For information on what transpired between the First and Second Voyages see, especially, Documents 50 to 77, pp. 281–300.

[2] The journal begins on this date, but wages began on 24 August 1699; see Document 91, pp. 312–3.

[3] D, Gallions. Halley also uses this form below, entry for 18 September.

[4] Ready-made clothing and other furnishings supplied to seamen from the ships stores.

[5] D, Downs. For this and many other English place names and locations used in all three of Halley's voyages see 'A New and Correct *Chart of the Channel between* England *and* France'. A copy of this map, which resulted from Halley's third voyage, is included with this volume as Figure 9 and as two folded sheets in a separate portfolio. See Documents 81 to 83, pp. 303–5.

such a Gale that we came against the Flood into Margate road that evening —

♃ 21 about 11 of the clock we came to an Anchor in the Downs the Middle of the Town bearing about West from us, the wind being about W S W obliged us to make severall boards[1] before we got to our Anchoring place

♀ ♄ ☉ 22. 23. 24. The wind continued blowing hard at W and W S W so that no ships could Stirr out of the Downs.

☽ 25 The wind came up at N W whereupon all the small Craft weighed — and stood to the Southward, and in the afternoon they were followed by the Winchester and another man of Warr bound to Cadiz-the Faulconbrid[2] bound to Guiney haveing promised to keepe me Company, and not[3] thinking fitt to weigh with so bare a wind I stirred not and before night the Wind returned to the W N W and afterwards to West

♂ 26. The Wind was at S S W. a gentle Gale and by Night it came by the South to the S b E Small Wind with thick Foggy Rain This day it was low water at Deale carefully observ'd at $5^{h}:15'$ post M and the

☽ South at $10^{h}:15'$. high water at deal S b W Moon ——[4]

[1] That is, tack.

[2] As Halley told Burchett, this vessell which promised to escort the *Paramore* for 800 leagues, Document 81, p. 303, was '. . . a Shipp of good force belonging to the Royall African Company . . .' (Document 82, p. 304). There have been several vessels named *Winchester* in the Royal Navy, but the one referred to here is described in J. J. Colledge, *Ships of the Royal Navy*, vol. 1, pl. 613, in these terms; 'Winchester 4th Rate 48, 673 bm 130 × 34½ ft Wells, Rotherhide 17.3.1698. Rebuilt Plymouth 1717 as 711 bm; hulked 21744. BU completed 5.7.1781 at Chatham.' The bm notation refers to the builder's measure, and BU means broken up.

[3] The word 'not' is careted in on the MS.

[4] D, South 10h. 15m. High Water at Deal S b W Moon.

Such notes, which in the MS are bracketed and run into the text of the MS, are in D placed clearly to the left hand side of the text proper and in type of about 7 picas, as opposed to about 10 for the text proper. The abbreviation 'm' for minutes is used by D only occasionally in favour of the symbol ′.

Streame ran to the Southwards from abo^{t}: two till past 8. ——[1]

☿ [2]27. About Sunn Rise we had a very fine Sky and a Curious Variation in the Downs this Morning 7°:32′ } Gale at E S E so I observ'd the Amplitude at riseing 16°½ and Then I order'd to unmore;[3] and weigh, and 3 min: before 9 we were aweigh the Falconbird was gott under Saile before us, and haveing made a tripp to weather the foreland was about and stood to the Southwards, so that we were apprehensive of loosing[4] him; but about 9 at night we fetch't him a little short of Beachy:

(f.10v.)

♃ — [5]28. This Morning the East part of the Land of Dunmose[6] bore North the Wind being come about to E N E and blowing a Stout Steady Gale, this Noon the Cliffs of Freshwater Bay bore North abo^{t} 8 or 9 Leagues off

[1] This entry well illustrates differences in the journal of Halley's second voyage and the transcription in D in which it is rendered: Tu. 26. The wind was at S S W a gentle gale, and by night it came by the S° to the S b E small wind with thick foggy rain; this day it was *low water* at Deal, carefully observed at 5$^{h.}$ 15$^{m.}$ P.M. and the stream ran to the Southwards from about 2 till past 8.

[2] D puts the variation note just below the date, abbreviating Variation to Var., which is usual with him, and below that adds: *Ther. Bar.* 28.0 30.1
A feature of D in the Second Voyage, not found in the MS, is the recording of readings from the thermometer and barometer. These are placed along with the notes on variation, etc. at the left margin of the text proper. They are in the smaller type used for notes (see n. 4, p. 123 above); such entries in both categories in D are from 27 September 1699, as indicated, to 10 March 1699–1700 after which they end abruptly.

[3] D, and then I ordered to unmoor . . . The catchword (or number), Then (in this case, capitalized), is set at the end of the sentence on the preceding page in the MS. D also has catchwords, but because of the pagination it would be fortuitous if they were the same word or figure as in the MS. Hereafter no attention will be called to catchwords, which are not a feature of the MS of Halley's First Voyage though they are of D in the case of both voyages.

[4] D, losing.

[5] D adds: 33.0 30.1. Thermometer and barometer readings, respectively, included in D often, as here, immediately before the date but without identification except for the first such entry on the page. See n. 2 above.

[6] D, Dunnose. There is a correction on the MS which may be an attempt to change from Dunmose to Dunnose or vice versa.

♀ [1]29. Yesterday at four of the Clock the land of Portland bore from us N ½ E abo^{t}: eight Leagues distant, hence I take my departure supposeing my Selfe in Lat 50°.4′ and Longitude West from London 2°:34′. Fryday Noon I am by a good observation in Lat 49°:14′ and have Sailed Since my departure 130. Miles by estimate, which with the diff of Latt: gives a Line W S W. Coarse,[2] and makes my Longitude 5°:40′ to the West of London so that I am much abo^{t}: the Meridian of the Lizard. Wind a Stout Gale from E to N E b E——

♄ [3]30. This 24 hou^{rs}: we have had a fine Gale of Wind at E to N E b E our Course West 40°. South Variation allow'd 154 Miles Latt. observed 47°.35′ Longitude W from Lon$^{\theta}$. 8°.38′—

Octo^{r}:

☉ — [4]1. by a very good observation I am in the Latitude of 46°.33′ and by reckon^{g}. we have made 1°:32′ to the Westwards, so I am Longitude from London 10°:10′ West; We have had little Wind since 2. in the Morning: severall small Birds flew on board us this day, blown off as I suppose from the French Shore by the late Strong Easterly winds. in the Evening I observ'd the Amplitud 4°:30′. whence the Variation 6°:7′ Westerly Course S W 88. Miles { variation this Evening 6°:7′ W.

☽ — [5]2. Latitude by a good observation 45°:22′ and have made by

[1] D adds: *Ther.* *Bar.* 33.0 30.0
As in p. 124, n. 5 above this is the first entry of these readings on a page hence, *Ther. Bar.* Hereafter, such additions from D will be made without explanation.

[2] D, . . . Latitude gives a true W S W course . . .

[3] D adds: 41.0 29.7

[4] D adds: 43.½ 29.7. Below this D puts the variation note which in the MS is at the end of this day's journal entry.

[5] D adds: 43.0 29.8. D places the variation note for this day below this entry.

reckoning 55′ of Longitude West, so am in Long 11°:5′ from London; Course South 30° West distance 78 Miles: in the Night the wind came up at N W and after W N W that we were forced to hall[1] all sharp. Evening amplitude observ'd 4½ South of the west.

Varia Evening Ampli 6°:34′ West

♂ [2]3. This 24h we have had a moderate Gale from the N W to the West, and have kept close hall'd the whole time, by an observation I find my Selfe in Latt: 44°:59′. and Longitude west 40 Minutes; in the whole 11°:45′. At 10.y^c Wind came about to W S W, when the Falconbridg Tackt[3] and stood to the Northward, which I did also, being unwilling to loose his Comp[4] at five next Morning we Stood to the Southward, the Wind Comeing up to W N W true Coarse is West 40° South, distance 36 Miles and halfe.[5]

☿ [6]4. This 24 houres we have had the Wind variable betweene the West and the North, till Sunn set 'twas much westerly, with Squalls of Wind, but after five, it came to N W b N, and Stood at N b W a Fresh Gale and fair Weather. Latitude by observation 43°:34′ Longitude 13°:28′ from London, we have made a Coarse S 41 West, distance 113 Miles —

(f.11)

♃ —— [7]5 This 24 houres we had the Wind variable from N b W to N E b N, where it Stood; since 10. at night a fine Steady Fresh[8] Gale, Lattitude by observat 42°:2′; difference of Longitude 1°:15′. in all from London 14°:43′ Course S S W ½ W, distance 106 Miles. This Morning we fell in with a fleete of Danes of

[1] D, haul.
[2] D adds: 46.0 29.8.
[3] D, . . . the Falconbird tacked . . .
[4] D, . . . to lose his company,.
[5] D, . . . distance 36′½.
[6] D adds: *Ther. Bar.* 41.0 29.9
[7] D adds: 46.½ 29.8. In the statement following (in MS), the word 'Fresh' is careted in.
[8] The word 'French' is careted in on the MS.

18 Saile, and by Noon we came up with an English Barke which the Danes reported to us to be a Sally man, and found him to be a poore Dartmouth Sloop —

♀ 6 This Morning in Lat 41°. or thereabouts I had a good Amplitude 16°.40′ Whence the Variation is 4°:42′ West; at noon by a good observation Lat 40°.29′ We have had a fine Gale of

Variation by a Morning Ampli is 4°. 42 West[1]

N E. Wind, excepting some squalls with rain. We lay by three houres to examine a a[2] Saile, which the Danes affirmed to be a Sallyman but proved a Dutch man, who hoisted French Colours: he was exceeding Sharp and promised to Saile like the Wind, but he made it appear that he came from Faro, and his Loading was Figgs. We have sailed this day and drove 100. Miles S S W ½ W which makes my Longitude West 1°.4′ in all from London 15.47.

♄ [3]7. We have had little Winds next to Calmes for the most part of this day, at Noon I find my Selfe in Lat 39°:52′ by observation, which is 15 Miles More than the Logg gives. I suppose the Sea heaves us to ye South westward, there being a greate Swell out of the N E board. I suppose our whole Westing to be 20 Miles, and Course S 29 W distance 42 Miles,[4] my whole Longitude 16°:13′ West from London. this Evening at Sun Sett the Amplitude was 9 degrees. Variat 32°:8′ West

Variation by Evening Ampl 3°:28. — —

[1] As before with similar notes in D, this is set out on the left margin in small type. Below it D adds: 43.0 29.7.

[2] D does not repeat the word 'a'.

[3] D adds: *Ther. Bar.* 51.0 29.6

[4] D, . . . to be 20′. and course S 29° W, distance 42′.

☉ [1]8. We have had this 24^h a Fine Gale of Wind from the West to the S W we have plyed to Windward with our Starboard tacks on board, Latitude by a good observation 38°.39′, distance Sailed 74 Miles, Course S 10° E. our Longitude from Lond°: 15°56′ West, Evening Amplitude was much about 9 degreese East, Variation 3.45 West —

Variã by our Evening Amp 3°45′ — —

☽ [2]9. We have had Squally uncertaine weather this 24^h the Wind from the S W to the S E b E by the Southward, soe have plied to the Southard and by a good observation I find my Selfe in 37°:43′ we have made our way good in all S 14° West 58 Miles our Longitude from London 16°:15 West This Morning about 7 we had Sprung our M Topmast in the Cap, and by Noon we gott him fisht, and[3] in a Condicõn to make saile the occasion of this mischance was a Short halow Sea made by the shifting of the Winds from S W to S E —[4]

(f.11v.)

♂ [5]10. We have had this 24 houres thick troubled weather, in the afternoon the wind was much Southerly with squalls, then it fell Calm to twelve at night, then a Gale of Westerly and afterward S West wind: dark — cloudy weather with rain, our course protracted, allowances made is S. 8° West, Distance 32 Miles, Lat: by Estimation 37°:11′. Long 16°20′ West.

☿ [6]11. We have had this 24 hours, the Wind at first west and

[1] D adds: 55.0 29.7. Immediately above he places the variation note for the previous day.

[2] D adds: 59.0 29.4. Immediately above he places the variation note for the previous day.

[3] The word 'fisht' is altered and the word 'and' careted in on the MS in another hand. See Journal of the First Voyage, p. 108 n. 1 for amplification.

[4] D renders this: This morning about 7 we had sprung our maintopmast in the cap, and by noon we got his fisht and in a condition to make sail; the occasion of this mischance was a short hollow sea made by shifting of the winds from SW to SE.

[5] D adds: 55.0 29.3½.

[6] D adds: *Ther.* *Bar.*
51.0 29.7

W b S, about 5 it came up to the N W, and by ten blew soe hard we were forced to scudd — under our fore Saile, and it continued Stormy all night, very violent. I allow for the greate Sea Setting me to the Eastward, and haveing by a good observation found my selfe in 35°.15′ I conclude we have made but 12 Minutes to the Westward; soe that I am in Long 16°:32′ West Course S 5°W, Distance 118 Miles. I reckon my Selfe 50. Leagues North from the East end of Madera:

♃ — [1]12. We have had a Fresh Gale at N W and N W b N for this 24 hours, at Noon by a good observation I am in Latitude 33°.29′, and have made o^r: way 107 Miles[2] S S W ¼ W, Difference of Long 1 degree; in all 17°:32′ West from London; at two this afternoon I took leave of the Falconbird and Shapt my coarse for the Madera, to have gotten Wine for my Men.

♀ [3]13. I stood till Midnight into the Latitude of the Island, haveing the Wind at N W, and at 12 a Clock N N W; Then bore away East, with an easy Sail till Day, when the wind came up the N b E and N N E so that we could Scarce keep the parallel; at noon by a very good observation we were in Lat 32°:11′ We have made this 24 hours 90 Miles on a Course S 30°E. Longitude from London 16°:37′ West; I resolved to Stand to the Eastwards till night, to see if we could raise the Land wch by o^r: observation we find[4] was to windward of us and our people chose rather to go without their Wine, than to his beating[5] it so much in danger of the Salley Rovers. —

[1] D adds: 60.0 29.7.
[2] D, . . . our way 117 miles . . . There is a difference of ten miles between the two figures.
[3] D adds: 66.0 29.8.
[4] D, which by our observation we found . . .
[5] That is, sailing against the wind.

♄ [1]14. Yesterday betweene 3 and 4 in the afternoone my poor Boy Manley White had the misfortune to be drowned, falling over board. We brought the Shipp immediately a Stays, and hove out an Oar, but the Sea being high and the Ship haveing (f.12) fresh way wee[2] lost Sight of him and cou'd not Succor[3] him; at 6 I bore away South West, not thinking it advisable to stay turning to Windward in the Latt of Madera This day at Noon by a good observation I am in Latitude 30°.52′ my Course protracted S 31′ W.[4] distance 94 Miles; whole Long West 17°.35′, wee have had the Winds this 24 hours at N. or[5] N b E a Steady Stoute gale.

⊙ [6]15. This 24 hours we have Stear'd away due South by Compass and at Noon by a very good observation I was in 29°.17′ Lat, Long. 17°.31′ West, Course South 2. degrees East 95 Miles.

♄ Evening amplitude	12°:00	
⊙ Morning Amp.– – –	16:00	
Variation – – – – – –	1:58 West.	[7]

☽ 16 Wee have Stear'd away this 24^h by Compass and at Noon by a very good observation I am in Lat. 27°.36′ yesterday at Sunn sett the Isle of Palma appear'd, the Highland on the North point bareing EbS, and the South point SEbS. or somewhat more Easterly: This Morning at 7^h the South point Palma bore ENE, and the North

Palma	N.End	28.48
	S.End	28.25
Ferro	N.End	27.50
	S.End	27.40[8]

[1] D adds: *Ther. Bar.* 68.0 267.
[2] D adds, soon. The whole of MS f. 12 is in another hand.
[3] D, succour. See Document 91, pp. 312–13, for additional information on this unfortunate accident.
[4] D, 31°. 0′ W.
[5] The word 'or' is careted in on the MS in another hand.
[6] D adds: 67.0 29.7½.
[7] In D this information is placed in the left margin under the appropriate dates.
[8] D adds, 70.0 29.9. Below this D renders the bracketed statement thus:

of Ferro ESE at 11^h ye South End of Ferro bore due East ending in a low point, ye North Part E 15.N I conclude by these observations, that I am ab^t^ 11 Leagues to the Westwards of the Isle of Ferro, the body of wch lies 27°.45′ & I find that I am two degrees more Westerly than Teneriff, or in the true Long. from Lond.^θ^ 19 degrees, haveing Erred 1°.30′ in my reckoning Course South. 101.Miles Wind NNE, ENE[1]

♂ [2]17 I have this 24 hours Shaped my Course S.b W. and have Sailed 150 Miles; by a good observation I was at Noon in 25°.8′ Longitude West from London 19°.29′; we have the Winds from N E to E and E b S a Fresh Steady Gale

☿ [3]18 We have Stear'd[4] away S b W this 24 ho. 143 Miles & at Noon I am in Lat 22°.47′, Long West from Lond^θ^ 19°.57′. We have had the Winds from E N E to E b S a Stout Steady Gale

♃ [5]19 We have had thick hazey weather this 24^h but a Fresh Gale between the East by North and N E Latitude observed 20°20′ Course S b W 149. Miles Long from Lond^θ^ 20°.26′

♀ [6]20 By a good observation I am in Latitude 18°.00′ my Course

Palma, N^o^. End 28°.48′.
S^o^. End 28°.25.
Ferro, N^o^. End 27.50.
S^o^. End 27.40.

[1] In the MS in the first line, the statement 'this 24^h' has been careted in, as have two lines in a miniature script between the second and third line in this entry, which makes interpretation difficult. D renders this passage: We have steered away due S this 24 hours, and at noon by a very good observation I am in Lat. 27°.36′. Yesterday at sun-set the Isle of Palma appeared; the high land on the North part bearing E b S, and the South point S E b E, or somewhat more Easterly; this morning at 7 the South point of Palma bore E N E and the North of Ferro E S E, at 11 the South end of Ferro bore due E ending in a low point, and the N part E 15°. N. I conclude by these observations that I am about 11 leagues to the Westward of the Isle of Ferro, the body of which lies in 27°.45′. and I find that I am 2° more Westerly than Tenneriff, or in true Longitude from London 19°. having erred 1°.30′. in my reckoning, course South 101 miles, Wind N N E. E N E.

[2] D adds: 72.0 29.8.

[3] D adds: *Ther. Bar.* 77.0 29.8½.

[4] D, steered.

[5] D adds: 82.0 29.7½.

[6] D adds: 87.0 29.7½.

S b W 143 Miles difference of Long. 29 Minutes Long from Lond$^{\theta}$. 20°.55′ West: we have had the Winds this 24 hours from N E b E to N E b N a Stout Steady Gale

♄ [1]21 By a good observation Lat 16°.55′ Course protracted is S W ¼ W 96 Miles—diffrence[2] of Long is 1°.14′ in all 22°.9′ from Lond$^{\theta}$: this night I lay by for the Isle of Sall from 2. till 5. in the morning, then bore away west in the Latitude thereof designing to take in some salt there for the use of the Voyage

☉ [3]22. Yesterday at 4 in the afternoon we made the Island of Sall[4] bearing West 8. or 9 Leagues off, we were up wth[5] it by eight in the Evening and lay off and on till day, then we made Saile and about nine we came to an Anchor in a very good road a little to the Southward of a Bluff point about the Midle[6] of the West Side of the Island. here I went on Shore and found a Portuguese there wth. Some few Blacks Servants, who assured us there was no Salt to be had the Salt panns being all in the Water, we had leave to Hunt, and our people Kill'd and brought aboard two Cabritos,[7] one very fatt and good Meate. We saw Turtle in the road, and their Tracks on Shore, so 4. of our hands stay'd on Shore this night, and next morning they brought off

Sall long 23:00 }
NE end 16.55 }
S End 16.35 }

(f.12v.)

☽ .23 two Turtles, a Hawksbill and a Green. The Portuguese promised me some Salt but made me stay till Evening for it, and it was not much above a Bushell when it came, bad Salt mixed

[1] D adds: 89.0 29.7.
[2] D, difference.
[3] D adds: 90.0 29.7½. Below this he puts the note for this day which on the MS is bracketed, but in D it is rendered: Sal, Longitude 23°. 0′. N°. N.° End, 16.55. S.° End, 16.35.
[4] D, Sal. So rendered here, and in the note referred to in n. 3 above.
[5] D, with.
[6] D, middle.
[7] Either antelopes or goats (Spanish *cabrito*: kid).

Bonavista. 23°:00′ NE end 16.20 S End. 16.00 Evening Amp 15°:00[1]	w^th^: Dirt, he sent me alsoe some Cabritos, and two of his servants went on Board to Skin them, but the Sea riseing suddenly, they cou'd not get a Shore but by swiming[2] w^ch^: they did

♂ 24. At 7 in the morning I had weiged and stood away due South, and Soon raised the Island of Bonavista; at ¼ past .11. we were up w^th^: the North end of it at ¼ past 2 we were abrest w^th^:

Morning 17°:00W Variat: 1:55W at Sall road	the South End of it, at Noon Lat. by a good observation 16°:18′. 91:29:7[3]

♀ [4]25. Yesterday about one of the clock a Ledge of Rocks that lies off of Bonavista about ⅓ part of it from the South end obliged us to goe away S W b S for one hour, then I shaped my Course for St. Iago, so as to stear clear of a Sunk Rock that is said to lie between Bonavista and it, and haveing Sailed in all 66 Miles S S W by a protracted Course, I fell in with the Island about 2. in the morning, about ye Midle of the North East side. then tackt musled w^th^: the head off to sea, till broad day, then made Sail along Shore and ab^t^: 11. this morning came to an— Anchor in Praya Road. I find that the three Islands of Sall,

[1] D, swimming.

[2] D places this note in the left margin beside the entry for 24 October where it is rendered: Bonavista 23°.0′. N°. End 16.20. S°. End 16.0. M. Even. 15.0. Tu. Morn. 17.0. Variat. 55′. W. in Sall Road.

D adds below this: *Ther. Bar.* 91.0 29.7.

As can be seen above, parts of two notes from the MS have been combined and added to; some differences will be noticed. On the MS the W, after 'Varia. 1.55″ is repeated probably to clarify a correction of the original from a letter 'N' to 'W'. The statement in D, Variat 55′, is closer to the plotted data; see the Atlantic Chart in the portfolio of maps.

[3] D omits these figures which appear to be related to those indicated in ns. 5, 6, p. 131 and n. 1, p. 132, if so they are among the relatively few such readings reported in the MS. They are in another hand.

[4] D adds: 91.0 29.6. This in the left margin of the entry for this day, centered; there would be confusion with the preceding entries if it were in line with the date as was the practice previously.

Bonavista and May. lie as near as may be under a Meridian and not above Six or Seaven Leagues to the Eastward of the East Side of St Iago; La Praya lies in Latitude 14°.50′. Longitude from London 23°.30′ West. Here I found an English Merchant-man bound for Guiney/Mr Jn° Taylor Master,[1] who came on Board me to give an Account of himselfe, and Sailed that Evening. In the afternoon I went on Shore to desire leave of the Governour to fill—Water wch he granted Im̃ediately./.[2]

♃ ♀ [3]26:27 Our people rummaged the Hold, gott all their Water fill'd and Stow'd, and a clear Shipp. They ashore observed that the Portugeese were more stiff than usuall, vallueing their things high and ours low in Truck:[4] and it seemed to me that

♃ Evening 16°½ } Variation 0.8′ } the Governour had a designe to furnish—all wee wanted and Buy up any thing we can

(f.13) Spare at at his own price; tho I presented him to the value of five Dollers, wch I thought might purchase his favour, besides what I gave his Sergeants to protect our people from Injurys, (which they did with greate Content) and none of my[5] Folks had any thing taken from them ♃ Morn amp 16°½ Va 0°.0′

♄ 28. I allowed my People this Morning to repose them, and get such refreshments as the Shore would afford them; but to our greate Surprise, wee found noe markett, the Country people being I suppose forbid to come downe; and they would not let my Boatswain dispose of Some Cheese he had agreed to deliver,

[1] D, . . . Guinea, Mr John Taylor, Master.

[2] D, . . . the Governor to fill water, which he granted immediately.

[3] D has no thermometer or barometer readings but adds below: Th. Morn. Ampl. 16½ Variation 0°.0′. Note difference in variation figure.

[4] D, truck. The term refers to trading value.

[5] D, our. D often changes a personal pronoun to a less personal form.

nor go up into the Country to buy fowles for us: This Treatment I was obliged to put up, on the score of my Small force, perhaps more men and Gunns might have procured better useage from them. The boat comeing on board with this news, I order'd after dinner to weigh, and we were a weigh by $3\frac{1}{2}^h$ and made Saile $4^h\frac{1}{2}$ I ordered y^e Course S E b S in order to pass the line in the proper place.[1]

☉ [2]29. At noon by observation I am in Latt 13:18. and have gone upon an S E b S Course 112 Miles, which makes my difference of Long 1°:4′ and my Long 22°:26′ West, a fine Fresh Gale and Smooth water Wind at N E and N E b N.

☽ [3]30. At Noon by observation I am in Lat 11°:52′ course this 24 hours S E b S. 104 Miles difference of Long 1°:00′ my Whole Long: 21°:26′ from London a fine Gentle Gale at N E and E N E and very Smooth Water —

♂ [4]31. at Noon by a very good observation Lat 10:21. Coarse this 24 hours S E b S 110 Miles Difference of Long 1°:3′ Long from London 20°:33′ West, a fine Steady Gale N E b E; with Smooth water. I find the Shipp behind the Logg about ten Miles p Diem Memo: to examin the Logg line ——

Novem^r [5]1. a^t Noon was[6] by a good observation I am 8°.47′ Lat, Coarse

☿ this 24^h S E b S — whereof 63 Miles a point from the Wind, the rest Large; Wind at E N E to N E b E, I allow $\frac{1}{2}$ point Leeway

[1] Presumably to cross the equator at the optimal place in respect to the winds; see entry for 16 November, below. Before leaving St. Iago, Halley sent a letter to Burchett briefly summarizing his voyage up to that point and indicating his immediate plans. See Document 83, p. 305.

[2] D adds: *Ther. Bar.* 95.0 29.6½.

[3] D adds: Even. Ampl. *Ther. Bar.* 96.0 29.7.

[4] D adds below: 96.0 29.6½.

[5] D adds below: Morn. Ampl. 98.0 29.6.

[6] There is attempt to delete the word 'was' in the MS.

for the s^{d} 63 Miles, and make my diff of Longitude 5′6,[1] and whole Long 19°27′. True Course S 30 E Distan 110 Miles. Correct, a Fine Gale and Smooth water.

♃ [2]2 by a very good observation I am in 7°40′ North Latt: Since yesterday noon we have had the Winds from E b N to N E b E a fine gentle Gale; in the night we had much Lightning; but no Thunder. We have made our way S 24° E Distance 73 Miles, Diffrence of Longitude 30′ East, My Long from Lon$^{\theta}$: 18°:57′ West

♀ [3]3. I am by good observation in Lat: 6°:18′ yesterday between 2 & 3 in the afternoon we had a Smart Tornado at about E S E, it put us under our Courses, but the Violence thereof was soon over, it continued cloudy thick weather wth Thunder and Lightning for severall houres; at Night it proved little Wind, but we durst not Trust it, but made provision by Shortning Saile, in the Morning the Gale Freshn'd at E and E b N We have made our way good S 12 E Distance 84 Miles, Longitude 17′ East; Long from Lond$^{\theta}$ 18°:40′ —

(f.13v.)

♄ [4]4. By a good observation I am in Latt 5°:14′ Toward Night and in the Night we had two or three Squalls out of the E b N and E N E, that put us to the Southward; between them but little Wind. we have made our Course protracted S 13 E 66 Miles Longitude 0°15′ East Long from Lon$^{\theta}$ 18°25′ or 5°:5′ East from St Iago. This Night we had perpetuall coruscations of Lightning but no Thunder —

[1] D, 56′. This is probably intended in the MS.
[2] D adds below: 101.0 29.6.
[3] D adds below: 99.0 19.6.
[4] D adds below: *Ther.* *Bar.* 93.0 29.6½.
In the MS in this entry there is an erasure of 'and' after the word 'them'.

☉ [1]5 By observation I am in Lat 5°:9′ We have had it Calm till eleaven at night, then sprung up a Gale at S S E which shifted to South and S b W. we have made by account 10 Minutes Westing, and our whole Long is 18°:35′ from Lond$^{\theta}$ Course S 27 W 11 Miles —

☽ [2]6. By a good observacon I am in the Latt 4°:55′. We have had the winds only by Squalls out of the S S E. N W. and S W the greatest pte[3] of the time Calme, And Soe little winds as Scarce to be perceived[4] true course protracted is S 35 W 20 Miles, Longitude West 11 Miles in all 18°:46′ a' London to the Westward —

♂ [5]7. By a good observation I am in Lat 4°30′ We have had the winds only by Squalls out of ye S S E. N W and S W the greates[6] part of the time Calme True Coarse protracted is S 20 W 24 Miles Longit west is 8. Minutes in all 18°:54′ —

☿ [7]8 By a good observation I'm in Latt: 4°15′ haveing been Sett to the Southward very considerably this 24 houres We have had the Winds all Southerly and S b E wth Calms, and have made by Logg noe more than 16 Miles on a S W b W course nearest Long West 15 Miles[8] Long from London 19°:9′ or 4°:21′ from St Iago True Course S W 21 Miles —

♃ [9]9 By observation I am in Latt 3°:45′, we have had the Winds

[1] D adds below: 96.0 29.6. [2] D adds below: 95.0 29.6½. [3] part.

[4] D renders this passage: We have had the winds variable from the South to the NE, with calms and so little winds as scarce to be perceived.

D then begins a new sentence. Of course the *Paramore* is in the Doldrums, hence little wind.

[5] D adds below: 93.0 29.7.

[6] D, greatest. The terminal letter is missing from the MS.

[7] D adds in line with the date: 94.0 29.6½. Only two lines are left on the page, hence he resorts to his earlier practice.

[8] D, . . . Longitude W 15 minutes. D is, of course, correct.

[9] D adds below: *Ther. Bar.* 94.0 29.6½.

from S b E to S E b S a fine Moderate Gale true Course protracted and Leeway allow'd is W 39° S 48 Miles; Difference Long: West 38 minutes or from Lon$^{\theta}$ 19:47.

♀ [1]10 By a good observation Latt 3°:20′ agreeing wth y^{e} Logg exactly Differ of Long 0:2 Minutes West Course protracted is S 5° W Distance 25 Miles little Winds and Calms in the Morning much Thunder & Lightning &[2] Rain when a Small Gale Sprung up at E and afterwards E b S and E S E This noon we (f.14) were Taken Short by the Wind at South but it Soon came to S E b S Long 19°||49′

♄ [3]11. By a good observation I am in Latt 2°:42′. We have had the wind mostly at S S E and have made our way good W 38 S. 62 Miles diffr of Long 48 minutes Long West from Lon$^{\theta}$. 20°:37′ a Fine Gale and fair weather Saturday Morning and Evening I had a good observation of the Variation Morn Ampl 18°:50′ Even 21°:30′. —

☉ — [4]12. By a good observation I am in Lat 2°:21′, We have had the wind continually at S S E and S b E a Fine Gale, we have plyed to windward and our true Course protracted is W 29 S. 44 Miles, Differ of Long 38 Mils[5] Long: from Lond$^{\theta}$ 21°:15′. about 10. this Morning we had a seveer Squall of Wind with much rain, which put us by our Topsailes for about halfe an hour Ampli this evening 22°:00′[6]

☽ [7]13. I am by observacon in Lat 2°:5′. The winds continue as

[1] D adds below: 88.0 29.6.

[2] On the MS there is a blot on the first of these two ampersands which may be intended as an erasure; there is no ampersand or comma here in D. The second ampersand in the MS is careted in, and is included in D as the word 'and'.

[3] D adds below: 91.0 29.6. [4] D adds below: 89.0 29.6½. [5] D, miles.

[6] D, . . . about 10 this morning we had a severe squall of wind with much rain which put us by our topsails for about half an hour; Amplitude this evening 22°.

[7] D adds below: *Ther. Bar.* 92.0 29.7.

before at S S E and S b E we made a tripp to the Eastward of 6 hours the wind comeing far Southerly True Course protracted is S 37 W 20 Miles Diff of Longitude is 12 Minutes West Long from Lond$^{\theta}$ 21°:27′ W —

♂ [1]14. I am in Latt by observation 1°:40′ Yesterday in the afternoon the wind came about to N N E a small gale with very much rain this morning it came again to S E b S a Fresh Gale and fair weath^{r} true Course is S W 36 Miles Diff of Longitude is 25 Minutes Long a' Lon$^{\theta}$ 21°:52′ I find my Selfe Sett to the Northward this 24 houres noe less then 16 Minutes.

☿ [2]15. I am in Latitude by observation 0°:56′ to the Northward of the line This 24 hours we have had a Fine Steady Gale of S E Wind we have gon close haled S S W and Sailed 75 Miles, which makes Westing 48 Miles correct Course is W 43 S 65 Miles I am again set to the Northwards 14 Miles Long from Lon$^{\theta}$. 22°40′ West I suspect a Strong Current Setting W N W —

♃ — [3]16. By a very good observation I am in Lat 0°12′ North, we have had a fine steady Gale at S E b E and steered away S S W 72 Miles I have observed the Shipps wake very carefully, and find her course correct to be S 36 W which makes 42 Miles Westing but I am again Set 14 Miles to ye Northwards this day Longitude West from London is 23°:22′ or 8 Minutes to the Eastwards of St Iago in the Merridian of which I shall Cross the line by my Acco^{t}. Correct Course is S W 60 Miles —

♀ [4]17. By observation I find my Selfe in Lat 0°:30′ S: we have had a

[1] D adds below: 88.0 29.7.
[2] D adds below: 90.0 29.7.
[3] D adds below: 89.0 29.7.
[4] D adds: *Ther. Bar.* This entry, with no figures immediately below, is at the top of a page. In

Steady Gale at S E b E and have gone away S S W a point from the Wind distance by Logg 72½ true Course is S 36 W which gives 42½ Miles Westing my correct course is Due S W 60 Miles the Current Still Setts to the Northwards 16 Miles this Day Long West from London 24°:4′ Yesterday in the Evening the Amp was 23 Degrees and this Morning 19° whence the Varriation 2° West[1] I begin to be apprehensive that we shall scarce weather the Island of Fernando Loronho.

(f.14v.)

♄ [2]18. By a good observation I am in Lat 1°:22′ South we have had a Steady Gale of S E b E and E S E Wind, and have Sailed S b W 52 Miles and 23 Miles S S W, a point from the wind; the whole course I allow is S S W ¾ West the Variation Considered. which gives my Westing 38 Miles Difference of Latt by observa is 52 Minutes Still 12′ less than Logg[3] the Current Still Setts Northward Correct Course S 36 W 64 Miles last night the Varriation was as before or not Sensibly more than 2 Degrees The Longitude by Acco^t from London is 24°:42′ West this[4] Evening the Amplitude was 24° —

☉ [5]19 By observation I am in Latitude 2°:17′ The Wind has Come forward this Morning to S E and S E b S the Gale the Same as before I find not the Current so Strong as before we have made 48 Miles Westing p Logg[6] which with the difference of Latt:

the middle of the margin of the entry for 17 November, D adds: 88.0 29.7. As mentioned in p. 133, footnote 2, above (and usually indicated in subsequent ns.) after 24 October D has such figures set below the date opposite the middle of the entry, where there is more room, rather than as earlier, typically, in line with the date. In either case, they are in small type in the left margin of the page.

[1] D . . . variation 2°. E. This appears to be more correct according to Halley's Atlantic Chart.

[2] D adds below: 88.0 29.7.

[3] D, . . . than per log:.

[4] D, Saturday. Here D uses the day rather than the word 'this'.

[5] D adds below: 88.0 29.7.

[6] D, per log:. After this point the abbreviation for per is used fairly frequently in the MS.

gives the Correct Course S 41 W 73 Miles Longitude from Lond$^{\theta}$: 25°:30′ last night the Amplitude was 24° and this Morning twas 19° Varriation 2½ East

☽ 20. By observation I am in Lat 3°:10′ S I reckon we have made our way good S 40 West 70 Miles the Wind much the Same as — yesterday, we make much Lee way being overgrown wth Barnacles as the last Voyage Long 45′ West a' London 26°:15′[1]

♂ [2]21. I am In Lati by observation 3°:50′ we have had small Gales at S E, and Shaped our Course S S W But by Reason of Lee way and Varriation I allow no better than S 40 W. 52 Miles which makes differ of Longitude 34 Minutes and my whole Longitude from London 26°49′ West Yesterday Morning a Tropick bird and a man of Warr flew about the Ship but this day all the fouls are gon[3] we are now in the Latt of Fernando Loronho but see it not.[4]

☿ [5]22. By a very good observation I am in Latt 4°:58′ We have had fine weather Wind at E b S and E S E a Moderate Gale, I find the Current wholly Ceased and this day out runn the Logg to the Southard My correct Course Lee way and Variation allowed is S 20 W Miles 72 whence my Diff of Longitude is 25 Minutes and my whole long: from Lon$^{\theta}$. 27°:14′ My Variation observed last night and this Morning was much about 3°. Easterly whence I cannot be farr from the Coast of Brasile —— (f.15)

♃ [6]23. By a good observation I am in Lat 6°:7′ This day had a

[1] D, Longitude 45′ W. from London 26° 15′.

[2] D adds below: *Ther.* *Bar.* 84.0 29.7.

[3] D, . . . fowls are gone.

[4] The last three words of this entry in the MS are placed above the line in smaller writing.

[5] D adds below: 86.0 29.7¼.

[6] D adds below: 88.0 29.7½.

Moderat Gale of Wind at E S E, and E b S[1] and have lain away South: But Lee way and variation allow'd S 15 W 72 Miles Diff of Long 18 Miles and from London 27°32′ last night the Evening amplitude very carefully observed was 25°:30′

♀ [2]24 By a very good observation I am in Lat 7°:22′ We have had very fair weather and Wind a Curious Gale at E S E and S E b E. We have made our course correct S 17 W 78 Miles Diff Long 23 Minutes and Longitude from London 27°:55′ Amplitude this Morning 18°:00 This Morning a Tropick Bird and two white Birds like the St Helena Pidgeons flew about the Shipp —

♄ [3]25. by observation I am in Lat 8°:18′ A fine gentle gale E S E and E b S we have made our way good S 19 W 60 Miles Difference of Longitude 20′ and whole Long from London 28° 15′ West The Amplitude this Morning was 18 and last night 26½

☉ [4]26 By observation I am in Lat 9°:12′ Very fair Weather and smooth water Wind at E b S, we go away a point from the Wind and variation and Lee way allowed have made our way good S b W 55 Miles[5] which gives Long 11 Minutes and makes from London 28°:26′ Last night the Amplitude was 27°:00′ and this Morning 17°:30′ about tenn this Morning the wind came off to East and E b N.

☽ [6]27. By observation I am in Lat 10°:55′ a fine Gale of wind at E b N and E N E I have gon away South by Compass, by

[1] In the MS 'and EbS' is careted in.

[2] D adds below: 87.0 29.7.

[3] D adds below: *Ther.* *Bar.* 86.0 29.7.

[4] D adds below: 86.0 29.7½.

[5] D, 56 miles.

[6] D adds below: 90.0 29.7½.

Variation allow'd S ½ W 103 Miles Difference of Long 10′ West from Lon$^{\theta}$: 28°:36′ we have been very much set to the South ward this 24 houres Varia was Curiously observed last night p amp 27°½ and this Morning 17°.20′[1]

♂ [2]28 By observation I am in Lat 12°:51′ haveing a Fresh Gale at E N E I hald away S b E to give the Abrothos the better birth[3] and to allow for the Varriation wch is N E halfe a point I have made my way good S ½ E 117 Miles Diff of Long. East 12′ Long: from Lond$^{\theta}$. 28°.24′ w^{t}[4] Last night the Amplitude care fully observ'd 28°.30′[5]

☿ [6]29. By a good observation I am in Latt 14°:36′ I have made my course[7] good S 2 ½ E 105 Miles, which gives Difference of Long East 5 Min or from London 28°:19′ West this Morning the wind (f.15v.) came to East, so I orderd the Course South by Compass last night ye Ampl was very exactly taken 29°.00′ whence the Variation 5°:30′ East this Morning the Sunn rose in a Cloud—

♃ [8]30 By a good observation Latt: 16°.22′ We have Steer'd away South with the Wind at E b N But Variation allow'd my corect Course is S b W,[9] 106 Miles which gives Difference of Long 11 Minutes West, that is from Lond$^{\theta}$. 28°:30′ Last night the Amplit was 30 Degrees and this Morning 17°:00′ Varia 6½ as near as can be observ'd ——

[1] D, . . . per Amp. 27½ and this morning 17°20′.

[2] D adds below: 90.0 29.8.

[3] D, 'I hauled away S b E, to give the Abrolhos the better birth, . . .' For explication of this, see entry for 2 December, p. 144, and Appendix B, p. 356.

[4] In the MS this abbreviation for West is careted in.

[5] D, Longitude from London 28°.24′ W; last night the Amplitude carefully observed was 28°.30′.

[6] D adds below: *Ther. Bar.* 90.0 29.8.

[7] D, way. This in place of, course.

[8] D adds: 91.0 29.8½. This is in line with the date in this case.

[9] D, S 6 W. This might be also interpreted from the MS; see p. 111, n. 3, Journal of the First Voyage.

Decem^r^ [1]1. By observation I am in Lat 17°:55′ We have had the Winds at
♀ E b N and East and have Stood away S and S b W Course protracted and Varriation allowed is S 11 West 95 Miles, Diff of Long is 19 Minutes West Long a′ London 28°:49′ Varia very accurately observed and adjusted by Morning and evening Amplitudes 7°:10′ Suppose in Latitude 17°: —

♄ [2]2. by a good observation I am in Lat 19°:6′ We have had this 24 hours two or three Squalls and than again little Winds a^d^ variable from the N E to E S E[3] I went away South by West till Sunn Sett, when being abreast of the Abrothos or Shoals of Brasile I Sounded, and had noe ground at 110 Fath Then I bore away S S W designing to recruite my Wood and Water and gett Some Rum for my Men at Rio Janeiro. Course protracted and corrected by Variation is S 25 W Diff of Long 35 Min. and totall Longit from London 29°:24′. The Evening amplitude last night was 31°:40′ This Morning could not observe the Sunn rose in Clouds.

☉ [4]3. Lattitude by observa 20°:00′ Very fair Weather and a Gentle Gale at N E, I have made my course good S 42 W. 73 Miles which gives diffrence of Long 52 minutes and my whole Long 30°:16′ W Varia by Evening Amplitude was 8 Degrees

☽ [5]4. Latitude by observation 20°:58′ Wind and Weather as before we Stear away S W b S p Compass which makes a S 43 W Course correct Distance 79 Miles Diff: of Long 57 Minutes Long a′ London 31°:13′ West Last night the Amplitude was 34½

[1] D adds below: 89.0 29.9.
[2] D adds below: 88.½ 29.9.
[3] D, and then again little winds and variable from the NE to the ESE.
[4] D adds below: *Ther.* 92.0 *Bar.* 29.8½.
[5] D adds below: 95.0 29.8½.

and this Morning 15½ very good observation, the Sea being very Smooth and the Ship quiet True Variation Stated from both is 9°:30′ West in 20°:30′ This Morning the Moon Aplyed to a Starr in Virgo of the 4 Mag: whose Longitude is ≏ 0°:39′[1] Lat 1°:25′ The Moon did exactly Touch this Starr with her Southern Limb At 3^{h}:15′ in the Morning, and at 3^{h}:20′:20″[2] (f.16) the Southern horn was just 2 Minutes past the Starr haveing carefully examin'd this observation and Compared° with former observations made in England I conclude I am in True Longitude from London at the time of this observation 36°:15′ and at this Noon 36°35′. That is according to the Acco^t I have of it, about 5 Degrees East of Cape Frio

♂ [3]5. Lattitude by a good observation 21°:49′ Very fine setled weath^r[4] Wind from N E b N to N b E a Gentle Gale, Variation allow'd S 43 ½ W. 70 Miles which gives diff. of Long[5] 52 Minutes Corect Long a' Lon^θ 37°:27′ West last Night the Amplitude was 35° and this morning 15°[6] the Moon apply'd to Mars who was in a Line wth her horns at 4:3 or when Cor M was 8°:6′ high in the East — Lat 21°:30′[7]

☿ [8]6. By observation I am in Latt 22°:44′ We have had a Stout Gale at N N W and N b W, and have made W S W ¼ S Course

[1] D, . . . of the 4th Magnitude whose Longitude is ≏ 39′.0°. This reversal of minutes and degrees in D is inconsistent with other entries, but if read as shown, agrees with the MS in fact, though not in form.

[2] D, 3h.20m.20s. This is the only example of a recording involving seconds in the MS or D.

[3] D adds below: 92.0 29.8.

[4] D, settled weather.

[5] There is a space after Long in the MS because of an erasure of the word 'from'.

[6] This figure is careted in on the MS.

[7] D, renders this: . . . difference of Longitude 52 minutes; correct Longitude from London 37°.27′. W last night the Amp. was 35°. and this morning 15°. This morning the Moon applied to Mars who was in a line with her horns at 4h. 3m. or when cor. M. was 8°.6′. high in the East Latitude 21°.30′.

[8] D adds below: *Ther. Bar.* 92.0 29.7½.

129 Miles. Diff of Long is 2°:5′ West and Long a' Lond$^{\theta}$. 39°32′ being near the Lat of Cape Frio I clapt upon a Wind fearing to fall to the Southards: of it as the wind now Stands. Amplit: last night was 35 degrees

♃ [1]7. By observation I am in Lat 22°:41′ We have had the Wind fresh at N and N b W, till 6 this Morning when it came up at W N W — And we Tackt and Stood to the Norward we have made our Course correct[2] W ¼ N 66 Miles whence the Diff: of Longitude is 1°:12′ and our Long from Lond.^{m} 40°44′ last night the Amplitude was 35°.40′ and some time 36° Variation near a point East

♀ [3]8. By Acco^{t} I am in Lat 22°:46′ We have had small Gales from the W to the N W and have plied to windward this 24 hours: and have made our way 8 Miles W 40 S: Diff of Long 7 Minutes, Longitude a' Lond$^{\theta}$. 40°:51′ W, Last night the Amplitude was full 36°. The riseing Sunn Cloudy —

♄ [4]9. By Acco^{t}: I am in Latt 22°50′ We have had the Winds from the North to the N W b N, sometimes a Fresh Gale we have made our correct course W ¼ S 89 Miles Diff of Long 1°:37′ Totall from London 42°28′ This morning we fell into such a Smooth, notwithstanding it blew a Stout Gale at N N W that we conclu^{d}d[5] we were gotten under the Shelter of the Land and about 7 in the Morning we all smelt a very Fragrant Smell of Flowers which the Wind bro^{t}. of the Land: and Severall Butterflies flew on board us haveing had noe observation this

(f.16v.) 2 dayes I concluded that we then past by Cape Frio; and that

[1] D adds below: 88.0 29.8.
[2] D, correct Course.
[3] D adds below: 91.0 29.7.
[4] D adds below: 85.0 29.7.
[5] This word is not clear in MS; probably the past tense, concluded, is meant.

we had been Sett so farr to the Southard by Some Current, as not to See it, it being thick Hazey weather —

☉ [1]10. By observation I am in Lat 22°15′ The wind coming forward to N W and after to West and W b S, I stood to the Northward to make the land, and this Morning we gott Sight of the Main Land of Brasile being Cape St Thomas, to the N E of Cape Frio. and by noon we raised low land cover'd with Trees which I take to be the Island of St Ann. This 24 houres we have made our Correct course N 27° W 40 Miles, whence diff of Long 19 Minutes, and from Lond on[2] 42°:47′. At noon we Sounded and had Ground at 15 Fath water, the high land of Cape St Thomas bearing N W last night the amplitude was 36°:40′.[3] 11th By observation I am

☽ — [4]11. in Lat 22°20′ At yesterday noon the wind came up at S. and then S S E and died away before night; we being in 11 Fathom Water, and a very dark Storm of Rain and Thunder riseing from the Shore, I thought it adviseable to anchor till there was more wind and a clearer Sky: But it continued rainy and foggy till day, when we got up our anchor and Stood to the Southward with an air of E N E Wind But it Stood not Long there, but before noon came forward to the S E b S. we have made our way W 19° S 15 Miles, which gives 16 Minutes of Longitude and from London 43°:3′ W —

♂ 12. By Observation I am in Latt 22°:28′. We have had very little winds at S E and E S E, and almost calm all night: about

[1] D adds below: *Ther. Bar.* 84.0 29.6½.

[2] D, . . . London.

[3] D puts the statement following this under the new entry for the next day, 11 December, where it belongs.

[4] D adds below: 88.0 29.6.

$10^{h}.\frac{1}{2}$ in Morning a fine Gale Springing up at East and before Noon we raised Cape Frio about 10, or 11 Leagues distant at Noon my correct course is W 30 S 16 Miles which gives diff of Long 15 minutes and y^{e} whole Long 43°.18′. we found by the Land y^{t} we had been Sett during the Calme night very considerably to N W.[1]

☿ [2]13. We are in Lat p $Acco^{t}$ 23°..2′[3] we have had a very fine Gale between the E b N and N b E. about 8 h y^{e} Island of Cape Frio bore W by Compass and about ten it bore N. at Noon the Sugar loaf at the Entrance of Rio Janeiro bore N W b W p Compass. True Course protracted is W 28° S $72\frac{1}{2}$ Miles whence diff of Longitude is 1°10′ and from London 44°:28′ The Island of of[4] Cape Frio wch is very remarkable Land and high, lies in Lat 22°:55′ and — Longitude correct from London 43°:40′ —

(f.17) ♃ — [5]14. Lattitude by a very good observation is 23°:8′ we have had a very fine Gale of wind from W S W to W N W and have plied to the Westward all day. True Course protracted is W 26° S, 14 Miles. whence Diffrence of Long 13 Minutes and from London 44°:41′ We are right before the Entrance of Rio Jeneiro[6] which at Noon bears from us N N W Last night the Amplitude was 37°:30′ and this Morning 14°30′ variation 11°:30′. Let the Longitude of Rio Jeneiro be 44°:45′ West from London.

[1] D renders this: . . . about $10^{h}.\frac{1}{2}$ in the morning a fine gale sprung up at E, and before noon we raised Cape Frio about 10 or 11 leagues distant. At noon my correct Course is W 30° S 16 miles, which gives difference of Longitude 15 minutes and the whole Longitude 43°.18′. We found by the Land that we had been set during the calm night very considerably to the N W.

[2] D adds below: *Ther. Bar.* 87.0 29.7.

[3] D, W. 13. We are in Latitude by account 23°.2′.

[4] D has only one 'of'; the MS might imply 'off of'.

[5] D adds below: 86.0 $29.7\frac{1}{2}$.

[6] D, Rio Janeiro, here and below in this entry.

☉ —— [1]29

[2]29 This Morning before day we weighed out of the Harbour of (f.17v.)

♀ Rio Janero[3] and by 6 we were over the Barr. The Sea breeze coming in at S S W obleiged us to go to the S E wards. in The Night it proved Calm so that we were still before the Harbour the next day at Noon

♄ 30. About 3 of the Clock after noon the midle of the Entrance of the Harbour between the fortt[4] and the Sugarloaf bore due North whence I take my departer.[5] being then in the Latt. of 23°:20′ South

☉ 31 Latitude by Acco^t 23°:46′ We have had the Winds all day S S E and S E & b S[6] at Night E N E and N E a gentle Gale. Correct Course is S 41 W 34½ Miles Diffrence of Longitude West 25 Minutes a' London 45°:10 No observation these two days, it being Dark gloomy weather and the Sun never[7] appearing from Morning to Night

Janua^r [8]1. Lattitude by observation 24°:6′ We have had the Winds

☽ from S S E to S b W, a Small gale, we have plied to the Southards and o^r[9] true Course protracted is S 14 W. 20 Miles

[1] Following the entry for 14 December, which occupies approximately the top quarter of the page (folio 17) the MS is blank except for the symbol and date which are not in D. These entries are about two-fifths of the distance from the top of the page, and the symbol for Sunday is incorrect, as can be inferred from subsequent entries on folio 17 verso, following. D also leaves a space between the entries for 14 and 29 December, the latter beginning on a new page. As indicated in Document 84, p. 306, Halley wrote a letter to Burchett before he left Rio de Janeiro which does not seem to be extant and perhaps never reached England.

[2] D adds below: F. Even. Ampl. 36°.0′ Var. 11°.46′.

[3] D, Rio Janeiro. Note difference in spelling of this place name in the MS between this entry and that of December 14. Obviously the same settlement is referred to.

[4] D, Fort.

[5] D, departure.

[6] D, all day S S E and S E b S.

[7] D, scarce.

[8] D, January, $\frac{1699}{1700}$ M.1.

[9] D, our.

whence diff of Long 5. Minutes West and my totall Longitude from London is 45°:15′ at 7 of the Clock this Morning Island Grande[1] bore N b W or North by correct Compass; and is 38 Minutes to the West of Rio Jeneiro —

♂ 2. Latt: by observation 24°:28′. We have this day had the winds from S S E to S S W a gentle gale This Morning observing the Winds to Continue as it were trade at South[2] blowing in upon the land of Brasile. I resolved to Stand to the Eastward with the Wind on the beam, hopeing to find Easterly winds without Cape Frio. Our Correct Course is S E b E 40 Miles, whence Diff of Longitude 36 Minutes East but from London 44°:39′ West Last night the Amplitude was 36°:00′ Variation 12°:4′ East

☿ 3 Lattitude by observation 25°:8′ Till Sunn sett the wind — continued Southerly and I stood to the Eastwards with the Night a gentle Gale of Easterly wind Sprung up with^{ch}[3] afterwards — came to E N E and N E so I shaped my Course S b W by Compass. My correct Course protracted is S $\frac{3}{4}$ W 40 Miles Diff of Long 6 Minutes West. So that this Day at Noon I am in Longitude 44°:45′ or Due South from Rio Janeiro. Last Night by a very good observation the Amplitude was 36°:00′ Varia 12°:10 East.

(f.18) ♃ 4. Lattitude by Observation 26°:10′. We have had a fine Gale of Wind from the East to N N E and have Steerd away S b W by Compass, that is S 23 $\frac{1}{2}$ W — 68 Miles: Whence differ: of Long: is 30 Minutes West and totall Longitud 45°:15′ Last Night at Sunn sett the Amplitude was 36°:30′ Varia 12°40′ East

[1] D, Isle Grande. See Atlantic Chart and Appendix B, p. 356.

[2] D, *Trade* at *South*, . . . That is, the southeast trade wind.

[3] D, which. On the MS it looks like an amendment from with to which; the latter, as in D, makes more sense.

♀ [1]5. Latt by Acco^t: is 26°:50′ We have had the Winds from N N E to N N W till mid night then it fell Calm[2] and a little before day a gale Sprung up at S E which came afterwards to, East. Our correct Course is S 24 W 44 Miles Diff. of Longitude 20′ Totall Long a' Lond^θ. 45°:35′ West. Last night the Amp was 37°:00′ and this Morning 11°:00′: whence the Varia 13°:00′ both very good Obser

♄ 6. Latt by Acco^t 27°:18′. We have had the wind for the most part at S E b E a gentle gale; and have gon S b W close hauled. but our correct Course is — S 43° W 38 miles whence diffr: of Long: is 29 minutes West and our Totall Long is 46°4′. Last night the Amplitude was 37°:00′. —

☉ 7. Latt by a good observation 27°:57′. we have had the winds from the S: to S E b E and have plied to the Southwards, True Course protracted is S 19° W. 41 Miles: hence diffrence of Longitude is 15 Minutes and totall Long from London is 46°:19′. —

☽ [3]8. Latt by a good observation 28°:29′. We have had the Winds S and S S E till 6 this Morning than[4] E S E and have plied to the Southards, Our true Course is S 15 W 33 Miles. Whence diff of Long is 10 Minutes and Totall Long a' Lon^θ. is 46°:29′ Last night the amplitude was very curiously 37°:00′

♂ [5]9. Latt by observation 29°:14′. We have had the winds from E S E to E b N a fine Gale we have made our Course S b W by Compass: Butt Variation and Lee way allowed our Correct

[1] D adds below: *Ther.* 92.0 *Bar.* 29.8.

[2] D, came. In the context D's interpretation makes no sense.

[3] D adds below: *Ther.* 77.0 *Bar.* 29.9.

[4] D, then.

[5] D adds below: 82.0 29.8½.

Course is S 31° W 53 Miles: Diff of Long is 31 Minutes West, and Totall Long a' Lond$^{\theta}$ 46°:50'. Last Night the — Amplitude was 37°:00' and this Morning 9°:00'. whence the Variation is 14°:00' Easterly this take to be very exact. —[1]

☿ [2]10. Latt by observation 30°:32'. We have had a fine fresh Gale at East to E N E and N E and have Steard away this 24 houres S b W by Compass — S 25° ½ W 87 Miles. hence Difference of Long: 43 Minutes, and totall — Longitude from Lond$^{\theta}$ 47°:33'. Last Night the Amplitude was 37°:30' and Variation 14°:5'. —[3]

♃ [4]11. Lattitude p observation 31°:45' We have had very fair Weather and a fine Gale from the N E to East, and have continued our Course S b W by Compass, that is S 26° W 81½ Miles. Diff of Long is 42 Minutes W and totall Long 48°:15'. The Amplitude last night was 38° and this Morn^{g}: 8° whence the Variation 15° Easterly.[5]

(f.18v.) ♀ [6]12. Latt by observation 33°:41'. We have had very fair Weather and a Fresh Gale from the East to the N E, Course as before S b W p Compass but Correct Course S 26° ½ W. 130 Miles Diff of Longitude 69 Minutes and Long from London 49°:24'. Amplitude last Night 38½ —

♄ [7]13. Latt by Acco^{t}: 35°:35'. We have had a Stout Gale of Wind at N N E and gon before it S b W by Compass or S 27°W. Varria allowed 128 Miles hence difference of Long 1°:11' Minutes and Totall Longitude from London 50°:35'. Last night the Amplitude was very near 39° perhaps 39°:15' —

[1] D, this I take to be very exact.
[2] D adds below: 80. 029.7½.
[3] D ... and the Variation 14°.5'.
[4] D adds below: 77.0 29.7.
[5] D has a full stop after 15°. Such minor punctuation differences are common.
[6] D adds below: *Ther.* *Bar.* 79.0 29.9.
[7] D adds below: 75.0 29.7½.

☉ [1]14. Lattitude by a good observation 37°:10′ Yesterday in the afternoon it blew a hard Gale at N N E and towards Evening it Came to North and blew so hard that we were obliged to Scudd before it: about Nine it began to lighten and from ten till half an hour past eleaven we had Terrible Thunder lightning and rain with vehement Squalls of wind first from the North and after from the N W: By twelve the Storme was over and it began to clear up and a fine Gale sprung up at W S W. so I orderd the Sailes to be sett and to goe away S S E with the Wind on the beame. Our true Course correct is S 15° W. 98 Miles Diff of Long 32′ W and our Longitude from London 51°:7′ and from Rio Janeiro 6°:22′ —

☽ [2]15. Latt: by a good observation 37°:44′. We had the Winds all round the Compass this 24 hours, we have made the best of our way to the S: True Course protracted is S 1° W. 34 Miles: Diff of Long 1 Minute. Long a' Lond$^{\theta}$ 51°:8′. These two last days I find we are Sett to the North about 15 p Diem, perhaps a Current may sett North East a long Shore.[3]

♂ [4]16. Latitude by Account 38°.6′. We have had the Winds this 24 hours from the S E to E b S a fine fresh Gale till after middnight then little winds next to Calm; we hoisted out our boat to trie the Current but found none. We have Stood to Windward with our Larboard tack on board.[5] and our correct

[1] D adds below: '72.0 29.7'. Immediately below this after several spaces there is a dagger; the dagger refers to a footnote at the bottom of the page which reads: 'In the original is a black lead circle with 1 in it'. None of this is in the MS; see subsequent footnotes referencing such enigmatic circles with numbers in them.

[2] D adds below: *Ther. Bar.* 63.0 29.9½.

[3] D, perhaps a Current may set N E alongst shore.

[4] D adds below: 61.0 29.9.

[5] D, . . . our larboard tacks on board, and . . .

Course is S 35 W 27 Miles. Diff'rence of Long: 20′. and Long from London 51°:28'. The Sea run soe high yesterday that the observation I took ought not to be Consider'd, the Sea over topping the Eye:[1] Last night the Amplitude was 41°:00'. —

☿ [2]17. Lattitude by a good observation 39°:27′. We have had a Fresh Gale of Wind from the N E to the N W, and have made our way good S 3° E 81 Miles: hence Diff of Longitude 4 Minuts East, and Long from London 51°:24′: The Season of the Year being farr[3] lapsed I think it not adviseable to go any more to the Westward, and accordingly at 7 last night I steard away S S E with intention to follow that Course till I gott the

(f.19) Lattitude of 50°.[4] The Evening Amplit 41°½ and the Morning 6°½ both very well taken, whence the Varia is 17°½

♃ — [5]18. Latt by observation 41°:40′. We have had a Stout Gale a Stout Gale[6] of Wind from the N N W to the W N W and have Stear'd away before it S S E by Compass but Variation allow'd S 4 ½ East 133 Miles. whence diff of Longitude 14′ Minutes East, and Totall Long: from London 51°:10′ After Midnight it blew extream hard at N W. with much Lightning, and again a little before Sunn rise with very terrible Lightning which seemed to be just on board us but God be thanked we received no damage by it.[7]

[1] D, The sea run so high yesterday that the observation I took ought not to be confided in, the Sea overtopping the Eye:
[2] D adds below: 74.0 29.8.
[3] D, far.
[4] D, . . . get the Latitude of 50°.
[5] D adds below: 72.0 29.6. Following this, after several spaces, is a dagger which refers to a footnote at the bottom of the page which reads: In the margin the original has in black lead a circle with 2 in it. (This is not in the MS; see p. 153, n. 1 above).
[6] D does not repeat this statement as in the MS.
[7] This is the first reference to the Deity in the journal.

♀ [1]19. Yesterday in the afternoon the wind came to the Southards of the West and brought very fair weather. Latitude by observation 42°:32′. The wind Southing upon us we could make no better of it then a Correct Course S 40 E. 69 Miles, though by the Logg we had 15 Miles more. Our differ[2] of Longitude is just one degree East and our Long from Lond$^{\theta}$ 50°:10′ West. This day the Wind being at S W b S we begin to feel it coolish Last night the Amplitude was 43½ and this Morning at 5^{h}:00′ the Azimuth was 3°½ to the Southard of the East variation limited 19°‖ 16′ at midnight[3]

♄ [4]20. Latt by a very good observation 43°:12′ We have had the Winds S W b S and S W a gentle gale and very fair weather. In the morning little wind at S and S b W so we hoisted out our boats and made a roomage for water. Our correct course is S 35 E 49 Miles which gives difference of Longitude 38 Minutes, and Long from London 49°:32′. yesterday at Sunn Sett the Amplitude was 44½ and this morning but 4 to the Southward of the East, both very good observations Variation limited at Midnight 20°:15′ The Colour of the Sea is Changed to pale green[5]

☉ [6]21. Latt by a good observation 44°.22′ Yesterday about two in the afternoon there sprung up a fine Gale at N W and we

[1] D adds below: *Ther. Bar.* 54.0 29.8

[2] D: '. . . than a correct Course S 40 E 69 miles, though by the Log we had 16 miles more. Our difference . . .' The word 'correct' is over an erasure in the MS and it is difficult to decipher.

[3] In the MS the phrase 'at midnight' is added above the phrase 'limited 19°‖16″' at the end of the line without a caret symbol; all of this and the preceding word 'variation' in another hand – possibly Halley's.

[4] D adds below: 62.0 29.8.

[5] In the MS the word, green, is careted in after the word, pale, at the end of the line and in D both words are italicized, probably for emphasis to suggest the existence of land.

[6] D adds below: 59.0 29.8. Below this after several spaces is an asterisk; see p. 156 n. 2 for an explanation of this.

Steard away S S E by Compas ie S 2 E 70 Miles Diff of Long East 3 Minutes Longitude from Lond$^{\theta}$. 49°:29′ last night the Sea appear'd very white and abundance of small Sea Foule about the Shipp and severall beds of weeds drove by the Ship of which we took up some for a Sample being what none of our people had Seene eles where[1] This Morning the Amplitude at Sunn riseing was scarce 3°$\frac{1}{2}$ very curiously observed: Variation

* 21°:10′ East*[2] The Alcatrosses[3] which we first mett with in about 27° South have now left us, we see noe more of them —

☽ [4]22. Latitude by a good observation 46°20′, we have had a Stout Steady gale of Wind at W N W and W b N and have gon away S S E by Compass that is Variation allowed due South 118 Miles Longitude as be fore. 49°:29 West from London

♂ [5]23. Latt: as well could be observed for the hight of the Sea

(f.19v.) 47°:48′. We have had the Winds from the N W to the W S W with much violence as obliged us scudd under a fore saile and being in unknown Seas we tried under a Mizzen from 9 to 3 in the morning.[6] Correct Course Variatio and drift allowed is

[1] D renders this passage: Last night the *Sea appeared very white and abundance of small Sea Fowl about the Ship* and *several beds of weeds drove by the Ship*, of which we took up some for a sample being what none of our people had seen elsewhere.

This last may refer to sargasso, but experienced seamen would surely have seen this before. See p. 155, n. 5.

[2] Both on the MS and in D there is an asterisk here and in the margin as shown and indicated in p. 155, n. 6. This asterisk refers to a footnote contained in D only, which reads: *So in the Original. This variation figure is approximately correct for this latitude and longitude at the time of Halley's voyages as shown on his Atlantic Chart (in portfolio).

[3] i.e. albatrosses.

[4] D adds below: *Ther.* *Bar.*
52.0 29.3$\frac{1}{2}$.

[5] D adds below a dagger and below this after several spaces: 47.0 29.3. The dagger refers to a footnote at the bottom of the page which reads: In the Original in black lead a circle with 3 in it. (This is not in the MS.)

[6] D renders this passage: Tu. 23. Latitude as well as could be observed for the height of the Sea 47°.48′. We have had the Winds from the N W to the W S W with so much violence, as obliged us to scud under a foresail and being in unknown Seas we tried under a mizzen from 9 to 3 in the Morning.

Of course the *Paramore* was now in the middle of the notorious 'roaring forties'.

S 31° E, 104 Miles. whence diff of Long 1°:18′ East and Long from London 48°:11′wtt[1] Multitudes of Sea Birds are everyday about the Ship, they are of five or Six severall kinds, but none of them settle on the Shipp. In the hardest of the Weather the Barometr Sunk to 29°2′½

☿ [2]24 Latt by Accot 49°:5′ We have had the Wind from the W b S to the West by N very fierce which obliged us to continue Scudding before it S E and E S E: we tried this night under a Mizzen from 10. to 3. and and[3] in the morning it blew so hard as to oblige us to lower and reef our fore saile, and we shipt such Seas as made it necessary to put before it Towards noon the Wind came up at S S W and blew as fierce as before. We have made a correct course S 28 W[4] 94 Miles which makes diff of Long 1°:7′ and Longitude from London 47°:4′ about Noon the barometer began to rise haveing been down somewht[5] below 29:00 Inches ——

♃ [6]25. Latitude by a good observation 48°:42′. We have had the Winds from S S W to S yesterday in the afternoon it blew so hard as to make us bear away E N E, but towards night the wind abated to a Moderate Gale We have run by Logg this 24 hours nearly East 82 Miles and tried under Mainsaile and Mizzen from ten to two drift E N E five Miles, in all 87 Miles East, which makes 2°:13′ Longitude and from London 44°:51′. so that we are in the Merridian of Rio Jenerio[7] by my reckoning. This

[1] D, 48° 11′ W. In the MS the abbreviation for the word 'West' is careted in, in another hand.

[2] D adds below: 37.0 29.0. Below this a dagger which refers to a footnote at the bottom of the page which reads: In the original in black lead a circle with 4 in it. (This is not in the MS.)

[3] D does not repeat the word 'and'.

[4] D, S 28 E. Dalrymple is, of course, correct.

[5] D, somewhat.

[6] D adds below: *Ther.* *Bar.* 13.0 29.6½.

[7] D, Meridian of Rio Janeiro.

Morning the Wind blowing Moderately at S, it was so cold as to be scarce tollerable to us used to the warm Climates; and in my Cabbin which had been kept from the Air the Thermometer stood but 11°[1] above freezing, but it blowing dry made us some part of amends: I find by my observation that we have been set to the Nortwards this 2 days near halfe a degree more than by reckoning —[2]

♀ [3]26. Latitude by Acco^{t} 49.37′. which I find[4] to be near the truth by a glare of the Sunn taken 5 Minutes before noon. We have had the Winds far Southerly till midnight, then from the West to N W a fine Gale and Smooth water Course S 36 E. 68 Miles Diff of Long 1°:1′ East and Long from London 43°:50′ last night the amplitude was 47° and this Morning but 3° to the Southwards of the Magneticall East. Variation 22°:00′ About 6 in the (f.20) Evening the Thermometer was sunck to 7° in my Cabbin, and it was so cold upon Deck that I beleive it froze in the wind, which is very extraordinary in this Climate in the hight of Summer. The Cold abates not much by the Wind comeing to W N W —

♄ [5]27. Latitude by account 50°:45′ South We have had the Winds from the N W to the S W a gentle gale, we have Steard away S E p Compass ie S 23 E. 74 Miles, allowing the drift of four

[1] D, but at 11°.

[2] D renders this: I find by observation that we have been set to the Northwards this 2 days near half a degree more than by Reckoning.

[3] D adds below: 14.0 29.7.

[4] D, found. In this as in other passages there are differences in tense between D and the MS; also in spelling of certain words as (in D), Sun, believe, Cabin, sunk, height, etc. D also supplies the definite article before certain words and abbreviations when the MS does not. However, as before, only if it is judged that there is a chance of misunderstanding are these differences footnoted.

[5] D adds below: *Ther. Bar.* 14.0 29.5½.

hours from ten till two; which makes diff of Long 45'. and Long: from London 43°.5' All this Morning we have had a greate Fogg, so have gone — away with my foretopsaile only, lowred down on the Capp, and Sounded every two hours, apprehending myself near Land; and the rather because yesterday and to day severall fowls, which I take to be penguins, have passed by the Ship side, being of two sorts; the one black head and back, with white neck and breast; the other larger and of the Colour and siz of a young Cygnett, haveing a bill very remarkable hoocking downwards, and crying like a bittern as they — past us. The bill of the other was very like that of the Crow, Both swam very deep, and allwais dived on our approach, either not having wings, or elce not commonly useing them[1] At Noone haveing passed the Latitude of 50°. I orderd to Stear away East p Compass ie E S E, till I attain the Latt. of 55°. being the limitt prescribed in my pticular Instructions.[2] This day I allow my Men whole allowance while the Cold lasts

⊙ [3]28. Latitude by an indifferent good observation 51°.1'. We have had the Winds from the W S W to W N W, a moderate gale; our Course has beene East ie E 22 S, 61 Miles, Diff: of Longitude 1°.30', Longitude from London 41°.35' We have had a Continuall thick ffog for this 24 hours, which obliged us to goe away with our fore top saile only, on the Capp; and to

[1] From the description it is hard to determine what these birds might be; the first could be Gentoo penguins (*Pygoscelis papua*) and the second, young King penguins (*Aptenodytes patagonica*). Among several species of penguin found in this area these two seem best to match Halley's description.

[2] See Document 78, p. 301.

[3] D adds below: *Ther.* 5.0 *Bar.* 29.7.

Sound every two hours, We have had Severall of the Diveing birds with Necks like Swans pass by us, and this Morning a Couple of Annimalls which some supposed to be Seals but are not soe; they bent their Tayles into a sort of a Bow thus ⌓ and being disturb'd shew'd very large Finns as big as those of a Large Shirk The head not much unlike a Turtles.[1] This Morning it was very cold and the Themometer at but 4 above frezing in my Cabbin

(f.20v.) ☽ [2]29. Latitude by account 51°:40′. We have had the Winds from the N W to the West a fresh Gale with a Continuall Fogg for this 24 hours We have Steard away East by Compass that is E 21 S 108 Miles, allowing the drift of 6 hours that we lay under a Mizzen from 9. to 3. in the Morning. Diff of Longitude is 2°:41′ and o♈ Long from Lond^θ 38°:54′. it continues very cold — misty rainy uncomfortable weather, though the hight of Sumer here[3]

♂ [4]30. Latitude by observation 51°:52′ We have had the Winds — variable from the West to S. with thick Fogg till night. We lay by under a Mizzen from 9 to 3 in the Morning A[5] nine in

[1] D, Turtle's. It is not clear what creatures are referred to here. Two of the 'diveing birds' are pictured on Halley's Atlantic Chart poleward of 50° S latitude with the statement: The Sea in these parts abounds with two sorts of Animals of a Middle Species between a Bird and a Fish, having necks like Swans and Swimming with their whole Bodyes always under water only putting up their long Necks for Air.

According to Dr L. Harrison Matthews, formerly Director of the Zoological Society of London, the second creature described may be the bottle-nosed whale (Porpoise or dolphin – genus *Tursiops*), particularly if for 'Turtles' we read 'bottles'. However, it is clearly Turtles in the MS. Interestingly, in D there are two drawings of bows, one immediately above the other, rather than one, as in the MS. See Halley's statement on these creatures, Document 97, pp. 316–317, and p. 317, n. 1.

[2] D adds below: 11½. 29.4½.

[3] D, it continues very cold, misty, rainy, uncomfortable weather, though the height of Summer here.—

[4] D adds below: —4.0 29.5.

[5] D, At. Probably this is also meant in the MS.

the Morning the Wind came up at East extream Cold, The Thermometer being below in the Frezzing point in my Cabbin[1] so I stood to the N Eastwards, in hopes of warmer weather; and the rather because it being at present so cold; if the Easterly winds should sett In I should have a long passage to Cape Bon Esprance,[2] and endure the Severity of the weather in these cold tempestuous Climates, and endanger my mens healths who are all very tender by being so long near the Sun. We have made our Course this 24 hours E 10° S 74 Miles which gives diffrence of Long 1°:58′ Long from Lond$^{\theta}$ 36°:56′ Yesterday a Seale swam after the Ship. —

☿ [3]31. Latitude by acco^{t}: 52°:6′ from yesterday noon till 8 at Night, we have had the winds at E. and E b S. then Calm till Midnight: when a Gale sprung up at N and Came to N W b N when I steard away E S E Correct Course all allowances made is E 18° S. 48 Miles which gives diff of Long 1°:14′ Long from Lond$^{\theta}$ 35°:42′ Yesterday afternoon we had very Serene weather but though the Sunn Shone out very clear for 7 houres, he had not force enough to warm the Air, but the Thermometer continu'd below the freezing point; and this Morning the Wind being at N W b N, which is nearly N b W and ought to bring the warm Air, we find no abatement of the Cold so that for ought appears this Climate is what Horace means when he saies pigris ubi nulla Campis arbor æstiva recreatur Aura. . Sever^{ll} beds of ye Weeds we took up ye 21st

[1] D, the Thermometer being below the freezing point in my Cabin.
[2] D, Cape Bon Esperance. The Cape of Good Hope; see Appendix B, p. 356.
[3] D adds below: *Ther: Bar.* —3 29.7½.

Inst past by ye Ship, Amplitude at o Sett 43 & this Morn^g at riseing 5°. Variation 19° well observed[1]

(f.21) Februr 24 21[2]. Latitude by Account 52°.24′. Yesterday in the Afternoon with a fresh Gale at N b W, I steard away E S E, and between 4 and 5 we were fair by three Islands as they then appeard; being all flatt on the Top, and covered with Snow. milk white, with perpendicular Cliffs all round them, they had this appearance, and bearing[3]

The greate hight of them made us conclude them land, but there was no appearance of any tree or green thing on them, but the Cliffs as well as the topps were very white, our people calld A[4] by the Name of Beachy head, which it, resembled in form and colour, and the Island B in all respects was very like the land of the North-foreland in Kent, and was as least as high[5] and not less than five Miles in Front, The Cliffs of it were full

[1] D renders this interesting passage: . . . says, *Pigris ubi nulla Campis – Arbor æstivâ recreatur Aurâ*; several beds of the Weeds we took up the 21st instant pass by the Ship. Amplitude at Sunset 43°. and this Morning at Rising 5°. Variation 19°. well observed.

In the extremity of his situation he seems to be recalling that experience when he quoted from Horace, *Ode* 1.22, line 17, 'Place me on the lifeless plain where no tree revives under the summer breeze'. In the MS the quotation and subsequent data are in small writing, possibly Halley's, squeezed into two lines at the end of the page.

[2] D adds below: *Ther. Bar.* o. ± 2.4.

[3] D adds: [Vide Plate H]. The square brackets are Dalrymple's, who places the illustration of icebergs (which is below in the MS) in a separate plate with other drawings from the journal. The direction designation on the illustration C, (unclear in the MS) is E S E in D.

[4] This letter and others following refer, of course, to those on the sketch above.

[5] D, and was at least as high. Halley estimates 200 feet which is reasonably close to the actual height on Beachy Head; he also suggests that if it were floating ice only one eighth of the mass would be visible. See Documents 84 p. 306, and 94 p. 315.

of Blackish Streaks which seemed like a fleete of Shipps Standing out to us. Wind[1] blowing fresh, and night in hand, and because our vessell is very leewardly, I feard to engage with the Land or Ice[2] that night, and haveing Steard[3] in as farr as I durst, I resolved to Stand off and on till day, when weather permitting I would send my boat to See what it was. In the night it proved foggy, and continued so till this day at noon, when by a clear glare of Scarce $\frac{1}{4}$ of an hour we saw the Island wee called beachy head very distinctly to be nothing else but one body of Ice of an incredible hight, whereupon we went about Shipp and Stood to the Northward. True Course to this day noon is S 44 E. 25 Miles. Difference of Longitude 29 Minutes East: Longitude from London 35°:13′. —

♀ [4]2. Lattitude by Account 51°:54′ we have had the winds from the W N W to the N W b W, a moderate Gale. We Stood to the Norward all day close hald, at night we tackt and Stood to the Southards to spend the dark: between 11 and 12 this day we were in iminant danger of loosing our Shipp among the Ice,[5] for the fogg was all the morning so thick, that we could not See a furlong about us, when on a Sudden a Mountain of Ice began to appear out of the Fogg, about 3 points on our Lee bow: this we made a Shift to weather when another appeared more on head with severall peices of loose Ice round about it; this obliged us to Tack, and had we mist Stayes,[6] we had most (f.21v.)

[1] D, It (instead of 'Wind' as in MS).

[2] In the MS 'or Ice' is careted in, suggesting that Halley might have had second thoughts on this matter.

[3] D, stood.

[4] D adds below: —1 29.2. Below that, but on the next page: *Ther. Bar.*

[5] D, . Between $11^{h.}$ and $12^{h.}$ this day we were in imminent danger of losing our Ship among the Ice.

[6] D, mist stays. That is, failed to bring her head to windward for tacking.

Certainly been a Shore on it, and we had not beene halfe a quarter of an hour under way when anoth^{r} mountain of Ice began to appear on our Lee bow; which obliged us to tack again, with the like danger of being on Shore: but the Sea being smooth and the Gale Fresh wee got Clear: God be praised This danger made my men reflect on the hazzards wee run, in being alone without a Consort, and of the inevitable loss of us all, in case we Staved our Shipp which might soe easily happen amongst these mountains of Ice in the Foggs, which are so thick and frequent there.[1] This 24 hours we have made a N E b N Course 36 Miles. Diff of Long 33′[2] Long: from London 34°:40′.

♄ [3]3. Latitude by observation 50°59′. we have had the winds to the N W and N b W from the W b S, and have mad our way good N 36°: E 68 Miles. Difference of Long: 1°:4′ East, and Long. from London 33°:36′ Yesterday in the Afternoon we past by abundance of Ice in greate and Small peices; some we saild very near to was was[4] in appearance very hard and white as Alabaster, and we — fear'd very much to strike against them, so in the night it being a greate Fogg, we tried under a mainsaile and Mizzen, and watcht all hands to be ready on occasion but it happen'd that we saw noe more till toward this day Noon, when a greate high Island past by us to windward, which we had seen near 4 Leagues from us it resembled a booth in a fair all Cover'd with Snow

[1] D, here.

[2] D, . . . 33 minutes. In the MS the number and symbol are careted in.

[3] Immediately preceding this entry one and half lines have been erased from the MS. D adds below: ±0.0 28.9.

[4] The word 'was' is not repeated in D.

☉ [1]4. Latitude by Acco^{t} 50° 26′ from yesterday Noon till night we had a moderate Gale at W b N, all night little Wind, and with the day the wind cam up fair Northerly when we desern'd 3 Islands of Ice to windward, bearing about N E from us; we made two boards with the Wind at North, and this day noon they bore from us E N E and N E b E : Course this 24 hours is N 30 E 38 Miles Difference of Long 30′ East and Longitude from Lond$^{\theta}$ 33°:6′ The weather reasonably clear from Fogg but very cold cloudy uncomfortable[2]

☽ [3]5. Latitude by Account 49°:55′ Yesterday in the afternoon the wind being N b E and North we stood off to the westward it being foggy, and we haveing observed the Ice to lie to the Eastward of us, After Sunn Sett it clear'd up and we had a very Sereen Night[4] till towards morning, Wind at N W b W I stood to the Northward close hall'd; about Noon it veer'd to the S W a fine Gale I order'd the Course North p Compass Course this 24^{h} is N 22 E 33 Miles, diff of Long 19′ Min and Longitude from London 32°:47′ W — (f.22)

♂ [5]6. Latitude p observation 48°:10′ as well as the hight of Sea would permitt. We have had a very hard Gale of wind this 24 hours at S W a^{d} S S W, so that we Scudded away N with

[1] D adds below: *Ther.* *Bar.*
—2 29.1.

[2] D renders this passage: Su. 4. Latitude by account 50°.26′ From Yesterday noon till night we had a moderate gale at W b N, all night little wind, and with the day the Wind came up far Northerly, when we descried three Islands of Ice to Windward, bearing about N E from us; we made two boards with the wind at N. and this day at noon they bore from us E N E and N E b E: Course this 24 hours N 30 E 38 miles. Difference of Longitude 30′ E. and Longitude from London 36°.6′. The Weather reasonably clear from fog, but very cold, cloudy and uncomfortable.

The above passage well illustrates differences between D and the MS, in form especially.

[3] D adds below: +4 28.7.

[4] D, serene night.

[5] D adds below a dagger, and below this: +12 29.6. The dagger refers to a footnote at the bottom of the page which reads: The original has here in black lead a circle with 5 in it. (This is not in the MS).

our Fore sail & in the morning took in two Reefs in him; all night we lay a tryundr. a mizzen ballast.[1] True course drift and variation allow'd is N 16° E 109. Miles. Diffr of Longitude is 45 Minutes East and Long from London 32°.2'. It was very remarkable, that the Baromerter,[2] which had been very Low with moderate North and N W: winds began to rise assoon as the wind vered to the Southard, and rose all the time of the Storm, contrary to what I ever observ'd of it; which is, that it never rises till the Storme begins to abate, it is to be observ'd also, that this Southerly wind warmed the Air and the Thermometer Started upon it, when all the late Northard winds had no effect, Contrary to any apparent cause —

☿ [3]7. Latt: p Accot : 47°24'. We have had the winds this 24 hours from the S W to the N W., and from 3h. to 7h In the morning due North; It being very little wind in the night we went away under our fore top saile. Towards noon the wind coming up to West, I order'd to goe a way N N E, to recover the warm Sunn, whom we have Scarce seen this fortnight; the weather being comonly foggy with so penetrateing a moysture that our linnen, our Cloaths, our papers &c feel wett with it, even in our Cabbins.[4] True Course this 24 hours is E 43 N 67 Miles. Diff: of Long is 1°.12' East Longitude from London 30°.50' West. The dark Moon in these unknown Seas — obliges us to lie by every night does very much retard our progress —

[1] D renders this: We have had a very hard gale of Wind this 24 hours at S W and S S W, so that we scudded away North with out foresail, and in the morning took in two reefs in him; all night we lay a try under a mizen ballast.

This was done to keep the ship's bow to sea and prevent her rolling to windward.

[2] D, Barometer.

[3] D adds below: *Ther.* *Bar.* +15 29.4.

[4] D renders this: ; the Weather being commonly foggy, with so penetrating a moisture that our Linnen, our Cloaths, our Papers, &c. feel wet with it, even in our Cabins and Chests.

♃ [1]8. Lattitude a good observation 46°:19′. We have had the winds this 24 hours a fresh Gale at W. and W N W This Morning pretty clear Sunn Shine, Our Course, Variation drift and Lee way allow'd is N 43 E 89 Miles. difference of Long 1°:30′ East and Long from London 29°:20′. — (f.22v.)

☿ [2]9. Latitude by observation 45°:13′. We have had the Winds from the W N W, to the South west a Steady Fresh Gale. and have gon[3] away N N E by Compass, and have lain by 4 hours in the Night; drift and Variation allowed our correct Course is N 38° E. 84 Miles Difference of Long is 1°:15′ and Long from London 28°:5′. It was this Morning fine Clear weather, but in the Wind it was very cold. We have not been able to gett the Variation observed since the 31 past, it being cloudy alwaies morning and evening —

♄ [4]10. Latitude by observation 44°:10′. we have had the Winds from the W S W to the W N W a Fresh Steady Gale, We have Steard away N N E and N E b N p Compass. True Cours Drift and Variation allow'd is N 39° E 81 Miles. Difference of Long 1°:12 East Long from London is 26°:53′ Last night I observed the Amplitude of the Setting Sunn to be 28°½ whence Variation 12°:53′ or in a round Number 13 degrees

☉ [5]11. Latt by Account 43°:51′ We have had the Winds this 24 hours from the N W to North a Moderate gale we have gon upon a wind with our Larboard Tacks on board True course protracted is E 23 N 49 Miles. Difference of Longitude 1°:3′ East Long from London is 25°50′ West. It has been Foggy all this

[1] D adds below: 16.0 29.5.

[2] D adds below: *Ther. Bar.* 21.0 29.6.

[3] D, gone.

[4] D adds below: 250. 29.7.

[5] D adds below: 33.0 29.4.

morning. Yesterday in the afternoon we had above 20. Alcatrosses[1] about the Shipp, and this morning our people saw one of those annimalls, we saw on the 28th. past which swam twisting its tayl into a bow. I suspect wee are now near some land or Rock by the birds: this Morning we see noe more of them

☽ [2]12. Latitude by observation 43°:3′. We have had the Winds variable from the N N W to the W S W, a fresh Gale, towards night it blew very hard at West, so as to oblige us to try all night under a Mizzen not dareing to scudd in these dark nights, and unfrequented Seas, especially So many birds being Seen about us. True Course protracted drift &c allow'd is E 41 N 73 Miles. Difference of Long is 1°:16′ East Log from London 24°:34′ West. —

♂ [3]13. Lattitude by Accot: 42°:12′: We have had the Winds this (f. 23) 24 hours from the N W to the W N W a fresh Gale, and have gon away by Compass N N E and N E b N. True Course, variation, drift &c allow'd is N 43 E. 70. Miles Difference of Longitude is 1°:5′ and Longitude from London 23°.29′. This night wee tried again from, Nine till day light under main saile and Mizzen it blowing pretty hard at W b N dark gloomy weathr

☿ [4]14. Latitude by an observation taken by a Glare through the Fogg 40°:55′ We have had a Fresh Steady Gale from the West to W N W we went away all day N N E by Compass, and by

[1] D, Alcatrasses. The albatross, a frigate bird.

[2] D adds below: *Ther.* 25.0 *Bar.* 29.7½.

[3] D adds below: 33.0 29.8½.

[4] D adds below: 38.0 29.9.

night close halld to the Northard True Course protracted N 32° E 91 Miles, which gives diffr of Longitude 1°:4′ East. Long from London 22°:25′. I take the Islands of Tristan d'acunha to bear N E 120 Leagues, and being not much out of my course I design to See and Discover them. The Thermometer is this day no higher than it was in the Latitude of 49°. on the 24th past. It is evidently Colder to the Easter part of this Southern Ocean near the Coast of America:[1]

♃ — [2]15. Latitude taken as yesterday through the Fogg 39°:37′. We have had a Steady Gale at N W b W and N W, and have made our true Course N 33 E 93. Miles; which gives Difference of Long 66 Minutes or 1°:6′. East Long: from London 21°:19′. Finding it Scarce possible to gett an Amplitude in this cloudy and Foggy Climate, I am forced: to take the Sunns Azimuth when he is low, and Yesterday afternoon at 5^h 16′½ The Sunn being due West in the heavens, was 9°: to the Southwards thereof, and so much is the Variation, and at 5^h:54′. The Sunn was 15°: by Compass to the Southard[3] of the West.

♀ [4]16. Latitude taken as yesterday, but with more Certainty 38°:16′. We have had the same Gale at N W b W without any deflection, and have Steard away N N E, a point from the Wind; the weather allwais overcast but pretty clear. True Course Variation and Lee way allowed is N 35 East 99 Miles. Diffrence of Longitude 1°:13′ Long from Lond 20°: 6 West At noon today

[1] A good generalization; the ship was nearing the cool Benguela Current.

[2] D adds below: *Ther. Bar.* 43.0 29.9.

[3] D, Southward.

[4] D adds below: 53.0 29.9.

we saw an inumerable quantity of birds about the Shipp & many Alcatrosses —[1]

♄ [2]17. Latitude by a Good observation 37°:22′. We have had the Wind from the N W b W to the N N W. a very Fresh Gale; at night we kept close upon a wind to Slacken our way. At 5 this morning we made the Southermost of the three Islands of Tristan da Cunha, bearing N b E from us not above 4 Miles, the top of it cover'd with a very black Coud[3] I immediatly tackt, till I was more certain which of the 3 Islands it was: and about 6^h Steard[4] in with it again, where we saw the Wester most (f.23v.) Island being very Steep and high at the Southern point. When that high point of it Shutt in behind the Island close by us, the Southerly — point of one to the Southern of the other, bore W N W ½ N p Compass. The Northermost and Principall Island of Tristan da Cunha we could not now See, being cover'd in the Foggs and Haizy Air.[5] At 8 of the Clock, being leeward[6] of all these Islands and it blowing fresh at N N W, and a great Sea withall, I boar away for the Cape of Good hope at 12^h. the greate Island appear'd, the South point thereof bearing due W N W; we then being 26 Miles Distant from the Island we first Saw, due East b N p Compass. Yesterday Evening I took the Variation of the Compass p Azimuth, and at 5^h.2′ the Sunn was 3°½ to the Southward of the Magneticall west, and at 5^h50′ he was just a point, or W b S p Compass, whence the Variation is 5.48′ 5‖36′ / 6‖00[7] True course protracted is E 40° ½

[1] D, At *noon to-day we saw an innumerable quantity of Birds about the Ship*, and many Alcatrasses.

[2] D adds below: 57.0 29.8.

[3] D, Cloud.

[4] D, stood.

[5] D, ... foggy and hazey Air.

[6] D, being to Leeward.

[7] D, whence the Variation is 5°.48′ E. between 5.°36′ / 6. 00. Double spacing of the type in D is

N 83 Miles, whence Diffrence of Long: is 1°:20′ East and Longitude from London 18°46′. I Determine the Latitud of the most Southerly of the Isles of Tristan da Cunha 37°:25′ and its Longitude from London 19°:20′ West; which I have reason to beleive may be 3 degrees to much, by the Account I have of its distance from the Cape, and St Helena —[1]

☉ [2]18. Latitude by observation 36°:44′. We have had the Winds from the N N W to the West a Stout Gale. We have gon away with it E b N. and N E b E to make the Wind fill our Sailes to the best advantage: True Course protracted is E 18 N. 124 Miles, which gives difference of Longitude 2°:28′ East. correct Long from London (i.e. abateing 3°) is 13° 18′ West from Tristan da Cunha 3°:2′[3] Since we are past these Islands the Foggs clear up and we begin to have a dry comfortable Air, thô ye Thermometer be now Sunk 10 degrees Since yesterday noon by the Winds veering from N W and N N W to West —

☽ [4]19. Latitude by observation 36°:13′ We have had the Winds from the West to S W a fresh Gale, Wee have made our correct course E 17′ N 108 Miles which gives difference of Longitude 2°:8′. Long from London is 11°:10′ and from Tristan da Cunha 5°:10′. Severall beds of Weeds, pass by us, most of that sort we took up on the 21 past.[5] Yesterday at 5^h:17′ post

necessary to accommodate this notation. In the MS one set of figures is squeezed in above the others.

[1] D renders this: ; which I have reason to believe may be 3°. too much, by the account I have of its distance from the Cape and St. Helena.

Actually, it is about 37° 6′ South, and 12° 15′ West of London, thus Halley was about 7° short in longitude.

[2] D adds below: *Ther. Bar.* 47.0 29.8½.

[3] D, . . . from *Tristan*, &c. 3°.2′. As mentioned previously, D often italicizes place names, but such abbreviation is unusual.

[4] D adds below: *Ther. Bar.* 48.0 30.0½.

[5] See p. 156 and n. 1.

Merid: the Sunn being truly West his Magnaticall Azim was 4 degrees to the South, that is soe much East Variation as well as could be taken for the greate Sea and rouling Motion of the Shipp[1]

(f.24) ♂ [2]20. Latitude by Account 36°:1′. We have had the Winds variable from the S W to the N N E. Shifting gradually half round the Compass to the Eastwards we have made our correct Course protracted E 13 N 52 Miles whence Diffrence of Longitude is 1°:2′ and Longitude from London 10°:8′ from Tristen da Cunha 6°:12′;[3] Last night at Sunn Sett the Amplitude was 12°:00′, and this morning 7°:00′. to the Southard of the West ad East:[4] whence Variation is 2°:30′ East. I could not See the Sunn last night, but I estimated the point of his Setting by the obliquity of his beams, appearing between the Clouds that Cover him[5]

☿ [6]21. Latitude by a good observation 36°:3′. We have had the Winds from the N E b N to the N b W a fine Gale, we have our Correct Course E 1° S $82\frac{1}{2}$ Miles. Difference of Longitude 1°:42′, and Longitude from London 8°:26′ from the Islands 7°:54′; for the most part close overcast weather the Sunn scarce appearing all day. —

♃ [7]22. Latitude by observation 35°:53′. We have had the Winds

[1] D renders this: Yesterday at $5^{h.}$ $17^{m.}$ P M. the Sun being truly West, his Magnetical Azimuth was 4°. to the South, that is so much East Variation as well as could be taken for the great Sea and rowling motion of the Ship.
The fifth word from the end of this entry in the MS and D means 'rolling'.

[2] D adds below: 48.0 29.9.

[3] D, and Longitude from London 0°.0′ 10.0′; from Tristan da Cunha 6°. 12′. Perhaps the first figures here in D are merely an indication of the Longitude of London.

[4] D, . . . Southward of the West and East.

[5] D, that covered him.

[6] D adds below: 57.0 30.0.

[7] D adds below: *Ther.* *Bar.*
59.0 30.0.

from the West to S W a gentle gale towards noon Calm true Course is E b N 50. Miles, whence difference of Longitude is 1°:1′ East Longitude from London 7°:25′. from the Islands 8°:55′. Cloudy weather still continues

♀ [1]23. Latitude by Account 35°:53′. We have had the Winds from N N E to N N W. a fine Gale. this morning about 9^{h} the wind came about to the S S W with a Squall that made us lett fly both our Top saile Sheets. about noon nearly Calm The true Course this day is East 100 Miles, which gives difference of Longitude 2°:3′. Longitude from London 5°:22′. This Morning I hoped to have Seene the begining of the Eclipse of the Moon, but the Sky was all overcast, as is usuall in these Climates. —

♄ [2]24. Latitude by an observation taken 12′ after Noon 35°:38′. We have had the winds variable; till 5 yesterday dead Calme, then N N E and N E b N; about Midnight a Squall of Wind and rain brought the Wind to S W, whence it gradually came to the S b E. Course protracted is E b N 71 Miles which gives difference of Longitude 1°:27′ East Longitude from London 3°:55′. from Tristan da Cunha 12°:25. West[3] Yesterday at Sunn Sett the Amplitude was 6°:40′ to the Southwards of the West whence the Variation is halfe a degree Westerly. The weather squally and uncertain with rain. No variation 11½ to the Eastwards of the Islands. —

[1] D adds below: 57.0 29.9.

[2] D adds below: 50.0 29.8. Below this in the margin is an asterisk in line with the entry in n. 3 below, which see.

[3] D '. . . from Tristan da Cunha 12°.25′.W* . . .' The asterisk refers to a footnote at the bottom of the page which reads: '**West*, this is an error for *East*'. Of course, this location is east of Tristan da Cunha but it is west of London as was all of Halley's open sea sailing once out of the eastern part of the English Channel. See Atlantic Chart (in portfolio) with track of Halley's second voyage.

(f.24v.) ☉ [1]25. Latitude by a good observation 34°:44′. We have had the Winds this 24 hours from the S S E to the E S E a Fresh Gale; we have gon close halld with our Starboard taks on board. Our Correct Course is N E 76. Miles. Difference of Longitude is 1°:6′ Longitude from London 2°:49. West

☽ [2]26. Latitude by Acco^t: 33°:20′. We have had the Winds from the S E to the S S W a moderate Gale till five in the afternoon, when the Wind came to S b W fresh[3] with much rain but before night we were forced to go under a forcsale only; by Midnight we were forced to Scudd before it; the Storm encreasing till daylight with a Terrible high Sea about Six this Morning a greate Sea broke in upon our Starboard quarter, and withall threw us to that we had likt to have oversett; the Deck being full of Water, which had a clear pasage over the Gunnell, but it pleased God She wrighted again.[4] So we handed our Fore-topsaile and Scudded a hull[5] till this day Noon; The Fury of the Storm Seeming to abate, but the Sea running Mountains high We have made our way N 43 E 115. Miles Difference of Long 1°:35′. and totall Longitude from London 1°:14′ West—

♂ [6]27. Latitude by observation 31°:18′. The Storm Continuing and blowing very hard at South: and we scudded A Hull till three When wee set our spritsaile reeft, and Scudded right afore it all Night; by day the Wind being somewhat moderated, we

[1] D adds below: *Ther.* *Bar.* 55.0 29.7.

[2] D adds below: 48.02 9.7.

[3] D, first.

[4] D renders this: . . . that we had like to have overset; the Deck being full of Water, which had a clear passage over the Gunnel; but it pleased God she righted again.

[5] D 'So we handed our Foresail and scudded a-hull'. That is, they made their way with sails furled.

[6] D adds below: 49.0 29.8.

Sett our foresail and by Noon we found we were Shott to the Northwards of the Cape 60 Leagues,[1] the wind Still Blowing fresh at South: and wee being 300 Leagues to the Westwards of the Cape; and our Water not to be Come at without romaging[2] (which is not practicable in these Tempestuous high grown Seas) and withall to Save time, fearing to go hom in the Winter, which would Expose my weak Shipps Comp^tt^ to greate hard ships.[3] I orderd to Continue our[4] Course North to fill our water at St Helena, our Stock being nearly spent haveing been now 9. Weeks at Sea Correct Course this 24 hours is N 2 W 122 Miles — The Difference of Long 5 Minutes and Longitude from London 1°:19′ West —

☿ [5]28. Latitude by Acco^t^ 29°:35′. We have had the Wind due South this 24 hours and have gon away right before it North 103 Miles but correct by Variation N 2 W: Difference of Longitude (f.25) 4 Minutes, and Long from London W 1°:23′. The late Storm haveing twice filld my Cabbin knee Deep, the Water found Some leaks into the Bread roome, my Steward gave me an Acc : that a Considerable quantity of bread was spoiled, and would Damage more if it were not immediately removed so I order'd a Survey by my Officers and they found 6 C^wt^ Cwt of Bread and 30. of Flower, and 30. of Cheese to be perished and unfitt to be eaten, and it was accordingly cast over board,

[1] D '. . . shot to the Northwards of the *Cape*'. They were now well north of the latitude of the Cape of Good Hope (34° S Latitude).

[2] i.e. rummaging.

[3] D 'fearing to go home in the Winter, which would expose my weak Ships company to great hardships'.

[4] The word 'our' is careted in on the MS.

[5] D adds below:

Ther.	*Bar.*
57.0	29.8.

the weather close over cast the Sunn Scarce appearing all Day.

♃ [1]29. Latitude by observation 28°:8′. Wind South till Midnight, then come to S S E and E b S; we now entring on the Trade Wind of S E. our Correct Course is N 2° $\frac{1}{2}$ W 87 Miles: Diff of Longitude 4 Min[u]ts and Long from London 1°:27′ West fine Smooth weather but still cloudy, that it is not possible to observe the Variation: and with greate difficulty the Lattitude by help of my Glass. —

March ♀ [2]1. Latitude by Account 26°:46′ we have had the winds from the S S E to the East a moderate Gale and very Smooth water. Correct — course is N 3° W 82 Miles Difference of Long: is 5 Minutes, and Long: West from London is 1°:32′ from Tristan da Cunha 14°:48′ East This day towards Sunn Sett, the Sunn being 3° high was 1°:30′. to the Northard of the Magnaticall[3] West, and Seem'd to goe down due West, by Compass allowing for the Obliquity of his Descent. whence Variation West 3°:30′ —

♃ [4]2 Latitude by observation 25°:14′. We have had the Winds from the East to S E b E a fine Gale, and have gon a way North p Compass, i e N 3° $\frac{1}{2}$ W 92 Miles, Difference of Longitude 6 Mintues, and Long from London West 1°:38′ Memorand: that Variation mencond yesterday ought to be reckon'd as of this day being observed in Lat 26°:30′[5]

⊙ [6]3 Latitude by observation ++ ++ 23°:30′. We have had the

[1] D adds below: 62.0 29.8.

[2] D adds below: *Ther. Bar.* 65.0 29.9.

[3] D, Magnetical.

[4] D adds below: 66.0 30.1.

[5] D renders this: Memorandum the Variation mentioned yesterday ought to be reckoned as of this day being observed in Latitude 26°.30′.

[6] D adds below: 70.0 30.0.

Winds from the S E to the East a Fresh Gale we have gon away N p Compass ie N 3 ½ E[1] 104 Miles: Difference of Long 7′ and Longitude from London West 1°:45′ The Cloudy weather still Continues that we rarely See the Sunn or Starrs especially in the Morning hours —

☽ [2]4. Latitude by observation 21°:58′. We have had the Winds from S E to E as yesterday a fine Steady Gale our Correct course this 24 hours, in N 4 W 92 Miles, difference of Long 7′ and Long: from Lond^θ 1°:52′ West Yesterday near Sunn Sett, with much Difficulty I observed the Sunns magneticall Azimuth vizt at 5^h:30 the Sunn was 5° to the Northard of the West & at 5^h:50′ he was 3°00′ to the Northward in Latt 23°:15′. Varriation West 4°:10′ — (f.25v.)

♂ [3]5. Latitude by a good Observation 20°:25′. We have had the winds at S E all this 24 hours a Fresh Gale and Smooth water. Course by Compass is N b W but Correct p Variation N 15° W 96 Miles wch gives difference of Longitude 27 Minutes and Long from London 2°19′ West I reckon my Selfe this Noon to be 4 degrees to the East of the Island it bearing N 41 W 116 Leagues distant by my Account.

☿ [4]6. Latitude by a very good observation 18°:26′. We have had the Winds from the S E to E b S, a Fresh Gale. We have Steer'd away N b W p Compass or N 15° W correct Course, 123 Miles. diff of Long: 34′ and Longitude from London West 2°:53′. At Sunn Sett the Magnetick Amplitude was 2°½ to

[1] D, i.e. N 3½ E*. The asterisk refers to a footnote at the bottom of the page which reads: '*E for W'. D is correct, as Halley was veering slightly to the west while attaining the latitude of St Helena (see Atlantic Chart, in pocket).

[2] D adds below: 72.0 30.0.

[3] D adds below: *Ther. Bar.* 75.0 30.0

[4] D adds below: 77.0 30.0.

the Northard of the West, but the true Amplitude was 1°:36′. to the South; Variation 4°:6′ West

♃ [1]7. Latitude by a good observation 16°40′: We have had the Winds at E b S and S E b E this 24h and have made our Correct Course N 15° W. 110 Miles: Diff of Long 30′, and Long from Lond^θ^ 3°:23′. Last night at Sunn Sett the Amplitude was 2°:30′ to the Northard of the West and this Morning the Sunn rose 4°:30′. to the Southard of the East p Compass, from which the Variation is Concluded — 3°:30′ to the Westward of the North —

♀ [2]8 Latitude by a very good observation 16°:1′ We have had the Wind from the South b E to the E S E, a fine Gale. By Sunn Sett we were able to See into the Lattitude of the Island, it being very Clear on the Northern board, so I order'd to Stear away N N W till we were in the Latitude which was by two this Morning, when we bore away due West. Our Correct Course is W 34° N 70 Miles, which gives the Diffrence of Longitude one degree just Long from London 4°:23′ West

(f.26) ♄ [3]9. Latitude by a good observation 15°:55′. We have had the Winds from the S b E to the East a moderate Gale we have gon away due West 87½ Miles allowing for the drift of four hours from 12 to 4 in the Morning that we lay by: Diff: of Longitude 1°:31′ and Long from London 5°:54′. Last night and this Morning by good observations I found the Variation nearest 3°:00′. or rather 2°:50′ West

☉ [4]10 Latitude by a good observation: 15°:54′ We have had the

[1] D adds below: 77.½ 29.9½.

[2] D adds below: 79.0 30.0.

[3] D adds below: *Ther. Bar.* 78.0 30.0.

[4] D adds below: 82.0 29.9.

Winds from S b E to East a fine Gale and have made our way due W. 70 Miles haveing lain by 4 hours with our head to the Southards Difference of Longitude 1°:13′. Long: from London 7°:7′ Variation well taken by the Morning an Evening Amplitude 2°:30′ West: this morning we Saw many of the St Helena white birds[1] flying about the Shipp I conclude by them and by the Variation I am not to Leeward of the Island though my reckoning be now out

☽ 11. Latitude 15°:52′. by a good observation. We had[2] the Winds S S E to S S W a Small Gale and have made our way good West 52 Miles Difference of Longitude 0°:54′ Long: from London 8°:1′ West. last night the Variation well taken was as near as might be 2°:00′ West at 11 this Morning We raised the North part of St Helena, the topp thereof only just appearing Due West from us and by Noon we Saw the high land in the middle of the Island being then about 13 Leagues distant from us as we found afterwards by our Logg. And it cannot be Seen above 15 Leagues up Deck in all —[3]

♂ 12. By Sunn rise this Morning we were close under the Land. but the winds being far Southerly we were becalmed under the high land of the Barn point, and Masts Mount,[4] So that it was near noon when we gott to an Anchor off Chapell valey in 23 Fathom Water. by my Account of the Ships way this Island Should be 8°:40′ more Westerly than London, which is two

[1] From his earlier residence on the Island Halley would have recognized these birds, possibly terns (*genus Sterna*).

[2] D, We have had . . .

[3] D, and it cannot be seen above 15 Leagues in all upon deck.

[4] Halley first saw the northeast coast of St Helena – Barn Long Point – and above that feature The Barn, *c.* 650 metres, and Flagstaff Hill *c.* 725 metres to the west.

degrees more than by Celestiall observation I have found it formerly,[1] and so much I conclude I have been Sett to the Eastwards by Some Current since the 17th February when I left the Isles of Tristan da Cunha, from wch I have mad 7°:40′ Longitude East to this Island which by Concurrent accounts is nearest 9.[2]

(f.26v.) ♄ 30 In the afternoon I weighed out of St Helena road and by 6 of the Clock the Westmost part bore South I reckon I depart from Latitude[3] 15°52′ and Long west from London 6°:30′ —

☉ 31. Latitude by observation 16°18′ I Stear away W S W in order to get into the Latitude of Trinidad[4] much to windward thereof, to see if there be any such Isles as the Maps lay down, Winds from the East to the E N E a fine Gale Course W 24° S 63 Miles whence difference of Long 1°:00′ Long from London 7°:30′ At noon we laid[5] the Island and saw noe more of the white birds. —

Aprill ☽ 1. Latitude by observation 16°:53′ We have had the winds at E N E & E b N a Fresh Gale True Course W 20 S 103 Miles which gives diff of Long 1°:41′ Longitude from London 9°:11′

[1] This would make the longitude about 6° 40′ W. In reality it is approximately 5°.40′ W.

[2] D, . . . from which I have made but 7°.40′ Longitude E to this Island; which by concurrent accounts is nearest 9°.

After this statement in D there is a blank half page with only a capital letter, H, centred at the bottom of the page and the catchword, In. As in the MS, D picks up the log again as Halley leaves St Helena after about a two week stay, on 30 March. On this day, just before leaving, Halley wrote Burchett summarizing his voyage from Rio de Janeiro through the South Atlantic to St Helena (Document 84, pp. 306-7).

[3] The word, 'Longitude,' has been crossed out and 'Latitude' put above it on the MS.

[4] D, *Trinidad* – italicized but the same spelling as in the MS. It is rendered as Trinidada on the Atlantic Chart and refers to a volcanic island at Latitude 20°.30′ S, Longitude 29°.20′ W. now Trinidade, belonging to Brazil. See Appendix B, p. 356.

[5] D, layed. That is, sailed out such a distance that the Island was brought to and below the horizon.

West. Yesterday at Sunn Sett the Varriation was 1°:00′ West by good Amplitude

♂ 2. Latitude by a good observation 17°:21 We have had the Winds from the E b N to the S E b S. a Fresh Gale and Smooth Water. We have made our true Course W 15° ½ South 104. Miles. Difference of Long: 1°:45′ Long from London 10°:56′. Yesterday Evening the Sunn Sett in a Cloud

☿ 3. Latitude by observation 18°:00′. We have had the Winds from S E b S. to S E b E a Fresh Gale and Some squalls. Our true Course is W 19° S 120. Miles diff: of Long 1°:58′. and Long from London 12°54′. Yesterday Evening by a good Amplitude I found there was no Variation of ye Needle

♃ 4. Latitude by observation 18°:34′; we have had the winds from the S b E to E b S a Stout Gale. Our Course[1] W 16° S 127 Miles whence Diff of Long 2°:6′. and Long from London 15°:00′. Yesterday Even Amplit gave 1°:00′ East variation. —

♀ 5. Latitude by Observation 19°:18′. We have had a Stout Gale of Wind from E b S to E N E. Our true Course W 20° S. 130 Miles which gives diffrence of Long 2°:10′ and Long from London 17°:10′. the Evening Variation was full 2°. East and this Morning 2°½ East

♄ 6. Latitude by Observa 19°:48′. We have had the Winds from the E b S to S E. b S. a Gentle Gale. True Course W 18° South 99. Miles Diff of Longit 1°:40′. and Long from London 18°:50′.[2]

☉ 7. Latitude by Observation 20°:13′ We have had the Winds

[1] D, Our true Course . . .

[2] D renders this: We have had the Winds from E b S to the S E b S a moderate gale. True Course W 18 S 99 miles; gives difference of Longitude 1°.40′. Longitude from London 18°.50′.

Following this are erasures on the MS decipherable as the concluding statement of the entry for the following day.

from S E b S: to E S E a Gentle Gale. True Course W 18° ½ South 79 Miles Diffrence of Long 1°:20′ and Long from London 20°10′ This Morning the Magna Amplitude just 15° —[1]

(f.27) ☽ 8. Latitude by Observation 20°:24′. We have had a Gentle Gale at E b N and have made our True Course W 9° South 69 Miles; whence the Diff: of Longitude 1°:14′ and Long from London 21°:24′. I am now gott[2] into the Latitude of Trinidada, but find my self continually sett to the Northwards of my Acco^t: so Conclude a Current Setting W N W or thereabouts

♂ 9. Latitude by a good observation 20°:24′. Wind at E b N a Gentle Gale We have made our Course due west 58 Miles which gives Diff of Longitude 1°:2′ and from London 22°:26′ we found that Stearing W ½ South kept the paralell exactly and Soe went away by Compass 12 hours West and 12 hours W by South. The ☉^s Amplitude at riseing this Morning 16°:30′[3]

☿ 10. Latitude well observed 20°:23′. We have had Gentle Gale at E b N and E N E and made our Course due West 66½ Miles, whence the differ: of Longitude is 1°:11′. and from London 23°:37′. This Morning the Ampl was 17°:00′ —

♃ 11. Latitude by observation 20°:25′. We have had a fine Fresh Gale at E N E and have made our Course due West 96 Miles Diffrence Long 1°:43′ and Long: from London 25°:20′. The Evening Amplitude was 8°:00′ and the Morning Amplitude was 18°:00′ Last Night the Moon Apply'd to the Contiguæ in facie Tauri, and I got a very good observation, whence I

[1] D, This Morning the Magnetical Amplitude was just 15°.
[2] D, gotten.
[3] D, The ☉ Amplitude at rising this morning was 16°.30′.

conclude my Selfe 2°:00′ more to the Westward than by my Account —

♀ 12. Latitude by observation 20°:24′ We have had the Winds shiffting[1] about between the N E, and N N W, a gentle Gale but with Some threatning Clouds. We have made a due West Course 55 Miles which gives Difference of Long 1°:00′. and Long from London 26°:20′. Yesterday Evening the Amplitude was again 8°:00′ —

♄ 13. Latitude by observation 20°:21′. We had very little Winds this 24^{h}: and for the most part Calme, Shuffling all round the Compass,[2] we have made our way due W 17 Miles, which gives 18 Minutes of Longitude and from London 26°:38′. This Morning the Sunns Amplitude was 20°:00′ —

☉ 14. Latitude by observation 20°:25′ we have had little winds from the E to the E S E and have made our true Course due West 41 Miles, in Long 43 Min & from London 27°:21′ This Morning about halfe an hour past 10, we raised the Islands or rather the Rocks of Martin vaz[3] distant about 6 Leagues & bearing W from us, at Noon they had this position & figure being in all 3 in Number[4]

[1] D, shuffling.

[2] D, 'We have had very little winds this 24 hours, and for the most part calm; shuffling all round the Compass.' Here we do have the word 'shuffling' in the MS.

[3] D, *Rocks* of *Martin Vaz*. These islets were named after the Portuguese pilot who discovered them in the early sixteenth century.

[4] D renders this: At Noon they had this position and figure [Vid. Pl. H N1] being in all 3 in number.

The square brackets are Dalrymple's; the bracketed material refers to the plate in D where all illustrations in the Journal of Halley's Second Voyage have been placed together. Because the illustration is separated from the immediate text, D has a heading above it, *Rocks of* (f.27v.) ☽ 15. Yesterday in the afternoon about 2 we were up with the three Isles of Martin Vaz, which lie nearly North and South unless — the Northermost (which is but a Small Rock) be some what more westerly they are in all not much more than a Mile asunder and about the same time we discover'd the Island of Troindada bearing from us by Compass between the W b S and W S W — wee Stear'd in w:th it till Sun Sett and about 5. at the dist. of about 4 Leages it Appeared thus bearing West from us[1]

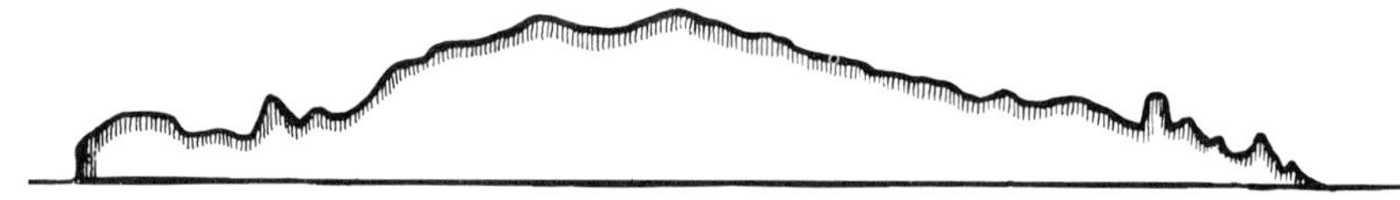

Wee plyed to Windward under an easey Sayle all night, it blowing pretty fresh at S E, with the day wee bore away, and about. 8. in the Morning wee came to an Anchor in 30 Fathome above a mile From the Shore on the West side of the Island: I went on Shore in the Boat to looke for Water, which wee soon found, and Im̄ediately sent the Boate, a Board to get the Cask ready, and the pinnace went and Sounded and Found Graduall

MARTIN VAZ; and adds the notation, *S.* following the latitude, and the notation, *N⁰ i*, on the left hand side though it is not the first illustration (see n. 3, p. 162). In the MS it is difficult to decipher the script under the sketch, which might be directional or possibly interpreted as W 6 L. L may mean leagues. This statement in the MS is omitted in D who adds instead: These *Islands* lie nearest N. and S. only the Northernmost is somewhat more Westerly, and are not above a mile in length, they are no better than Rocks and no way accessible. About 10 in the morning the Wind came up at S E b S and blew fresh.

[1] D renders this: M. 15. Yesterday in the afternoon about 2 of the Clock we were up with the three *Isles* of *Martin Vaz*, which lie nearly N. and S. unless the Northermost (which is but a very small Rock) be somewhat more Westerly, they are in all not much more than a mile asunder, and about the same time we discovered the Island of *Trinidada* bearing from us by Compass between W b S and W S W. We steared in with it till Sunset and about 5. at a distance of about 4 Leagues it appeared thus [Vide Plate N N2] bearing W from us.

As before the square brackets are Dalrymple's and the bracketed material refers to the plate in D containing all the illustrations from the log of Halley's Second Voyage. This illustration is labeled No. 2, and within the profile is titled, *TRINIDADA Lat 20° 27′ S.*

Shoalings to .8. and .10. Fathome. By my account I reckon but 21°.20′ from St Helena to Trinidada, but by my observation of the Moon on the 11th Ins^t^., I allow it 23°.20′ West, and from London 29°.50′., the North part in 20°.25′South, and the South in 20°.29′: at most. The Island being about 1½ League in Length, lying nearest N W and S E. the North and West Part is nothing but Steep Rocks Scarce Accessible.

♂ 16 The Boate went and brought us .3. Turns of water but it was difficult to gett it into the Boate by reason of the Rocky Shore wch Staved some of our Cask: Finding wee had drove into deeper water, I order'd to Weigh and Stood all night to Windward wth a Fine gale at E b S, and by morning we had the North point of the Isle fair under our Lee

☿ 17 This morning wee moored in 18 Fathom on the west Side of the Isle the north part being[1] E N E, the South part S E, and the high Steep Rock like a Nine=pinn E S E. Whilest the Long Boate brought more Water on Board I went a Shore and put Some Goats and Hoggs on the Island for breed, as alsoe a pair of Guiney Hens I carry'd from St Helena. And I tooke possession of the Island in his Maj^ties^ name as knowing it to be granted by the Kings Letters Pattents leaving the Union Flagg flying[2]

♃ 18, The water of this Island being very fine and good I (f.28) emptyed my Cisterns of their brackish St Helena Water, wch by reason of the great Raines whilest I was there, was so turn'd[3]

[1] D, bearing.
[2] D '... King's Letters Patents, leaving the Union Flag flying.'
[3] D, turbid.

sometimes as not to be fitt to take on Board. The watering place we used was a little to the Southward of the high Steep Rock, where the water rann all the time wee were there wth a plentifull Stream but the Shoar being very Rocky much endammaged our Cask

♀ 19. I rowed round the Island in the pinnace and found it of the —following forme and position.[1]

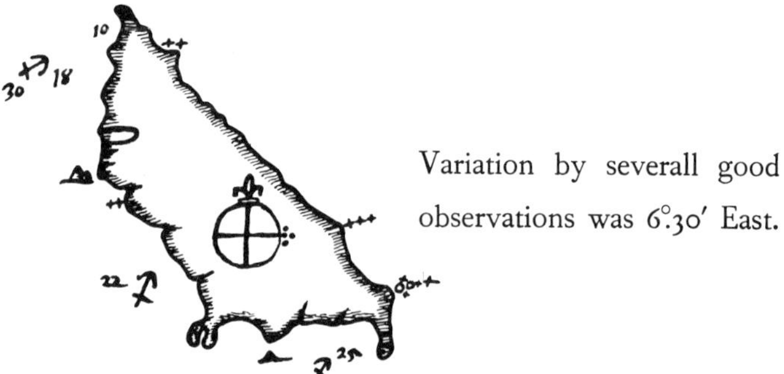

Variation by severall good observations was 6°.30′ East.

T[2]

This afternoone I went up to the topp of the Island and found it very Steep and Laborious to ascend it but fresh watter rann downe in Sever^{ll} places plentifully perticularly at A where I went up. On Board they Stowed every thing away and made ready to Saile,

♄ 20. This morning I weigh'd from Trinidada about .7. and at .9. made Saile with wind at E b S: at Noon the Island was about 4

[1] D follows this statement with: [Vide Plate H.]. Again, the square brackets are Dalrymple's and this refers to the plate in D, mentioned previously, containing engravings of all of the illustrations from Halley's Second Voyage. This last illustration of the plate in D (unnumbered) is a fair copy of the one in the MS. However, it lacks the compass, but in its place has the identification '*TRINIDADA*'. The letter 'A' referred to in the text below (in the MS and in D) is shown shoreward of the anchor marked by the 22 fathom reading on the plate, but not on the MS map. The variation statement is not present in D, and on the MS map appears to be in a different hand than most of the text, possibly Halley's

[2] The writer of the MS started this line so high that it would interfere with the map if continued. Thus he began again on the line below. Understandably the extra T is not in D.

Leagues distant bearing[1] S E b S, though wee had Steared away N N W; for the Port of Pernambuc[2] in Brasile; but I find by the Land that a Current Setts us to the Westwards: Lat. by the observations 20°:15′ Longitude from Lond.$^{\theta}$ 29°:56′ Nothing occurring remarkable in this passage, it may Suffice to Set it downe in the following Table

		Wind	Course	Miles	Latitude Cor.r	Long′: Cor.r	Amp.	Var. East
☉[3]	21	E.ENE.	N22W	93.	18.49.	— 30.33	E10.00	6.27
☽	22	EbN.	NbW	106	17.05.	— 30.55	E11.00	5.36
♂	23	E.EbS.	NbW	113	15.14.	— 31.19	M22.30	5.51
☿	24	E.NE.	NbW	82	13.54.	— 31.41	E12.00	5 4
♃	25	ESE.	NbW	106	12.10.	— 32.00	M22.30	5 31
♀	26	SSE.	NbW	114	10.18.	— 32.20	E12.00	5 15
♄	27	SEbE.	N24W	107	8.40.	— 33.5	----	
☉	28	ESE.	W15N.	83	8.19.	— 34.25	----	

From Saturday Noone I bore away West by Compass that is W 5°.[4] North at Night for one watch I Stood NE close hal'd, then bore away West again about Noone the water begann to (f.28v.) be discolloured, and heaving the Lead we had 30 Fathome Sandy Ground in Lattitude 8°.19′, before one in the afternoone we discover'd the main Land of Brasile first right on head then 4 points on both Bows, about 5 Leagues distant, wee Stood in w.th it till 4^{h} then clapt by the wind[5] and stood N E b E till night

[1] D, bearing. In the MS the word 'being' has been altered to 'bearing' by the letters 'ar' being careted in.
[2] Could be Fernambue in the MS. It is hard to decipher but it refers to D, *Pernombuc* (or *Pernambouc*), modern Recife. See Appendix B, p. 356.
[3] D adds: April. above this and below, as is his usual practice, the days of the week are abbreviated, not symbolized. There are lines boxing in the various columns of the table in D.
[4] D, W 5 N. D introduces this statement with 'Su. 21'.
[5] That is, brought the ship close to windward.

when knowing the Current at this time of the year to Set to the Norwards and not being assured of the precise Latitude of Pernambue,[1] I feared to drive past it in the night soe came to an Anchor wth Small bower[2] in 12 Fathom water about a League from Shore

☽ 29 By day breake wee were a peek[3] and heaving the Anchor out of the ground our Cable broke wth in a Few Fathom of the Clench, and for want of light wee — cou'd not Find our Bouy so made Sail along Shore for Pernambue wch wee deserned to the Norward of us, about Sun rise I went on Shore in the Boate for a Pilot, who brought us in ab^t^ 10. of the Clock, and Moored us under the Portuguese Cannon and by two of their men of Warr. Waiting on the Governour I found him very obligeing and I had Liberty to Supply my self wth what Wine and other things I wanted, and was Informed that all was at — peace in Europe wch I was most desirious to be assured of

♂ 30. This day one Mr Hardwick who calls himselfe English Consull begann to shew himselfe Suspitious that we might be Pirates, and told me the Governour had promised to detain us, till wee had acquitted ourSelves to him, wch my two Commissions and Subsequient orders woud not doe though he had noe objection against them[4]

May ☿ 1st Mr Hardwick took two of my Seamen under Examination, a part & wrote downe the Account they gave him wch he told me did agree wth what I had told him my Selfe wherefore I

[1] There is no question about the initial letter P in this case in the MS, but the final letter might be e or c. See p. 187, n. 2.

[2] One of the two small bow anchors.

[3] apeek, i.e. the ship vertically over the anchor.

supposed him Satisfyed, and gott my Wine & other things on Board intending to Saile the next day. This morning the Suns Magnetical Amplitude[1] was 23°.00 to the Northward of the East Variation East 4°.38′.

♃ 2 Mr. Hardwick pretending further Jealousie, desired me to call on him at his house this afternoon, where instead of Business he caused me to be — Arrested, and a Portuguese Guard Sett over[2] me whilest he went and Searched my Shipp, wch he did without ever acquainting me, but Finding no Signes of of[3] Piracie on Board he came and discharged me of my Guard begging my pardon and Excusing it that what he had Done was to give Satisfaction To the Portuguese who were Jalouse (f.29) of me, as not comprehending my Business

♀ 3. The next day resolving to Saile I Found the Pilot wou'd not put us out of the Harbour wthout the Goverours order wch I this day — obtained, and I was given to understand that Mr. Hardwick had Acted in my Affair wthout Authority being only impower'd to Act For the Affrican Company,[4] and the Owners of the Shipp Hanniball[5] wch had been Seized there as a Pirate and had no Commission of Consul

♄ 4. Wee Weighed out of the Harbour of Pernambue wch they call the Reciff.[6] The Towne of Villa Olinda wch lyes about a League to the North is at pesent almost deserted, but was heretofore the Seate of the Portuguese This day at noon the

[1] The letter m in Amplitude has been careted in.
[2] D, on.
[3] D has only one 'of'.
[4] D renders this: . . . Mr. Hardwyck had acted in my affair without Authority, being only empowered to act for the African Company.
D only spells Hardwyck in this way in this instance; otherwise it is spelled as in the MS.
[5] D, Ship Hannibal.
[6] See p. 187, n. 2 above, and Appendix B, p. 356.

Reciff bore about W S W distant about 10 Miles — The Latitude of the Reciff is 8°:10′ South Correct Longitude From Lond$^{\theta}$ 35°:30.

☉ 5 Latitude by observation 6°:25′. Wee have had Winds from the S E b S. to the East a Small Gale, I Stear'd away N N E when the Wind would permitt it to gett an Offing and this 24^{h} have made by Logg 70 Miles Course N N E ½ N diff of Latitude 1°:07′ but by observation I find 1°:40′. So that the Current Setts to the Norward^{s}: about 1:[1] Miles p hour diff of Long 21 minutes East Long From Lond 35°:00′ This morning the Amplitude was 23½ and this Evening but 15°½ hence Variation

☽ 6 Lat by observation 4°:32′ Wind between the E S E & S E a fine Gale, I kept a point from the Wind till Sunn Sett, then Stear'd away N N W. designing for the Carribie Isle[2] Course protracted N b W 102 Miles diff of Latitude 1:40, Latitude by account 4°:45′ So we have been Sett 13 Miles by the Current to the Norwards. diff of Longitude[3] 21′ West Long from London 35:21 West, This Evening the Amplitude was as Yesterday. 15½ This morn^{g} ☉ rose Clouded[4]

♂ 7. Lat. by observation 2°:58′, Wind at S E b. E and E S E a fresh Gale and. — Smooth water I Stear'd away N N W till Midnight then W N W Course — protracted N 38 W 108 Miles diff of Lat 1°:25 Lat by acco$^{\theta}$: 3°:7 Current to the Norwards 9 Miles Diff of Long 1°:7′ Long From London 36°:28′. This — Morning the Amplitude was 24°½

[1] D, 1⅓ mile per hour. In the MS there is an erasure after 1: which might have been ⅓, but it is hard to decipher.

[2] D, Caribbe Isles. In the MS, nd has been erased after Isle, suggesting that originally the word Island had been entered.

[3] The n in Longitude is careted in.

[4] D, This Morning the sun rose clouded.

☿ 8 Latitude by observation 2°:4′ South Wind at E S E and S E b E a fine Gale Course W N W 76½ diff of Lat 34 Lat. p Acco$^{\theta}$: 2°:24 Current to the North. 20′ Diff of Long. 1°:8′ Long from London 37°:36′: this Morning the Sun rose Clouded, but in the Evening the Amplitude was 15°:40′ accurately[1] (f.29v.)

♃ 9 Latitude by observation 1°:4′[2] Wind from S E b E to East a Steady Gale and very Smooth Water Course W N W 95 Miles Difference of Latitude 43 Miles. Lat by Acco^{t}: 1°:21′ Current 17. Miles to the Norwards Diff of Longitude[3] 1°:25′ Long from London 39°:1′ In the Evening the Amplitude was 15°00′ but not So Certainly as last Night.

♀ 10 Lat. by Estimate 0°:00′ Darke Cloudy Weather Wind till Midnight E b S then E b N to N E a fresh Gale Course W 32 N 90 Miles, Diff of Latitude 48 Miles Lat by account 0°:16′ South Difference of Long. 1°:16′ Longitude from London 40°:17′ Morning Amplitude 25°½ and this Evening 15¼ both well taken —

♄ 11. Lat by observation 1°:37′ North. Winds Variable from S b E[4] to N E a gentle gale Course protracted N 30 W 74 Miles diff of Latitude .64. Miles and from Thursday noon 112 Miles but by observation 161 Current 49 Miles in 48 hours to the Norwards. Diff. of Longitude 37 minutes Long from Lond$^{\theta}$ 40°:54′ I allow this Current to Sett N W b W along Shore at the rate of 30 p diem and this day Correct my Longitude adding to it 2°:51′ so that my true Longitude from London is 43°:45

⊙ 12. Dark Cloudy Weather Wind from N E b E to East with Squalls and Violent Raines. Course N W b N 76 Miles Diff of

[1] D, 15°:48′ accurately.
[2] The 1° is corrected from 2° in the MS.
[3] Corrected from Latitude on the MS.
[4] D, E b S.

Latitude 63 Miles Lat. by Acco^{t}: 2°:40′ North Diff of Long 42′ Long from London 44°:27′

☽ 13. Wind and Weather as Yesterday onely Sometimes lunn gales next to Calme, Course N W 47 Miles Difference of Longitude and Latitude 33 Miles Latitude by acco$^{\theta}$: 3°:13′ North Longitude from London 45°:00′.

♂ 14 Latitude by a good observation 5°:21′ Wind and Weather as before Course N 32 W 66 Miles. diff of Latitude 56 miles lat by acco$^{\theta}$: 4°:9′ Current to y^{e} Norwards in 3. dayes 72 Miles, Diff of Long 35′ Long from London 45°:35′ Wee can Seldome See the Sun the Sky being wholly overcast wth Violent raines by Squalls

☿ 15 Latitude by observation 7°:11′, Wind from the E N E to N E a fresh Gale I goe away N W, to gett off the Lee Shore of Guiana. Course due N W .112. Miles Diff. of Long and Lat 81′ minutes Lat by acco$^{\theta}$: 6°:42′, Current this 24 hours 29 Miles (f.30) to the Norward,[1] that is 100 miles Since my Correction on the 11th day. Longitude by Acco$^{\theta}$: 46°:56′ I allow the Current to have Sett 2°:00′ Since the 11th day to the Westward and my Correct Longitude will be 48°:56′ West from Lond$^{\theta}$. Variation this day in the evening, the amplitude being 16½ was

♃ 16 Latitude by observation 8°:25′ Wind at N E a Steady Gale and fair Weather Course N W 79 Miles Difference of Latitude 1°:1′ of Long 51′ Latitude p acco$^{\theta}$: 8:12 Long by acco$^{\theta}$: 49°:47′ I allow 30 Miles for the Current, Long Correct 50°:17′ from London Morning Amplitude was 26½ and this Evening 17° but not soe certain as this Mornings

[1] D, Current this 24 hours 29′. to the Northward, . . .

♀ 17 Latitude by observation 9°:27′ Wind from E N E to N E fair weather Course N. W 77 miles diff of Latitude 1°:00′ of Long. 51 West Lat by acco$^{\theta}$: 9°:25′ Long by acco$^{\theta}$: 51°:8′ but allowing the Current 51°:38′ this Morning the Collour of the Sea changed from Blew to a darke Green or Somewhat Brownish, and we Saw many Birds both Nodies[1] and Men of Warr the Evening Variation well taken was 17°.00′ The Current now Setts wholly West

♄ 18 Lat by observation 10°:55′ Wind as Yesterd from N E to E N E a fresh gale. Course N W 105. Miles Diff of Lat 1°:20′ Diff of Long: 1°:9′ minutes Latitude by Acco$^{\theta}$: 10°:47′ Long p Acco$^{\theta}$: 52 47 Long Correct 53°:17′ This Evening in the Latitude of 11°:15′ the Sea again recover'd its Blew Colour after wee had runn over a Bank of Oazy bottom for ab$^{\theta}$: 50 Leagues on a N W Course

☉ 19 Lat by observation 12°:29′ Wind at E N E and East, a fresh gale Course N.W. N W 109 miles, Difference of Latitude 83. Miles, of Long 1°:11′ West Lat. by by acco$^{\theta}$: 12°18′ Long by acco$^{\theta}$: 54°:28′ Correct by Current 54°.58′ this Evening many men of War Birds seen befoe Sunn Sett. w^{ch}: makes me Conclude that I have not allowed Enough for the Current and that wee are near Barbadoes The Sunn rises and Setts thick

☽ 20 Lat by observation 13°:7′ Wind at East and E N E a Steady Gale I went. away N W till last night at 8^{h} then W b N till midnight Course protracted — W 23 N 95. Miles Diff of Latitude 37. Miles Lat by acco$^{\theta}$ 13°:6′ so that the Current setts

[1] Soot-coloured sea birds (*Anous stolidus*) of tropical regions.

wholly to Westwards Diff of Long 1°:29′ Long by acco$^{\theta}$.[1] 56°.27′ but allowing the Current 56°:57′ West from London. The Horison still thick and hazey

♂ 21. Yesterday about 5^{h} in the afternoone wee raised the Island of Barbadoes the midle of it bearing West halfe South by Compass 10 Leagues off wee Stood in wth it till midnight, then wee Stood off and on till day. I reckon that on Yesterday Noon

(f.30v.) wee were 20 Leagues distant from the Bridge Towne[2] to the Eastwards So that by Correct acco$^{\theta}$: I can make no more than 22½ degrees of Longitude between Pernamboue and Barbadoes wch by — Celestial observation is 23°½ and although I have allowed 7°½ of Longitude for the Current it does not Suffice by 20 Leagues and wee have Sett full 10 Leagues a day to the Westwards in this whole Course wch must be observed by all those that goe from — Brasile to Barbadoes about noon wee ankor'd in Carlisle Bay in 5 fathome Water. here I found his Majesties Shipp the Speedwell[3] under Saile for England

☿ I went I went up[4] into the Country to Wait on the Governour the hon^{able} Ralph Grey Esqr. who advised me to make no more Stay than was absolutely Necessary by reason the Island had not been knowne so Sickly as at p^{e}sent, the Bridge Towne Especially and for that reason to take care to keep my Men on

[1] The word 'acco^{t}:' careted in on the MS.

[2] D, *Bridgetown.* Halley's instructions called for him to visit the 'English West India Plantation,' for the purpose of determining their 'Geographical Scituation'; see Documents 33, pp. 268–9, and 78, pp. 301–2, and Appendix B, pp. 358–9.

[3] D, . . . his Majesty's Ship Speedwell . . . 'SPEEDWELL Fireship 8, 120 bm, 94 × 25 ft, Gressingham, Rotherhide 3.4 1690. Rebuilt Deptford 1716 as 6th Rate 20, 274 bm. Wrecked 21.11.1720 on Dutch Coast.' So described in Colledge, *Ships of the Royal Navy*, p. 518.

[4] The words 'I went' are not repeated in D. In place of the first two words in this line in D is the expected date, W. 22. which is missing in the MS although the symbol for Wednesday is there.

board[1] I order'd the Water Caske to be gott ready and Some of them carried a Shore This evening the Amplitude in Carlisle Bay was 17°.30 Variation 5°:25′ East

♃ 23. This Morning the Ampiltude was 28¼ allowing for the Change of ☉ Azimuth — from the riseing to his Appearance over the Land, by night our people had gotten 2 turnes of Water on board and all Stowed away. The Wind these 3. dayes Variable from the East to S. E

♀ 24. I weighed from Barbadoes this Morning and whilst busey getting under Sail I found my Selfe Seized w:th the Barbadoes desease, w:ch in a little time made me So weake I was forced to take my Cabbin. I order'd my Mate to Shape his Course for St. Cristophers,[2] without the Islands; we left our Stream Anker in Barbadoes. road, the hawser we rode by, being fretted in two and the Bouy rope likewise by Some Corrall Rocks there.[3] Wee made Sail alongst Shore, Wind from East to S E; the body of the Island bearing S E 5 Leagues off at 6 of the Clock.

♄ 25. Latitude p observat 14°:43′ Wind at S E a fine Gale Course N 9 W 64 — miles Longitude West from Bridgetowne 20′ Long from London 59°:35′

☉ 26. Latitude by observation 16°:47′[4] Wind from E S E to East a fresh gale Course N. 2°. E diff of Long 3′ East Long from London 59°:32′

☽ 27. Latitude by observation 16°:52′ Wind S. E. to E S E a

[1] Halley again shows himself to be a concerned as well as sagacious commander in following this good but difficult advice as well as he could under the circumstances.

[2] D, *St. Christopher's*. Now St Christopher or, more often, St Kitts. For this and other West Indian place names see Halley's Atlantic Chart (in portfolio) and Appendix B, pp. 358–9.

[3] D, by some Coral Rocks there.

[4] Corrected from 16° 46′ in the MS.

gentle fine gale Course West and W b S 79. miles difference of Longitude 1°:23′ Long from London — 60°:55′ at 11. hour this morning wee made Antego baring W N W about 5 — Leagues off[1]

♂ 28 No Observation. Winds E S E and E b S Course W 22 N.75. miles Difference of Latitude 28. minutes; Lat by acco^θ: 17°:20′ Diff of Long 1:13 Long from London 62°8′ We have the Logg home to the old rode of St Christophers where Anchor'd at 8. this morning in 15. fathom water[2] I continued here in hopes to recover my health. till Wendsday June the 5th. in which time we fill'd all our Water Cask, and my Boatswain overhaled the rigging, and repaired what needed; the wind being out at S E and Sometimes further Southerly, made a greate Suff on the Beach of the old Road,[3] so that it was not without difficulty that we gott the Water off; and on Munday Morning June the 3 we had the misfortune to Stave the pinnace on the Beach, by the Grapnells giving way, that shee could not be made Serviceable, Wood and Fresh provisions being Scarce here, and finding my Strength return but Slowly, and the Island being likewise sickly, I Departed —

(f.31)

☿ 5. June for Anguilla, we were under Sayle by 7 in the Morning and at Noon we had past the Isle of Eustachia[4] (which lies in the

[1] D, At 11^h. this morning we made *Antego* bearing W N W about 5 Leagues off. The island referred to is now Antigua; see Appendix B, p. 358.

[2] D, . . . *Old Road* of *St. Christophers* where anchored at 8 this Morning in 15 fathom water. D ends the paragraph here.

[3] D, . . . sometimes farther Southerly, made a great Surf on the beach of the Old Road.

[4] D, *Eustachia*, Now Sint Eustatius, Eustatia, Eustachius, etc. in Latitude 18°31′N and Longitude 64°21′W. See Appendix B, p. 358.

— Latitude of 17°:40'). Saba bareing W b N about 4 Leagues —

♃ 6. D$^{\theta}$ This Morning about halfe an hour past Tenn, we Anchored in the road of Anguilla, in 7 Fathom water, about halfe a Mile from Shore[1] the 7th and 8th. we gott a good quantity of dry wood on board and what fresh provision the Island afforded us,[2] the 9th I allowed the men to go on Shore to recreat themselves, and the[3] Tenth in the morning we stood out of the channell to the Eastwards of Dogg Island at Noon Latitude 18°:30' Dogg Island bareing S E ½ S two Leagues[4] Longitude from London 63°:00' West: I Steard away N W b N and in hours we were up with the Island of Sambreo[5] lying in Latitude 18°:40' it is not a Mile in Length, Low and Flatt with Some rocks on the topp that look like old buildings; the Sea birds are in numerable from hence I shaped my Course for the Island of Bermoodas[6] in which passage nothing occuring but a fair wind and fine weath^{r} it may Suffice to give a Table thereof —

[1] D ends the paragraph here with a full stop and inserts before the new entry:

F. 7.
Sa. 8.

[2] D ends paragraph here with a full stop and inserts before the new entry:

Su. 9.

[3] D ends paragraph here, without punctuation, and inserts before the new entry:

M. 10.

[4] D, *Dog Island* bearing S E ½ S 2 Leagues.
Dog Island, as it is today, is in about Latitude 18° 17' N and Longitude 63° 15' W. See Appendix B, p. 358-9.

[5] D, I steared away N W b N and in 3 hours we were up with the Island of *Sembrero* . . .
Now Sombrero, Latitude 18° 30' N and Longitude 63° 28' W. See Appendix B, p. 358-9.

[6] D, *Bermudas*.

June 1700.	Wind	Course	Miles	Lat:Cor:[1]	Long:Cor:[2]	Amplit.	Morn[3] or Even	Variat.n[4]
☽ 10[5]	ENE	NWbN	6	18:30	63:00	20:30	E	4:27E
♂ 11	ENE NEbE	N13W	113	20:20	63:26	----	--	----
☿ 12	ENE EbS	N9 ½W	115	22:13	63:46[6]	30:00 22:00	M E	4:36 3:35
♃ 13	EbS	N7W	98	23:50	63:59	22:37	E	3:17

(f.31v.)

June 1700	Wind	Course	Miles	Lat:Corec:	Long:Cor:	Amplit	Morn or Even	Variat
♀ 14	ESE to SSE	NbW[7]	106	25:35	64:11	28:30 24:00	M E	2:25 2:16
♄ 15	SSE	N7W	76	26:50	64:21	28:00 25:00	M E	1:40 1:30
☉ 16	SSE	N8 ½W	73	28:2	64:33	25:30	E	1:17
☽ 17	SSE	N10 ½W	69	29:10	64:47	28:00 26:00	M E	1:7 1:2
♂ 18	SE EbN	W15 ½E	57	30:5	64:30	28:00 27:00	M E	0:52 0:14E
☿ 19	ENE	N	58	31:3	64:30	27:40 27:30	M E	0:22E 0: 2W
♃ 20	ESE East[8]	N26E	61	31:56	64:00	27:50	E	0: 9W

This[9] Day about 11 of the Clock we made the Island of Bermoodas, the Southermost part there of bearing N b W, Distant between five and Six Leagues, the Wind being Easterly we kept close haled till 4, then Stood in with the Land, and

[1] D, Lat. Corr.
[2] D, Lon. Cor.
[3] D, Morning or Evening.
[4] D, Variation.
[5] As before, D renders this 'M. 10' etc., so it continues down the column.
[6] D has brackets following this entry and below in this column wherever, as in this case, two numbers appear in the Amplitude column following.
[7] D, N b W. It may be N b W in the MS; it is hard to decipher.
[8] D, E S E, E.
[9] As before, D indents and precedes this with the date, in this case: Th. 20.

about 5 fired two Gunns for a Pilott, who got on board us about 7, we plied to windward all night, and — next morning we bore away for St Georges harbour where we Anchored about 8. before the Town in 6 Fathom water vizt ♀ June 21. 1700[1] This harbour being very convenient for the purpose, I resolved to clean and fitt the Shipp for the homeward voyage, expecting blowing weather to the Northward, we careen'd and Scrubbed her as well as we could and our Decks and upper-works being leaky by being so long in the heats, I hired three Caulkers to assist my Carpenter, who in Six days had finished their work, and I gave a new coat of Paint to our Carved work which was very bare and parcht.[2] I made Severall observations to determine the Longitude of this Island, which I — find to agree with my reckoning account, vizt that the Longitud of St Georges Island is 63°:45′ from London and the Latitude thereof 32°:24′ which is the Northermost part of the Land ——
The Islands of Bermoodas Streach[3] in Length about 8 Leagues N E and S W and the Southermost part which we first raised when we made it lies in Latitude 32°:10′. To the North and N W are Rocks and Shoals above 4 Leagues off to Sea, so that those that intend to make these Islands ought to be very carefull of being to the Norward[4] and if they come from the Westwards they ought to Keep the Lat′: Latitude 32°:10′,[5] nor to Exceed (f.32) 32°.20′ if they Come from the Eastwards. The S E Side of the

[1] D, viz. Friday June 21st 1700. Opposite the line in which the above statement occurs, D has a marginal entry, F.21. The following entry beginning 'This . . .' (in D) begins a separate paragraph which is indented.

[2] parched. Presumably Halley had someone do this work for him.

[3] D, stretch. The beginning of the sentence in which this word occurs is the beginning of a new paragraph which is indented.

[4] D, Northwards.

[5] D, Latitude of 32°.10′. There is no abbreviation, Lat:′ or repetition of the term in D

Islands are clear from dangers at any distance — from the Shore. An E S E Moon makes high water and it flows about four foot on a Spring in the Harbour. — Haveing lost our Stream Anchor at Barbadoes as above I Bought another of the Governour here weighing 315 lb wait for which I paid him £7:17:6.—[1]

♄ 6 July All things were in a readiness to Saile but the Wind continuing to blow at E and S E, there is no Turning out of this Harbour by reason of the narrowness of the Channell among Sunk Rocks —

♃ 11 July in the Morning the Wind came Southerly[2] a Gentle gale next to Calm. my Mate Edward Sinclair haveing desired his Discharge for Some preferment offer'd him here, and one Mr St George Tucker an able Bermoodas Master, wanting a passage into England I entertained him as my mate, and gave Sinclair his Tickett;[3] This Morning in the Afternoon the Pilott gott us out of the Harbour, and we Stood off to Sea with a gentle Gale at S S E, in the night little wind

☿ 12 July in the Morning at 8h. St Georges Isle was seen from top mast head bareing S S W, 8 or 9 Leagues, then I Shapt my course for Cape Codd in New England N N W,[4] and at Noon we were in Latt 32°.59′ Longitude from London 63°.37′

[1] D, I bought another of the Governor here weighing 315 lb. for which I paid him 7*l.* 17*s.* 6*d.* D has eliminated the word, wait (i.e. weight). See Document 133, p. 341, where the price is £7. 17*s.* 0*d.*

[2] D, In the Morning the wind came far Southerly . . . In a very informative letter sent to Burchett from Bermuda, Halley recounts his experiences since his last letter from St Helena; he included accounts of his incarceration at Pernambuco, the disease afflicting Barbados, and the care he had received from his doctor, Surgeon George Alfrey. See Document 85, pp. 307–8.

[3] See Document 91, p. 313 for data on Edward Sinclair (Edwd St. Claire) and his replacement as mate St George Tucker (St Geo Tucker).

[4] D, . . . *Cape Cod* in *New England* N N W.

Morning Amplitude 23°:00′ Evening 25½ by the former Variation 1°:10′ by the Latter 1°20′ West

♄ 13 July Latitude by observation 34°:12′ Wind[1] Variable from S E to S W Course by Compass N N W true Course N 24 W 80 Miles Longitude from London 64°:16′ —

☉ 14 July Latitude by observation 36°:00′ Winds variable from S to S W a Stout Gale[2] Course by Compass N N W true Course N 25 W 119 miles hence the Difference of Longitude 1°:2′ and Longitude from London 65°:18′.—

☽ 15 July latitude by Account 37:21 Wind from S W to W S W this Morning it came up at N b E we Stood to the Eastward Course protracted N 13 W 83 Miles true Longitude from London 65 42 Dark over cast Weather —[3]

♂ 16 Latitude by observation 37°:56′ Wind from the N b E to N E b E, at four yesterday we tackt and Stood to the N Westwards, true Course protracted is N 43° W 48 Miles. Longitude from London — 66°:23′ this Evening at 6°52′ the Azimuth of ye ☉ was 27°½ to the Norwards of the Magneticall West. — (f.32v.)

☿ 17 July Latitude by observation 38°36′, Wind at N E and N E b E we ply to the Norwards Course protracted W 42 N 60 Miles. Difference of Longit 0°:57′ West Long: from London 67°:20′. This Evening the Amplitude was 30½ whence the Variation 6:00 proxime —

♃ 18 July Latitude by Observation 38°:10′, Wind from the N b E to N E We tackt and Stood to the Eastwards this 24 hours, Course protracted is E 24 S 64 Miles difference of Long

[1] D, Winds. This word begins a new sentence.
[2] On the MS 'a Stout Gale' is careted in.
[3] D renders this: . . . we stood to the Eastwards, Course protracted N 13 W 83 miles true Longitude from London 65°.42′. Dark overcast weather.

1°:15′ East Long from Lond$^{\theta}$ 66°:5′ this Evening the Amplitude was 30 degrees Variation 6° West

♀ 19 July Latitude by observation 39°:8′. Wind from the E N E to East We tackt and Stood to the Norwards true Course N b W 59 Miles Long from London 66°:20′ Morning Amplitude 18°½ Variation 5°½ West

♄ 20. July Latitude by observation 40°:30′, Wind from the S E b E to S S E, after Midnight S, and before Noon W S W, by Midnight we had runn 54 Miles p Logg Course N N W p Compass when being in the Lat: of 40°, and the Wind blowing a fierce Gale at S, I tried under a Mizen till day with head to the Eastwards when the Gale Still encreased and blew a meer frett of Wind till Noon;[1] wee being near the Banks of Nantucket, upon which there is Ground in 40°40′, at about 50 Fatho and being not able to bear Saile, in Such Weather uncertain Winds and a high grown Sea I was unwilling to runn any hazards, and bore away for Newfound Land[2] Longitude this day at Noon 66°40′ West.

☉ 21. Latitude by observation 41°00′. The Wind came up to N W then N N W. but in the Morning W S W, I bore away East then E N E, True Course E 19 N 92 Miles Diff of Longitude 1°55′ East Long from London 64°:45′ Variation by the Azimuths of the Sunn and Moon this Evening 7°:45′

☽ 22. Latitude by Acco^{t}: 41°28′ Wind between the W S W and South a Small Gale Course Correct E 30 N 56 Miles Longitude from Lond$^{\theta}$: 63°:41′. This Evening the Amplitude was 32½.

[1] D, '... blew a meer fret of Wind till noon'. That is a sea squall or flurry.

[2] D renders this: ... in such uncertain winds and weather, and a high grown Sea, I was unwilling to run any hazards, and bore away for *Newfoundland*.

♂ 23. July Latitude by observation 41°:24′, Calme all day with a Mighty swell and the Sea ripling & breaking in a fearfull (f.33) manner[1] in the Night a Small breeze of E N E and N E, Course E 31 S 8 Miles Longitude 63:32. Even Amplitude 32°:30′ —

☿ 24. July Latitude by observation 41°:40′; A Gentle Gale from W N W to S W b S, True Course E 24 N 40 Miles Longitude 62°:44′ Morning amplitude 15 Variation Evening 32°45′ whence Variation

♃ 25 Latitude by observation 42°21′ Wind W S W to S E, a fine Gale and Smooth water True Course E 30 N 82 Miles Longitude 61°:8′.

♀ 26 July Latitude by Observation 43°:22 Winds from the S W to the N N W a fine Steedy[2] Gale, Course E 39° ½ N 96 Miles, Long from London 59°27′. Variation this Morning 9°:30′ West. —

♄ 27 July Latitude by Observation 43°:18′ Wind from N to N N E a fine Gale Course E 3 ½ S 63 Miles Longitude 58°:00′. —

☉ 28 Latitude by Observation 43°:37′ Wind from N to N W a Small Gale and sometimes Calme. Course protracted N 44 E 29 Miles. Longitude at Noon 57°32′ This Evening the Amplitude well taken was 33°15′ thence Variation

☽ 29 July Latitude by observation 44°22′ Little Wind till Morning then a fresh Gale at W N W, Course N 28 ½ East 51 Miles, Longitude from Lond° 56°:58′ Morning Amplitude

[1] D, '. . . and the sea ripling and breaking in a fearful manner.' The symbol and word '& breaking' are added above in the MS without a caret symbol.

[2] D, steady.

11°30′ well taken. In the Evening 34°:00′ hence Variation This Morning I observed the Moon aply to ye Hiades —[1]

♂ 30 Latitude by Observation 45°:56′ A Stout Gale of Wind at W and W S W Course N 35 E 115 Miles Longitude from London 55°:23′; Last Night at 7^h we had ground at 40 Fathom. and again this Morning at 9^h:45′ Fathom all this Night we went away East This Morning the Amplitude was 10°:00′ and the Evening Amplitudc 37°:00′ hence Variation

☿ 31 July Latitude by Account 46°:42′ A fresh Gale from the W S W to S W. Correct Course is N 41 E 61 Miles, Longitude 54°:25′ This day about Noon we fell in with the French side of Newfound Land about Cape Anglois w:^ch^ is the Southern point of the Bay of St Maries. It was all this Morning a very thick Fogg that we could See nothing, and had we not fell in with som French Fishermen we might have been on Shore.[2] Yesterday afternoon at 2 we had 53 Fathom, and at 8 at Night 40 Fathoms — Then we lay by under a Mizen till 4, Then made Sayle at 6 we had 35 Fathom and at 8^h in the Morning 70 Fathom not foure Leagues from the Shore. —

(f.33v.) August ♃ 1. Latitude by Acco^t^: 46:25′ Wind S W and S W b S a moderate Gale all Yesterday and this Day one Continued Fogg without intermition[3] so thick wee could not see 100 yards about us, only about Sunn rise it cleard up for an hour and

[1] D has as a separate paragraph under the first entry for 29 June: This morning I observed the Moon apply to the Hyades.

In the MS there is a big separation between this and the preceding sentence, which is not terminated with a full stop.

[2] D renders this: , and had we not fallen in with some French Fishermen we might have been on Shore.

[3] D, intermission. The letter r is careted in on the MS.

Shew'd us the West Coast of Newfound Land and the Bay of S Maries out of which we had been turning all the afternoon and the Night. it is about 6 Leagues from Cape Anglois to Cape pines and this Noon we were about five Leagues[1] to the Eastward of Cape pine not much Short of Cape Raze Longitude 53°:53′

♀ 2 Aug^st Yesterday afternoon we went about Cape Raze and Stood to the Northwards alongst the English Shore till night, Wind at S W b W off Shore then lay by all Night, in the Morning it proved little Wind and foggy with fair weather till 10 Then it Cleard up with a fresh Gale at N N E at Noon Latitude 47°:6′ Longitude from London 53°:34′ The Bay of Bulls bore N N W by Compass and as the Wind was we could fetch no nearer than the Isle of Sphere called by our people the Isle of Despaire,[2] bareing at Noon W N W about 2 Leagues. We hald in with the Land and being come near the English Fishboats they all fled from us, takeing us, as we found afterwards, for a Pyrate; Being come into the harbour of Isle of Sphear calld Toads Cove, one Humphry Bryant a Biddiford[3] man fired 4 or five Shott through our rigging, but without hurting us: here we Anchored in 15 Fathom water, and I sent my boat to fetch Bryant on board, who excused what he had done, by giveing me an Account of a Pirate that had lately cruised on the Coast, and plundred a vessell but a few dayes

[1] This statement (from the word 'from') is careted between lines in the MS. Some of the Newfoundland place names, e.g. St Maries (now St Mary's) Bay and Cape Raze (now Cape Race) are shown on Halley's Atlantic Chart, which see in portfolio; also see Appendix B, p. 358.

[2] D, '. . . the Isle of *Sphere*, called by our people the Isle of *Despair*.' Probably present Cape Spear.

[3] Bideford, Devon.

before. I forgave the affront finding the said report Confirmed: I conclude the Longitude of this place by my Account from Bermoodas, and by my Observation of July 29 AM to be 54° from London

♄ 3 Here being Excellent good water, and Birch Wood easy to come at I gave order to rummage for the Cask, and to carry them on Shore and wash them and a boats crew went to Cutt Wood. Wind North a fine Gale.

☉ 4. Wind at N W and N N W. moderate weather

☽ 5 This Morning I had a good Amplitude the Sunn riseing clear 5°½ to the Northwards of the Magnaticall East and the true Amplitude being 20°:30′ the Variation is 15° West and So much I found it on Shore by my needles.[1] Wind most Westerly —

(f.34) ♂ The 6 Yesterday and this day we had gott as much wood and Water on board as was necessary, so this day noon I ordered to Stow all away and make ready to Saile. wind a fine Gale at N W. —

☿ 7. Yesterday about 5^hpM I weighed out of Toads Cove for England and as soon as we were gott out, the Wind came about to N E and N E b N a Fresh Gale, so we Stood away by the Wind E b S and E S E all night, at Sun rise it fell dead Calme. and at noon we were by observation in Lat 47°:00′ Cape Broyle bareing W 5° North by correct compass; distant 10 Leagues Longitude from London 53:20. ——

♃ 8 Latitude by observation 47°:52′ Yesterday about 1^h Sprung up a fine Gale of S b E wind which came round with the Sunn

[1] See Documents 25, p. 265, and 106, p. 321.

to W S W and — freshn'd I Steard away E b N by Compass. but Correct course E 23 N 132 Miles Difference of Longitude 3°:00' East Long from London 50°:20' West' By[1] Amplitude last night and Azimuth this Morning, I conclude the Variation 14°:40' West at Midnight last past

♀ 9 Latitude by Account 48°:38' Winds from W b S,[2] Correct Course E 24° N 113 Miles, Diffrence of Longitude 2°:35' East Longitude from London 47°45' all this day a Steady Gale with a Continuall Fog

♄ 10 Aug^st^ Latitude by Account 49°:8' Wind at W S W a Fresh Gale and continuall Fogg Course East by Compass, but Correct E 14° N 124 Miles diffrence of Longitude 3°:5' Longitude from London 44°:40' West. —

☉ 11 Aug^st^ Lattitude by Account 49°:48'. Wind at W S W and S W a Stout Gale Correct Cource E 13° ½ N 172 Miles. The Fogg still continues as before and no observation. Diffrence of Longitude 4°20' East Long: from London 40°:20' —

☽ 12 Aug^st^ Latitude by Account 49°56'. Wind as before till Morning, then from N N E to E N E I plied to the Eastwards. Correct Course E 4° N 120 Miles Difference of Longitude 3°:5' Long from London 37°:15'. —

♂ 13 Aug^st^ Latitude by observation 49°:6' but by Acco^t^ 49°:26' (In 14 degrees of Longitude we have not Err'd above 20 Minutes in Lattitude) Wind at E N E and N E b E Course Correct[3] S 40° E 65 Miles Difference of Longitude 1°:4' Longitude from

[1] D, W. by. In the MS there is an erasure after West; a full stop after this word may have been intended.

[2] D, from W b S to S b W. Halley is now getting into the latitude of southern England for parallel sailing home as shown on the track on the Atlantic Chart (in portfolio) and Figure 4.

[3] D ,Correct Course.

London 36°:11′ This Morning the Fogg clear'd up for a few hours. —

☿ 14 D$^{\theta}$ Latitude by Account 49°30′ Wind S S W a Stout Steady Gale Correct Course E 10′. N 142 Miles, Difference of Longitude 3°33′. Long: from London 32°:38′ —

(f.34v.) ♃ 15 Latitude by Account 49°45′. Wind as yesterday till Morning, then small Gales at W b S Course E 10° N 87 Miles Difference of Longitude 2°13′ Longitude from London 30°:25′ —

♀ Augst 16 Latitude by Account 49°:50 Small Winds a variable[1] Course Correct E 9 N 31 Miles Diff of Longitude 48 Minutes East, Longitude from London 29°:37′ The Foggs still continue.

♄ 17. D$^{\theta}$ Latitude by a Good observation 50°:16′ but by Account 50°:00′ Winds Variable from West to South. Correct Course E 9° N 62 Miles — difference of Longitude 1°:37′. Long from London 28°:00′ West. This morning being above halfe away over Sea the Foggs cleard up for good and all —

☉ 18 D$^{\theta}$ Latitude by observation 50°:22′ A Fine Gale from S to S W Course E 4° N 81 Miles. Difference of Longitude 2°:6′ and Longitude from London 25°:54′. Yesterday about Sunsett the Moon then allmost full arose clear. being about full then her Altitude was 2°:0′ her Azimuth from the East Southerly, was 31°:00′ her place — 28°:00′[2] Latitude North 0°:34′ by which I compute the Variato^{n} 9°:10′ Westerly.

☽ 19 D$^{\theta}$ Latitude by Observation 50°:8′. Wind as Yesterday Course correct E 9° S 93 Miles; Difference of Longitude is 2°:24′ Longitude from London 23°:30′ This Morning the Colour

[1] D, Small Winds and variable. The sentence ends here in D.

[2] D renders this passage: Yesterday about sun-set the Moon then almost full arose clear. When her Altitude was 2°.00′ her Azimuth from the E. Southerly, was 31°.00′. her place ♒ 28°.00′.

of the Sea changed into greenish. I hove the Deepsea Lead but had no Ground at 75 Fathoms. I doubt not but it is a Bank of Shoaler ground the out side thereof is 220. Leagues West from Scilley[1]

♂ 20. Latitude by Account 49°:34′ Wind from S W b S to W S W a Stout Gale, in the night Especially. Correct Course E 14° S 144 Miles, which Gives Difference of Longitude 3°:35′[2] from London 19°55′ Yesterday, in the Evening by two good Azimuths I conclude[3] the Variation 8°:15′ West.

☿ 21. Latitude by a good observation 49°25′ Wind at W b S till 10^{h} at Night then N E and N E b N a Fresh Gale Course E 5° S. 103. Miles Difference of Longitude 2°:38′ and Longitude from London 17°:17′ —

♃ 22 Augst Latitude by a good Observation 49°8′. Winds variable from the N E b E to S E b E we ply to the Eastwards Correct, Correct Course[4] protracted is E 28° S 36 Miles, Diffrence of (f.35) Longitude 49 Minutes Longitude from London 16°:28′ West. Last night the variation by a good observation was 7°:32′[5] and this Morning again 6°:17′ Westerly. —

♀ 23. Augst. Lattitude by Account 49°:19′ Wind from South to West — variable a moderate Gale Course Correct E 7 N 93 Miles. Difference of Longitude 2°:20′ Longitude from London 14°:8′. —

[1] D renders this passage: , I doubt not but it is a *bank of shoaler ground* the outside thereof is 220 Leagues West from *Scilly*.

This refers to a shoal, or shallow waters west of the Scilly Islands: on rocks off these Isles a few years later Sir Clowdisley Shovell was to suffer disastrous shipwreck; see Introduction: The First Voyage, p. 39, n. 3.

[2] D, '... of Longitude 3°.35′. Longitude from ...' The longitude figure is careted in on the MS.

[3] D, concluded.

[4] D, '... the Eastwards, Correct Course ...' The catchword Correct is incorporated in the line here but is not repeated in D.

[5] D, Last night the Variation by a good Azimuth was 7°.32′. and ...

♄ [1]24 D$^{\theta}$ Latitude by a very good Observation 49°18′. Winds variable from the North to E N E Course protracted E 1° S 66 Miles differ: of Long 1°41′[2] Longitude from London 12°:27′.—

☉ 25 D$^{\theta}$ Latitude by observation 49°:39′. Wind variable from N N W to W S W a Fine gale Course protracted E 14° N 88½ Miles. Difference of Longitude 2°:12′ Long from London 10°:15′ West Yesterday abo^{t}. Sunn Sett viz 6°:17′ the Azimuth of the Sunn from the West was 15° Northerly and we then Sounded and had no Ground with 80. Fathom; But at 8 this Morning we had Ground in 70 Fathom Scilly bareing Due East as wee found the Next Day full 50 Leag^{s}.[3]

☽ 26 Augst Latitude by a very good observation 49°:49′. Wee have had the Winds variable from the S S W to the N W, a Fresh Gale. Correct Course is E 4° ½ N 131 Miles, Difference of Longitude 3°22′ Longitude from London 6°:53′ West. Last Night at Sunn Sett we had ground in 60 Fathom, and this morning at 4^{h} the Same Depth; at 9^{h} Wee made Scilley the Light house bearing E b N 4 Leagues off at Noon wee were past the Bishops and Clerks and the West part of St Agnes Isle[4] bore Due North of us. The South part of Scilly lies in 49°:50′ past Dispute[5]

♂ 27 D$^{\theta}$ This Morning at 9^{h} wee came to an Anchor in Causon bay in Plymouth Sound, Wind at W N W and N W; I went forthwith to look for orders at Comisoner St Low's but found

[1] D heads a new page April, 1700. This should, of course, be August 1700. D omits the ditto symbol following the dates: Sa. 24.; Su. 25.; Tu. 27.; W. 28.; and Th. 29. as shown in the MS.

[2] This figure is corrected from 2.°41′ in the MS.

[3] D, : *Scilly* bearing due E as we found the next day full 50 Leagues.

[4] See Halley's Chart of the Channel in portfolio for this and other English place names.

[5] D, . . . *past dispute*.

none[1] Yesterday at Sunn Sett. the Amplitude was 17°:00 Variation 7°:13′ and this Morning off of the Eddistone the Amplitude was 3°:00′ Variation 6°:33′. —

☿ 28 D$^{\theta}$ This Morning I weighed out of Plymouth Sound: Wind at S W b S I made a Tripp to the Westward fearing I should Scarce weather the Start,[2] and at noon went about again to the Eastwards —

♃ 29 D$^{\theta}$ Yesterday evening abo^{t} 6 of the Clock we came up with the Bolt Wind fair Southerly and blowing Fresh we could not weather the Start, So Stood to the Westwards till 10^{h} at Night then Tackt and weathered the Start, by Noon we were fair by Portland

♀ 30. Yesterday in the afternoon was Foggy till Sunn Sett then (f.35v.) clearing up wee were faire by the Isle of Wight, Wind S W. The Morning prov'd calme but after Sunn rise an Easterly gale Sprung upp, so between 8^{h} and 9′ it being high water we chopt to an Anchor in 28. Fathom off of the Ourse,[3] being out of Sight of Land, at noon Lat. by a good obs[4] 50°:28

♄ 31. Augst the Wind continued Easterly a small Gale and Sometimes calme wth Fogg: We Tided it to windward The Sunn Rose this Morning due East by Compass, variation 7°:14′ at Noon we were thwart of Beachy The west part of the head

[1] D, '... Commissioner St. Low's but found none.' Presumably Captain George St Loe, R.N., who had been appointed as Extra Commissioner at Plymouth in April, 1695. Actually two letters had been written anticipating Halley's return but they were not sent to the Commissioner at Plymouth. See Documents 86, pp. 308–9, and 87, p. 309. Halley wrote a short letter to Burchett from Plymouth; see Document 88, pp. 309–10.

[2] Start Point; see Halley's Chart of the Channel for this and other English place names.

[3] The shoal to the south of Selsey; see inset of the Isle of Wight on Halley's Channel Chart (in portfolio) and Appendix C, p. 363.

[4] D, Observation.

Land bearing North a league from us, by an exact observation Latitude 50°:42′.

☉ 1 September The Wind continuing E and E b S we Tided it to windward this Morning with the Flood we had a Gentle of S and S S W which brought us by noon a brest of Dunginess —[1]

☽ 2 Septem^r Yesterday in the afternoon it fell Calme about 4^h we came to an Anchor to the Eastwards of the Ness to Stop the Tide. The Ebb being done we weighed with a Gale of N W. wind. and this day about one of the Clock p M came to an Anchor in the Downs —

♂ 3 Septem^r This Morning I received the L^ds Comison^rs Orders to make the best of my way to Long reach there to putt my Gunns and so to Deptford to be laid up.[2] accordingly I weighed with the Flood about 3 and at high Water came to an Anchor off of Ramsgate. Wind at N b W —

☿ 4 Septem^r This Morning we weigh'd with the Wind at W N W a Stout Gale which when we came open of the foreland[3] blew so hard that the Pilott not fitt to bear saile So bore up and anchored again under the Shelter of the North foreland —[4]

♃ 5 Septem^r Wind at W S W This Morning we weighed with the Flood and by high watter were gotten into Westgate Bay with the Night Flood soe turn'd it into the Gore —[5]

[1] D, '. . . had a gale of South and S S W Wind a small breeze which brought us by noon abreast of *Dunginess.*' That is, Dungeness (see Channel Chart in portfolio and Appendix C, p. 362).

[2] Halley sent a letter to Burchett, from the Downs (Document 89, p. 310) on the previous day, and now he had obviously picked up his mail. D, This Morning I received the Lords Commissioners orders to make the best of my way to *Long-reach* there to put out my Guns and so to *Deptford* to be laid up. See Documents 86, pp. 308-9, and 87, p. 309.

[3] D, *Foreland.* Probably refers to the South Foreland; see n. 4 below.

[4] D, *North-foreland.*

[5] D renders this passage: . . . high water were gotten into *Westgate Bay*, with the night flood we turned it into the *Gore.*

♀ 6. Septem^r the Wind at S W and S W b S we turn'd it through the Narrows and went over the Flatts, we found so little water at the red Sand that we were forced to Stay till the Tyde was — more flown.[1] About Noon it being near halfe Flood we had 10 Foot & ½ Water[2] over the Barr and the Wind Southering we were able to Stem the Ebb. and the next Morning by high water we came to an Anchor at Gravesend. the Wind being at W S W——

Septem^r 7 About Noon we weighed and with the Flood came to an Anchor in Long reach about 3 of the Clock. I sent up my — Gunner to give notice at the Tower of our Arrivall, but it being night before he gott to Town 'twas Munday Morning before they had Notice —[3] (f.36)

☉ ☽ 8. & 9 We Continued in Long reach Wind S W and W S W
10 September We Deliver'd our Gunns and Gunners Stores and the Pilott being on board by lowe Water, We — weighed from Long reach and Deliver'd the Pink this Evening into the hands of Captn William Wright Mast^r of Attendance at Deptford[4]

[1] D renders this passage: F. 6. Winds S W and S W b S we turned it through the narrows and went over the *Flats*, we found so little water at *Red Sand* that we were forced to stay till the tide was more flown.

[2] D, . . . near half flood we had 10 foot water over the bar . . .

[3] D renders this passage: . . . the *Tower* of our Arrival, but it being night before he got to Town 'twas Monday Morning before they had notice.

Obviously the Tower of London is referred to, see p. 212, n. 2. Halley wrote to Burchett on this day from Long Reach (Document 90, p. 311). The entries which follow for 8, 9, 10 September to the end of the MS are omitted in D.

[4] Although the journal ends here the crew was not paid off until 18 September 1700 (Document 91, pp. 312–13). Burchett replied to Halley's letter of 7 September on the 19th, Document 92, p. 314.

ABSTRACT OF DR. HALLEY'S VOYAGE.[1]

1699.

Sept. 16. SHIP sailed from *Deptford* to *Gallions*

18. Dr. *Halley* embarked at *Gallions*, sailed from thence and anchored in *Gravesend Reach* a little below the *Town*

20. Sailed from *Gravesend* and anchored in *Margate Road*

21. Anchored in the *Downs*

26. ☽ S°. 10^{h} 15^{m}. High Water at *Deal* S b W Moon — *Low Water* at *Deal* carefully observed at 5^{h} 15^{m} PM. and the Stream ran to the *Southwards* from 2 till past 8

27. *Variation* in *the Downs* 7°.32′. — Sailed from *the Downs*

28. Past *Dunnose*: Took a departure from *Portland* bearing N ½ E about 8 Leagues distant[2]

Oct. 1. Some small Birds flew on board

5. Fell in with a Fleet of *Danes* of 18 sail; and spoke with a *Dartmouth* Sloop

6. Examined a *Dutchman* from *Faro*, who hoisted *French* Colours

11. Violent Storm

13. Missed *Madeira*

14. Lost his Boy *Manly White* overboard[3]

15. Saw *Palma* — N. End 28°.48′N. S. End 28°.25′N.[4]

16. Saw *Ferro* N. End 27.50 S. End 27.40

[1] This Abstract is found only in D, not in the MS, which is also the case in Halley's First Voyage. However, in the MS journal of Halley's First Voyage there is a Table of Latitudes and Longitudes which might be taken to be an Abstract of sorts. There is no such table in the MS journal of Halley's Second Voyage.

[2] Some events reported retrospectively in the journal are placed under their correct date in Dalrymple's Abstract, as here.

[3] Manley White.

[4] Entered on 16 October in MS and D.

21. Saw *Sal*
22. Anchored in a very good *road* on the W. Side of the Island. Variation 0°.55′W.[1]
    Sal N End 16°.55′N
    S End 16.35 Longitude 23°.0′W
24. Sailed from *Sal*, saw *Bonavista*,
    N. End 16°.20′N
    S. End 16.0 Longitude 23°.0′W[2]
25. Anchored in *Praya Road, St. Iago*, Latitude 14°.50′N Longitude 23°.30′. Variation 0°.0′. Found an *English* Merchantman bound for *Guinea*, which sailed that Day
28. Sailed from St. *Iago*.

Nov. 17. Passed the *Equator*
20. Saw a *Tropick Bird* and a *Man of War Bird*.
21. No Birds this day —
24. Saw a *Tropick Bird* and two *white Birds* like *St. Helena Pigeons*.

Dec. 2. *Sounded* no ground 110 fathom, abreast of the *Abrolhos*[3]
4. Observation of Longitude by ☾
5. Observation of ☾ and Mars
9. Got into *smooth water*, under shelter of the *Land*; a fragrant smell of Flowers, and several Butterflies
10. Saw the *Main Land* of *Brasile*, being Cape *St. Thomas* to the N E of *Cape Frio*. *Sounded* and had 15 fathom.
    The *Highland* of Cape *St. Thomas* bearing N W.
    Anchored in the Night.
12. Saw *Cape Frio* —
13. Saw the *Sugar Loaf* at the Entrance of *Rio Janeiro* —
    The Island of *Cape Frio* lies in 22°.55′S.
14. Anchored in *Rio Janeiro*[4]
29. Sailed from *Rio Janeiro*
30. Took a departure from thence, the middle of the Entrance bearing due N.

[1] Variation entered as 1°.55′ W on 24 October in MS and in D, 55′.
[2] See p. 133, n. 2, Halley's Second Voyage, above, for explication of this entry.
[3] See journal entry for this day for amplification of this feature.
[4] This can only be surmised, not inferred, from the MS or D.

1700.

Jan. 14. Hard Gale of Wind

16. Tried the *Current*, found *none*

18. Hard[1] Gale of Wind

20. Colour of Sea changed to *pale green.*[2] — At night Sea appeared very white and abundance of small sea-fowl about the Ship and several beds of Weeds. — Alcatrosses which first met with in 27°S. now left them

23. Violent Gale of Wind — Multitudes of Sea Birds every day about the Ship, of 5 or 6 several kinds.

24. Violent Gale of Wind

25. Very cold with a S. Wind — set near 30′ to N^{d}[3] in 2 Days

27. Great Fog — Sounded every two hours, apprehending himself to be near *Land*; yesterday and to-day several fowls which he took to be *Penguins* passed by the Ship

28. Continual thick Fog. — Several *Diving Birds* and a *couple* of *extraordinary Animals.*

29. Very cold, misty, rainy, uncomfortable weather — a *Seal* swam after the Ship[4]

30. Thick Fog

31. Clear Weather[5] with Easterly Winds — Several beds of Weeds

February 1. Saw 3 *Islands* of *Ice*; *one* of them *at least* as *high* as the *North-Foreland*, and not less than 5 miles in front — To-day Latitude by account 52°.24′S. which is the farthest *South* they went

2. Thick Fog — amongst the *Ice*

3. Fog — more *Ice*

4. The weather reasonably clear from Fog, but very cold, cloudy and uncomfortable — descried 3

[1] Stout, in MS and D.

[2] All of the entry following this actually appears under 21 January 1700 in MS and D, where it is reported retrospectively.

[3] Northward.

[4] The event noted in this last clause is reported retrospectively on 30 January in MS and D.

[5] Halley actually reported 'Serene Weather' retrospectively for the previous day, though we might infer that it continued clear through 31 January.

Islands of Ice. Observed the *Ice* to lye to the *Eastwards*[1] of them. The last Ice they saw but little to the Southward of 50°S.[2]

6. Hard Gale of Wind — *Southerly*[3] Wind *warmed* the air. Barometer rose with it
7. Weather commonly foggy, and great damps
9. Fine clear weather but Wind very cold
10. In the afternoon above 20 Alcatrasses about the Ship
11. Foggy; in the morning saw one of the Animals mentioned the 28th. Suspect near some *Land* or *Rock* by the *Birds*; saw no more of them this morning
12. Many Birds
14. Colder in the *Eastern Part* of this Ocean than near the *Coast* of *America*
16. In 38°.16′ S°. at noon an *innumerable quantity of Birds* about the Ship, and many Alcatrasses.
17. Saw *Tristan da Cunha.* — The Latitude of the *Southern Island* 37°.25′S. Variation 5°.48′E
18. Fogs clear up since past the Islands[4]
26. Storm
27. Storm continuing

March 10. Saw many of the *St. Helena White Birds* about the Ship
11. Saw *St. Helena*
12. Anchored at *St. Helena*
30. Sailed from *St. Helena*

April 14. Saw *Martin Vaz* — in the afternoon saw *Trinidada*
15. Anchored at *Trinidada*
17. Put ashore some *Goats* and *Hogs* for breed; and a pair of *Guiney Hens*; took possession of the Island.
18. *Fine Water*
19. Went up to the top of the Island

[1] E N E and N E b E, in MS and D (though, of course, generally eastward, as reported retrospectively).

[2] Actually this inference relates to 4 February and is reported retrospectively 5 February in the MS and D.

[3] S W and S S W; and later in the day, Southard and later Southerly, in MS and D

[4] Tristan da Cunha.

20. Sailed from *Trinidada*

29. Got *Soundings* on the Coast of *Brasile*, saw the *Land* and anchored in the night,[1] lost an anchor; in the morning anchored at *Pernambuc*

May 4. Sailed from *Pernambuc*, Lat. 8°.10′S.

17. Colour of Sea changed from *blue* to *dark green* or somewhat *brownish*; saw many *birds*, both Noddies and Men of War.

18. In the Evening the Sea recovered its *blue colour*, after running over a *Bank* of *ouzy Bottom* for about 50 leagues on a *N W Course.*

19. Many Men of War Birds

20. In the afternoon saw *Barbadoes* — *Strong*[2] *Currents*

21. Anchored in *Carlisle Bay*. — Variation 5°.25′E.

24. Sailed from *Barbadoes* — Lost an anchor there

27. Saw *Antego*

28. Anchored in the *old Road* at *St. Christopher's*

June 3. Stove[3] the Pinnace

5. Sailed from *St. Christopher's*, passed *Eustachia* in 17°.40′N

6. Anchored at *Anguilla*

17. Sailed from thence, passed *Sombrero* in 18°.40′N[4]

20. Saw *Bermudas*

21. Anchored in *St. George's* Harbour, Northermost Part of the Land 32°.24′ N. Longitude from London 63°.45′W.

Bermudas from 32°.10′. to 32°.24′N.[5]

July 11. Discharged *Edward Sinclair* his mate, and engaged Mr. George Tucker. — Sailed in the afternoon.

12. Lost sight of *Bermudas*

29. Observation of ☾ and the Hyades

31. Fell in with *Newfoundland* about *Cape Anglois*

Aug. 2. Anchored in *Toad's Cove* in the *Isle of Sphere*

5. Variation 15°W.

6. Sailed from *Toad's Cove*

[1] The preceding events took place on 28 April.

[2] An inference; MS and D '. . . the Current sets wholly to the Westwards.'

[3] That is, staved.

[4] Actually this occurred on 10 June.

[5] The extreme latitudinal extent of the Islands.

7. Lost sight of *Newfoundland*
17. The Fog cleared up for good and all, being half way over-sea.
19. Supposed they passed over a *Bank* 220 Leagues W from *Scilly*.
25. Got Soundings.
26. Saw *Scilly*
27. Anchored in *Causon Bay* in *Plymouth Sound*
28. Sailed from *Plymouth*

Sept. 2. Anchored in the *Downs*
6. Anchored at *Gravesend*
7. Anchored in *Long-reach*

[THE THIRD VOYAGE]

(f.37v.)

Paramore Pinks Journall
Anno 1701.[1]

(f.38)

A Journall of a Voiage in his Ma:ties Pink
The Paramore: for discovery of the Course
of the Tides in the Channell of England.
By Edmond Halley Commander. Anno. 1701.

1701

♄ June 14°. I fell down from Deptford with the Afternoon Ebb and at night came to an Anker off of Gravesend, wind at WSW a steady gale[2]

☉ · 15. about noon with the same wind we weighd and saild down the river and about 8:h P.M. we ankered in the first deeps between the Redsand and Spanyard.[3]

[1] Unlike the other two voyages, this one was never printed as far as is known. Also, unlike the others, this journal is entirely autograph. There are internal variations in spelling in this journal as in the two earlier ones. In Halley's handwriting it is sometimes difficult to distinguish e from o and a from u, etc. It is also hard to tell whether or not a word is capitalized in some cases. These and other similar problems are more difficult to resolve in this journal than in the other two because we have no other source, such as Dalrymple, with which to compare it. As before, repeated headings and catchwords are not transcribed.

[2] Although the journal starts officially on 14 June 1701, rigging for the voyage had begun a few weeks earlier on 26 April. See Document 129, p. 337.

[3] For this and other place names on Halley's Third Voyage see Appendix C, pp. 362–4, A New and Correct *Chart of the Channel between* England & France. A reproduction of this map is included in the portfolio accompanying the present volume as two folded sheets.

☽ · 16 Wind between W and SW. we past the Flatts, and about four P.M. came to an anker in the Downs, where the wind being westerly I continued the 17th and 18th and procured four men from Rear Admirall Munden then in the Downs, in the Plymouth.[1] Whilst I rode here I observed the Course of the tide in the Downs. viz. that a SbE and NbW Moon makes high water by the shore but the stream setts to the Northward till a SSW moon or somewhat later.[2]

♃. 19 I weighd out of the Downs this Evening with a small gale of SW wind at $9^h\frac{1}{2}$,[3] the tide then turning to the Southward and drove all night with the Tide

♀ 20 a little before Sunrise I ankered under the pitch of ye South foreland, about a mile from shore, the middle between the two Light houses baring NNW. here I saw the turn of the Tide both ways, and observed that it ran to the Westward till a SE moon, and to the Eastward which is commonly calld the Flood till a SW or III^h Moon, but that it was high Water by the Shore with a S $\frac{2}{3}$ E ☽ or XI$\frac{1}{2}$. the set of the Flood between ENE and NEbE. The tide being done about 11^h, I weighd with an easy gale at NEbN and at 5^h I came to an anker off of Dunginess a small mile from the Beach the Light house baring NbE. Here I rode till the next day morning when I found it was

[1] At this time there were at least two ships of the name *Plymouth* in the Royal Navy. The ship referred to is probably the one detailed by Colledge, *Ships of the Royal Navy*, vol. 1, p. 427, in these terms: 'PLYMOUTH 60-gun ship, 752 bm, 140 × 34½ ft. Taylor, Wapping 1653. Rebuilt, Blackwall 1705 as 900 bm, 64 guns. Foundered 11.8 1705'. T. D. Manning and C. F. Walker, *British warship names* (London, 1959) p. 345, describe the ship as a 3rd rate vessel. Another *Plymouth* in use at this time is described by Colledge as: 'Sheer hulk, 524 bm, 121 × 32 ft. Purchased 19.5 1689. BU 1730'. However, it is unlikely the Admiral would be aboard this vessel.

[2] See Document 120, pp. 329-30, referring to events described in the journal, 16 June 1701.

[3] Beside the symbol, h, a letter has been scratched out.

(f.38v.) ♄ 21 high water by the Shore a little before eight that is with a SbE moon: but that the Eastern tide held out to a SWbS or II½ Moon.

about 9^h in the Morn I weigh'd and stood off to Sea, with a gentle gale of ENE wind, and about One after noon came to an anker in 18 fath. the Ness Light baring NNW; and Calis[1] cliff ENE. here the westward tide was done at 5^h. 35′, or three hours and half before the Moons Southing. whence I concluded the course of the Tides here the same as at the Ness. viz that a II½ Moon ends the Eastern Tide. at 6^h I weighd and stood to the eastward with a small gale of SSW Wind, and about 9^h fell with the West end of the Riprapps which is a narrow rigd of soft and sand.[2] I crost it severall times in 9,8 and 7 fath and the Eastern tide being near done, I came to an anker in that depth the Ness light baring WNW and that of the South Foreland NbE p Compass. here I rode two tides and found the Eastern tide done on a SW or NE Moon nearest. that it flowed about three fath. that it runs half tide here as by the Shore and that the Sett of the Stream is nearest NE and SW.

⊙ 22 The Eastward tide being done about 1^h P.M. I stood against the Tide with a fine gale at SSW following the Ripraps till 3^h when we got over the East end of them, where the bank is double and found no less than 4½ fath on them at Low water then I stood over to the French coast and at 7^h½ P M ankered in 30 fath. two leagues to the westwards of the Land, Dover Castle baring NbW, and Calis cliff NEbE truly. here we found the flood to 3½ Miles p hour NNE and the Ebb or western tide as strong

[1] Calais, on the Channel Chart.
[2] See Channel Chart for a delineation of this feature.

SW. when I ankered this even the Western Tide was just done at 7½ PM, and again

☽ 23. At eight this morning precisely twas just still water and the Moon being south at 10^h 32′ it follows that it ebbed till a IX½ Moon and the other tide held out to a III½ Moon or SW ½ W. about 11^h I weighd and stood in with a gentle gale at North for the French Shore. being got within a league of Ambleteuse the wind came up fresh at NE so I hal'd in close under the Land (f.39) and saild along shore as farr as Bullogne designing to anker off of EStaples then the wind flew out to NNW a stout gale so that we could not ride to any purpose so I went away SSW and SbW for Diepe[1] where there is a very good peire in case it overblew. by sun set we were a breast of the cliffs of Treport and found the Tide of flood so strong against us that we scarce got a head by the Land.

♂ 24 Before day we came before the town of Deipe, and ankored — in 6 fath water a large mile from the Shore: the sea ran so high by reason of these out winds that is was hard to determine the still water but comparing three tides to gather[2] I concluded a SbE Moon to make high water and that here the tide ran true that is that the whole flood came from the East, and run about 3½ miles p hour on the Spring, alongst the shore.

☿ 25 The Ebb being done at ¼ before six, and the flood half an hour before noon, I weighd and drove with the tide to the westward, with little wind off shore, about 6 I ankered — Deipe baring SEbE distant 10 miles in 13 fath and having

[1] Dieppe, on the Channel Chart.
[2] *i.e.* together.

seen both ebb and flood I concluded that a S $\frac{1}{2}$ E or XI$^h\frac{1}{2}$ Moon made high water, the tide run here about 4 miles p hour.

♃ . 26 /.at One after midnight I weighd, and with the wind off Shore a gentle gale and the Ebb, by 8^h in the morning Feschamp or Fackam bore South distant about 3 Leagues; here I ankered in 16 fathoms and found it was high water at 20 minutes after Noon that is at XI^h Moon: then I fell with the Ebb a breast with Cape Caux, calld by the French cape Antifer,[1] and about 5^h ankered in 15$\frac{1}{2}$ fath[2] the cape baring SEbS and the Seyn head SbW where twas low water at 6$^h\frac{3}{4}$ that is about XI^h Moon makes high water.

♀ 27 I weighd from thence about 1 in the morning, with a small gale of SW wind, and having made 7 Leagues in the time of an Ebb and flood, on a correct NbE course, I ankered in 20 fathoms water, being nearly land too. here it was high water at half an hour past one and low water at 7^h. 40′. and the Moon that day Southing at 2^h. 20′ after noon it follows that a SbE moon makes high water here. the strength of the Ebb which runn about 3$\frac{1}{2}$ miles p hour set WbS.

(f.39v.)

♄ 28 The morning early we weighed, and in an ebb and flood with[3] a small breze next to calme we made five leagues NNE. here again I ankered in 21 fath. Beachy Head as farr as it is could be seen baring due North from us, and it was high water just at 2 after Noon, that is a SbE $\frac{1}{2}$ E Moon made high water. and by Sunset the tide of Ebb was just done. then I weighed and stood

[1] 'Cap d'Antifer on cap de Caux' on H. Jaillot's 'carte de la Manche', 1692.

[2] The statement 'in 15$\frac{1}{2}$ fath' is careted in.

[3] It appears that the word 'and' has been deleted and the word 'with' is placed above the deletion.

due North for the head[1] the Wind being Easterly very small. and

☉ 29 By seaven in the Morning I came to an anchor in 24 fathoms two Leagues south of Beachy head where the Tide of Ebb was done at $9^h\frac{1}{4}$ whence a SbE ☽ makes high water. Then I went on Shore on the head and found the Variation with my Needle 7°.40′ by one observation, and 7°.45′ Westerly by a second. the Latitude therof I observed 50.45 and the High water as near as could be guessed for the motion of the Sea was about an hour sooner on shore than in the Offing. Then with a fine gale of ENE wind I ran alongst shore as far as Brighthelmston,[2] where it being near Low=water I came to an anker to trie the Tide and found it was dead Low-water at $8^h\frac{1}{2}$ this evening that is a SSE moon makes Highwater

☽ 30 I weighd early and with the same wind saild alongst shore to Selsey, and about ten came to ankor in the Park about half a league from Shore, Selsey bill and Dunnose in one, at Noon the Tide to the Eastwards was done, and the Westward Tide at 6¼ P.M. but on Shore it was High water at ¼ past three. that is with a SSE Moon; but here it flows three hours after the Tide is made to the Westward, and tis Low water in the middle of the Eastward Tide. contrary to what it is between Dover and Calis where tis highWater at 3 hours flood.

July About Midnight I weighed from the Park and with the wind

♂ 1 at NEbN a fine gale I stood out to Sea to weather the Oares or Ourse,[3] which having done, I bore away for St Helens where

[1] That is, Beachy Head.

[2] Brithelmston on the Channel Chart. This place, spelled in various ways (at that time a fishing village), is modern Brighton.

[3] Owers on the Isle of Wight; inset of the Channel Chart in portfolio.

I ankered in 12 fath: about nine this morning. and about $9^{h}\frac{1}{2}$ the Westward Tide was ended. At 3^{h}. 25′ the Eastward Tide was done, but by the shore it was not highwater till past five.

(f.40) ☿ 2 About four this Morning the Eastward Tide came to an end so I weighed and the wind coming up at NWbN we turned it in to Spitt head, where I found Sr Clowdsly Shovell Admirall of the Blew in the Triumph.[1] I continued

♃ 3 here this day and y^{e} third; and found the course of the Tides much the same as at St Helens. viz: that the Eastward tide ended at a IX$\frac{1}{2}$ Moon or rather SEbS but that it flowed till a SbE Moon or rather later

♀ 4 Having a small gale Easterly I weighd from Spithead about 8 this morning, and came to an anker in midd=channel off of South hampton creek, just as the Westward Tide was ended. viz at 10^{h}.$\frac{3}{4}$. and the Stream ran to the Eastward till half an hour past five, that is at a IX$\frac{1}{2}$ Moon the Moon now southing at 8^{h}.

♄ 5 I observd the same course of the Tides in Cows[2] road viz that a IX$\frac{1}{2}$ Moon or SEbS, makes the turn of the Tide to the westward and that it flows by the Shore about two hours longer, or to a SbE Moon. In the afternoon having a fine gale, I weighd and came again to an anker off of Hurst castle it baring WSW two miles distant.

☉ 6 This morning about a quarter before two the Ebb or Westward tide was done; and exactly at 7^{h}.55′ the Eastward or flood tide ended. whence a X$\frac{1}{4}$ Moon or a SSE $\frac{1}{2}$ E Moon makes the turn of the Tide in the Channel between Hurst castle and the Isle of

[1] Colledge, *Ships of the Royal Navy*, p. 571: 'TRIUMPH 2nd Rate 90.1,482 bm, 160 × 46 ft. Chatham DY 1698 Renamed PRINCE 27.8.1714. Rebuilt Chatham 1750 as 1,677 bm. 168$\frac{1}{2}$ × 48 ft. BU 1775 at Plymouth'.

[2] Cowes, on the Channel Chart.

Wight. then I weighd and sayled out at the Needles, and anchoring Dunnose baring EbS, and Christchurch steeple NbW, the Ebb or western Tide was done at half an hour past two, and the Moon then Southing at ten, a SSE Moon makes high water here. The flood being made I stood for Dunnose with a small gale of Northerly wind, and at 5 minutes before nine it was high water: Dunnose baring NE and the Needles NW here at X$\frac{3}{4}$ Moon made highwater.

☽ 7 West Dunnose baring NE about 4 miles, it was low water at $3^h\frac{1}{4}$ in the morning and driving with the flood till East Dunnose bore NNW two leagues off, the Tide was done at $9^h.15'$ whence a X$\frac{2}{3}$ Moon made high water. then I stood in with the Land, and went on shore and took the Latitude at Bunchurch[1] 50°.32′ and the Variation 7°.25′ west. I found that it had flowed longer (f.40v.) by the Shore than in the offing, and had been high water about a SbE Moon or later; that moon making high water all over the Isle of Wight. After noon I steard off to sea SbE and SSE with the Tide of Ebb, and when the flood was made it hove us away to the Eastward, so that by night West Dunnose bore NW $\frac{1}{2}$ W, and the Culver cliffs, then just down, NNW. and the Eastward Tide was just done at $10^h.20'$ or a SbE Moon then having little wind at East we lay by and drove with the Ebb.

♂ 8. This morning at 4^h 50′ the ebb tide was ended, and we came to an anchor in 36 fath. to stopp the flood and it was high Water precisely at eleaven a clock,[2] or XI$\frac{1}{2}$ Moon. Then I weighed and drove with the Ebb, making very little way to the South ward there being very little wind. I rode the boat, and

[1] Bunn Church, on the Isle of Wight, inset of the Channel Chart.
[2] The words 'a clock' are careted in.

the ebb tide was done at five and seaven min: or a SbE Moon nearest. at $6\frac{3}{4}^h$ for a short space we had sight of Dunnose land, baring from the North almost a point Easterly, 8 or 9 Leagues off. Then with a small gale at E and EbS and having made about 4 Leagues in the night we found it, by riding the Boat, to be Low water at 5^h next Morning

☿ 9 The Ebb being done at 5^h this morning, we stood over to the — French coast, and about 8^h we saw Cape Barfleur, baring about SSW 3 Leagues off. I then rode the Boat to trie the — strength of the Tide of flood in 37 fath. water, and there ran such a Tide that we could not recover our grapnell till high Water which was at 11^h or rather five minutes later nearest a SSE Moon. at the middle of the Flood it ran $3\frac{3}{4}$ Miles p hour. By our course since we last saw the Isle of Wight I conclude Cape Barfleur to be N&S with the middle of Dunnose land, but could have been more certain had the weather been clear, and more Wind. At $5^h\frac{1}{4}$ the Ebb was done. being now off of Cherburg, and fair in with the Bay, I lay by and sent the boat on shore to enquire concerning the Tide there and found that an ESE or VII$\frac{1}{2}$ Moon makes high water by the Shore tho the Stream ran to the Eastward till a SSE Moon in the offing. All night it proved little wind and we found the Tides both ways to set in to the Bay, so ankered off of Querqueville about 11 fath:, amile and half from the Shore, here the flood was done at a quarter past Ten or a SE Moon on Thursday Morning (f.41)

♃ 10 This Morning with the Ebb sprung up a small gale at NW and with it we stood off to Sea, and so doing found that we came again into the flood which lasted above an hour longer in the offing than by the shore. At noon cape Hague baring West by a good observation I found the Latitude 49°.46′. The afternoon proved foggy so we drove with the Ebb till half an hour past 4. then ankoring it was low water precisely at $5^h.20'$. at 7 it cleard up and I found the Isle of Aldernay[1] to bare from SSW ½ W to near SW and the bluff land calld the Nez de Jouberg S E b S easterly. We found our selves open to the Race of Aldernay, but that both Ebb and flood ran to the Northward of the Island. setting WSW and ENE at first and afterwards WbS and EbN. I–rode here two Tides, because of the Night, and the flood was done at $11^h.25'$. so that a SEbS Moon makes high water in the race

♀ 11 This morning early, the Ebb slackening, I weighd and stood in for the Island, but having little wind, the flood came so quick, that I was obliged to anker again, Aldernay baring WSW and Cape Jouberg SSE in the middel of the Race. but even here the flood came without the Island. The Tide ran with great violence between 8 and 9 this morning, and by the Logg better than five knotts. About 11 resolving to pass the race I got under saile with the last of the flood and at twelve Aldernay baring due west I observed the Latitude 49°.47′. Assoon as we were through the race and had gotten the French land NE of us the strong tide abated and the Ebb sat SSW between Sark and Jersey. in the afternoon the wind came to W and WSW so that we could not lie better than South, and withall it began to blow fresh so I resolved to put in to Jersey. but the wind Southering I was put to Lee ward of the Island, and being come within two leagues of the Island we found a (f.41v.) strong flood set to the Eastward upon the Rocks of the

[1] Alderney, on the Channel Chart.

Dirouilles and Ecrehou,[1] but the Wind freshning and the tide abating about Sunsett I came to anker in Boulay bay on the NE side of Jersey, wind at WSW off shore.

♄ 12 I went to Jersey town to get me a Pilot acquainted in these parts and the Dept. Governour gave me one Peter St Croix of St Aubin's, who came on board the 13th but it blowing fresh — Westerly we did not weigh. Here we found that an E $\frac{1}{2}$ North or a V$\frac{1}{2}$ Moon made high Water, and that the Tide ran true alongst shore to the Eastwards till full Sea. and that it flowed here about six fathoms.

☽ 14 It was high water about $9^h\frac{1}{2}$ this morning. when having a fine gale at SW we weighd and stood over for Guernsey with the Ebb and being a breast with the Paternosters or Pierres de Leche we found the Ebb continue till $6\frac{3}{4}$ this Evening or to a SE $\frac{1}{2}$ E Moon, as we observed it coming to an anchor about 6^h of y^e clock off of the Stack of Sark: Sark Mill baring North about five miles.

♂ 15 This Morning little Wind at SW and the flood setting NE without Sark we could not stirr till the Eastward Tide was done which was at a quarter past one, then with the Ebb and a gentle Gale we fetcht in under the South side of Guernsey, and before the Tide was done came to an anchor, St Martins point baring NEbN one league. Here the Westward tide ended at $7^h\frac{1}{2}$ this evening or a SE $\frac{1}{2}$ E Moon. I continued here this day

☿ 16 and the next, to observe the situation of the adjacent Islands, and the Tides about them, and observed that an E and West Moon nearest makes full sea by the Shore, but that the Tide

[1] Dirouille and Erehou, on the Channel Chart.

♃ 17 runs through the Russell to the N Eastwards three hours Longer or to a IX^h or SE Moon; and the same is on both sides of Sark: I found the Variation of the Needle full eight degrees westerly and I refitted my small Anker whose stock had been twisted round when we rode in the Race of Aldernay.

♀ 18 A little before Noon we weighed with an easy gale at SW and the Stream running hard to the NE we had scarce wind enough to keep clear of the Russell rock, but it being near full sea we had no need to fear it. We drove to sea with the Eastern Tide till about four, when the Western Tide hove us away to windward. Being desirous to see the Caskets[1] about Sun sett we came to an anker about 4 miles South West from the Westmost of those Rocks. (f.42)

♄ 19 It was high Water 20′ minutes past four or at a SE Moon and the stream to the West was done about half an hour past Ten. assoon as this Tide was done, I weighd and made Sayle for Portland. At $11\frac{1}{2}$ this Morn, the Casketts bore due East about $\frac{1}{4}$ of a Mile distant, and I found these Rocks to lie nearest East and West with Aldernay, and due North from the West side of Sark. The wind freshning at SW, I kept the Casket rocks baring due south from me, chequing the flood as the gale and Tide required. By two we could but just discern them, and a 4^h having steard NbW $\frac{1}{2}$ W we raised Portland baring due North by Compass, we hauled in with it and being come within three leagues of it bearing NbW it fell little wind and I anchored in 25 fath: where the evening flood was done a little before seaven, and the next morning precisely

[1] Casquetts, on the Channel Chart. Halley communicated with the Royal Society from the Channel Islands, in a letter dated 18 July. See Document 123, p. 332.

☉ 20 at $7\frac{1}{4}$.[1] I weighd to stand into Portland road when the wind came up very fresh at SWbW and made it necessary to seek harbour, we ankered under the high land the Eastern part baring SSE. It blew very hard at WSW all this day and the 21th and 22th. During my stay here I observed on the 21th the Latitude of the Stone peer to be 50°.32′, that it was high water by the shore at Portland Castle at a EbS[2] or a VII^h Moon thô the flood ran to the Eastward till XI, in the offing. And in Portland Castle I observed the Variation very Curiously 7°.33′ Westerly.

☿ 23 This Morning the wind moderated and came about to WNW an easy gale, about noon I weighd and stood out to Sea, but it falling little wind I came to an anker about five Leagues from Portland baring NbE in 28 fath: and rode all night becalmd the Stream ran to the Eastward till $10^h\frac{1}{2}$ PM or an XI^h Moon and the Western Tide ended about three quarters past four.

♃ 24 This morning before six we got under sayle and I steard South p Compass for Aldernay being desirous to see when it was full sea by the Shore on that Island: Wind WbN a gentle gale. About 11^h we say[3] the Island, it being hazey baring SSW from us, the flood having horsed[4] us to the Eastward, then having but little wind, we stood SSE to cheque the[5] Ebb. and about 5^{h}P.M. the Eastward Tide being made, I ankered in 16 fath: near the NE point of Aldernay. I went on shore on the Norther-

(f.42v.)

[1] Following this figure is a space from which nothing appears to have been erased.
[2] A correction of the original entry here has made it unclear, so Halley rewrote EbS above.
[3] Sic, obviously 'saw' is meant.
[4] To carry with force (a ship or its crew).
[5] Following this the word 'flood' was written (which has been erased from the MS) and the word 'Ebb' added as the first word on the following line.

most point of all the Island, by the Pierre de Bray,[1] and found Cape de Hague and the Casket rocks to lie very near East and West from thence, or rather somewhat Southerly: and the outermost of the rocks that lie off of the west end of the Island are not above two thirds of a point or W $\frac{2}{3}$ N which I note to show the error of the Neptune Francois[2] The variation I observed carefully 8°.10′, and at 7^h this Even it was high Water by the shore. or at an EbS Moon. — wheras in the race I had found it SEbS. so that here it runs just half Tide. Before night I got under saile and stood over for the English Coast.

♀ 25 This Morning having had but little wind all night we had still Aldernay in sight about eight, it being Low water, we had both lands in sight. viz: Cape de Hague and the high Land of St Albans. It being little wind I ankered in 31 fath and observed curiously St Albans to bear North one degree West and Cape Hague S 12°$\frac{1}{2}$ E whence being in the middle the Lands bare one from other N.6°$\frac{3}{4}$ W. Here the Eastward Tide was done at 11^h.35′ and the Westward Tide at 5^h.20′ whence a SSE[3] Moon ends the Eastern Tide here and it runs half Tide here in the middle of the Channell as well as on both shores. I then weighd and stood to the Northwards.

♄ 26 . This morning at Sunrise we ankered about a league South of Swanwick[4] point, where I observed exactly Dunnose to bear E4° $\frac{1}{2}$ N from portland bill,[5] we riding precisely in the same line

[1] Not shown on the Channel Chart, but Braye Rocks on modern British nautical charts.

[2] *Le Neptune François* was the name applied to the sea atlas which resulted from the observations and mapping of the French coast by Jean Picard, Gabriel Phillipe de La Hire and other members of the Académie Royale des Sciences. Using astronomical observations these surveyors delineated the coast of France with much greater accuracy than on any previous charts but not, apparently, entirely to Halley's satisfaction.

[3] The word, Tide, is erased after this and Moon entered.

[4] Swanage, on the Channel Chart.

[5] Bill of Portland, on the Channel Chart.

between them. Here the Westward Tide was done at $5^{h}.20'$ this Morning, and the flood at $11^{h}.45'$ or a SEbS Moon. Then the Wind freshening at SW, I weighd and ran in at the Needles, and came to an anchor in Cows road. It continuing to blow hard for severall days, I spent them in observing what I could, between the Isle of Wight and the Main, and found all over that[1] Channell that a SEbS or rather, a IX½ Moon makes high water, as I had formerly noted. And not without admiration I observed, that as both here and in the race of Aldernay the Eastward Tide is done nearly as the same Moment, yet tis but a quarter flood on the Isle of Wight, when tis high Water or full Sea on Aldernay & Cape de Hague. On the 31th I observed carefully the Variation on the point of the Isle of Wight over against Hurst and found it nearest $7^{\circ}.30'$.[2]

(f.43)

♄ Aug 2° The stormy winds being over, there sprung up a gentle gale at NNE, and the Eastern stream ending at five this morning, I past the Needles, and anchored in 17 fath: Dunnose baring E. Saint Albans Land due West, and Hurst castle NE. I came to an Anchor a little before noon and found the Tide run to ye Westward till 25′ past Twelve, but the flood or Eastern Tide lasted till 6½ P M or to a SSE Moon. I then weighd and drove to the westward with the Ebb, having little wind, and stopt the night flood: it was foggy that we could not see the Land but the Tide ended about $7^{h}\frac{1}{2}$ this morning

☉ 3. We drove with the ebb till Noon, then came to an anchor three Leagues SbE from Portland, I observed the Latitude to be

1 Sic, obviously 'the' is meant.

2 On 29 July Halley wrote to Burchett summarizing the results of his voyage up to that point, Document 122, p. 331.

50°.23′, the Ebb held till $1^{h}\frac{1}{2}$ P.M. as near as could be discerned the slack being long and the Tide very easy I rode out the flood and about Sunsett fell down again with the Ebb, it being almost calme.

☽ 4. About midnight there sprung up a fresh gale at NE. so I stood away W.S.W. against the flood, and by two in y^e afternoon came to an anchor in Plymouth sound: here I found but very little Tide; but it was full sea on shore at three this afternoon; and the next morning it was Low Water at $9^{h}\frac{1}{2}$ AM.

♂ 5. At noon I found the Latitude of Plymouth town 50°.20′ and the Variation from 7°.20′ to 7°.35′ by three distinct observations. In the Evening I sailed out of the Sound for the Eddistone and about midnight came to an anchor under the Lighthouse baring SE, in 29 fathoms water.

☿ 6. I went on shore at the Lighthouse, and found the stream to the Eastward done at $7^{h}\frac{1}{4}$ this morning, that it was low water by the stone at $10^{h}\frac{1}{2}$: but that the westward Tide ran down till a (f.43v.) quarter past one. Hence a SEbE Moon makes the turn of the streame, but it flows no longer than an EbN or $V^{h}\frac{1}{2}$ Moon nearly as in Plymouth sound. I observed the Latitude on the stone 50°.8′, and the Variation by one observation 7°.15′, by another 7°.25′ about two after Noon I weighd and Stood to the Southwards

♃ 7[1] and came to an anchor about 7^{h} PM in 38 fath. the — Lighthouse baring NNE from us about 5 Leagues and at $7^{h}\frac{3}{4}$ PM it was high water or the Eastern Tide done, and the Next Morning about 8^{h} it was again so. I gott up my Anchor, with the wind at SbW a fine gale, and stood to the Westwards,

[1] The symbol and figure are repeated three lines below on the MS.

hoping with the ebb to weather the Lizard, but before we reachd the Deadman[1] it blew so hard as to put us by our Topsailes, and the wind at once shifting to the WbS put us to leeward of Falmouth so I was forced to bear up for Foy[2] where I anchored about 6 in a very good harbour. It continued to blow hard between the West and SW till the 11th during which time I observed the situation of the adjacent Coast and that an EbN or $V^h\frac{1}{4}$ Moon made full sea.

☽ · 11 · Wind at NNW a pleasant gale I stood out of Foy harbour and the same evening ankered by the Lizard point baring west of us in 21 fath:[3] about a league distant. Here the Eastward tide was done at $7^h.45'$ P.M. Variation on shore $7^\circ.45'$ West.

♂ 12 Next morning it was Low water at 50 minutes past One and again High Water at 8^h this morning, wherfore a V^h or rather at ENE $\frac{1}{2}$ E Moon makes high water as well on shore as where we rode. I weighd and stood away South and by two we laid the Lizard baring North, the very point somewhat westerly p compass distant — about 8 leagues. Then I lay by and in 45 fath rode the Boat by her grapnell, but it was not low water till a quarter after four. At eight we hove the Lead and had 50 fath: being about Mid channell, at Midnight

(f.44) ☿ 13 we had 52 fathoms.[4] At four Aug. 13° Mane we had 55 fathoms and the boat coming to ride we found the Tide of flood made strong, so I ordered the shipp to an ankor with two cables to an end, and rode it till high water, which this morning fell out at $10^h.7'$. the water being then perfectly slack at Noon by a good

[1] Dodman Pt., on the Channel Chart.

[2] Fowey, on the Channel Chart.

[3] On the MS 'in 21 fath:' is careted in.

[4] As before, several spaces (three ems in this case) have been left after the end of the sentence and before the new day's entry.

Observation I was in Lat. 49°.10′ the Tide ran about 7^h in the morn not above a mile and half p hour, this was a very good observation by reason the whole Tide was very Calme By noon I weighd and a small gale springing up at EbS I Stood away SbW to allow for the Variation and some small matter I was to the Eastwards of the Lizard when we lost sight of it, but the wind afterwards coming ESE and SEbE I could not keep the Meridian as I desired but fell a little to the Westwards.

♃ 14 In the Morning early we made Ushant[1] from the fore yard about 7 or 8 leagues distant; upon the Ebb the wind did Souther so that we were obliged to go about, and the Tide being under our Lee we neared the Island, so that by noon we were about 4 Leagues distant from it, baring SbE in Lat 48°.42′ by a good observation. In the night we stood off and on.

♀ 15 This morning Ushant bore South of us about 2 Leagues off. the weather thick and little wind at WSW. about 7^h I came to an anchor to observe the Tides here depth 52 fath: about 9^h in[2] cleard up and it was high water at ten minutes before eleaven: Moon then South at 5^h.35′ wherfore an EbN Moon make high water, between 8 and nine the strength of the Tide was not more than $1\frac{1}{2}$ mil p' hour. I observed the Latitude at noon 48°.36′. Then I Stood in with the Island and being come within half a league, the wind came up at SW and blew so hard that I concluded I could not with any conveniency carry my instruments on Shore to observe the Variation, as I hoped to have done on Ushant. Having the wind fair for it, I stood over (f.44v.) for the Isles of Silley[3] to have observed there, but the Wind

[1] Ushent I, on the Channel Chart.
[2] Sic, obviously 'it' is meant.
[3] Isles of Scilly, on the Channel Chart.

coming to the West and after NW and blowing very hard obliged me to bear away for the Coast of England.

♄ 16 . This morning was very thick and foggy and withall a hard gale at W and WSW. We had made 26 Leagues due North from Ushant, and were very near the Lizard but could not see it, till about Noon when it cleard up a little, and we were about four miles to the SSE of the Lizard point we then stood into Falmouth till better weather. In this harbour I found that an E $\frac{1}{2}$ N or rather a $V^{h}\frac{1}{2}$ Moon made high water. and

♂ 19 This morning I went on Shore under Pendennis castle & observed the Variation precisely 8° degrees. and it was low water as near as could be judged at $8^{h}\frac{1}{2}$. about Noon the Wind came up at WNW with fine weather, so I stood out to sea & finding little wind with great rains and Thunder and Lightning I came to an anker before twas dark, the night was very terrible for the Thunder but calme.

☿ 20 This morning proved thick & foggy, but still calme. wee could not see the Land, but found the Eastward Tide ended at $5^{h}\frac{3}{4}$, or at an Eight-a clock Moon. The Ebb ran down till — Noon, but the whole Tide was very easy and the slack long. about 2^{h} it cleard up and we found the Deadman baring NNW 3 Leagues and the Lizard West S.W. depth 31 fathoms. about 5^{h} there sprang up a gale at SW, so I weighd and stood for the Start[1]

♃ 21 This morning at Sun rise the Start bore ENE and the Light house on the Eddistone NbW. We stood for the Start and sometimes could scarce get on head against the Tide. Yet the wind freshening we got to anker by Noon, the Start baring

[1] Start Point and Bay.

West[1] by Compass and the Berry head NNE. The Latitude of the Start was found 50°.10′. The Ebb Tide ended nearly about One, Then I went on shore, and found the High water about four of the Clock, in the Sandy bay just within the Start; and the variation was 7°.35′ carefully observed. returning on bord, the flood ended about half an hour past 7^h or at a SEbE Moon, tho it had been full Sea by the Shore 3 hours sooner or at an EbN Moon. It beginning to blow I weighd before the sea rose, (f.45) and lay by all night with the head to the Southward wind at SW. This evening the Navy Royall under Sr George Rook came into Torbay being taken short with this Wind.

♀ 22. It continuing to blow, so that I could not conveniently anchor I put into the haven of Dartmouth, and was obliged to stay there till Thursday the 28th, it blowing all the time very hard at SW and WSW or thereabouts. I found here that an EbN or rather a V½ Moon made full Sea, and that this harbour was somewhat difficult by reason of the flaws of Eddy winds occasioned by the Mountains.[2]

♃ 28 Wind at NW a gentle gale, I saild out of Dartmouth about Noon, and by Sun sett the Start bore WNW, and the Berry NbW. I then stood over South for the Sept Isles on the Coast of Bretagne,[3]

♀ 29 and having run 11 Leagues. next morning, we discovered the Island of Guernsey baring East from us, about 7 or 8 Leagues. soon after the wind freshned at North, and not

[1] Corrected from 'East' in the MS.

[2] Halley wrote again to Burchett from Dartmouth summarizing his voyage from the time of his last letter to the Secretary (29 July) up to this point. See Document 124, pp. 332–3.

[3] Brittany; see Channel Chart.

thinking it advisable to deale with the Lee shore of France with so much wind, I put into Jersey road, and abode there all the next day. Here I found that a VI^h or East and west Moon makes full sea.

☉ 31 It was high water by the shore a quarter before two, then I stood out of Jersey road to the Southward with the Ebb and a gentle gale at NW, and at Sunsett came to an anchor in 20 fath, Sark baring North as far off as it could be seen, Grosnez point NNE ½ N and St Clements on Jersey NEbE correct barings. Here the Ebb was done. half a quarter after Eight this Evening and as far as could be seen in the night it was high Water at Two in the morning. The Time very calme.[1]

☽ Sept 1 This morning at ¼ past 8^h, 'twas again Low-water or at a South Moon somewhat Westerly. So that a VI¼ Moon makes high Water here. I weighd on the flood and stood to the Southwards wind at WNW a gentle gale and about one came to an anchor Cape Frehell[2] baring due South, in Latitude 48°.53′ about 4 leagues from shore. Here it was high Water five minutes before three a very smooth Tide. I weighd and drove with the Ebb, and in the Night the wind came off shore at SWbS so I stood to the west wards against the Flood.

♂ 2 At Seaven this Morn, Cape Frehell bore SE from us as far as we could see it, and the middle of the Isle Brehat[3] WSW; the wind much southerly but small; about 9^h we saw Rock (f.45v.) douvre[4] about 3 Leagues to Leeward. the wind freshning we

[1] That is, at the time very calm.
[2] Trelrell, on the Channel Chart, and usually Frehel to-day.
[3] I. Brehaut, on the Channel Chart.
[4] Rock Daure, on the Channel Chart. See subsequent renderings of this in the Journal and Appendix C, p. 364. It could be 'danure' in the MS.

made head against the flood and by 11^{h} were abreast with the half=Tide rock cald La Horraine[1] or Canyn; which we saw about a league to the southward. At Noon the Heaux[2] de Brehat baring West somewhat Southerly I observed the Latitude exactly 49°.00′, which is the Latitude of the most northerly rocks of all the Coast of Bretagne. About 3^{h} I came to an anchor in 18 fath, the East part of Brehat baring South about two leagues distant and found the flood done here at a VII^{h} Moon, or at half an hour past 4^{h} this day. Then I weighd with the Ebb and by ten at night came to an anchor the Eastmost of the Sept Isles baring SW about a league in 30 fath: and we found the Ebb to run down till 11^{h} this night.

☿ 3 This Morning the flood lasted till 5$^{h}\frac{1}{2}$ or to an ESE Moon then I weighd, and with the wind S.Westerly stood off to Sea to speak with a saile[3] that stood with us, he proved a French man bound from Dieppe for Marseilles. Then I stood in again as near as I durst (there being much broken ground about the Sept Isles) and went on Shore on the most Easterly calld Rousie.[4] here we found store of Connies. I gott on Shore about Eleaven, hoping to have seen the Low water time on land, but found it to flow very fast. I observed the Variation on this Island to be 7°.27′ Westerly, and at Noon the Latitude 48°.57′. I staid to see the high water by the shore, which as near as could be judged, was at half an hour after 3 or rather sooner so that an EbN moon makes full sea here as at the Start which lies over

[1] Le Haraine, on the Channel Chart.

[2] Les Heux, on the Channel Chart, which is not quite the most northerly of the rocks of Brittany shown on the chart.

[3] The word 'stood' is deleted and the word 'saile' added after the deletion.

[4] The reference is to Rochabell as shown on the Channel Chart.

against it. I found the Heaux de Brehat which are the most northerly rocks of Bretagne to bear truly E $\frac{1}{2}$ Northerly, and the Treaclepots or Triagons[1] W $\frac{1}{2}$ half southerly about two leagues distant: and the Isles of Bass[2] as far off as we could see WSW $\frac{1}{2}$ W or W. 17° South. I went on board about 4, and found the flood still ran strong to the Eastwards[3] designing with the Ebb to fall down to the Isle of Bass. I stood off to Sea, but by night the wind came up at WSW and blew fresh, so I lay all night under a mainsaile with the head off.

♃ 4 By sunrise the flood, which runs in the offing. about an hour longer than near the shore, had brought us in sight of Rock Doure. Then the wind and Sea rising with rain and dirty weather I put back again for Jersey. I observed Rock Doure to bear truly from Guernsey SSW westerly and from the middle of Jersey WbS $\frac{1}{2}$ Southerly and the rock Barnoüy about two Miles SbE from Rock Doure. This Rock Doure is a patch of Rocks like Hay stacks with some little Island among them, — about 7 Leagues from Jersey. There are on this coast severall such patches of Rocks as the Treaclepots the Minquiers[4] to the South of Jersey and the Ecrehou to the N.E. thereof and the Casketts to the West of Aldernay. About two we came to an anchor in the bay of St Hilary, and about 5 came in to the peer of St Aubin which dries at half Ebb.[5]

(f.46)

♀ ♄ 5 · 6 Finding our shipp very foul, and having the convenience to clean here, we spent these days in scrubbing and cleaning. I observed

[1] Les Triagnons or Treacle Potts, on the Channel Chart.

[2] I. de Bass, on the Channel Chart.

[3] The 'r' in 'Eastwards' is careted in on the MS.

[4] Mincquors, on the Channel Chart, apparently. It is difficult to read because a rhumb line passes through the word.

[5] Off the Isle of Jersey.

the Latitude at St Aubin to be 49°.15′, and the variation 7°.50′ very exactly.

☉ 7 It blew hard at SSW with much raine.

☽ 8 The wind being moderate at SW, I turned out of the Bay and with the Ebb weatherd the Island, but whilest the boat sett the Pilot on shore, the flood came out of the WNW and drove us right on the Corbiere rocks, so that we were obliged to anchor till about sunsett then the Tide slackning we weighd and stood into the half-Tide that runs between Jersey and Sark, which served us till past Ten; then the wind blowing a stout gale we made good way against the Ebb and before Sunrise past the race of Aldernay.

♂ 9 I stood over for the coast of England and that same evening came to an anchor in St Helens road.

☿ 10 About noon with the Western Tide I weighd wind at West, and turned it up to Spitthead.

♃ 11 My provisions being nearly spent, I this day got an order from Comiss^r. Greenhill[1] for a months provision

♀ 12 I received the sd provisions from the Victualling Office.

♄ 13[2] With a small gale northerly, I sailed for the Ourse, to take account of that Ledge of Rocks, which is the only considerable danger on the English side of the channel. About Two at the End of the Eastern Tide (which runs but slack within the Ourse) I came to an anchor in 10 fath: at the West entrance of the Loo[3] channel, Chichester baring NbE, and the marks for the

[1] Henry Greenhill was appointed Commissioner at Portsmouth in April 1695, in which post he seems to have remained until transferred to Deptford and Woolwich in August 1702.

[2] Halley took the opportunity of writing to Burchett from Spithead a very optimistic letter in which he summarizes his voyage from the time of his last letter to the Secretary (23 August) to the present. See Document 125, p. 333.

[3] Looe, on the Isle of Wight.

(f.46v.) Loo, viz the Cardinalls hat and Swan cliff precisely in one, baring truly W $7\frac{1}{2}$ S or two thirds of a point to the Southwards of the West. I went in my boat and sounded the Puller which lay to the South of us and is the Westermost of three banks of sand calld the Barrows lying off of Selsey and found not above 16 foot in many places.

☉ 14 This morning the flood came about 9^h and withall a fine gale at ENE. The Loo being narrow I durst not venter to turn through it; but stood to the Southwards and went in between the East barrow head and the Middle ground where there is a good channell of 6 fath: above half a mile wide. I followed the bank of the Eastbarrow head with the Tide and crost it severall times sounding 3 and $2\frac{1}{2}$ fathoms the Tide being aloft. There is very little water at Low water on the east end of this Shole. On the Ebb I came to an anchor in 5 fath in the Park of Selsey.

☽ 15 This morning the wind came up at East and EbS and blew very fresh and we rode open to the Sea. Assoon as the Flood Tide was made I weighed, and in the afternoon the wind and Tide serving I came directly into portsmouth harbour where I continued by reason of hard Easterly winds till

♃. 18 About 11^h this morning I sailed again out of portsmouth harbour for the Ourse, wind at ENE, and turned it through the Bouys and stood all night off to Sea with an easy gale.

♀ 19 With the day, the wind came up at SW, with fair weather, about ten this morning, the ebb being made, I came to an anchor about a mile without the breach of the overfall of the Ourse. in 20 fath: Swan=cliff baring W $\frac{1}{2}$ N by the correct Compass and Chichester Steeple NbW westerly, Variation allowed. Here it was low-water $3^h.12'$ P.M. or at a WSW Moon. The Tide slackening, I went and sounded the outward or Sea-Ourse which I found to be a ledge of Sunk rocks in some places very little covered at a low water time.

♄ 20 and ⊙ 21th I spent in sounding and taking the marks in order to describe exactly the severall dangers of these Sholes and the channells through them, and found the best mark to avoid them to be the Swan=Cliff on the Isle of Wight; There is a small (f.47) hummock B that lies to the Northward of the Cliffland A, if they appear as in the figure with a Dalke[1] in the middle as at C, you are in a line with the Sea Ourse and may be in Danger

But if the same lands appear closed in one, as also if the Culver Cliff[2] which faces the South begin to appear on the South point of the Swan cliff thus at D.[3] you are safe without. and have nothing to fear.

In thick and dark weather tis best to keep off to sea, but if you turn down there is a bank above a mile without the Ourse on which there is not above ten or twelve fathoms: the Sounding^{s} wherof will give notice to tack in time.

☽. 22 It beginning to blow hard at SSE I this morning got under Saile and the Tide being aloft turned it over all the Sholes. and that evening came to an anchor at Spitthead.

[1] Dalke, dalk, delk, or daulke = a hollow or depression.
[2] On the Isle of Wight; see inset of this island and its environs on the Channel Chart.
[3] The statement 'at D' is careted in with the full stop below the letter.

♂ 23 It continuing to blow hard I went into portsmouth harbour and for the same reason stayd there till Friday 26th.

♀ 26 This morning at the desire of Cōmissioner Greenhill, I went and sounded and described the Middle-sand, which lies away to the Eastward of East Cows point.[1] On it at Low water I found in some places not above ten foot. It reaches almost half way from Cows to Gilkicker point, and has two points on the East end, but ends in a narrow Tayle to the westward, almost as far down as the East Cows point. If you Shut in West cows castle behind the point you go clear of it to the Southward.

♄ 27 I went over to the North side of the Channell, to sound the Bramble, which lies at the mouth of South-hampton creek: but the wind coming up fresh at WSW, we could not use our boats for that purpose, with any conveniency. Wherfore finding the nights become long, and the weather uncertain and boisterous, and my provision almost spent, I resolved to return for the River, and accordingly this night I sailed through the Bouys and gott to Sea.

(f.47v.) ☉ 28 This morning was thick dirty weather and sometimes Squally wind at WSW, about noon the wind shifted to NW and it did clear up and we found Beachy head to bear NbW about 3 Leagues. before four we were up with Dunginess and by Nine gott to an anchor in the Downs.

☽ . 29 Wind much Westerly having gotten a Pilot on bord I saild for the River and this night anchored in Margate road.

♂ 30 This morning early before day we weighd and turned it into the Gore where we anchored about 8 and the — wind being

Octob far Westerly we continued there all that day.

[1] On the Isle of Wight.

☿ 1. About one the wind came up at SbW a fine gale so with the first of the flood we got through the narrows and over the Flatts.

♃ 2 This morning by day we were at the Lower end of the Hope and before highwater we came to an anchor in Long-reach.

♀ 3 I gave notice of my arrivall to the Admiralty office and at the Ordnance,[1] and sent for a pilot to bring us up the River.

♄ 4 I received an order to deliver my Gunns and Ammunition in Gallions and this night John Frost the Pilot came on board.

☉ 5. After midnight there arose a severe Storm at WbN, so that it was not[2] adviseable to make saile, it blowing exceeding hard all this day and the next.

♂ 7 We weighd with the flood, but it blew so hard, that we were forced to come to an anchor again, by the half=way-house.

☿ 8. We weighd and gott into Gallions, and delivered there our Gunners stores and Ammunition.

♃ 9. It blew again so hard that we could not make sayle.

♀ 10 We came to Deptford, and I delivered the pink into the Custody of Capt Wright, Master of Attendance.[3]

♃ 16 The pink was paid off at Broad street.[4]

Edmond Halley[5]

[1] See Halley's letter to Burchett of this date, Document 126, p. 334, and the quick official response to this, Documents 127, pp. 334-5, and 128, p. 335.

[2] The two words, was not, are in the margin, on the MS.

[3] Presumably Captain William Wright, R.N., one of at least two officers of this name and rank serving in the Royal Navy at this time.

[4] Wages ended on this day as shown in Document 129, p. 337.

[5] Halley used his full signature, without abbreviation, which is unusual.

DOCUMENTS RELATING TO HALLEY'S VOYAGES AND AFTERMATH

Manuscript journals of Halley's *Paramore* voyages used in this work are now in the British Library, but most of the other documents pertaining to Halley's three voyages are to be found in the Public Record Office, the archives of the Royal Society, or the National Maritime Museum, Greenwich. In the Public Record Office are several classes of documents fundamental to an understanding of these expeditions, notably: Captains Letters to the Secretary of the Navy (in this case Halley to Burchett), Secretary's Letters (Burchett to Halley), Lords Letters to the Navy Board, and Treasury Papers, while the National Maritime Museum contains the Navy Board Minutes, etc. In the Royal Society archives are valuable letters and entries in the Journal and Minute Books of the Society. All of this material is manuscript, and much of it (especially letters, etc., to Halley) has not hitherto been published. To avoid unnecessary footnoting of the documents, if a person, event, etc., is adequately dealt with in the other sections (Introduction with footnotes, Journals with footnotes, etc.) the information is not repeated, only cross-referenced in the Document section. Small entries from diaries, etc., are included in the Introduction.

Most of the documentation is self-explanatory and is divided below into four sections corresponding to some of those of the Introduction and/or Journals, viz: Halley's Voyages – Preparations; Halley's First Voyage; Halley's Second Voyage; Halley's Third Voyage and the aftermath. If there is an address, or if a document is endorsed or minuted these items are included, but their absence is not specifically indicated. Not all of the correspondence is complete; we can infer that a few letters have been lost and some which are judged to be irrelevant are omitted. However, the important documentation is included and it is remarkably complete considering the period. It gives a good picture of Halley's voyages even when considered by itself, but if read in conjunction with the journals greatly enriches these accounts.

PREPARATIONS

I

ROYAL SOCIETY, COLLECTANEA NEWTONIANA.[1]
(Vol. IV. No. 425)
March [1692/1693]

Whereas this Honble Society has at all times, according to Its Institution, appeared ready and willing to promote any Designe tending to the Advancement of Usefull Arts or the Discovery of Nature. And whereas the variations of the Magneticall Needle are as yett unknowne to Us in all that vast Tract of Sea betweene America and China, being neare halfe the Globe, none of our Journalls giving the Least Account thereof. And whereas the Vibrations of the Pendulum in Clocks are found to be Swifter and Slower in differing Latitudes, hindring the Discovery of the Longitude at Sea by that meanes, unless this Difference be adjusted by Accurate Observation in Severall Places. And whereas there has of late been Severall other Methods thought of for discovering the Longitude at Sea by the Motion of the Moone and other Celestiall Bodys, which have not as yett been effectually put in Practice, Soe that it cannot be as yett concluded how farr the Same may be relyed on for the use of Navigators. It is therefore most humbly prayed that this Honble Company would please to Lend their Assistance and Good offices to Obtaine of their Ma^tys^ a vessell which may be Secure in all weathers, but not exceeding. 60. Tunns burthen for a voyage to be undertaken by Benjamin Middleton Esqr and Edmond Halley in Order to discover what may be Learnt in the abovesd^d^ Particulars: the designe being to compass the Globe from East to West through the great South Sea. And the said Benj: Middleton for promoting the said Undertaking does oblige himself to goe the Voyage and to Victuall and Man the said Vessell at his owne proper Costs and Charges, and Likewise to render an Account of his Proceedings to the Rt. Hon^bles^ the Lords of the Admiralty and to this Society. And the Care

[1] On the cover of the folded sheet the following appears: 'March 1693 – Proposal of Mr. Middleton and Mr. Haley to compasse the Globe for Improvement of Navigation'. The letter was bought at Sotheby's May 1809 from the collection of James Stewart, Esq., FSS. The Sale catalogue lists it as, 'Draft of Proposals presented to the Royal Society in 1693 for a voyage of discovery under the scientific conduct of the great Dr. Halley. Endorsed in Mr. Secretary Southwell's hand. An interesting record of a forgotten project from the Southwell Sale.' Of course this was not a forgotten project unless we think of this proposal as unrelated to the *Paramore* voyages as reported by Dalrymple, Burney, etc.

of Making the Necessary Observations is undertaken by the s^d Edmund Halley, whose Capacity for Such Purposes is Supposed to be Sufficiently knowne to this Honble Company.

2

ROYAL SOCIETY JOURNAL BOOK COPY[1]

Vol. VII p. 164

12 April 1693

The President was pleased to propose to the Society a paper lately offered him by Mr Benjamin Middleton, requesting the assistance of this Society to procure for him a small vessell of about 60 Tuns to be fitted out by the Government, but to be victualled and manned at his own proper charges. And this in order to compass the Globe, to make observations on the Magneticall Needle, &c. The President in the name of the Society promised to use his endeavors towards obtaining such a vessell.

3

TREASURY PAPERS

T 54 14 p. 202

May it please your Ma^ty
In obedience to your Ma^ts Comands signified to Us by Sr John Trenchard Kn^t[2] one of your Ma^ts Principall Secrys of State upon the annexed Pet^n of Benj^a Middleton Esqr wherein he proposes to goe about the world to

[1] Thomas Birch in his *History of the Royal Society*, Four Vols. (London, 1756–7), reproduces the contents of the MS of the Royal Society Journals down to December 1687. In the third and fourth volumes there are many entries relating to Halley. MacPike, 1932, Appendix VIII, pp. 210–238, contains extracts from the Journal Book from 11 January, 1687/8 to 1 July, 1696 pertaining to Halley, though this list is not exhaustive. (Interestingly the extract above is not included). Therefore the MS Journal Books at the Library of the Royal Society were searched and items copied referring to Halley's voyages both before and after the terminal date of entries from this source in MacPike, which of course does not cover the actual period of the voyages.

[2] Appointed in 1692 as one of the Principal Secretaries of State taking the place of Henry, Viscount Sidney, afterwards Earl of Romney. In turn Trenchard was succeeded in this position in 1695 by Sir William Trumbull; see p. 268, n. 3.

discover the variacons of the Needle &c Wee have considered the same and are humbly of Opinion that soe good and publick an undertaking deserves encouragm^{t} All which is most humbly submitted to your Ma^{ts} great wisdome

G. Sff. ES. CM.[1]

June 23. 1693

[Minuted]

Report on the Pet^{n} of Ben: Middleton

4

ADMIRALTY ORDERS TO THE NAVY BOARD

ADM/A/1797.[2]

Admiralty Office 12th July 1693.

Gentlemen,

A petition has been lately presented to this Board by Benjamin Middleton Esqr Wherein he proposes, that he will together with Mr Edmond Halley, undertake a Voyage, wherein he purposes to incompass the whole Globe from East to West, in order to the describeing and laying downe in their true Positions, Such Coasts, Ports and Islands, as the Weather will permitt, to some of which possibly an Advantageous Trade may be found. And also to endeavour to gett full information of the Nature of the Variation of the Compasse over the whole Earth, as Likewise to experiment what may be expected from the Severall Methods proposed for discovering the Longitude at Sea. And praying that he may be furnished with a Vessell of about Eighty Tuns Burthen fitted out for the said Voyage, & maintained therein at their Ma^{ts} Charge, excepting only for Victualls & Wages, which he will be at the Charge of; Which Petition having been laid before the Queen Her Ma^{ty} is graciously pleased to incourage the said undertakeing. And in pursuance of her Ma^{ts} pleasure Signified therein to this Board. We do hereby desire and direct you forthwith to cause a Vessell of about Eighty Tuns Burthen to be set up and built in their Ma^{ts} Yard at Deptford assoon as may be, and that

[1] Sidney, Lord Godolphin; Sir Stephen Fox; Sir Edward Seymour, Baronet; Charles Montagu.

[2] This letter, from the National Maritime Museum, compares closely with the Public Record Office copy, ADM. 2. 173 p. 374.

Mr Midleton be consulted with about the conveniencies to be made in her for Men and Provisions, and that when she is built She be fitted out to Sea, and furnished with Boatswains and Carpenters stores for the intended Voyage, & delivered by Inventory to the said Mr. Midleton to be returned by him when the Service proposed shall be over.

So Wee remain,

Your affectionate friends
Falkland
J. Lowther
H. Priestman
Robert Austen.[1]

Navy Board.
Read 17th.

[Minuted:]

12 July 1693

Admty Office
Commrs

Mr Middleton's
Proposal of Discovery
on ye Globe.

To Build a Vessell at Deptford, fitt her out to Sea & furnish her with Stores as Mr Middleton shall advise; She being to be employed by him in making further discovery's on ye Globe.

5

NAVY BOARD MINUTES. SERGISON /37

17 July 1693

[Admiralty Order]

An other, of the 12th – To cause a Vessell of about Eighty Tuns to be sett up & built at Deptford & fitted out for Sea for the Voyages intended for her by Mr Middleton to whom she is to be deliver'd by December,

[1] Anthony Cary, Viscount Falkland, First Lord of the Admiralty; Sir John Lowther, Baronet; Henry Priestman; Robert Austen.

& to be return'd when the Service as proposed shall be over – Send a Warrant to the Offc at Deptford to go in hand in building & fitting the said Vessell accordingly, & to submitt Us an Estimate of the charge thereof.

6

ADMIRALTY – NAVY BOARD

Deptford Yard Letter Books. Series 1

ADM 106/3291

Honord Sir/

According to your Order here of ye dimensions of the Masts and Yards which I think proper for the new Vessell building here for Esqr – Midleton vizt/

	Masts		Yards	
	Length in Yards	Diamtr in ins.	Length in Yards	Diamer in ins.
Main Mast –	16–	$12\frac{1}{2}$	$13\frac{1}{3}$	$9\frac{1}{8}$
Top Mast	$9\frac{2}{3}$	$7\frac{3}{4}$	$7\frac{1}{3}$	$5\frac{1}{4}$
Top galt mast	$3\frac{5}{6}$	$3\frac{1}{8}$	$3\frac{2}{3}$	$2\frac{3}{8}$
ffore Mast	$14\frac{1}{6}$	11	$11\frac{2}{3}$	8
Top Mast	$8\frac{2}{3}$	7	$6\frac{1}{2}$	$4\frac{3}{4}$
Top galt mast	$3\frac{1}{2}$	$2\frac{7}{8}$	$3\frac{1}{4}$	$2\frac{3}{4}$
Mizen Mast	$13\frac{1}{6}$	$8\frac{1}{4}$	10	5·
Top mast	$4\frac{2}{3}$	$3\frac{1}{4}$	$3\frac{2}{3}$	$2\frac{3}{4}$
Bowspritt	$10\frac{1}{2}$	$10\frac{1}{2}$	$7\frac{2}{3}$	$5\frac{3}{4}$
Sprit Saile topmast	3	3	$3\frac{2}{3}$	$2\frac{3}{4}$
Cross Jack	–	–	$7\frac{1}{2}$	$3\frac{3}{4}$

Octer 13
1693 To the Surveyor H.H.[1]

[1] H. H. seems to refer to Fisher Harding, for he subsequently signs himself H. Harding. Harding was Master Shipwright at Deptford from 30 October 1686 to 5 November 1705. Prior to this he had served as Assistant to the Master Shipwright at Deptford for some nine years and also held appointments at Woolwich and Harwich.

7
ADMIRALTY – NAVY BOARD
Deptford Yard Letter Books, Series 1
ADM. 106/3291

Rt Hono^ble^

Their Maj^ts^ New Pinke building here will be ready to Launch any day which your Hon^r^ will please to Appoint these Spring tides . . .[1]

Deptford 29
March, 1694

H.H.[2]

8
ADMIRALTY ORDERS TO THE NAVY BOARD
ADM/A/1806

From the Princip^le^ Officers
& Commiss^rs^ of their Ma^ty^

Adm^ty^ Office
1st April 94.

Navy.
These

Gentlemen,

You having acquainted me that the New Pink ordered to be built at Deptford for Colonel Middlleton may be Launched this Spring; We do hereby desire & direct you to cause her to be Launched accordingly, And that she be named the Paramour & entered on the List of the Royall Navy by the same name.

So we remain

Your affectionate Friends

Pembroke,
J. Lowther,
H. Priestman.[3]

[1] The remainder of the letter has to do with other matters, vessels, etc.

[2] See n. 1, p. 254.

[3] Thomas Herbert, Earl of Pembroke and Montgomery; Sir John Lowther, Baronet; Henry Priestman.

[Minuted:]

Adm^{ty} Office 1° April 94.

Comm^{rs}

To cause y^{e} New Pink built for Colon. Middleton to be Launched and Named y^{e}

Paramour

9

ADMIRALTY – NAVY BOARD

Deptford Yard Letter Books – Series I

ADM. 106/3291

Honr. S^{r}

According to your Order of the 9th Ins^{t} here is the Dimensions and Tunnage of the Vessells foll$^{\theta}$ Viz^{t}[1]

	Length	Breadth	Depth	Burthen
	ft. ins	ft. ins	ft. ins	Tuns
	. . .	. . .	. . .	. . .
Paramour Pinke	52.00	18:0	9:7	89
	. . .	. . .	. . .	. . .

Our Boate makers haveing but little to doe, I desire to know your Hon^{rs} pleasure, if we Shall Sett up in their Maj^{ts} Yard here, Boats for the New b^{t} Charles ordered to be built in their River. I Remain

H. Harding
To the Surveyor

Deptford 14th
May 1694

[1] The dimensions of thirteen ships are given in the table: *Torbay*; *Canterbury*; *Phoenix*, fireship; *Fire brand*; *Mary & Ann*, Pinke; *True Love*; *Grey hound*; *Endeavour*; *Owners Ashore*; *Society*; *Angell*; *Paramour*, Pinke; *Jersey*. Among these vessels the *Paramour* was one of the smallest; they ranged from 1184 tons for the *Torbay* to 52 tons for the *Endeavour*. Although this last name, like many others, was in turn to be used for a number of Royal Navy vessels, apparently the name *Paramour* (in its many variations) was applied to only one Navy vessel – the pink commanded by Halley.

10

ADMIRALTY - NAVY BOARD

Deptford Yard Letter Books – Series 1

ADM. 106/3292 f.17

Rt Honorble/

In Obedience to yor Honor Warrt of ye 4th Inst: Wee have been on board ye Parrimore Pink and all ye Yachts in ye River & made a Strict search but find none of their load Ballast wanting and having no Brigantines now, can give your Hons noe acct of them.

We have viewed ye Rings and Boles[1] and find they are not Marked wt ye Kings mark but ye Lords are in Severall places.

Wee are
Your Honrs Most Obedt Servt
WW: T.H.: T.H.: JJ.

Deptford ye
11th January [1695/96]

11

COMMISSION AND WARRANT BOOK

ADM. 6/4 f.5

Commission without Instructions for Mr Edmund halley to be Master and Commandr of his Mat –
Pink the Paramour, Dated ye 4th June 96.

ER. RR. JK.
By & JB.[2]

[1] Refers to the fastenings for the guns.

[2] Admiral Edward Russell, later Earl of Orford, First Lord of the Admiralty; Sir Robert Rich, Baronet; James Kendall. The last initials J. B., refer to Josiah Burchett, Secretary of the Admiralty. Burchett's initials, which will become familiar, are not hereafter footnoted.

12
ADMIRALTY ORDERS TO THE NAVY BOARD
ADM/A/1831

To the Principall Officers
& Com^ds^ of his Mats Navy — Admiralty Office 4th June 1696.
These

Gentl^n^

Haveing granted Warr^ts^ to William Maunder, William Cornwall John Mathews, appointing them Boatswaine, Guner and Carpenter of his Ma^ty^ Pink the Parramore, for the better performance of the Voyage on which shee is going under the Comand of Mr Edmund Haley, Which officers are to bee payd by the persons who are concern'd with him y^e^, sayd Halley, We doe therefore herby desire & direct you, to take sufficient security for him for the payment of the sayd Officers, before you passe their Warrants at your Office, wch Warr^ts^ are herewith sent you.[1]

....

wee are your affectionate friends
Russell
J. Kendall
R. Rich[2]

to the Navy Board.
read 5th.

[Minuted:]
Adm^ty^ Office 4 June 1696
Com^rs^ Wm Mander
Wm Cornwall — Office^r^ of ye Paramore
John Mathews

Total security of Halley for paying their Wages before Wee pass their Warrants./

[1] There is a further paragraph dealing with another ship, the *Oxford*.

[2] Admiral Edward Russell, later Earl of Orford, First Lord of the Admiralty; James Kendall; Sir Robert Rich, Baronet.

13
NAVY BOARD MINUTES SERGISON 34.

5 June 1696

Com^{rs} of ye Adm^{ty} of yesterday – For takeing Security of Mr Edm^{d} Haley for ye Payment of ye Boatswaine, Gunner & Carpenter of his Ma^{t} Pink ye Parramore . . .

14
ADMIRALTY ORDERS TO THE NAVY BOARD
ADM/A/1831.

Adm^{ty} Office 15^{t} June 1696.

Gentlemen,

Whereas wee did sometime since direct you to take Security from Mr Edmond Halley for the payment of such Wages as shall bee due unto the Officers appointed by this Board to the Parramour Pink, which is going on a private Affaire under his Command:– And hee haveing since applyed himselfe to this Board, concerning the Men which hee shall entertaine to sayle his Ma^{ts} sayd Vessell, desireing that for the better keeping them in Discipline, and they may bee borne on her in his Ma^{ts} Pay, and that Security may bee taken from him, for the makeing good to his Majesty what Wages shall bee due unto them at the end of the Voyage, Wee doe hereby desire and direct you to cause them to bee borne on the said Vessell accordingly, And that sufficient security bee taken of Mr. Halley for paying them their Wages at the end of the Voyage as aforesaid. Wee are

Your^{r} affect^{t} Friends
Russell
R. Rich
J. Kendall.[1]

To the Navy Board.
Read 17th.

[1] Admiral Edward Russell, later Earl of Orford, First Lord of the Admiralty; Sir Robert Rich, Baronet; James Kendall.

15

[Halley to the Navy Board]

ADM/A/1831

[Enclosure]

Right Honorable.

The Right Honorble the Lords Commissrs of the Admiralty having been pleased to appoint me Commander of his Maties Pink the Paramore and to order me to give sufficient security for the wages that shall become due to the Shipps Company: and your Honours having commanded me to lay before you a list of the Number and Quality of the persons I design to take with me; they are as follows

1 Chief Mate
1. Mate and Gunner
1 Chirurgeon
1 Boatswain
1 Carpenter
10 Foremast men
2 Boys.

Which with myself, Mr Middleton and his servant will be in all twenty persons. The Voiage entended being about Ten Months according to the common Course of Navigation.

Sir John Hoskyns of Harwood in the County of Hereford Bart undertakes to give the security desired.

I am your Honours most obedient sert

Edm. Halley.

Received the 19 June 96 & read

[Notes and calculations on the security desired]

Parramore	Months Lunary			Months Calendar		
	£	S.	D.	£	S.	D.
1 Chief Mate	27.	7.	6.	25.	4.	0.
1 Gunner and Mate	27.	7.	6.	{ 24.	0.	0.
				15.	12.	0.

1	Surgeon.	65.	3.	6.	60.	0.	0.
1	Boatswain.,	26.	1.	5.	24.	0.	0.
1	Carpenter.	26.	1.	5.	24.	0.	0.
10	Foremast men	156.	8.	4.	144.	0.	0.
2	Boys	12.	7.	8.	11.	8.	0.
	for 12 months.	340.[1]	17.	4.	A bond of £600.		

[Enclosed with Halley's letter received 19 June 1696.]

16

ADMIRALTY ORDERS TO THE NAVY BOARD

ADM/A/1833

To the Principall Officers and Comp^t of his Ma^ty Navy
Adm^ty Office 15° Aug^st 96

Gentlemen,

We do hereby desire and direct you to cause his Majestys Pinke the Paramour to be laid up in the wett dock at Deptford untill further order, notwithstanding any former directions to the contrary. So Wee remaine

Your Affec^t Friends
Robt Austen
G. Rooke
J. Kendall.[2]

To the Navy Board.
read 17th.

[Minuted:]
Adm^ty Office 19th August 1696
Com^r Paramour Pinke
To Cause her to be layd up in y^e
Wett Dock at Deptford

[1] Some erasures here.
[2] Robert Austen; Admiral Sir George Rooke; James Kendall.

17

LORDS LETTER BOOK

ADM. 2 178 p. 462

Adm^ty 16 Mar: 97/8

Gent^n

The Czar of Muscovy having desired that his Ma^tis Pink the Paramour at Deptford may be Riggd and brought afloat, in Ord^r to make Some Experim^t about her sayling. Wee do therefore hereby desire & direct You in pursuance of his Ma^tis pleasure signified to this Board, forthwith, to give the necessary Orders for Rigg^g and bringing afloat the said Vessell, & Employing her in such maner as the Czar shall desire so Wee remaine

Navy Board.

Your &c

O: h P: GR:[1]

[Endorsed:] Paramour Pink to be ffitted &^c, & Employ^d as the Czar of Muscovy shall desire

18

ROYAL SOCIETY COUNCIL MINUTES

Vol. 2 p. 133

6 July 1698

It was Ordered that the Treasurer pay to Edm: Halley 50 £ ~ full for his Salary to 27th October 1696

19

[Burchett to Halley]

SECRETARY'S LETTER BOOK

ADM. 2 395 p 47

Sr Admiralty 7th July 98

My Lords of the Admiralty desiring to speak with, upon occasion of

[1] Admiral Edward Russell, Earl of Orford (7 May 1697), First Lord of the Admiralty; Henry Priestman; Admiral Sir George Rooke.

your late letter, I send this to acquaint you that Saturday morning will be a proper time for it between ten and eleven a Clock. I am

Mr halley Sr

: Y^or &c.

JB

[Endorsed:] That Saturday Morning will be proper for his attending the Board.

20

LORDS LETTER BOOK

ADM. 2 179 p. 12

Adm^ty 23^d July 98.

Gent^n

His Majestys Pink ye Paramour being designed on a Particular Service, & it having been represented to Us that she is very Crank, We do hereby desire & direct You to cause her to be Girdled in such manner, as shall be thought^t most proper for making her Carry ye Better Saile & in ye Doing thereof, regard is to be had, that it may hinder her sailing as little as possibly may be. We are

Navy Board.. Y^r & ^c

H P: G R. J H: J K.[1]

[Endorsed:] Cause the Paramour Pink to be Girdled.

21

NAVY BOARD MINUTES, SERGISON PAPERS/39

Satturday 23rd July 1698

Adm^ty Ord^r of this day for causing the Paramore Pink to be Girdled in such manner as may make her carry the better Sayle – Give Order therein to the Off^rs at Deptford.

[1] Henry Priestman; Admiral Sir George Rooke; Sir John Houblon; James Kendall.

22

LORDS LETTER BOOK

ADM. 2 179 p. 30

Admty 9° August 98.

Gentn

Whereas his Majesty has been pleased to lend his Pink the Paramour to Mr. Hawley for a Voyage to the East Indies or South Seas, Wee do hereby desire and direct you, to cause her to be forthwith Sheathed and Fitted for such a Voyage, and that shee be furnished with Twelve Monthes Stores proper for her. And you are also to allow her Twenty men on the Service shee is going, and order her to be Victualled for Twelve months, for the said voyage. So Wee remain

Navy Board. Yor &c. J H. G W. J K.[1]

[Endorsed:] Cause the Paramour Pink to be Sheathed & Fitted for a Voyage to the East. Indies.

23

[Burchett to Halley]

SECRETARY'S LETTER BOOK

ADM. 2 395 9. 140

Admty Office 11 Augt 98.

Sr

By Comand of my Lords of ye Admty I am to signifie their Directions to You, to attend their Lordships here on Saturday next at ten of ye Clock in ye forenoon.

I am

Sr Yr &c

J.B.

Mr Hawly – In Town

[Endorsed:] To attend next Saturday

[1] Sir John Houblon; Goodwin Wharton; James Kendall.

24

COMMISSION AND WARRANT BOOK

ADM. 6/5 f. 27 verso

Commission for Mr Edmund Halley to be Master and Commander of his Ma^{ty} Pink the Paramour dated the 19th day of Augt 98

O: JH. JK[1]
By&^{c}JB

25

NAVY BOARD MINUTES, SERGISON PAPERS/39.

Wednesday 14th September 1698
Mr Halley's Lre of this day read – Send a Warrant to the Officers at Deptford to supply the Parramore Pink with two Azimouth Compasses & with such a small yawle as he shall desire.

26

NAVY BOARD MINUTES, SERGISON PAPERS/39.

Wednesday 21 September 1698
Mr Halley of this day desireing a Supply of ffishing Geere, as also that one George Alfry may be appointed his Surgeon – Send a Warrant to Deptford to Supply the former, and lett the Person he recomends be appointed his Surgeon.

27

ADMIRALTY ORDERS TO THE NAVY BOARD

ADM/A/1857.

Admiralty Office 22 September 1698.

Gentlemen,

My Lords of the Admiralty have commanded me to signify their

[1] Admiral Edward Russell, Earl of Orford, First Lord of the Admiralty; Sir John Houblon; James Kendall.

directions to you forthwith to consider and report to them your opinion what numbers and natures of guns will be fitting to be allowed his Majesties Pink the Paramour, which is bound on a long voyage under the command of Captain Halley.[1]

I am Gentlemen your most humble servent.

J. Burchett.

To the Navy Board.
Read 23rd
Answrd 26th

[Endorsed:]

A copy given to Capt. Willshaw[2] the surveyor who will consult Capt. Halley about it

28

NAVY BOARD MINUTES, SERGISON PAPERS/39.

Friday 23rd September 1698
Mr Burchett of the 22nd for our opinion what Numbers & Natures of Guns will be fitting to the allow'd to the Paramour Pink – A Copy of it was given to capt Wilshaw[3] who with the Surveyor will contact Capt Halley about it.

29

LORDS LETTER BOOK

ADM. 2 179 p. 71

Admty Office 23d Sept: 98.

Gentmn

Wee do hereby desire and direct you, forthwith to Impress unto Capt Halley Commandr of his Matys Pink the Paramour, ye sum of one

[1] This appears to be the first official reference to Halley as Captain, although there are several unofficial ones.

[2] Captain Thomas Willshaw, who was Controller of the Storekeepers' Accounts from June 1693 to September 1702.

[3] See note 2 above.

hundred pounds for contingency on ye Service he is Ordr. So wee remaine.

Yr &c:

Navy Board HP: JH: GW:[1]

[Endorsed:] Imprest unto Capt. halley of ye Paramour pink one hundred pounds.

30

NAVY BOARD MINUTES, SERGISON PAPERS/39

Monday 26th September 1698
Another of do date (23rd) for Impresting £100 for Capt Hally Commander of the Parrimore Pink – Let it be done.

. . . .

A report made to the Lds of the Admty what Numbers & Natures of Guns are fitting to be allow'd to the Paramour Pink for her intended voyage in answer to Mr Burchett's Lre of the 22nd instt.

31

LORDS LETTER BOOK

ADM. 2 179 p. 72

Admty Office 27th Sept 98

My Lord.

His Matys Pink the Paramour, now in ye River, being designed on Private Service, Wee desire your Lordsp will give Necessary Orders for her being Supplyed, as soon as may be, with the Guns under mentioned, with Guns stores proper for a Forreigne Voyage, to be delivered into ye charge of her Master Gunner, and his Indent taken as is usual, Vizt.

Six three Pounders of about four hundred Weight Each.

[1] Henry Priestman; Sir John Houblon; Goodwin Wharton.

Two Pattereroes,[1] or two small Guns, in swivells, carrying a Pound Shott.

Wee are

Yr &c:

H:P : J:H : J:K :[2]

Earl of Romney Mas Genl of ye Ordnance.[3]

[Endorsed:] To furnish ye Paramour Pink with Six Pounders of 4 hundred Wt Each & two Pattere roes or two small Guns & Gunrs stores proper for a Forreigne Voyage.

32

COMMISSION AND WARRANT BOOK

ADM. 6/5 f. 31 recto

Commission for Lieutent Edward Harrison to be Mate & Lieutenant of his Majs Pink ye Paramour, dated ye 4 Octr 1698

JH: JK: GW.[4]

By &c

JB

THE FIRST VOYAGE

33

ORDERS AND INSTRUCTIONS

ADM. 2 25 pp. 155–156

[15 October 1698]

Whereas his Maty. has been pleased to lend his Pink the Paramour for your proceeding with her on an Expedition, to improve the knowledge

[1] Peterero, pateraro, etc.: variants of *pedrero*, a small gun.

[2] Henry Priestman; Sir John Houblon; James Kendall.

[3] Henry Sidney, Earl of Romney (1641–1704), fourth son of the second Earl of Leicester. See John Macky, *Memoirs of the Secret Services of John Macky Esq.* (London, 1723), pp. 33–4.

[4] Sir John Houblon; James Kendall; Goodwin Wharton.

of the Longitude and variations of the Compasse, which Shipp is now compleatly Man'd, Stored and Victualled at his Mats Charge for the said Expedition; you are therefore hereby required and directed, forthwith to proceed with her according to the following Instructions.

You are to make the best of your way to the Southward of the Equator, and there to observe on the East Coast of South America, and the West Coast of Affrica, the variations of the Compasse, with all the accuracy you can, as also the true Scituation both in Longitude and Latitude of the Ports where you arrive.

You are likewise to make the like observations at as many of the Islands in the Seas between the aforesaid Coasts as you can (without too much deviation) bring into your course: and if the Season of the Yeare permit, you are to stand soe farr into the South, till you discover the Coast of the Terra Incognita, supposed to lye between Magelan's Streights and the Cape of Good Hope, which Coast you are carefully to lay downe in its true position.

In your returne home you are to visit the English West India Plantations, or as many of them as conveniently you may, and in them to make such observations as may contribute to lay them downe truely in their Geographicall Scituation And in all the Course of your Voyage, you must be carefull to omit no opportunity of Noteing the variation of the Compasse, of which you are to keep a Register in your Journall.

You are for the better lengthning out your Provisions to put the Men under you Com̃and when you come out of the Channel, to Six to four Mens Allowance, assureing them that they shall be punctually pay'd for the same at the End of the Voyage.

You are dureing the Term of this Voyage, to be very carefull in conforming your selfe to what is directed by the Generall Printed Instructions annex'd to your Com̃ission, with regard as well to his Mats honor, as to the Government of the Shipp under your Com̃and, and when you returne to England, you are to call in at Plymouth and finding no Orders there to the contrary, to make the best of your way to the Downes, and remaine there till further Order. Giving Us an Accot. of your arrivall. Dated &c 15 Octor. 98.

H P. J H: J K. GW[1]

By &c. J. B.

To Captn. Edmd Halley Comandn of his Mats Pink the Paramour-River.

[1] Henry Priestmen; Sir John Houblon; James Kendall; Goodwin Wharton.

[Minuted:]
Instructions for proceeding to Improve the knowledge of the Longitude and Variations of the Compasse.

34
[Burchett to Halley]
SECRETARY'S LETTER BOX
ADM. 2 395 p. 332

Adm^{ty} 15° Oct. 98.

S^{r}

In answer to your Letter of ye 4th Ins^{t}, wherein You desire an addition of five Sailors, I am to acquaint You, that my Lords do not think fitt to allow more men than is already appointed: But as to your Officers Servants, in case they are not able Bodyed Men & fitt for Service, their Lordships direct that You do forthwith discharge them, and Enter able Seamen in their room. I am

Captain Halley – Paramour Pink. S^{r} Y^{r} &^{c}.

JB

I desire you will own ye Rec^{t} of ye Enclos^{d} Instructions for ye proceed^{g} with ye Pink und^{r} y^{r} Com̃and on your Intended Expedition.

35
NAVY BOARD MINUTES, SERGISON PAPERS/39

Tuesday 18th October 1698
Mr Burchett of this day for causeing Capt Halley of the Paramore Pink to be presently paid the Mony upon account of what Beer he takes short of the Proporcon ord^{d} him – Write to the Com^{r} of the Vict^{g} to doe it.

36

[Halley to Burchett]

CAPTAINS LETTER BOOK

(Admiralty-Secretary. In-Letters)

ADM. 1. 1871

[Address] To the Honble Josiah Burchett Esqr
Secretary to the Admiralty, London
These ~ humbly present

Portland Road Novemb 1°. 1698.

Honoured S^r

Last Saturday afternoon I past through the Downs to the Westwards, without anchoring, being unwilling to loose the opportunity of a fair wind; the next day it blew so hard as to put us by our Topsails, and yesterday being gott the length of Portland the Wind came up at West and W.S.W. which obliged us to putt in here. The Pink proves an excellent Sea-boat in bad Weather, and sails reasonably well Large, but goes to windward but indifferently, which perhaps may be amended by finding her trimm. During the bad weather on Sunday, her streining opened some leaks which are considerable for a new shipp, and have discovered an evill wee did not foresee; for having only hand pumps, and our ballast being Sand, the bilge water with the motion of the shipp brings the Sand to the pumps and choaks them, and we have pumpt up abundance of Sand with the Water, which galls and wears the pumps. Wherefore my Officers have remonstrated the necessity of shifting the ballast for shingle as also of caulking her upper works, which wee find very leaky. I therfore humbly entreat that their Lopps please to send their Order to the Docks at Portsmouth and Plymouth, that if the Paramour pink come in there, they with all possible dispatch cause her ballast to be shifted for Shingle, and the vessell brought on the Wey's, and searcht and caulked where need shall require. I hope two or three days may suffice for all we have to do.

I am your most obedient servt
Edm. Halley.

[Minuted:]
Portland Road – 1 Nov 98

Capt Halley advisith of his being forced in here of his being leaky & that he shall be obliged to shift his Ballast for shingle, by the reason that the sand choakes the Pumps – & that Orders may be sent to Plim° & Portsm° to that purpose & for the Caulking of his Decks

37

[Halley to Burchett]

CAPTAINS LETTER BOOK

(Admiralty-Secretary. In-Letters)

ADM. 1. 1871

[Address:] To the Honble
Josiah Burchett Esqr
Secretary to the Admiralty
These ~ present

Honoured Sr.

When I wrote to you from Weymouth road, it was so dead calm that it was impossible for me to guess whether the next wind would be fair for Portsmouth or Plymouth, but soon after a strong Westerly wind sprung up, which brought us hither yesterday. I waited on the Commissioner[1] and gave him the account I wrote you, of the ill condition of our ballast in relation to our pumps, and it was his opinion that my demand to have the ballast shifted and the leaks search'd, was so necessary that he needed not to stay for an order from above, however their Lopps letter will have effect to get me the sooner dispatcht, which therfore I humbly hope will not be denied to

Your Honours most obedient Servt.
Edm. Halley.

Spitt head
Novemb 4°
1698.

[Minuted:]
Paramore Pink – Spith
4 Nov – 98

Capt Halley advisith of his being forc'd both from Weym° road and that the Com^m^ here will comply with his desire in the shifting his Ballast &c

[1] Henry Greenhill; see p. 243, n. 1.

38

LORDS LETTER BOOK

ADM. 2 179 p. 100

Admty Office 5th Novr 98

Gentmn

Capt Halley, who is going on a Private Service with his Matys Pinke ye Paramour, having acquainted us, that during ye late bad Weather, he discovered some Leakes in her, which are considerable and desiring therefore yt she may be brought on the Wayes Either at Portsm°, or Plymouth, that She may be Searched, and that the Ballast he now has, which is Sand, may be Exchanged for Shingle, We send you herewith an Extract of his Letter and desire and direct you, forthwith to send Ordr to Portsmouth and Plymouth, that if the aforesaid Vessell Shall come to Either of those places, Shee be without Loss of time brought on the Wayes, her Leakes Stopt, and the Ballast Shifted, as her Comander desires. Wee are

Yr &c:

Navy Board. HP: RR: JH: JK:[1]

[Endorsed:] To stop ye Leakes of ye Paramour Pink at Porst° or Plym° & shift her Ballast.

39

NAVY BOARD MINUTES, SERGISON PAPERS/39.

Saturday 5th November 1698
Admty ordr of this day for sending Orders to Portsmouth & Plymouth to bring the Parramore Pink on the Wayes to have her Leakes Stopt. & her Ballast shifted [so l]et it be don.

40

[Burchett to Halley]

SECRETARY'S LETTER BOOK

ADM. 2 395 p 403

Admty 5° Novr 98.

S/

This comes to acquaint you, in answer to yor Letter of the 1st Instant,

[1] Henry Priestman; Sir Robert Rich, Baronet; Sir John Houblon; James Kendall.

that ye necessary Orders are given to the Navy Board, to Shift the Ballast, and Caulk ye Vessell under your Coḿand, either at Portsm° or Plym° wch you Shall first come to, as you desire: I am

Capt hally – Paramour Pink – Porstm°.

Yo^r^ &c.
JB.

41

NAVY BOARD MINUTES, SERGISON PAPERS/39.

Wednesday 9th November 1698
Mr Burchett of the 8th inst^t^ for causeing the Parramore Pink to be carefully search'd, & that she be well fitted for her intended Voyage – order was given therein[1] to the Officers at Portsmouth, as also to let us know how long time 'twill take up to repair & refitt the Restoracon.[2]

42

[Halley to Burchett]

CAPTAINS LETTER BOOK

(Admiralty-Secretary. In-Letters)

ADM. 1. 1871

[Address:] To the Honble
Josiah Burchett Esqr
Secretary to the Admiralty
These
humbly present.

Portsmouth Novemb. 28° 1698

Honoured Sr.

In persuance of their Lopps orders, the Commissioner here has caused me to be dispatcht with all the Expedition I could desire, and on the 22th instant I joyned Admirall Benbow at St Hellens, who lies there only

[1] There is an erasure after 'therein'.
[2] *Restoration*, 3rd rate, of 1678, lost in the great gale of 1703.

expecting a fair wind. Our people were somewhat doubtfull of going alone, for fear of meeting with a Sallyman, but if we can keep the Admirall Company those apprehensions are over. He has promised to take care of us; but if their Lopps shall think fitt to recommend us to him, in their next letters, it will assure me of his protection; which the weakness of my own compliment in all respects, makes me very desirous of. This is the last favour I have to begg, and I humbly hope it will not be refused to

Honoured Sr.

Your most obedient servant

Edm: Halley.

P. S. Novemb. 29 mane. The wind is now come up at N.E. and I belive wee shall saile this day, but the Admirall calls in at Plymouth for the Dreadnought.[1]

[Minuted:]
Paramore Pink
St Hilary
28 Nov – 1698
Capt Halley adviseth of his Joyning R.Adml Benbow under whose Protection he desires to proceed, being under some apprehension of meeting the Sallyman of War & so are his people too

43

[Burchett to Benbow]

SECRETARY'S LETTER BOOK

ADM. 2 395 pp 487 & 488

Admiralty Office 30 Novr 98
Wednesday Night

Sr/
I have this day rec'd a Letter from Captn halley of the Paramour, whereby he desires, that he may have the Countenance of Your Squadron, soe farr as it shall lye in Your way, to protect him from the Sally Men of Warr, which I have comunicated to my Lords of the Admiralty, and am

[1] *Dreadnought*, 62 guns, 4th rate, of 1691, broken up 1748.

Comanded to signify their Lord^{pps} directions to you, that soe farr as Capt^{tn} halley's way an^{d} your's shall ly^{e} together, you doe take care to protect him from any of those Rovers; but herein you are not to impede your proceeding on the Service you are Ordered: Cap^{tn} halley has acquainted me that you have already promised him this assistance, but as I have already said, 'tis by their Lord^{pps} Com̃and I doe recom̃end it to your care, & not having opportunity of writing by this Conveyance to Cap^{tn} halley, I desire you will acquaint him with the Contents of my Letter, a Duplicate Whereof will be sent by to Morrow's Post to meet you at Plymouth, at which time I will write to him, I heartily wish you a good Voyage & am

Sr your. &c

JB

Reare. Adm^{ll} Benbow-Portsm°
Return'd & Cancelled
Duplicate sent to Plym°

44

[Burchett to Halley]

SECRETARY'S LETTER BOOK

ADM. 2 395 p 489

1 Decr 98

Sr.

I am directed by my Lords of ye Adm^{ty} to acquaint You, in answer to your late Letter, that Directions are given to R. Adm^{l} Benbow, to take care, so far as your way lies together, to protect You from ye Sally men of War, as You desire in your said Letter
So I remain

Y^{r} &c.

JB.

Capt Halley – Paramour Pink – Plym°
I wish you a prosperous Voyage
[Endorsed:]
Returned & Cancelled

45

[Halley to Burchett]

CAPTAINS LETTER BOOK

(Admiralty-Secretary. In-Letters)

[No Address]

Madera Decemb 19° 1698

Honoured Sr

On the sixteenth Instant I arrived at this Island together with the Glocester, the Falmouth, the Dunkirk and Lynn frigots,[1] under the Command of Rear Admirall Bembow.[2] By reason of the Holydays it was not possible for the Shipps to have their Wines on board before this day, wch occasioned the Admirall to leave the Island the same night he arrived, being unwilling to waite so long. I have gotten my self dispatcht, and shall persue my Voiage with the first wind it being now Calm. I thought I ought to give their Lopps an account of our arrivall here, not finding that there were any letters left for you by the Admirall here; who left the Island in all diligence.

I am

Your Honours most obedt Servant

Edm. Halley.

[Not Minuted]

46

ROYAL SOCIETY COUNCIL MINUTES

Vol. 2 pp. 145–6

8 February 1698/9

The Vice President and Secretary informing the Council that Mr Halley acquainting them that he had left a Deputy Dr Arburthnott[3] to

[1] *Gloucester*, 50 guns, 4th rate, of 1695, broken up in 1731; *Falmouth*, 50 guns, 4th rate, of 1693, surrendered in 1704; *Dunkirk*, 60 guns (ex *Worcester*, renamed in 1660), broken up in 1749; *Lynn*, 40 guns, 5th rate, of 1696, sold in 1713.

[2] Benbow.

[3] Presumably John Arbuthnot, M.D., who was later (1704) elected Fellow of the Royal Society.

officiate in his place as Clerk to the Society. The Council Ordered the Books to be Searched about this Office and what was done in it to be looked into next meeting of the Council

47
ROYAL SOCIETY COUNCIL MINUTES
Vol. 2 p. 146
15 February 1698/9

It was proposed and ballotted that Mr Halley being absent upon a particular Service and no provision being yet made by the Council for Supplying his place It was Ordered that Dr Sloan Should propose the Names of two or three persons to be Assistant to the Secretaries as Clerk:[1] And it was carried in the Affirmative Nemine Contradicente.

It was Ordered in the mean time that Dr. Sloan Should employ whom he pleases any where else but none at the Table ~ Where the Society Meets but whom the Council Agree to.

48
ROYAL SOCIETY COUNCIL MINUTES
Vol. 2 pp. 147–8
8 March 1698/9

In pursuance to the Order of last Council Dr. Sloane proposed Mr Israel Jones as the fittest person to officiate in Mr Halley's ~ place as Clerk and Assistant to the Secretaries during his Absence.[2] It was put to

[1] This paragraph is taken to mean that the voyage was no longer a private one. 'Dr Sloan' refers to Hans Sloane, M.D.

[2] Israel Jones served as Assistant to the Secretaries of the Royal Society from 8 March 1698/9 to 6 November 1700 when he was succeeded in this post by Humphrey Wanley.

the Ballot whether he Should be the person or not and it was carried in the affirmative

It was ordered that Dr Sloan Should Acquaint him with it.

49

[Halley to Burchett]

CAPTAINS LETTER BOOK

(Admiralty-Secretary. In-Letters)

ADM 1. 1871

[Address:] To the Honble Josiah Burchett Esqr
Secretary to the Admiralty of England
These ~ humbly present London ~

Honoured Sr.

I have had no opportunity to give their Lopps any account of my proceedings since my last of Decemb. 20° from Madera. That same day I sayled for the Cape de Virde Islands and arriving at St Jago on Jan. 2°, I found there two English Marchāt shipps, one of which calld the New Exchange, whereof one John Way is Master belonging to London, was pleased, insteed of saluting us, to fire at us severall both great and small shott. We were surprized at it, and beliving them to be pirates, I went in to windward of them and bracing our head sailes to the Mast, sent my boat to learn the reason of their firing. They answered that they apprehended we were a pirate, and that they had on board them two Masters of vessells, that had been lately taken by pirates, one of which swore that ours was the very shipp that took him; wherupon they thought themselves obliged to do what they did in their own defence. Then they sent on board me the two persons they said were the Masters of the taken Vessells, and soon after the two Masters came themselves, they said they were sorry that they had fired at the Kings Colours, but that Colours were not to be trusted. I told them I must acquaint their Lopps with what had past, and if their Lopps would put it up, as it hapned they had done me no damage. The next morning they both sailed, and upon our arrivall here we found the said Master John Way and his shipp in this road. From St Jago we proceeded to the southward and being gotten within 100 leagues of the line, we fell into such calmes and small southerly gales, that our shipp being very indifferent to windward, we were full seven weeks before we gott 100 leagues to the Southward of the line, in which time our water being near spent, obliged us to recruite it on the coast of Brasile. By this time twas March and we found the Northerly Currents made against us, and we upon the Lee-shore; so that it would have been scarce possible for a more winderly shipp than we, to turn it to the Southward. And the winter advancing apace in those Climates I principally entended to discover, I thought it not adviseable to proceed that way at this time of the year; hoping it may give their Lopps some satisfaction if I do curiously adjust the Longitude of most of the Plantations and see what may be discovered in relation to the Variation of the Needle in the Northern Hemisphere. Twas the last of November before we left the coast of England, wch considering the uncertainty of the Winds was I find above two months too late: but I hope to be in England time enough to proceed again this year if their Lopps shall think fitting to allow it. We watred in the river of Paraiba in Brasile where the Governour Dom Manuel Soarez Albergaria was very obliging and civill, but the Portuguez, as farr as I could guess, were very willing to find pretences to seize us, and tempted us severall times to meddle with a sort of wood they call Poo de Brasile which is an excellent dye, but prohibited to all forreigners under pain of confiscation of Shipp and goods. I being aware of their design absolutely refused all commerce with them, and having gotten our water we arrived here in three weeks, on the second of this month: Our whole shipps company is hither in perfect health and our provision proves very good.

I am
Honoured Sr
Your most obedient Servant
Edm. Halley.

Paramour Pink
In Barbadoes road
Aprill 4° 1699

[Endorsed:] Recd ye 9° of June
in ye morning mail
[Minuted:]
Paramour Pink –
Barbadoes
4 Aprill 1699
Capt Edmd ad= viseth of his Proceeding from Madera & or his design to return for Engld

50

[Halley to Burchett]

CAPTAINS LETTER BOOK

(Admiralty-Secretary. In-Letters)

ADM 1. 1871

[Address:] To the Honble Josiah Burchett Esqr
Secretary to the Admiralty of England
These present London

Honoured S^r^

I this day arrived here with his Maties Pink. the Paramore in 6 weeks from the West Indies, having buried no man during the whole Voiage, and the Shipp being in very good condition. I doubt not but their Lopps will be surprized at my so speedy return, but I hope my reasons for it will be to their satisfaction. For as, this time, it was too late in the year for me to go far to the Southwards, I feared that if I went down to Jamaica, and so to Virginia &c. the same inconvenience of being late might attend me in case their Lopps, as I humbly hope, do please that I proceed again for I find it will be absolutely necessary for me to be clear of the Channell by the end of August or at farthest by the middle of September. But a further motive to hasten my return was the unreasonable carriage of my Mate and Lieutenant, who, because perhaps I have not the whole Sea Directory so perfect as he, has for a long time made it his business to represent me, to the whole Shipps company, as a person wholy unqualified for the command their Lopps have given me, and declaring that he was sent on board here because their Lopps knew my insufficiency. Your Honour knows that my dislike of my Warrant Officers made me Petition their Lopps that my Mate might have the Commission of Lieutenant, therby the better to keep them in obedience, but with a quite contrary effect it has only served to animate him to attempt upon my Authority, and in order therto to side with the said officers against me. On the fifth of this month he was pleased so grosly to affront me, as to tell me before my Officers and Seamen on Deck, and afterwards owned it under his hand, that I was not only uncapable to take charge of the Pink, but even of a Longboat; upon which I desired him to keep his Cabbin for that night, and for the future I would take the charge of the Shipp my self, to shew him his mistake: and accordingly I have watcht in his steed ever since, and brought the Shipp well home from near the banks of Newfound Land, without the least assistance from him. The many abuses of this nature I have received from him, has very sensibly toucht me, and made my voiage very displeasing and uneasy to me, nor can I imagine the cause of it, having endeavoured all I could to oblige him, but in vain. I take it that he envys me my command and conveniencies on bord, disdaining to be under one that has not served in the fleet as long as himself, but however it be I am sure their Lopps will think this intollerable usage, from one who ought to be as my right hand, and by his example my Warrant Officers have not used me much Better; so that if I may hope to proceed again I must entreat their Lopps to give me others in their room.

Notwithstanding that I have been defeated in my main design of discovery, yet I have found out such circonstances in relation to the Variation of the Compass, and the method of observing the Longitude at Sea, (which I have severall times practised on board with good success) that I hope to present their Lopps with something on those articles worthy of their patronage. I humbly entreat yr Honour to expedite my orders into the Downs, and if it be their Lopps pleasure, that the Shipp continue there for some time, they please to give me leave to come up to waite upon them, to give them a fuller account.

I am

Their Lordshipps and

Your Honours most obedient serv[t]

Plimouth
June 23° 1699.

Edm. Halley.

[Minuted:]
Paramore Pink at
Plim[o]
23 June 1699.

Capt Edward [sic] Halley Reasons for his Sudden Return – Complains of his Lieu[t] & Officers – desires Orders to proceed to the Downs & leave when he arrives there to attend the Board and give acc[t] of his proceed[gs]

51

[Burchett to Halley]

SECRETARY'S LETTER BOOK

ADM. 2 397 p. 67

Admty 29 June 1699.

Sr:

I have recd your Letter of ye 23d inst from Plymouth & this comes to meet You in ye Downes to acquaint you that Orders are sent to Sr Clo: Shovell to try your Lieutent at a Court Martial upon ye Complaint made of him in your said Letter.[1] To which I have only to add, that when ye matter is over You will receive Orders from Sr Clo: Shovell for repairing to Longreach and from thence to Deptford where she is to be paid off & laid up. I am

Yr &c.

Capt. Halley–Paramour Pink – Downes J.B.

52

ORDERS AND INSTRUCTIONS

ADM. 2 26 p. 34

Whereas Wee have recd a Letter from Capt Halley Com̃and of his Maties Vessell the Paramour Pink, complaining of Lieut harrison, the officer which Acts as Mate and Lieutenant of the said Pink, a Copy whereof comes inclosed, which complaint Wee think fitting should be enquired into at a Court Martiall upon her arrivall in the Downes; You are therefore hereby reqd and directed, to cause the same to be strictly enquired into and Tryed at a Court Martiall accordingly, for holding Whereof You are Empowered by Our late Warrant to You.

And when the Court Martiall shall be over You are to order the Com̃andn of the said Pink forthwith to repaire with her to Longreach and there hasten the putting ashore her Guns Stores and Provisions, and from

[1] See Document 50, pp. 281–2.

thence to proceed to Deptford, where shee is to be paid off and laid up.
Dated 29 June 99
To Sr Clo: Shovell Knt Admll
of the Blew
Downes

[Minuted:]
To try the Lieut of the Paramour pink at a Court Martiall & Then Order her to Deptford.

53

LORDS LETTER BOOK

ADM. 2 180 p. 37

Admty Office 29° June 99

Gentn

Wee do hereby desire and direct you, to cause his Matys Pink ye Paramour, upon her arrivall at Deptford, to be paid off there and laid up. So wee remaine

Navy Board. Yr &ct
JB: H: R R: G R: D M:[1]

[Endorsed:] To pay off & lay up ye Paramour Pinck.

54

LORDS LETTER BOOK

ADM. 2 180 p. 37

Admty Office 29° June 99

Mr Lord:

Having ordered his Majesty's Pink ye Paramour to saile to Deptford to be laid up and paid Off. Wee desire your Lordship will upon her arrivall at longreach, cause her Gunns and Gunners stores to be taken out & lodged in his Majesty's stores under your charge, as also yt you

[1] John Egerton, Earl of Bridgewater, First Lord of the Admiralty; Sir John Thompson, Baronet, Lord Haversham; Sir Robert Rich, Baronet; Admiral of the Fleet Sir George Rooke; Vice Admiral Sir David Mitchell.

demand & receive from her Master Gunner an account of the Expenditure of ye Gunns & Gunners stores Committed to his charge, & cause ye same to be duly Examined and passed as is usuall. Wee are

y^r &c

JB: H: RR: G R: D M:[1]

Earle of Romney – Tower

[Endorsed:] To take out the Gunns & Gunners Stores of ye Paramour Pink.

55

[Halley to Burchett]

CAPTAINS LETTER BOOK

(Admiralty-Secretary. In-Letters)

ADM. 1. 1871

[Address:] To the Honble
Josiah Burchett Esqr
Secretary of ye Admiralty of England
— These present London

Honoured Sr.

I arrived yesterday morning in the Downs from Plymouth, whence I sayled on Sunday. I was obliged to waite on Sr. Cloudsley Showell[2] that day, to see if we had any orders; but finding none, I obtained of the Flagg leave to come up to London, so that to morrow I will be sure to wait upon your Honour, and hope to find an opportunity to present my self to their Lopps. Your Honour will please to excuse my not writing by the last post, the Admiralls house being about seven miles from hence, occasioned my loosing the advantage therof

I am

Your Honours most obedient serv^t

Deale Edm. Halley

June 29° 1699.

[Minuted:]

Capt Halley adviseth of his arrival from Plim and his leave from Sr Clo. Shovale to come to Town

[1] John Egerton, Earl of Bridgewater, First Lord of the Admiralty; Sir John Thompson, Baronet, Lord Haversham; Sir Robert Rich, Baronet; Admiral of the Fleet Sir George Rooke; Vice Admiral Sir David Mitchell.

[2] Admiral Sir Clowdisley Shovell.

56
REPORTS OF COURTS MARTIAL
ADM. 1/5261

At a Court Martiall held ab^{d} his Maj^{ties} Ship ~~~ ye Swiftsure[1] in ye Downes ye 3^{d} July 1699

Present

The Honble Sr Clowdsly Shovell K^{t} Adm^{ll} of ye Blew. President

	Beaumont	Knapp	Haddock
Capt^{t}			
	Haughton	Jumper	Trevanion
	Price	Wynn	Underdown
	Elwes	Symonds	

All duely Sworne pursuant to a late Act of Parliam^{t}

Enquiry was made into ye Complaint exhibited by Capt Edm^{d} Halley Commander of his Maj^{ties} Pink ye Paramour against Mr Edwd Harrison L^{t} & Mate & other Officers of ye S^{d} Pink for Misbehaviour & Disrespect towards him their Commander. Upon a Strickt Examination into this matter ye Court is of Opinion that Captain ++ ++ ++ Halley has produced nothing to prove y^{t} ye said Officers have at any time disobey'd or denyed his Comand thô there may have been some grumbling among them as there is generally in Small Vessels under such Circumstances & therefore ye Court does Accquitt ye S^{d} Lt Harrison & the other Officers of his Maj^{ties} Pink ye Paramour of this Matter giving them a Severe reprimand for ye Same.

A true Copy
Hen Rowlandson

[Minuted:]

Swiftsure in ye Downes
3 July 1699
Court Martials Enquiry
Into the Comp^{t} of Capt Halley
agast Lt Harrison. &c

[1] *Swiftsure*, 70 guns, 3rd rate, of 1673, renamed *Revenge* 1716, sold 1787.

57

[Halley to Burchett]

CAPTAINS LETTER BOOK

(Admiralty-Secretary. In-Letters)

ADM 1. 1871

[Address:] To the Honble
Josiah Burchett Esqr
Secretary of ye Admiralty of England
These London
humbly present

Honoured S^{r}

Yesterday at the Court Martiall I fully proved all that I had complained of against my Lieutenent and Officers, but the Court insisting upon my proof of actuall disobedience to command, which I had not charged them with, but only with abusive language and disrespect, they were pleased only to reprimand them, and in their report have very tenderly styled the abuses I suffered from them, to have been only some grumblings such as usually happen on board small Shipps. My Lieutenent has now declared that I had signally disobliged him, in the character I gave their Lopps of his Book, about 4 years since, which therfor, I know to be the cause of all his spight and malice to me, and it was my very hard fortune to have him joyned with me, with this prejudice against me. Howsoever their Lopps may resent it, I am sure that never any man was so used by a Lieutenant as I have been, during the whole term of the Voiage, nor could I any wais help my self when abroad: It remains for me to show their Lopps that as to the Principall business I went upon, my Voiage has not been ineffectuall, and I humbly hope they will suspend their censure till I can prepare for them the Theory of the Variation of the Compass and of the changes therof, for which I have now obtained a competent stock of Materialls. I have my sailing Orders, but it blows so fresh at North that the pilote thinks not fitt to weigh.

I am your Honours most obedt. Servt.
Edm. Halley

Paramore pink riding in the Downes
July 4° 1699.

[Minuted:]
Paramore pink – Downs 4 July 1699 Capt Halley adviseth of the Triale of his Offr^{s} at a Court Matial

58

[Halley to Burchett]

CAPTAINS LETTER BOOK

(Admiralty-Secretary. In-Letters)

ADM. 1. 1871

[No Address]

Long Reach July 8° 1699

Honoured Sr

These may serve to acquaint you, that in persuance of orders I received from Sr Clowdsley Shovell, I arrived this day with his Maties Pink the Paramour in this place, where having delivered her Gunn's and stores I am to proceed to Deptford: Which shall be performed with all possible Expedition.

I am
your Honrs most obedt Servt
Edm. Halley

[Not Minuted]

59

[Burchett to Halley]

SECRETARY'S LETTER BOOK

ADM. 2 397 p. 129

Admty 13 July 99

Sr

I have laid before my Lords of ye Admty your Letter of yesterday and in answer to it, am to acquaint You, that their Lordsps do give You leave to come to Town for a weak, You taking care to leave such Directions with your Officers as that his Majs Service may not Suffer by your absence. I am

Y &c
JB

Capt Halley – Paramour Pink: Deptford.

60
ROYAL SOCIETY JOURNAL BOOK
Vol. VIII p. 165
July 19 1699

A Branch of a Barbado's fig tree which having many Nerves or long fibers which falling downwards hang so that they touch the Ground when they take root and so grow up again, and then all the long Nerves are closed like a ______?______ [1] was presented by Mr. Hally who was thank'd, they are Closed by a Gummy Juice which they produce from whence the Country took its name

61
WAGES BOOK – Extract[2]
ADM. 33/196 f. 287–291
15 August 1698 to 20 July 1699

Paramour Pinck Comp^{t} 20 Men

Entry (1698)	Mens Names	Quality	D or R[3]
Aug 15	Jo^{n} Dodson	Boats & Gun^{r}	
19	Ed^{d} Halley	Com̃an^{d}	
20	Pet^{r} Ingoldsby	Ab	
22	Jo^{n} Hodges	Boats S^{t}	
26	Jo^{n} Thompson	Ab	R 16: Ap^{l} 99
27	Math Butts	Gun^{s} Ma^{t}	
	Robt James	Ord	R 8 Sber 98
30	Jo^{n} Dilley	Ord	R 15: Sber 98

[1] This word has not been transcribed and in the rough minutes it is not readable, but may be, trunke. This information was supplied by Mr N. H. Robinson, Librarian of the Royal Society, in a letter dated 30 October 1973.

[2] In the Admiralty Wages Books the names are listed in order of entry. The books are filled with detailed information concerning allowances, deductions, etc., which is summarized in n. 3, below and p. 291, n. 1.

[3] Discharged or Released. Originally thirty-three names were entered of which thirteen were discharged or released prior to the departure from England, leaving twenty for the Atlantic crossing. Samuel Robinson embarked in Brazil and was discharged in Barbados. John Thompson was released at Barbados being replaced there by another Ab, Henry Clarke. Thomas Paramour entered as a Carpenter's Servant at Anguilla. Two men, Robert Dampster and John Vinicot were discharged at Plymouth.

WAGES BOOK – Extract cont.

ADM. 33/196 f. 287–291

Sber 2	Jo^{n} Dunbar	Midsp^{n}	
9	Tho: Price	Carp^{t}	
10	Jam: Glenn	Ab	
	Jo^{n} Hughes	Carp^{t} S^{t}	D 16: Sber 98
12	Fra: Thracia	Ord	D 19: D° 98
	Dav^{d} Wishard	Ab	
	Richd Arnold	Ab	D 20: Sber 98
	Jam: Garret	Ord	D 25: Sber 98
	Jam: Canadie	Ord	R 13 Sber 98
	Tho Baley	Ord	D 1 Ober 98
14	Edwd Child	Ord	D 28: Sber 98
19	Sam: Withers	Ab	
21	Wm Dowty	CarpMa^{t}	
22	Geo: Alfrey	Chy^{r}	
26	Wm Harrison	Ab	D 14: Ober 98
	Caleb Harmon	Capt Cl	
Sber 26 98	Wm Edwards	Ord	R 9 Ober 98
29	Wm Jones	Ord	R 7 Ober 98
	Tho: Daviss	Ab	
Ober 10 98	Edwd Harrison	Ma^{t} & Lieu^{t}	
	Tho: Burton	S^{t}	
17	Robt Dampster	Carp S^{t}	D 24 June 99
19	R^{d} Pinfold	Capt S^{t}	
	Dan: Dewett	Ab	D 22: Sber 98
Ober 20	Jo^{n} Vinicot	Ab	D 24 June 99
Mar 8 1698/9	Sam Robinson		D 3: Apr^{l} 99
Apr^{l} 16 99	Hen: Clarke	Ab	
July 9 99	Tho: Paramour	Carp^{t} S^{t}	

[signed]
Edmond Halley
Edw: Harrison
George Alfrey[1]

Nett Book

Paramour Pinck

Began Rigg: Wages 15th August 98

[1] The surgeon signed for his allowances.

WAGES BOOK – Extract cont.

ADM. 33/196 f. 287–291

Sea. . . . . . D°	31	October 98
Ended Wages	20	July 1699

Being then paid off at Broadstreete
Present

Sr Richard Haddock Kt
John Clarke }
Wm Hogg } Clerks

Read the 21 November 1700 ++
Made up 23 Do ———

Full ———————	520.	2.	3[1]
Deductions ———————	43.	16.	10
Neat sume paid to ye 23d Novem° 1700	476.	5	5

The Rt Honble Edward, Earle of
Orford Treasurer

THE SECOND VOYAGE

62

ADMIRALTY ORDERS TO THE NAVY BOARD

ADM/A/1867.

Admiralty Office 21st July 1699.

Gentlemen,

Mr. Halley who is lately returned with the Paramore Pinke haveing this day attended my Lords of the Admiralty and desired that hee may bee a second time sent out for the perfecting his designe of discovering the variation of the compasse, which their Lordships (in consideration of the good that may thereby accrue to the publick) are inclinable to allow of; but hee haveing represented that the Vessell hee

[1] Of the full wages of £520.2.3 for the voyage, Halley received £168.0.0; Lieutenant Harrison £71.5.2; Surgeon Alfrey £50.16.6; the carpenter, Thomas Price £22.15.8; Midshipman Dunbar £17.0.4. No other crew member received more than this last figure, with the average per capita earnings of an Ab who made the whole voyage being about £14 for approximately eleven months service.

was last in, is crank, and that shee will not keep a winds, and praying therefore that he may bee furnished with one more proper for the service, their Lordships have commanded mee to signify their directions to you, that you doe cause a survey to be made of the PARAMORE Pinke, and report to them your opinion what alterations may render her fitt for the same, or if you shall judge that any improvements upon that vessell will not be effectuall, that you doe then lett them know what other vessell of his Majesties (of like charge to the Navy or thereabouts) may bee putt into a fitting condition for the aforesaid expedition by the middle of the next month, the time which Captain Halley says tis necessary he should bee going.[1]

I am Gentlemen your most humble servent

To the Navy Board. J. Burchett.

Read 22nd.

Answered 28th.

63

ROYAL SOCIETY JOURNAL BOOK

Vol. VIII p. 166

July 26 1699

Mr. Hally shewd part of a Viviparous plant as he called it, which grows by the Salt waterside called Guaparaira the Mangrove[2]

64

ADMIRALTY – NAVY BOARD

(Deptford Yard Letter Books – Series 1)

ADM. 106/3292 f.100 verso

Rt Hons^{rbles}

In obedience to yor Hon^{rs} Warr^{t} of ye 22^{d} Inst: Wee have taken a

[1] The urgency, of course, had to do with Halley reaching his farthest south close to the Southern Hemisphere's summer solstice.

[2] Presumably *Rhizophora mangle* or perhaps *Rhizophora candel* (the Red Mangrove) of the West Indies. By viviparous Halley probably meant that the plant reproduces from seeds which germinate while still attached to the parent plant.

Carefull Survey of his Ma^{ts} Pinck ye Parramore, having hall'd her a Shore to View her bottom, doe find she has keel and Gripe[1] enough and cannot perceive but that she has a good body to bear sayle (as the Warr^{t} Officer informs us she does) soe that wee believe there is noe Vessell may be more fitting than she is for that Service, when the Platform abaft is Raised and ye Ovlope taken away wch will give more room in hold for ballast or Provision and will settle her more in ye Water and will be a great Advantage to ye Vessell in triming her as they shall have Occasion wch Alterations may be done in ye time Proposed. Humbly leaving it to yor Hon^{rs} Consideration.

We Remain

Your most Obed Servt
W.W. S.M.
WB

Deptford
ye 27th July 99:/

65
LORDS LETTER BOOK
ADM. 2 180 p. 77

Adm^{ty} Offices 3^{d} August 99.

Gent^{n}

You having with your Lre of ye 28° past sent us a Copy of ye survey taken of his Majesty's Pinck ye Paramour, with an account of what alterations are proper to be made in her to render ye said vessell fitt to be sent out a second time with Capt Halley; upon Consideration thereof had Wee do hereby desire & direct you, to cause ye said vessell to be fitted accordingly with all ye dispatch ye possibly may be. Mann'd with ye Complement of Men formerly allow'd her, & furnished with as much provision as she can conveniently stow, for a Forreigne voyage to ye West Indies & Other parts, of proper species for ye same, and ye said Captain

[1] 'The gripe of a ship is the compass and sharpness of the stem under water, especially towards the lower part. The use whereof is to make a ship keep a good wind; and therefore sometimes when a ship will not keep a wind well they put on another false stem to the true stem to make her gripe well.' (*Seaman's Dictionary*, London, Navy Records Society, 1922, vol. II, p. 159).

Halley having Complained to us y^{t} she is a Leewardly Vessell, You are to give such directions thereupon in ye fitting her as you shall think necessary to prevent ye Inconveniency for ye future as much as may be. Wee are

Y^{r} &c

Navy Board J B.: H: D M:[1]

[Endorsed:] To fit ye Paramour Pinck & mann her for a voyage to ye West Indies, wth her former Complem^{t} of men allowed her.

66

LORDS LETTER BOOK

ADM. 2 180 p. 77

Adm^{ty} Office 3^{d} August '99

My Lord:

His Majesty's Pinck ye Paramour at Deptford being Order'd to be fitted out to sea againe, for a second Voyage on Captain Halley's Propositions, Wee do therefore hereby desire your Lordship will cause ye said Vessell to be furnished with ye same number of Guns She had in her late Voyage so soon as she shall be in a Condition to receive ye same, to gether with ye like proportion of Gunners stores for ye said voyage, ye same to be delivered into ye Charge of her Master Gunner, to his Indent taken for them as is usual. Wee are

Y^{r} &^{c}

JB: H: D M:[2]

Earle of Romney – Tower

[Endorsed:] To furnish ye Paramour Pinck with ye same number of Gunns as she had on her late voyage.

[1] John Egerton, Earl of Bridgewater, First Lord of the Admiralty; Sir John Thompson Baronet, Lord Haversham; Vice Admiral Sir David Mitchell.

[2] John Egerton, Earl of Bridgewater, First Lord of the Admiralty; Sir John Thompson, Baronet, Lord Haversham; Vice Admiral Sir David Mitchell.

67

COMMISSION AND WARRANT BOOK

ADM. 6/6 folio 10

Warrants Dated ye 9° of August 99
For William Brewer Cooke of ye Fowey[1] to be Boatswaine & Gunner of his Maty^s^ Pinck ye Paramour in ye roome of ye former who is now removed into another vessell.

68

ROYAL SOCIETY JOURNAL BOOK

Vol. VIII p. 169

9 August 1699

Mr. Halley shewd the seed of the Viviperous plant he brought from Brazile, Dr Sloane said it grew in Jamaica and was very well described as figured in the Hortus Malabaricus[2]

69

ROYAL SOCIETY JOURNAL BOOK

Vol. VIII p. 171

16 August 1699

Mr. Halley shewd the several Variations of the Needle he had observed in his voyage, sett out in a Sea Chart, as also he shew'd that Brazile was ill placed in the Comon Mapps, and he shewed some Barnackles which he observed to be of quick growth[3]

[1] *Fowey*, 32 guns, 5th rate, of 1696, captured by the French in 1704.

[2] Presumably this refers to *Hortus Indicus Malabaricus, continens Regai Malabaricus apud Indus celeberrim omnis generis Plantus Rariores*, Amsterdam, 1678. This work, by H. Henry Van Rheede and others, in three parts (first, 1678; second, 1679; and third, 1683) is the subject of a long review in the *Philosophical Transactions*, 13 (1683), pp. 100–9.

[3] This short entry illustrates part of the range of Halley's interests in natural history, geophysics, and cartography. There is no suggestion here that he had yet produced the curve lines (isogones) for the representation of the point observations on magnetic variation (declination) he had already compiled.

70

[Halley to Burchett]

CAPTAINS LETTER BOOK

(Admiralty-Secretary. In-Letters)

ADM .1. 1871

[Address:] To the Honble
Josiah Burchett Esqr
Secretary of the Admiralty
these — humbly present

London August 23° 1699

Honoured Sr:

The Paramore Pink being refitted and almost ready to come out of the Dock, I humbly entreat their Lopps would please to renew my Commission, in order to the Shipping my Complement of Men, which though small may require some time: For the expediting therof I humbly hope your Honours favour Being

Sr

Your most obedient servt
Edmond Halley[1]

[Minuted:]
London 23 Aug 1699
Capt Halley adviseth of his Ships being near ready to come out of the Dock & desires the renewing his Commission in order to get men

71

COMMISSION AND WARRANT BOOK

ADM. 6/6 f. 11

Commission for Capt Edmond Halley[2] to be Master and Comandr of his Matt Pink the Paramour Dated &c 23d Aug '99

JB H DM[3]
By & JB

[1] Here Halley's full signature is given, which he rarely used; it appears to be autograph. When others transcribe his letters, etc., the full name more often appears. See Documents 84, pp. 306–7, and 85 pp. 307–8.

[2] This is the first time the rank of Captain is applied to Halley on one of his commissions, although official reference is made to him as Captain in Document 27, p. 266.

[3] John Egerton, Earl of Bridgewater, First Lord of the Admiralty; Sir John Thompson, Baronet, Lord Haversham; Vice Admiral Sir David Mitchell.

72

[Halley to Burchett]

CAPTAINS LETTER BOOK

(Admiralty-Secretary. In-Letters)

ADM. 1. 1871

[Address:] To the Honble
Mr Secretary
Burchett
These
humbly present

Honoured S^r

The Paramour Pink is at present in such a forwardness, that I hope to be ready to saile in a Weeks time. Their Lordshipps were pleased to allow me 100 li impress money for ye former Voiage, which still remains almost entire in my hands; I humbly hope they will now please to give their directions to the Navy Board, that the residue therof may be allowed me for the same purposes in this present Voiage. And wheras their Lopps have been pleased to appoint me a Boatswaine with one Arm, who by consequence can be of little service in case of extremity, I am obliged to begg the succour of 3 or 4 men more; which as I content my self with a Mate only, will be born on the Shipp with the same charge as in the former Voiage, when I had a Lieutenent allowed me.[1]

I am
Your Honours most obed^t Servt
Edm. Halley

Sept 4°
1699

[Minuted:]

Capt Halley adviseth when he shall be ready to sail – desiring ye residue of the Imprests and to be allowed 2 or 3 more men.[2]

[1] The mate William Brewer eventually received £28.7.0 for the voyage in comparison with an able bodied seaman who averaged £16.0 0. Thus the wages of the Mate plus those of four able bodied men would total under £100.0.0 as compared with the £71.0.0 which Lieutenant Harrison received for his services on Halley's First (shorter) Voyage; see p. 291, n. 1, and p. 313 n. 1. Actually Halley received the extra men (he had requested three or four) and thus, with Brewer, there was a full complement of twenty-four on the Second Voyage as against twenty on the First Voyage.

[2] Note the discrepancy between the number of men in the request, above, and how it is minuted.

73

[Halley to Burchett]

CAPTAINS LETTER BOOK

(Admiralty-Secretary. In-Letters)

ADM. 1 1871

To the Hon^{obl}
Mr Secretary Burchett
These
humbly present
[Endorsed:]
Capt Halley adviseth when he shall be ready to sail – desires ye residue of his Imprest, and to be allowed 2 or 3 more men.[1]
[No date]

74

LORDS LETTER BOOK

ADM. 2 180 p. 105

Adm^{ty} Office 6° S^{ber} 99

Gent^{n}

Wee do hereby desire and direct you to cause an addition of four men to be made to ye present Complement allow'd his Majesty's Pink the Paramour on ye service she is Order'd.

Wee are

Y^{r} &c.

Navy Board. J B: H: D M:[2]

[Endorsed:] To add four men to ye present Complem^{t} of ye Paramour Pink.

[1] This information is on the cover sheet but the letter appears to be missing. See n. 2, p. 297.

[2] John Egerton, Earl of Bridgewater, First Lord of the Admiralty; Sir John Thompson, Baronet, Lord Haversham; Vice Admiral Sir David Mitchell.

75

LORDS LETTER BOOK

ADM. 2 180 p. 110

Admty Offices 8° Sber 99

Gentn

Whereas application hath been made unto us by Mr Edmd Halley, who Comands his Majesty's Pink the Paramour, yt he may have ye remainder of ye one hundred pounds now in his hands which was Impressed to him at his last going out, towards ye defraying the Contingencys of his present voyages, Wee hereby desire and direct you, to give ye necessary directions accordingly, for which mony you are to take care he be accountable at ye end of ye voyage. Wee are

Navy Board. Yr &c

JB: H: D M:[1]

[Endorsed:] To give Orders for Capt Halley's having ye remainder of ye hundd pounds yt was left in his hands ye last voyage.

76

[Halley to Burchett]

CAPTAINS LETTER BOOK

(Admiralty-Secretary. In-Letters)

ADM. 1 1871

[Address:] To Mr Secretary Burchett
These
humbly present

Honoured Sr

I entreat that in the orders their Lopps please to give me, it may be specified that I endeavour to make discovery of the South unknown lands, between Magellan Streights and the Cape of Good Hope, between

[1] John Egerton, Earl of Bridgewater, First Lord of the Admiralty; Sir John Thompson, Baronet, Lord Haversham; Vice Admiral Sir David Mitchell.

the Latitudes of 50° and 55° South, if I meet not with the Land sooner.[1]

I am

Your Honours most obed^{t} Servt

Edm. Halley.

Sept. 12°
1699
[Endorsed:]
Rec^{d} y^{e} .12° in ye morning – & read.

77

[Halley to Burchett]

CAPTAINS LETTER BOOK

(Admiralty-Secretary. In-Letters)

[Address:] To the [Honorable]
Josia [h Burchett]
Secret[ary of the]
Admir[alty London]

Honoured Sr.

You were pleased to tell me Yesterday that their Lopps were consenting to allow me the imprest money now in my hands, for the use of my present Voiage. I now humbly entreat your Honour would please to signifie their pleasure therin, to the Navy board, and I shall then be ready to waite on you for my last orders.

I am

your most obed^{t} Servant

Edm. Halley

I am bound to attend the Navy board this morning and therfore must begg your Honours excuse that I waite not on you my self.

[No Date]

[1] This specific latitudinal objective which Halley requested be written into his orders for the Second Voyage is a most important difference between these and the ones issued for his First Voyage (Documents 33, pp. 268–70; 78, pp. 301–2). It was to have great significance to the later expedition.

78

[Halley's Second Voyage]

ORDERS AND INSTRUCTIONS

ADM. 2 2 p. 128–9

Whereas his Majesty has been pleased to lend his pink ye Paramour, for your proceeding a second time wth her on an Expedition to Improve ye knowledge of the Longitude and variation of ye Compass, which ship is now Compleatly mann'd, stored and victualled at his Majestys Charge for ye said Expedition you are therefore hereby required and directed forthwith to proceed with her according to ye following Instructions.

You are without loss of time to sett saile with her and proceed to make a Discovery of ye unknowne southlands between ye Magellan Streights and ye Cape of good hope between ye Latt^{d} of 50 & 55 South, if you meet not with ye land sooner Observing ye variation of ye Compass with all ye accuracy you can as also ye True Scituation both in Longitude & Latt^{d}, of ye ports where you arrive.

You are likewise to make ye like observations at as many of ye Islands, in ye seas between ye aforesaid Coasts as you can (without too much deviation) bring into your Course.

In your returne home you are to visit ye English West India Plantations, or as many of y^{m} as conveniently you may, & in them to make such observations as may contribute to lay them downe Truly in their Geographical Scituation in all ye Course of your Voyage, you must be careful to omitt no opportunity of noting ye variation of ye Compass, of which you are to keep a Register in your journal.

Your are for ye better lengthning out your provisions, to put ye Men under your Comand, when you come out of ye Channell, to six to four Mens allowance assuring y^{m} that they shall be punchially paid for ye samt at ye End of ye Voyage.

You are during ye Terme of this Voyage, to be very carefull in conforming your self to what is directed by ye Generall printed Instructions annexed to your Commission, with regard as well to his Majesty's honour as to ye Government of ye ship under your Comand; and when you returne to England, you are to call in at Plymouth, & finding no orders there to ye contrary, to make ye best of your way to ye Downes & remaine there till further Order. Dated &c: 12 Sber 1699

JB: H: DM:[1]

By &c

JB

To Captain Edmund halley
Comand: of his Matys Pink ye
Paramour at
Deptford

[Minuted:]

Instructions for his [Capt. Halley's] proceeding a second time to improve ye knowledge of the Longitude and Variation of ye Compass

79

[Burchett to Halley]

SECRETARY'S LETTER BOOK

ADM. 2 397 p. 280

Admty 13 Sber 1699

Sr

I desire you'l owne ye rect of ye inclosed orders from my Lords of ye Admiralty for your proceeding on your design'd voyage. So I remaine

Yr &c

JB:

Captain Halley – Paramour Pinck – Deptford

80

[Halley to Burchett]

CAPTAINS LETTER BOOK]

(Admiralty-Secretary. In-Letters)

ADM. 1. 1871

[No Address] Downs Sept. 21° 1699.

Honoured Sr

I gott into the Downs this day, just time enough to make use of the

[1] John Egerton, Earl of Bridgewater, First Lord of the Admiralty; Sir John Thompson, Baronet, Lord Haversham; Vice Admiral Sir David Mitchell.

Post, to give you an account therof; as also that we find the Paramore, now we have her by the stern, to saile much better than formerly; and to goe much better to windward, so that my hopes are, I shall have no further cause to complain of her. With my humble duty to their Lopps I remain

Your Honrs most obedt Servant
Edm. Halley.

[Not Minuted]

81

[Halley to Burchett]

CAPTAINS LETTER BOOK

(Admiralty-Secretary. In-Letters)

ADM 1. 1871

[No Address]

Downes Sept. 26° 1699

Honoured Sr

Yesterday the wind coming up at NW most of the small craft weighd out of the Downs, and were followed afternoon by his Maties Shipp the Winchester,[1] but before Sunn sett the wind shifted to W and WSW, so that they were all taken short off of Folkston; A Guiney man of 30 Gunns having promisd to keep me company 800 Leagues, did not think fit to weigh with so scant a wind, [so] I remaine here. This morning the wind is at SWbS, so if it blow fresh, we expect the return of those that sailed yesterday. I am ready to saile with the first wind, but belive that their Lopps are not willing to hazard the Shipp to the Rovers of Barbary, by my going alone, before their ports, with so small a force.

I am
Honord Sr Your most obedt Servt
Edm. Halley.

[Not Minuted]

[1] *Winchester*, 48 guns, 4th rate, of 1698, broken up as a hulk in 1781.

82

[Halley to Burchett]

CAPTAINS LETTER BOOK

(Admiralty-Secretary. In-Letters)

ADM. 1. 1871

[No Address]

Honourd S^r^

This morning the wind coming up at ESE a fine gale, I am now under saile to the Westwards in Company of the Falcon bird a Shipp of good force belonging to the Royall African Company, and I hope this wind may carry us clear of the Channell, in which case I am morally assured of my passage to the Southward. I humbly entreat your Honour will please to afford me your good opinion during my absence, and at my return I am fully perswaded I may be able to answer the expectations of those who perhaps censure the performances of my last voiage without examining all the Circonstances.

I am
Honoured S^r^
Your most obed^t^ Servt
Edm. Halley.

Downs
Sept. 27°
1699.

[Not Minuted]

83

[Halley to Burchett]

CAPTAINS LETTER BOOK

(Admiralty-Secretary. In-Letters)

ADM. 1. 1871

[Address:] To the Honble
Josiah Burchett Esqr
Secretary to the
Admiralty
of England
humbly present
London

St. Jago Octob 28° 1699

Honoured S^r^

These are to acquaint you, that I left the Downs on the 27th past, and on the 12th Instant was got into the Latitude of Madera, where the wind shifting from NW to NNE, put me to Leeward of the Island, and I thought it not adviseable to beat to windward so much in the way of the Salleteens.[1] So I made the best of my way to these Islands and arrived here the 25th about Noon. I have already filled all my water, and this morning saile to the Southwards; my Ships company is all well and my Officers as forward this time to serve me, as they were backward the last, so that I now proceed with great satisfaction, and hope to see the limits of my Voiage before the New Year.[2]

I am
Your Honours most obed^t^ Sev^t^
Edm. Halley.

[Minuted:]
Paramore Pink – S Iago
Capt Edm^d^ Halley adviseth of his proceeding from the Downs designs so soon as he has waterd to proceed to the Southwar^d^ – his men & Officers are all well and willing to serve him

[1] Salleteen, presumably a variant of Sallee-man Salley-man, Salley rover, etc., a Moorish pirate-ship from the seaport Sallee, formerly of piratical repute.

[2] Actually this expectation was not to be realized.

84

[Halley to Burchett]

CAPTAINS LETTER BOOK

(Admiralty-Secretary. In-Letters)

ADM. 1. 1871

[No Address]

Honord S.

I must Intreat you to lay before the Lords of the Admty. this account of what I have done in execution of the Orders I Received from them. Since my last from St. Iago, which I hope came long since to Your hands, haveing not been able to fetch Madera by reason of the winds shifting upon me, I was Obleged to putt into Ryo Jennero in Brasile to gett some Rumm for my Ships company, from whence I wrote you a letter which I suppose will not be in Engld: soe soon as this. I left Ryo Jennero on the 29° of December last and stood to the Southward till the 1st of February when being gotten into my Station Vizt. in Lattd: 52½° and 35° west Longitude from London, we fell in with great Islands of Ice, of soe Incredible a hight and Magnitude, that I scarce dare write my thoughts of it, at first we took it for land with chaulky clifts, and the topp all covered with snow, but we soon found our mistake by standing in with it, and that it was nothing but Ice, though it could not be less then 200 foot high, and one Island at least 5 mile in front, we could not get ground in 140 fadtham. Yet I conceive it was aground, Ice being very little lighter then water and not above an Eight part above the Surface when it swims; It was then the hight of Summer, but we had noe other signe of it but long Days; it froze both nigth and day, whence it may be understood how these bodies of Ice are generated being allways increased and never thawing. The next day February the 2d. we were in Imminent Danger to looss our ship and lives, being Invironed with Ice on all Sides in a fogg soe thick, that we could not see it till was ready to strike against it, and had it blowne hard it had scarce been possible to escape it: Soe I stood to the Northward to get clear of it, which in the Lattd. of 50° I did, and their saw the last Ice. In my way hither I Discovered the Isles of Tristan da Cunha, and in Eleaven Weeks from Ryo Jennero I arrived at this Island, to fill my Water and refrezen my men, and in this whole course I have found noe reason to doubt of an exact conformity in the variations of the compass to a generall Theory, which I am in great hopes to settle effectually

I am
Honord Sr
Your most Obedt Servt
Edmond Halley[1]

St. Helena
March: 30th: [1699/]1700
[Not Minuted]

85

[Halley to Burchett]

CAPTAINS LETTER BOOK

(Admiralty-Secretary. In-Letters)

ADM. 1. 1871

[No Address]

Bermudas July 8° 1700

Honourd Sr

My last from St Hellena, gave your Honour an Account of my Southern Cruise, wherin I endeavoured to see the bounds of this Ocean on that side but in the Lattd. of $52\frac{1}{2}°$ was intercepted with Ice cold and foggs Scarce credible at that time of the Year. Haveing spent above a Month to the Southwards of 40 degrees, and Winter comeing on, I stood to the Norwards again and fell [in] with the three Islands of Tristan da Cunha which yeilding us noe hopes of refreshment, I went to St. Helena, where the continued rains made the water soe thick with a brackish mudd, that when settled it was scarce fitt to be drunke; all other necesarys that Island furnishes abundantley. At Trinidad we found excellent good water, but nothing else. Soe here I changed as much of my St. Hellena water as I could, and proceeded to Fernambouc in Brassile, being desirous to hear if all were at peace in Europe, haveing had noe sort of Advice for near eight months, here one Mr. Hardwyck that calls himselfe English consull, shewed himselfe very desirous to make prize of me, as a pyrate and kept me under a guard in his house, whilst he went aboard to examine,

[1] The signature, like this letter, is not in Halley's autograph.

notwithstanding I shewd him both my commisions[1] and the smallness of my force for such a purpose, from hence in sixteen days I arrived at Barbados on the 21st of May, where I found the Island afflicted with a Severe Pestilentiall dissease, which scarce spares any one and had it been as mortall as common would in a great measure have Depeopled the Island. I staied theire but three days, yet my selfe and many of my men were seazed with it, and tho it used me greatly and I was soon up again yet it cost me my skin, my ships company by the extraordenary care of my Doctor all did well of it, and at present we are a very healthy ship: to morrow I goe from hence to coast alongst the North America and hope to waite on their Lordsps: my selfe within a month after the arrivall of this, being in great hopes, that the account I bring them of the variations and other matters may appear soe much for the public benefit as to give their Lord^{sps} intire satisfaction:

I am Your Hon^{rs} most Obed^{t} Servant:
Edmond Halley[2]

86

LORDS LETTER BOOK

ADM. 2 180 p. 375

Adm^{ty} 20 Augt 1700.

My Lord.

Haveing Order'd his Maj^{ty} Ship the Paramour Pink to Deptford, to be laid up, Wee desire your Lord^{p} upon her arriveall there, to cause her Guns & Gun^{rs} Stores to be taken out and Lodged in his Maj^{ts} Stores under your Charge, and also that you doe demand & receive of the Master Gun^{r}[3] of the said Ship, an Acct. of ye expenditure of the Guns and Gun^{rs} Stores comitted to his charge, and cause the same to be duely examined and past as usuall. Wee rem^{n}

Yo^{r} &c.
H. DM. GC.[4]

[1] Presumably those dated 19 August 1698 and 23 August 1699. Alternatively he may have been referring to his Commission and the Orders and Instructions for the Second Voyage.

[2] The signature, like this letter, is not in Halley's autograph.

[3] Presumably Nicholas Whitbread, who is listed as Gunner's Mate (Document 91, p. 312), unless someone senior, such as William Brewer, the Boatswain, took this responsibility.

[4] Sir John Thompson, Baronet, Lord Haversham; Vice Admiral Sir David Mitchell; George Churchill.

Earl of Romney[1]
[Endorsed:] To take out the Guns of ye Paramour Pink at Deptford.

87

LORDS LETTER BOOK

ADM. 2 180 p. 376

Adm^{ty} 20 Augt 1700

Gent^n

Wee doe hereby desire and direct you, upon arriveall of his Maj^{ts} Ship the Paramour Pink at Deptford to cause her to be paid off and Layd up there.[2] Wee &^{c}

Navy Board. H. D M. G C.[3]

[Endorsed.] Pay off Paramour Pink at Deptford.

88

[Halley to Burchett]

CAPTAINS LETTER BOOK

(Admiralty-Secretary. In-Letters)

ADM. 1. 1871

[Address:] To the Honble
Josiah Burchett Esqr
Secretary to the Admiralty
of England humbly present London

Honoured Sr.

I this day arrived from Newfound land at this port and waiting on the Commisr.[4] I found no orders from their Lopps, so shall this night persue

[1] See Document 31, p. 268, n. 3.
[2] The crew was actually paid off 18 September (See Document 91, p. 313).
[3] Sir John Thompson, Baronet, Lord Haversham; Vice Admiral Sir David Mitchell; George Churchill.
[4] Captain George St Loe, Commissioner at Plymouth.

my voiage to the Downs where I shall waite for what further orders their Lopps shall please to give me

I am

Your Honours most obed^t^ Servt

Plymouth: Edm. Halley.

August 27° 1700

[Minuted:]

Plim° – 27, Augt 1700

Capt Edm^d^ Halley adviseth of his arrival from Newfoundland & meeting no Orders here designed to proceed to the Downs

89

[Halley to Burchett]

CAPTAINS LETTER BOOK

(Admiralty-Secretary. In-Letters)

ADM. 1. 1871

[No Address:]

Downs Sept. 2° 1700

Honourd Sr.

I am just arrived time enough to save[1] the post, and to give y^r^ Honour an account that having received y^r^ Lopps orders, I shall as soon as the Tide serves endeavour to putt them in execution: We were forced to tide it from the Isle of Wight, otherwise I had waited on you by this time.[2]

I am

Your Honours most obed^t^ Servt

Edm. Halley

[Not Minuted]

[1] That is, make.

[2] Problems with the tides, as here, recorded by Halley anticipate the investigations he was to carry out on the Third Voyage.

90

[Halley to Burchett]

CAPTAINS LETTER BOOK

(Admiralty-Secretary. In-Letters)

ADM. 1. 1871

[Address:] To the Honble
Josiah Burchett Esqr
Secretary to the
Admiralty of England
These
humbly present
Admiralty Office

Long reach Sept 7° 1700

Honoured S^r

The winds having been extreamly contrary, it has cost me five days to gett from the Downs hither, and in the passage I have had the dissatisfaction to see the Paramour fall to Leeward of all the Marchant men that turned it with us. I now humbly hope from yr Honours favour, to find at Deptford (where I shall be in a day or two) their Lopps leave to come up to waite on them.

I am
S^r,
Your Honours most obed^t Servt
Edm. Halley

[Minuted:]
Paramore Pink
Long^rch
7 Sept 1700
Capt Edm^d Halley Adviseth of his arrival from the Downs

91
WAGES BOOK – Extract
ADM. 33/206 f.

Parrimore Pinke — 16 September 1699 to 18 Sept 1700

Complem^t 20

Entry	Mens Names	Quality	D or R[1]
Augt 24 99	Edm° Halley	Com^d	D
	Wm Brewer	Boats^w	D
	Pet^r Ingoldsby	Carp^tr M^t	D
	Dav^d Wishart	ord	R 10^t Sbr 99
	Jams Glenn	able	D to ye 5th of March [1700] ye Midship^m
	Tho: Daviss	Ab	D
	R^d Pinfold	Capt^t S^t	D
	Tho Price	Carp^tr	D
28th	Wm Terry	ord	R 13th Sbr 99
	Jn° Simerley	ord	
	Nicoll Langmead	ord	D 5. Sbr 99
	Jn° Wattford	ord	
	Geo: Allfrey	Chyrg°	D
29th	Geo Brock	QM^r	D
	Jn° James	ord	D 5th Sbr 99
	Jn° Small	Cr^t M^t	D
	Den^ss Clossier	Bo^t S^t	R 31 Dec 99
30th	Nicoll Whitbread	Gun^rs mt	D

[1] Discharged or released.

Originally thirty-two men and one boy entered. Nine of this number (including Halley and Surgeon Alfrey) had been on the first voyage, but one of these (Samuel Withers) was discharged and another (David Wishart) released before the vessel sailed. A total of ten men were discharged or released before the *Paramore* left the Thames, but one was picked up at Deal, so that twenty-four sailed. The boy Manly White was drowned on the 13th of October off Madeira; the next day William Gothern entered 'at sea'. Dennis Clossier and Peter Abber were released at Rio de Janeiro in December 1699, leaving twenty-two men aboard for the journey to Latitude 52½° South. On 4 March 1700, Thomas Greenhaugh was relieved as Midshipman, this position being taken over the next day by James Glenn. William Burch entered 13 March at St Helena, being discharged at Barbados on 22 May. An ordinary seaman William French entered at St Kitts, 28 May 1700. The Mate, Edward St Claire, was discharged at Bermuda on the 11th July, his place being taken by St George Tucker, who entered the next day. Two men, Henry Humphrys and William Gothern, were discharged at Gravesend before the ship docked at Deptford on 10 September.

WAGES BOOK – Extract cont.

ADM. 33/206 f.

		Sam^{ll} Withers	ord	D 5 } Sbr 99
		Gabr^{ll} Green	ord	R 11 } Sbr 99
Sbr.	6.	Jn° Mackintosh	Ab	R
Sbr.	6.	Robt Leonard	Able	D
		Wm Curtiss	Capt Clk	D
	8th	Edwd St Claire	M^{t}	D 11: July 1700
		Hen° Humphrys	ord	D 7. Sbr 1700
	11	Wm Small	Ab	D
		Edwd Jackson	ord	D 27: Sbr 99
	12	Peter Abber	Ab	R 29: Dbr 99
	17	Manly White	Capt S^{t}	DD 13: Obr 99
		Wm Lang	Chy^{r} S^{t}	D 24: May :1700
		Thom Greenhaugh	Midship^{m}	to ye 4th March 1700
		Tho: Fenn	Carp^{tr} S^{t}	D
	19	Wm Browne	Pyl^{t} Ex^{t}	D 21: Sbr 99
	28	Jos: Phillips	Ab.	D
Obr:	14	Wm Gothern	Able	D 7: Sbr 1700
Mar	13 1700	Wm Burch	Bo^{t} S^{t}	S 22 May 1700
May	28	Wm French	Ord^{r}	D
July	12	St Geo Tucker	M^{t}	D

[Signed] Edm: Halley
William Brewer

Nett Book

Parrimour Pinke
Began rigging wages 24 Augt 99
Sea d° – – 16 Sepr 99
Ended d° – – 18 d° 1700[1]
Then paid off in Broad Street 18 Septr 1700

[1] Of the full wages of £537. 3.10, Halley received £100.7.0; Surgeon Alfrey £67.3.8; Boatswain Brewer £28.7.0; the carpenter, Thomas Price £28.7.0; and the Mate, Edward St Claire, who was discharged at Bermuda, £23.2.4. No other crew member received more than this last figure, with the average per capita earnings of an Ab who made the whole voyage being about £16 for approximately twelve months service.

WAGES BOOK – Extract cont.

ADM. 33/206 f.

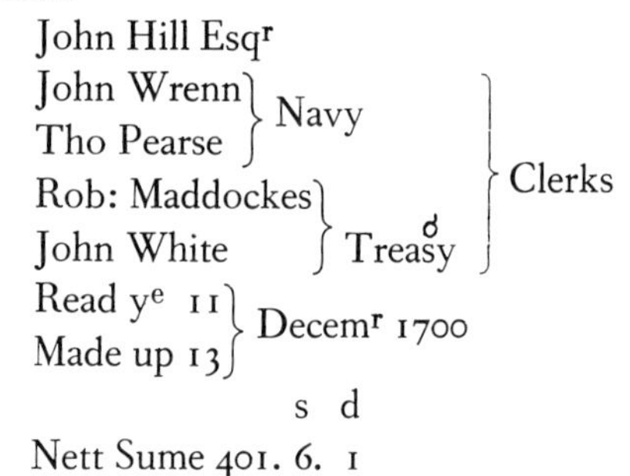

Present

John Hill Esqr

John Wrenn, Tho Pearse } Navy } Clerks

Rob: Maddockes, John White } Treas^{d}y } Clerks

Read y^{e} 11, Made up 13 } Decem^{r} 1700

s d

Nett Sume 401. 6. 1

92

[Burchett to Halley]

SECRETARY'S LETTER BOOK

ADM. 2 399 p 25

Adm^{ty} 19th Sep^{t} 1700.

S^{r}

I have rec^{d} your Lrs, and am sorry to finde the Paramore Pinke has such a tendincy to Leeward because I am apt to believe that quality in her, has put it out of your power to doe altogether soe much as otherwise you might have Pform'd.

There are Orders given for paiying her off; and thō my Lords doe not meet till tomorrow morning, yet I dare assure you that you will not offend in comeing to Towne; only lett me give you this Caution, To have ye Books in readiness and to attend at the payment of Vessell. I am

S^{r}

Yo^{r} very humble Servt

JB

Capt Halley – Paramore Pinke.

Deptford.

[Endorsed:] Is sorry his vessel has a Tendency to Leeward, he may come to Town with out offense.

93

[Halley to Sloane]

B.M. MS 4038 f. 82

Sr.

Having had the misfortune to omitt giving you notice of the favour I design my self on Munday night in enjoying your good company over a bottle of Wine, I now entreat you to forgive that neglect and that you will please to bestow your self on me at the usuall hour at the Kings Arms on Ludgate hill, as being a place in some respects more convenient for the Company and my self than at home:

I am Sr. Your most obedt. Servant

Edm: Halley.

Saturday morn
Octob. 26° 1700.

94

ROYAL SOCIETY JOURNAL BOOK

Vol. VIII p. 227

30 October 1700

Captain Hally produced a Map, and Shewed in it his Observation on the Variation of the Magnetick Needle which he rectified in the Chart, as it was curiously laid down with Marks etc in this Map.[1]

The same said he saw an Island of Ice, so high above the Sea, that they Saw it 7 Leagues off, in 52° South Lat. and they did not perceive it to move, so that they believed it to be fixed, tho they found no bottom when they Sounded Just by it, 140 fathoms[2] He was returned the Society's thanks for this Communication.

[1] This is probably the first reference to the Halleyan (Halleian) lines, or isogones as they became known later.

[2] Halley still had doubts about the character of the 'islands of ice' he had seen, but believed them to be fixed. He did not seem to have conjectured that these huge icebergs might be calved from some great unknown, larger body of ice to the south (Antarctica), nor that they might have floated a great distance.

95

ROYAL SOCIETY JOURNAL BOOK

Vol. VIII p. 234

27 November 1700

Capt Hally read an Account of Mr Patricks new Barometres and Thermometers.[1] The Same read his Report of Signr Albegettis Tables. And Dor Sloane was desired to Send him this report of Capt Hallys.

96

ROYAL SOCIETY JOURNAL BOOK

Vol. VIII p. 234

30 November 1700

An election of officers was held and: Mr. Charles Dubors Capt Edmund Hlly and Mr John Chile of Oxford were also balloted & Chosen Members of the Society.[2]

97

ROYAL SOCIETY JOURNAL BOOK

Vol. VIII p. 244

5 February 1701

Mr. Halley presented the Society with a Draught of the Course of a Comet in 1664/5 he was thanked. The Same Shewed a Map wherein was the Course they had held in his late Voyage and where were noted the Variations of the Needle in Several parts of the World; and also the true Longitudes & Latitudes of many places – he was thanked.

Mr. Halley Said that he saw a kind of Tortoises in the S: of Brasile,

[1] John Patrick, a London instrument maker with a great reputation for his thermometers and barometers. He published several broadsides on these instruments and their use and himself kept daily weather observations. Halley praised Patrick's work and may have used his instruments, one of which, a barometer, is now in the British Museum.

[2] Presumably Charles du Bois and John Keill, M.D., who were elected Fellows of the Royal Society 30 November 1700 (when Halley was reelected, having been first elected in 1678).

having Necks like Swans and all there Bodys under Water.[1] There was read an advertisement concerning the Latitude of the Lizard & Variation by Mr. Halley, he was thanked for this Communication which was Judged very useful to the publick.[2]

THE THIRD VOYAGE AND AFTERMATH

98
CAPTAINS LETTER BOOK
(Admiralty-Secretary. In-Letters)
ADM. 1. 1872

[No Address]
To the Right Honble the Lords Commiss^rs for Executing the Office of Lord High-Admirall of England.
It is humbly proposed

That if their Lopps shall think fitting to have an exact account of the Course of the Tides on and about the Coast of England, so taken as at one View to represent the whole; (which will be a work of generall use to all Shipping, especially such as have occasion to turn to Windward, and wch is wanting towards the compleating the Art of Navigation) there be provided a small Vessell such as their Lopps shall think proper, with all convenient speed, on board of which such an account of the Tides may be taken, as their Lopps shall direct; for which service their Lopps most obedient servant humbly offers himself.

Edm. Halley

Aprill 23°
1701.

[Minuted:]
Capt Edm^d Halleys Proposal for his taking an exact acc^t of the Tides about the Coast of England.

[1] It appears that Halley had now concluded that the creatures he first described in his Journal of the Second Voyage, 28 January 1700 as 'Severall of the Diveing birds with Necks like Swans', and portrayed and described on the Atlantic Chart in the sea off Patagonia, were tortoises (turtles). However two creatures are referred to in the Journal, and also on the map – but only one type portrayed, and one type described above. This confusion has led to interesting speculation on these creatures. See Journal of the Second Voyage, p. 160, and n. 1.

[2] See Journal of the Second Voyage, entry for 26 August 1700, p. 210.

99

[Halley to Burchett]

CAPTAINS LETTER BOOK

ADM. (Sec.-in-Letters)

[No Address]

Hon^rd^ S^r^

The Season of the Year advancing and Men being scarce, I humbly entreat my Commission to be dispatcht, in order to gett the Paramore Pink mann'd with such Compliment as their Lopps shall think fitting, which cannot be well less than it was the last time viz: 25 Men. She has been lately dockt & wants only rigging, which is but a little work. Two Boats and two spare Cables, for the small Bower and one spare Anchor, is all at present I can think may be needfull of Extraordinarys, being near at hand to be supplyed on occasion.

I am y^r^ Honours obd^t^ Servt
Edm. Halley.

Aprill 26°
1701

[Not Minuted]

100

LORDS LETTER BOOK

ADM. 2 181 p. 117

Adm^ty^ 26^t^ Aprill 1701

Gent^n^

Wee do hereby desire and direct you, to cause his Ma^t^ Pink the Paramour, at Deptford, to be forthwith Cleaned and fitted out to Sea for Channell Service, Man'd with Five and Twenty Men, and Victualled for three Monthes at whole allowance for the s^d^ Number of Men, or so much thereof as Shee can conveniently stow. And Captain Halley who is appointed to Comand the s^d^ Vessell having desired that Shee may be furnished with two Boates, and also two spare Cables for the small Bower, and one spare anchor Extraord^{ry} Wee do likewise desire and direct you to cause her to be supply'd therewith accordingly. Wee are

Navy Board. yor affect^{t} Friends.

P. H. DM.[1]

[Endorsed:] To ffitt ye Paramour Pink for Channell service Victuall'd for 3 mons for 25 men

101

LORDS LETTER BOOK

ADM. 2 181 p. 117

Usuall Letter to the Earle of Romney. M^{s} Genl of the Ordnance[2] to furnish the Paramour Pink with ye Ordnances Established on her, when in a condition to receive them, and a fitting proportion of Gunners Stores for Channell Service.

Dated & Sign'd as above.[3]

[Endorsed:] To furnish ye Param^{r} pk wth Gunns & Gun^{rs} Stores

102

COMMISSION AND WARRANT BOOK

ADM. 6/6 f. 91 verso

Commission for Capt Edmond halley to be Master and Comander of his Ma^{tt} Pink the Paramour Dated &^{c} 26th Aprile 1701

P. DM. GC.[4]
By &c JB

[1] Thomas Herbert, Earl of Pembroke and Montgomery, First Lord of the Admiralty; Sir John Thompson, Baronet, Lord Haversham; Vice Admiral Sir David Mitchell.

[2] See Document 31, p. 268, and n. 3.

[3] Refers to Document 100, pp. 318-9.

[4] Thomas Herbert, Earl of Pembroke and Montgomery, First Lord of the Admiralty; Vice Admiral Sir David Mitchell; George Churchill.

103

NAVY BOARD MINUTES. Vol. 44

Monday Morning 28th Aprill 1701
Another [Admiralty Order] of the do. 26th for causeing the Paramore Pink to be clean'd & fitted for Channell Service Mann'd with 25 Men, & Victualld for 3 Months, as also supplyed with two Boates, two spare Cables for the small Bower, & one spare anchor extraord[y] – Give Orders therein to the Officers at Deptford, & to the Com[rs] of the Vict[g].

104

[Halley to Burchett]

CAPTAINS LETTER BOOK

ADM. (Sec.-in-Letters)

To the Hon[b]
[Address:] Mr. Burchett
These
present

Hon[rd] S[r]

The Paramore Pink being so far fitted as to be ready to saile, if my Compliment of men were ready, I beseech you to lay before their Lopps the great difficulty I find to gett them, no men now offering themselves as usuall at other times. Eight or ten able hands before the Mast, is all I want necessarily, and I humbly hope that so small a demand will meet with no difficulty: The advanced Season of the Year makes me the more sollicitous in this matter.

I am
Your Hon[rs] most obed[t] Serv[t]
[29 April 1701] Edm. Halley

[Minuted:]
June 1701[1]
Capt Edm[d] Halley avis[th] of the Paramore Pink being ready to sail and desires he may be furnished with men

[1] No day is recorded for this late minuting.

105

LORDS LETTER BOOK

ADM. 2 181 p. 125

Admty 6 May 1701

Gentn

In obedience to His Mats Commands signified to this Board, Wee do hereby desire and direct you to cause to be be paid unto Captn Edward[1] Halley, out of the Money in the hands of the Treas of the Navy, upon Acct of the Tenths of Prizes[2] the Sum of two Hundred Pounds in consideration of his great Paines and care in the late Voyage he made for the discovering the Variation of the Needle. Wee are

Yrs &c.

N Board

P: DM: GC:[3]

[Endorsed:] To pay £200 to Capt Halley out of ye Tenths of prizes

106

ROYAL SOCIETY JOURNAL BOOK

Vol. VIII p. 256

7 May 1701

Mr. Halley tryed the Experiment of the Variation of the Needle this day with the two needles which he had with him on his late Voyage;[4] And by the one the Variation was 7° 40′ and by the other 8° 00′ W.

[1] *Sic.*

[2] This was a fund which arose from the balance of money received from the sale of captured vessels after certain prescribed allocations had been made.

[3] Thomas Herbert, Earl of Pembroke and Montgomery, First Lord of the Admiralty; Vice Admiral Sir David Mitchell; George Churchill.

[4] See Document 25, p. 265.

107
NAVY BOARD MINUTES. Vol. 44

Wednesday Morning 7th May 1701
Admty Ordr of the 5th for paying to Capt Edmd Halley out of the tenths of Prizes the sum of 200 in consideracon of his great paines & care in a late Voyage he made for the discovering the Variation of the Needle – Give a Copy to Mr Lyddell.[1]

108
NAVY BOARD MINUTES. Vol. 44

Monday Morning 12th May 1701
Capt Halley's lre of this day read, and Mr Erles appointed Chyrurgeon of the Paramore Pink according to his recomendacon.[2]

109
ROYAL SOCIETY JOURNAL BOOK
Vol. VIII p. 257
14 May 1701

Mr Halley Said, that ye Needle with a Counterpoise, he thought usefull in observing the Variations in these parts of the World where the Needle Dips, and that it Observ's more Exactly than the other sort of Needle.[3]

[1] Actually the order seems to have been dated 6 May rather than the 5 May as here indicated; see Document 105, p. 321. Dennis Liddell was Controller of the Treasurer's Accounts.

[2] As before, Halley requested a particular surgeon but made no other specific recommendations concerning personnel.

[3] Magnetic dip refers to the characteristic of the magnetized needle to incline from the horizontal to a greater or lesser degree according to locality. The phenomenon was described by Robert Norman in his *Newe Attractive* (1581), in which he indicated that he compensated for the dip by weighting the raised side of the needle with wax to make it horizontal. Later it was thought that the degree of inclination or dip of the needle might be used for finding the longitude if the latitude were known. Tables were compiled giving the dip at various places, but the method failed because of inadequate data and the difficulty of measuring the degree of inclination accurately. Actually the third use to which the isoline was put, after the isobath and the isogone, was to show the degree of dip of the magnetic needle, i.e. the isocline.

110

[Halley to Burchett]

CAPTAINS LETTER BOOK

(Admiralty-Secretary. In-Letters)

ADM. 1. 1872

[Address:] To the Honbl Mr Secretary
Burchett
humbly present

Honrd. Sr.

I have attended my Ld Lucas[1] according to their Lopps order, and find that his order of Councell for pressing Seamen has been discharged some time since. If their Lopps shall think fitting to spare me but two able Seamen out of four or five of the Ships of Warr, I will take care to return them where I had them in case the breaking out of a war oblige me to desist from my undertaking.

I am
Your Honrs most obedt Servt
Edm. Halley.

Maii 31°
1701
[Minuted:]
31 May 1701
Capt Edmd Halley for a supply of Able Seamen

111

[Burchett to Halley]

SECRETARY'S LETTER BOOK

ADM. 2 400 p. 223

Admty 31 May 1701

Sr

Your Lettr of this day has been comunicated to my Lords of the Admty, in answer whereto I have only to acqt you that their Lordps have directed

[1] Presumably Charles, Lord Lucas, who was Governor of the Tower of London under King William III. He was removed from this office on the accession of Queen Anne, J. Macky, *Memoirs of the secret services of John Macky, Esq.* (London, 1733), pp. 83–4.

Capt. Pichard Com^dr of the Namure[1] at Blackstakes to discharge into the Vessell under your Command to serve therein, those prest men which he has, according as you will find by the Inclosed, Lett^r which you will Send to Captn Pichard for the purpose So I remaine S^r Y^r &c

JB

Capt. Halley – Paramour Pink
In Towne

112

[Burchett to Captain Pichard – Namur]

SECRETARY'S LETTER BOOK

ADM. 2 400 p. 223

Adm^ty 31 May 1701

S^r

Your Lett^r of yesterday has been laid before my Lords of the Adm^ty and in answer thereto I am to Acq^t you, that 'tis the direction of their Lord^ps you do discharge the 3 Prest Men you have aboard the ship under your Com^d into his Maj^ts Pink the Paramour, Captn Halley Com^dr to serve therein and you are to give them Ticketts for the time of their Service So I remaine

S^r Y^r &^c
JB

Cap^tn Pichard
Namure[2] – Blackstakes

113

[Burchett to Halley]

SECRETARY'S LETTER BOOK

ADM. 2 400 p. 238

Adm^ty 4° June 1701

Gent^n/

My Lords of the Adm^ty Comand me to signifie their directions to you, that from the Ships you Command, you do spare Captn Halley of the

[1] *Namur*, 2nd rate, 90 guns; 1,442 bm, 161 × 46 ft, Woolwich D.Y. 28.4. 1697. Rebuilt at Deptford in 1729 as 1,567 bm. Wrecked 14.4.1749 in the East Indies. Colledge, 1, p. 376.

[2] See n. 1 above.

Paramoure Pink, so many Men as he shall have occasion of and Shall be willing to enter and serve with him. I am

Gentn Ys &c

JB

Captns of the Namure & Somerettt[1]

114

ROYAL SOCIETY JOURNAL BOOK

Vol. VIII p. 260

4 June 1701

Mr. Halley presented the Society with a Map of his late Voyage to the South, He was thanked for it and it was ordered to be hung up in the meeting room[2]

115

[Halley to Burchett]

CAPTAINS LETTER BOOK

(Admiralty-Secretary. In-Letters)

ADM. 1. 1872

[Address:] To the Honr
Mr Secretary Burchett
humbly present

Honrd. Sr.

I find myself disappointed in my Mate, who for great wages has been tempted to break his promise with me: and for 40 sh. p month I fear I cannot have a man capable to take charge of my Shipp, Marchants giving

[1] *Somersett*, 3rd Rate, 80 guns, 1,263 bm, 158 × 42½ ft. Chatham D.Y. 1698. Hulked 1715. BU 7. 1740 at Woolwich, Colledge, 1, p. 515. For *Namur* see p. 324, n. 1.

[2] This was presumably the Atlantic magnetic variation Chart with tracks of Halley's Second Voyage complete with dedication to King William III (See Figure 7 and Atlantic Chart in portfolio) but lacking the Description (Appendix D). It is particularly unfortunate that this map, one of the most important in the history of cartography, is no longer in the archives of the Royal Society which sponsored the project.

now so much to any able Seaman.[1] I humbly hope their Lopps will think it reasonable to allow me a warranted Master, well acquainted with the Channell in lieu of a Mate; and that they please likewise to give me leave to have out of the Shipps of Warr, under such restriction as their Lopps please, such men as shall be willing to serve on board me.

I am

June 4°
1701

Yr Honrs most obedt Servant
Edm. Halley

[Minuted:]
4 June 1701
Capt Edmd Halley signifys his being dissappointed of a mate & desires to be allowed a warranted mastr acquaintd with ye Chanel & be supplyd with such men out of the Men of War as are willing to go with him

116

[Burchett to Halley]

SECRETARY'S LETTER BOOK

ADM. 2 400 p. 250

Admty 9° June 1701

Sr/

When you did lately attend My Lords of the Admiralty you desired that you might have liberty to Hire a Pylott from time to time skilled in the Coast, the better to enable you to carry on your intended designe of observing the Setting of the Currents and other things remarkable in the Channell, to which their Lordps were then pleased to consent, and by their command I do hereby lett you know, that when you shall at any time find a want of an able Pylott, you are at liberty to hire such a one and to pay them our of the Mony remaineing in your hands that was formerly Imprested to you and their Lordps do not doubt that you will be as good a Husband therein for his Mastie as tis possible.[2]

I am

Sr Yr &c.

JB

Capt Haley – Paramore Pink

[1] A continuing complaint in the Service.

[2] On 12 July Peter St Croix, a pilot of Jersey, was picked up at St Hilary and served until 8 September. See Journal of the Third Voyage, p. 230, and Document 133, p. 341.

117

[Halley to Burchett]

CAPTAINS LETTER BOOK

(Admiralty-Secretary. In-Letters)

ADM 1. 1872

To the Honble
[Address:] Mr Secretary
Burchett
humbly present

Hon^rd^ S^r^

Being now in a condition to saile I addresse my self to your Honr: for the Instructions their Lopps please to give me; amongst which with all submission I entreat that these or to the same purpose may be inserted.

You are to use all possible diligence in observing the Course of the Tides in the Channell of England as well in the mid sea as on both Shores, and to inform your self of the precise times of High and Low Water; of the sett and strength of the Flood and Ebb and how many feet it flows in as many places as may suffice to describe the whole. And where there are irregular and half Tides to be more than ordinarily curious in observing them. You are likewise to take the true barings of the principall head lands on the English Coast one from another, and to continue the Meridian as often as conveniently may be from side to side of the Channell, in order to lay down both coasts truly against one another.[1]

What else their Lopps please to enjoyne me, I shall as is my duty perform to the best of my power, being

Your Hon^rs^ most obed^t^ serv^t^

June 11°
1701
Edm. Halley

[1] It has been suggested that this part of the mission was an intelligence operation designed to assist the Royal Navy in the impending war with France (Ronan, 1969, p. 185). This may be so, although a statement in Halley's Orders and Instructions seems to negate this idea unless by 'other Princes' (Document 119, p. 329), is meant allies: 'And in case dureing your being employed on this Service, any other Matters may Occur unto you the observing and Publishing whereof may tend towards the Security of the Navigation of the Subjects of his Maj^tie^ or other Princes tradeing into the Channell you are to be very careful in the takeing notice thereof.' However a statement in Halley's letter to Sir Robert Southwell, 'If it be an enemys Coast or otherwise inaccessible . . .' (Document 131 p. 339) might confirm the security hypothesis and suggest some intelligence activity.

Minuted:]

11th June 1701

Capt Edm[d] Halley advis[th] of his being ready to sail desires his Instructions and proposes what he thinks is proper to be added to them.

118

ROYAL SOCIETY JOURNAL BOOK

Vol. VIII p. 261

11 June 1701

Some foreigners were permitted to be present to whom Mr. Hally Shew'd and explained the Map of his late Voyage.

119

[Halley's Third Voyage]

ORDERS AND INSTRUCTIONS

ADM. 2 27 pp. 131–2.

Whereas his Majestys pink the Paramour is particularly fitted out and Put under your Command that you may proceed with her, and observe the Course of the Tydes in the Channel of England, and other things remarkable you are therefore hereby required and directed to proceed with the Said Vessel and use your Utmost care and Diligence in observing the Course of the Tydes accordingly as well in the Midsea as on both Shores As also the Precise times of High and Low Water of the Sett and Strength of the Flood and Ebb, and how many feet it flows, in as many, and at such certain places, as may suffice to describe the whole. And whereas in many places in the Channell there are Irregular and half Tydes you are in a particular Manner to be very careful in observing them.

And you are also to take the true bearings of the Principal head Lands on the English Coast one from another and to continue the Meridian as often as conveniently you can from Side to Side of the Channell, in order to lay down both Coasts truly against one another.

And in case dureing your being employed on this Service, any other Matters may Occur unto you the observing and Publishing whereof may tend towards the Security of the Navigation of the Subjects of his Maj^{tie} or other Princes tradeing into the Channell you are to be very carefull in the takeing notice thereof. And when you Shall have Performed what Service you can, with relation to the particulars before mentioned, you are to return with the Ship you Command into the River of Thames, giving us from time to time an Account of your Proceedings.

Dated this 12° June 1701.

To Capt^{tn} Edm^{d} Halley
Comd^{r} of his Maj^{ties}
Pink the Paramour

[Minuted:] Instructions for observing the Course of the Tides &c in the English Channell.

120

[Halley to Burchett]

CAPTAINS LETTER BOOK

(Admiralty-Secretary. In-Letters)

ADM 1. 1872

[Address:] To the Hon^{bl}
Josiah Burchett Esqr
Secretary to the Admiralty
of England &c
These
humbly present

Downs June 18° 1701

Hon^{ored} S^{r}

I arrived in the Downs on Monday last, and have to day gotten an order from the Admirall[1] for the four men their Lopps have appointed me

[1] Rear Admiral Sir John Munden, who had been knighted only a few days earlier.

here; They will be delivered me this night, and with them I shall be enabled to proceed according to their Lopps Instructions designing to sayle to morrow morning. I shall not fayle to give your Honr: an account of my proceedings as occasion shall offer, being

Your Honrs most obedt servt
Edm. Halley

Paramore Pink
Downs
[Minuted:]
18 June 1701
Capt Halley adviseth of his arrival shall be supplyd by the Admiral with 4 men ordered him & will sail ye next morning

121

ROYAL SOCIETY JOURNAL BOOK

Vol. VIII p. 263

18 June 1701

The Vice presidt [Sir John Hoskins] informed the Society that Mr. Hally was gon on a new Voyage, as he heard havg designed to make nice Observations on the Tides and Currents in the Channel, for the Improvement of Navigation that thereby by their different times, the going out of the Channel might be more easy against Contrary winds. Sir Robt Southwell[2] said that Sr Richd Ruth had sailed so often from England & Ireland that by his knowledge in the Tides Currents and Head-Lands, he could sail to England when nobody else could.

[1] See Document 131, pp. 338–40.

122

[Halley to Burchett]

CAPTAINS LETTER BOOK

(Admiralty-Secretary. In-Letters)

ADM. 1. 1872

[Address:]

To the Honble

Josiah Burchett Esqr
Secretary to the Admiralty
of England &c
humbly present
London

Spitt head July 29° 1701

Honoured S^r^

In obedience to their Lopps orders, I have since I left the Downs on the 19th of June, endeavoured to gett as exact an account of the Tides in the Channell as possible, and have ankered all over it, from the Forland to Portland, and from Blackness to the Casketts on the French side: and I have been particularly curious in this part between the Isle of Wight and Portland and the French Coast against it, where I find the Course of the Tides very extraordinary, but which I think I can describe effectually. I have been of late putt from my business by hard gales of Wind which drove me in hither, but still hope by the end of the Summer to give their Lopps a full account of the whole Channell, if not interrupted by the breaking out of Warr, which I find is suddainly expected here.[1] If their Lopps have any further orders for me, I shall call in at Plymouth for them, designing to saile hence as this day, and to tide it down, if the weather permitt it.

I am
Your Honours most obed^t^ Servt
Edm. Halley

[Minuted:]
Spitthead. 29 July 1701

Capt Edm^d^ Halley's Acc^t^ of proceedings in taking an acc^t^ of ye Tides in the Chanell – is forced in here by foul weather

[1] The War of the Spanish Succession did not become a general conflagration until the spring of 1702.

123
ROYAL SOCIETY JOURNAL BOOK
Vol. VIII p. 271
30 July 1701

A letter was read from Mr. Hally at Guernsey of the 18 July giving an Account of the Weather having been fair for a Month past, he had made good progress in the designs he had in making his Voyage

124
[Halley to Burchett]
CAPTAINS LETTER BOOK
(Admiralty-Secretary. In-Letters)
ADM. 1. 1872

[No Address]

Paramore pink at Dartmouth. Aug 23° 1701.

Honoured S[r]

By my last of July 29° from Spitthead I gave you an account that I had carefully observed the Course of the Tides in the Eastern part of the Channell of England; since then I have lost no opportunity, in order to do the like for the Western part, and I have ankered all along the English Coast in the Offing as far as the Lizard, and from thence in the midd Channell, and over to Ushant, where I was the last week. The frequent weighing my ankers in so deep water has been very hard service to my small company, but the greatest difficulty I find, is from the frequent gales of Wind, which, (especially without the Start) raise the sea to that degree that there is no riding, and which, in this month of August, have forced me four severall times into Harbour. I waite here for an opportunity of smooth weather, to anker in severall places between the Start and the Sept Isles; wherby I shall be able to compleat the sett of observations necessary to the description of the Tides in the Offing; of which I cannot find any of our books to give a tollerable account. When I return from the French coast, I entend to putt in to Spitthead, to receive any farther orders their Lopps may think proper for me. With my humble duty to their Lopps I remain

Your Honrs most obedt Servant
Edm. Halley.

[Not Minuted]

125

[Halley to Burchett]

CAPTAINS LETTER BOOK

(Admiralty-Secretary. In-Letters)

ADM. 1. 1872

[Address:]
To the Honble
Josiah Burchett Esqr
Secretary the Admiralty of England &c
London. These
humbly present

Paramore pink at Spithead Sept 13° 1701

Honoured Sr

These may serve to acquaint you that having observed the Course of the Tides in the Western part of the Channell, and my provision being almost spent, I came in here on the 11th Instant to recruite, and yesterday I received a months provision, with which I am going this morning to saile, to observe some particulars, which the circonstances of the Winds would not suffer me to do as I past down. I am in hopes I shall be so fortunate as to please their Lopps in this Summer expedition, wherin I have discovered, beyond my expectation, the generall rule of the Tides in the Channell; and in many things corrected the Charts therof. Before this Months provision expires the winter session will oblige me to return, hoping from yr Honour a favourable acceptance of the endeavours of

Honrd Sr Your most obedt. Servt.
Edm. Halley.

[Minuted:]
Paramore: Pink – Spith
13 Sept 1701
Capt Halley adviseth of his proceeding & of his comming here to recruit his provisions

126

[Halley to Burchett]

CAPTAINS LETTER BOOK

(Admiralty-Secretary. In-Letters)

ADM. 1. 1872

To the Honble

[Address:]

Josiah Burchett Esqr
Secretary to the
Admiralty
of England &c
humbly present
Admiralty Office

Paramore Pink in Long reach
Octob 2°. 1701

Honored S^{r}

Finding the season of the year too far lapsed to ride at anchor in the Channell; in persuance of their Lopps orders, I came into the River of Thames last night, and am at present moored in this place, where I waite their Lopps farther pleasure, hoping they please to allow me the Liberty to waite on them to render them an account of my Summers Expedition.

I am
Your Honours most obed^{t} Servt
Edm: Halley

[Minuted:]
Paramore Pink – Long^{r}
2 Ober 1701
Capt Edm^{d} Halley advisth of his arrival & waits further orders

127

LORDS LETTER BOOK

ADM. 2 181 p. 298

Adm^{ty} 2^{d} October 1701

Gent^{n}

Wee do hereby desire and direct you to cause his Ma^{ts} Ships the

Harwich and Roebuck,[1] and the Paramour Pink; which Pink is ordered up to Deptford to be forthwith pay'd off; but you are not to pay the Capt of the Roebuck his Wages till further Orders. Wee are

Navy Board.

Y^r^ &c. H. DM GC

[Endorsed:] To pay Harwich – Roebuck & Paramour Pink at Deptford but not to pay ye Capt of ye Roebuck till further Ord^r^

128

LORDS LETTER BOOK

ADM. 2 181 p. 298

The usuall letter to ye Earle of Romney[2] for taking ashoar the Paramour Pinks Gunns and Gunners Stores upon her arrivall at Gallions Reach Dated ye 2^d^ October 1701

[Endorsed:] Take ashoar ye Param^r^ Pink's Gunn &^c^

[1] *Roebuck* was a fireship of 1690, which became a 6th rate in 1695. Under Dampier's command she sank off Ascension Island, 22 February 1701. The crew stayed on the Island until 3 April when they were picked up by a convoy of warships and Eastindiamen bound for England. Mr Alan Pearsall suggested to the writer that the reference above may be to Dampier's crew. His lieutenant George Fisher, who had been incarcerated in Bahia, arrived in England before Dampier, where a Court Martial awaited the Captain. The court declared in favour of the lieutenant, and Dampier lost three years pay and terminated his naval career for a time although later he was reinstated.

[2] See Document 31, p. 268, n. 3

129

WAGES BOOK – Extract

ADM. 33/202 f.

26 Apl. 1701 to 16 Oct 1701

Paramore Pink Comp^{t} 24 men[1]

Entry	Mens Names	Quality	D or R[2]
Apr. 30 1701	Edm. Halley	Comand^{r}	
30	Richd Price	Boatsw^{n}	
May 5	Saml Pitts	able	
6	Mark Taylor	Boats Mate	
9	Charles Lucas	Boats Servt	
	Wm Tayler	Ord to 9 July. able	
12	Richd Stephens	able	
20	Wm Erles	Chirug^{on}	
29	Richd Cole	Carp^{t}	
	Wm Wright	Carp^{t} Servt	
	Moses Cathness	Chirug Servt	
June 4	Richd Pinfold[3]	Capt. Clerke	
	Thomas Cook	Cook	
7	James Calverly	} Comd^{r}	
	John Davis	} Servts	
14	John Rawlins	ord	
	Rich Davis	Mate	
	John Bradbury	Q. Master	
	Peter Drane	able	
19	Henry Bayly	Carp^{t} Mate	
	Alexander Jones	able	
	Job: Fake	Midssip Man	
	John Onyon	able	

[signed] Edmond Halley
Richard Price

[1] Although twenty-five men were allowed by the Lords letter dated 26 April 1701 (Document 100, p. 318), twenty-three are listed in the Wages Book. Halley picked up a pilot, Peter St Croix, in Jersey on July 12, 1701 so that, at most, twenty-four were aboard the *Paramore* for the Channel survey.

[2] None discharged or released before the crew was paid off.

[3] Other than Halley, the only name on the wage lists of all three voyages is Richard Pinfold. He was classified as a Captain's Servant and sailed on the third voyage, being first classified as 'Guner Mate' which is crossed out and 'Capt. Clerke' substituted.

WAGES BOOK – Extract cont.

ADM. 33/202 f.

Paramore Pink

Began Rigging Wages	26 Aprill 1701 –
Sea D° – — — ——	14 June 1701 –
Ended Wages[1] —— —— ——	16 Octor 1701 –

Then paid off at Broad street

Present

John Hill Esqr

Jn° Wrenn, Tho: Pearse	Navy	Clerks
R: Maddocks, C: Maddocks	Treary	

£142:8:1 Neat Summ paid

130

ROYAL SOCIETY JOURNAL BOOK

Vol. VIII p. 279

12 November 1701

Mr. Halley shewed a New Draught of the Channel of England, as lately observed by him And the Motion of the Sea thereof.[2]

[1] Of the full wages of £142:8:1 in total for the voyage, Halley received only three shillings at the payoff (he was recompensed later). Surgeon Erles received £24.0.4; Boatswain Price, £12.5.10; the carpenter, Cole, £10.3.11; the mate, Davis, £9.7.6. No other crew member received more than this last figure, with the average per capita earnings of an Ab being about £6.0.0 for some five months service.

[2] This was probably the manuscript of what became the Channel Chart (see two-sheet Channel Chart in porfolio, and Figure 9), which was not published before 20 May 1702.

131

ROYAL SOCIETY COLLECTANEA NEWTONIANA

Vol. IV (Ne. 4 27)

27 January 1701/2[1]

[Address:] From Captain Halley
to Sr R. Southwell:
About taking the Survey of
a Coast

Honourd Sr.

In obedience to your Commands I have endeavoured to draw up such plain directions for making the Survey of a Coast, as may be serviceable to any that have the will and opportunity to describe curiously any Shoals they are acquainted with:

In order to this Survey of a Sea coast and to lay down truly the shoals and dangers near it, if the land be accessible the best way will be to take with all possible care the true positions of as many remarkable objects such as Steeples, Mills, Rocks, Cliffs, Promontorys, or such like as you find most conspicuous along the Coast, that is their true barings from one another in respect of the true North and South; which is best done by measuring the angle with any proper instrumt. from the rising or setting sun, allowing his amplitude and according to the exactness of these angles will your survey be more or less true. I preferr this method of taking these angles by the Sunn rather than by the Compass or magneticall needle, because of the smalness of the radius of the Magneticall chart and the uncertainty of the variation on the Lands, the needle being affected with the neighbourhood of Iron Oars and Mineralls.

This done you may readily plott down all those objects on the Land, by any view of them from a vessell riding at Anchor off at Sea; for if you take their true position from your shipp, by help of the rising or setting Sunn as before, the intersections of those lines with those of the positions of the objects to one another, will give you the places and proportionall distances of the sd Objects one from another, to which afterwards a scale may be adapted, as shall be taught by and by.

[1] This important manuscript letter from Halley (autograph) to Sir Robert Southwell, President of the Royal Society (1690–5), is in answer to a request from the latter for a report regarding surveying of coasts. This letter with diagram annexed was bought from the Southwell sale at Sotheby's by the Royal Society in May 1809 from the collection of James Stewart, Esq., F.S.S.

Being thus assured of the plott of severall objects on the shore, it will be very easy to lay down the points of any sand or shole, or any sunk rock on that Coast, either by the position of two or more of those objects, from a vessell riding at those points; or more compendiously and easily by taking the angles between those objects, at the said places entended to be laid down in your platt. That this may be the better understood, take the following Scheme. On the Coast to be described Let A be a steeple, B a Mill, C a Rock D a remarkable Tree, E a steep Cliff &c. and lett each of them be seen from some other of the objects, and their positions truly taken. for example Let B bear from A West 12°. Northerly; C from B, W 30°. Southerly, D from C W. 20°. N. and E from A W 2°. Southerly. This done at a convenient distance off at Sea as at ⇞, let the position of A be North 20° Easterly, B. N 2° East, C. N 22° ½ W or NNW, D. N 40° W and E. N 53 West. I say the true platt of the aforesd places A, B, C, D, E &c. will be as in the Scheme, although as yet we know not the reall distances of them, and wee may use them with certainty to lay down any other places in their true position. As for example, let there be a shole at one end whereof E bares NNW and C, NE; this being protracted, tis plain tis at F that that point of the shole ought to be laid down. At the other end of the same shole which wee will call G, for want of the Sunn, wee can only take the angle DGB 60 degrees & the angle CGA 80 degrees, I say the point G will be nicely determined therby. For if the angle BDH be made 30 degrees or the Complement of DGB, and DH=BH, the arch of the Circle DBG described with the radius DH and center H, shall be such that wherever you take the point G therin the angle BGD shall be 60 degrees. In like manner makeing the Angle ACK 10 degrees the arck of the Circle AGC whose center is K passing through A and C, shall in all its points G make the angle AGC 80 degrees, and consequently the Intersection of those two Arches is the point G sought; this is demonstrated from 20.3. Euclid: the angle at the Circonference of a Circle being half of that at the Center. This is a very easy and expeditious way for putting down the soundings in Sea Charts in their proper places, and may be practisd in a shipp under saile.

If it be an enemys Coast or otherwise inaccessible, it will be necessary to make use of two Shipps or Boats, as two Stations, wherby to obtain the position of the objects on shore; which afterwards you may use as before. After your chart is made, you may adapt a scale to it, by help of the motion of Sound, which has been accurately tried both in England and France, and it is certain that sounds be they great or small move at the motion of Sound, which has been accurately tried both in England and France, and it is certain that sounds be they great or small move at the rate of a marine League in 15 seconds of time: and in still weather a gunn may be heard a great way, especially before a gentle gale of wind, and this I propose and recommend as a very usefull method of determining distances in these Hydrographicall Surveys. I shall be very willing further to explain any thing herin, that may appear obscure or difficult.

I am Your Honrs. most obedt. Servt.

Edm. Halley

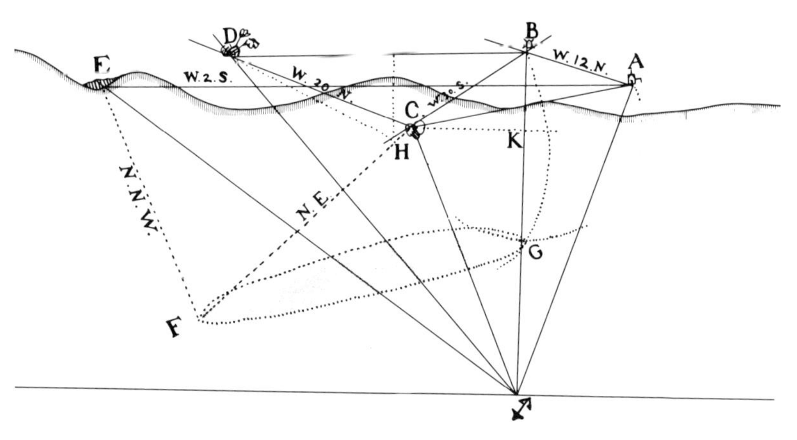

London 27 Jan. 1701/2.

132

[Burchett to Halley]

SECRETARY'S LETTER BOOK

ADM. 2 402 p 140

Admty 17 ffebry 1701/2

Sr/

I desire you will give me an opportunity of speaking with you tomorrow Morning between Eleaven and Twelve a Clock, I am

Sr

Yor &c JB

Captn Edmd Halley

133

[Halley to Burchett]

CAPTAINS LETTER BOOK

(Admiralty-Secretary. In-Letters)

ADM. 1. 1872

Paramore Pinks Acc[t] of Impres[t] Money

An Account of Monies expended for his Ma[tis] Govt. on board the Paramore Pink by Edm. Halley Comd. in three severall Voiages in the years 1698. 1699. 1700 & 1701.

viz

By presents to severall Portuguese Governors and Officers at St. Jago, Paraiba, Rio Jennero and Pernambouc at the prime coast	13.	16.	0.
P[d] severall Portuguese Pilots at Paraiba, Rio Jennero and Pernambouc	5.	17.	0
P[d] severall Coopers at severall times for trimming our Cask	1.	14.	8.
P[d] severall Caulkers for caulking our Decks and Upper-works at Bermodas in July 1700	4.	6.	4
P[d] then refreshing the paint of our Carvd work	0.	10.	2
P[d] Samll: Day Esqre: Governour of Bermudas for a small Anchor wt 315 lb wt: as per Voucher	7.	17.	0
P[d] Zachary Briggs Pilot, of Bermudas	2.	2.	8.
P[d] for Timber for a small Anchor stock	0.	5.	0
P[d] Peter St. Croix pilot of Jersey for 58 days service on board the Pink last summer in the Channell as p Voucher	11.	10.	0
Totall	47.	18.	10.

And wheras the late Lords Commiss[rs] of the Admiralty were pleasd to pay me 100 li Imprest money, it appears that there still remains 52 li thereof in my hands. But I humbly hope his Excellency my Ld High Admirall will please to consider the smallness of my wages in my late Channel cruise ammounting not to 50 li in the whole.

Edm. Halley

Feb. 18°
1701/2
[Minuted:]
18 Feb 1701
Capt Edm^{d} Halleys Acc^{t} of Disbursm^{t} in the Paramore Pink

134

LORDS LETTER BOOK

ADM. 2 182 p. 51

Admiralty 20th Feb^{ry} 1701/2

Gent^{n}

Captain Edm^{d} Halley late Comander of the Paramour Pink, having acquainted me that hee has not yet received his pay for his two last voyages; and for as much as he is not esteem'd as a Captain in the Navy,[1] but only Employd by Particular Order from his Majesty for the Improvement of Navigation; I do therefore hereby desire and direct you to cause him to be forthwith pay'd the Wages due to him for the time he Comanded the said Vessell provided he has pass^{d} his Acc^{ts} but if he has not, that then he be payd as soon as he has done the same. I am

Yours &c. P[2]

Navy Board.

[Endorsed:] Pay Capt Halley his Wages

135

LORDS LETTER BOOK

ADM. 2 182 p. 51/52

Adm^{lty} 20th Feb^{ry} 1701/2

Gent^{n}

Capt Halley late Comander of the Param^{r} Pink who has been Employd by particular Order from his Majesty for the Improvement of Navigation,

[1] That is, not a regular Captain in the Royal Navy.
[2] Thomas Herbert, Earl of Pembroke and Montgomery, Lord High Admiral of England, an office to which he had been appointed on 26 January, 1701/2.

having lay'd before me an Acco^{t} of the disbursements he has made out of the one hundred pounds formerly impressed to him for ye better carrying on of his bussiness, I send you inclosed a Copy of the said Acco^{t}, amounting in the whole unto seven and fforty pounds eighteen shillings and ten pence, and have directed him to deliver to yor Board what Vouchers he has for the Same: I do therefore hereby desire and direct you to consider of the said Acc^{t} and to allow thereof if you Judge it reasonable But if not, you are then to Report to me your opinion thereupon, in order to my considering of the Same, and giving Such further Orders therein as shall be thought ffitting.

I am Yours etc. P[1]

Navy Board

[Endorsed:] Pay Capt Halleys Bill of Expenses or Report their opinion of it

136
NAVY BOARD MINUTES, Vol. 46.

Monday Morning 23rd February 1701/2

Lord High Admirall's[1] Ord^{r} of the 20th for paying Capt Edmond Halley late Commander of the Paramour Pink the Wages due to him for the time he Commanded her provided he has passed his acc^{ts} – Give a Copy to Mr Lyddell.[2]

Lord High Admirall's Ord^{r} of the 20th incloseing an account of Capt Halley's Disbursments amounting to 47, 18.10 (L s d), and directing us to allow thereof if Wee judge reasonable, but if not, to report our opinion thereupon – Give a copy of it with the said account to Mr Lyddell. Another of the 21st for causeing the Paramore Pink to be fitted & Mann'd as Wee proposed to attend on the Muster Master of the ffleet & Victuall'd from time to time in the same manner as the shipps of the Fleet – send a Warrant to the Officers at Deptford to fitt her, & to the Com^{r} of the Victualling to Victuall her accordingly, & Give a Copy of the Order to Mr Lydell.

[1] Thomas Herbert, Earl of Pembroke and Montgomery, Lord High Admiral of England.
[2] Dennis Liddell, Controller of the Treasurer's Accounts.

137

LORDS LETTER BOOK

ADM. 2 182 pp. 85/86

Admrlty 11th March 1701/2

Gentn

I have considered of your Letter of the 20th of the last Month with the state of the Accot of Disbursements made by Capt Halley late Commander of the Paramour pink out of the money Imprested to him: and I do hereby desire and direct you to cause him to be allow'd such part of the said Disbursements as are rightly vouched, as also the thirteen pounds sixteen Shillings and six pence charged in ye said Acct, for severall presents to Portugues Governours and Officers at St. Iago &c.

I am

Yours &c

P[1]

Navy Board.

[Endorsed:] To allow Capt Halley his disbusements

138

NAVY BOARD MINUTES, Vol. 46.

Satturday 14th March 1701/2

Lord High Admirall's Ordr of the 11th to allow Capt Halley late Commander of the Paramore Pink such part of his Disbursements as are rightly vouch'd, as alow the £13.16.6[2] charged by him for Presents to severall Portuguese Governs & Offrs at St Jagoe &c.

[1] Thomas Herbert, Earl of Pembroke and Montgomery, Lord High Admiral of England.

[2] Greater by sixpence than the amount in Document 133, p. 341.

139

LORDS LETTER BOOK

ADM. 2 182 p. 164

20th April 1702

Gent^n^

It being her Ma^ts^ Roy^l^ Will and pleasure[1] that the Summ of two hundred pounds shall be payd to Capt Edm^d^ Halley (over and above his Pay as Captain of her Pink the Paramour) as a reward to him for his Extraordinary pains and care he lately tooke, in observing and setting down the Ebbing, and Flowing, and setting of the Tydes in the Channell as also and bearing of the head-Lands on the Coasts of England and France. I do therefore in obedience to her Ma^ty^ Commands hereby desire and direct you, to cause the sayd summ of two hundred pounds to be payd unto Him the sayd Capt Halley accordingly

I am Yo^r^ &

P[2]

Navy Board

[Endorsed:] Pay Capt Halley £200

[1] The reference is to Queen Anne who ascended the throne 8 March 1702 on the death of King William III.

[2] Thomas Herbert, Earl of Pembroke and Montgomery.

APPENDIXES

APPENDIX A

Selected Place Names: Halley's First Voyage

Note: The criterion for inclusion of place names on the list revolved around such matters as whether some interesting fact or observation related to it, whether there might be confusion in location, significant differences in spelling in various sources and, in a few cases, a change of name between modern and earlier forms. Only a few of the considerable number of English place names are included because these will receive special treatment in connection with Halley's Third Voyage (see Appendix C, p. 362-4). In the following list, place names from the Journal of Halley's First Voyage are given (generally in order of appearance) in the first column, followed by Dalrymple's version (if given), followed by the rendering on Halley's Atlantic Chart (if given), followed by an acceptable modern form. Variants are included in round brackets indented below the more usual spelling of the name, in the appropriate column. All proper names in the columns have been capitalized, whether or not they are so rendered in the original; and italics, commonly used by Dalrymple for place names, are not employed in the list. On the opposite page in line with the appropriate place name are co-ordinates from the MS journal (if given) and from modern sources. If a location is too large for a single co-ordinate, then the limits are given, e.g. latitude 13.02–21 N. Halley reckoned his longitude from London, hence its inclusion, with co-ordinates, so that the proper correction can be made for comparison with the modern longitude from Greenwich. Discrepancies between Halley's MS journal observations in the body of the work and the table at the end of the MS and, in two cases, with Dalrymple's versions are included in round brackets. All figures are in degrees and minutes only, because Halley did not use seconds of latitude and longitude in his MS. The co-ordinates listed are only a very small proportion of those detailed in the journal because most latitude and longitude observations were made at sea (by dead reckoning) and are therefore not tied specifically to a place name. The same is true of the observations on magnetic variation from the journal (final column in table), which represent only about one fifth of the total observations of this phenomenon. Modern magnetic variation (declination) of places is not given because temporal changes would not allow meaningful comparisons. Most modern place names and co-ordinates are from *The Times Index-Gazetteer of the World* (London, 1965). Abbreviations: I = Island; Is = Islands; C = Cape; P = Point; T = Table (at end of MS); D = Dalrymple's versions; directions: N = North; S = South; E = East; W = West (supplied, where missing, without square brackets).

MS	*D*	*Atlantic Chart*	*Modern*
London	London	London	London
Portland	Portland		Portland
Portsmouth	Portsmouth		Portsmouth
Ilhas Desiertas	Ilhas Desiertas		Deserta Grande [I]
Madera [I]	Madeira	Madera	Madeira
Fonchiall	Fonchiall		Funchal
Sall [I]	Sall	Sal	Sal
Bonavista [I]	Bona-vista		Boa Vista
St Iago	St Jago	S Iago	San Iago
May [I]	May	May	Maio
Praya	Praya		Praia
Trinidada [I]	Trinidada	Trinidada	Trinidade
Fernando Loronho [I] (Fornondo Loranho)	Fernando Loronho	Ferdinando Loronho	Fernando de Noronha
Pernambuco	Pernambuco	Pernambuc	Recife
Dello [C]	Dello		Cabedelo
Paraiba (Pariaba)		Paraiba	João Pessoa
Barbadoes [I]	Barbadoes	Barbados	Barbados
Carlisle Bay	Carlisle Bay		Carlisle Bay
Martinica [I]	Martinica	Martinico	Martinique
Desseada [I]	Desseada		Désirade
Antegoa [I]	Antegoa	Antego	Antigua
St. Christopher's [I]	St. Christopher's	S Christopher	St Kitts

MS		Modern		MS
Latitude	*Longitude*	*Latitude*	*Longitude*	*Magnetic Variation*
		51.30 N	0.10 W	
		50.33 N	2.27 W	6.30 W
		50.48 N	1.05 W	7 W
		32.32 N	16.30 W	
32.30 N	16.45 W	32.45 N	17.00 W	
32.30 N	16.45 W	32.40 N	16.55 W	4 W
16.40 N	22.00 W	16.36 N	22.55 W	1/2 W
(T 16.10 N	22.00 W)			
		16.00 N	22.55 W	
15.18 N	22.40 W	15.07 N	22.40 W	
15.05 N	22.00 W	15.08 N	23.13 W	
14.50 N	22.30 W	14.53 N	23.30 W	
		20.30 S	29.20 W	
3.57 S	23.40 W	3.50–2 S	32.25 W	3 E
(T 3.57 S	34.00 W)			
		8.06 S	34.53 W	
7.00 S	36.00 W	6.58 S	34.50 W	
7.00 S	36.00 W	7.06 S	34.53 W	3.30 E
				(D 2.44 E)
	59.[0]5 W	13.02–21 N	59.00–12 W	
T 13.10 N	59.05 W	13.05 N	59.37 W	5.00 E
14.20–50 N	60.30 W	14.20–50 N	60.30 W	
(T 14.35 N	60.20 W)			
16.23 N	60.30 W	16.08 N	61.03 W	
17.10 N	61.27 W	17.09 N	61.49 W	5.00 E
(T 17.30 N	62.25 W)	17.25 N	62.45 W	5.30 E

MS	*D*	*Atlantic Chart*	*Modern*
Nevis (Mevis) [I]	Nevis		Nevis
Redondo [I] (T Redando)	Redondo		Redonda
Monteserrat [I] (T Monte serrat)	Monteserrat		Montserrat
Guadalupe [I]	Guadalupe	Gadalupe	Guadeloupe
Anguilla	Anguilla	Anguilla	Anguilla
St. Eustachia [I] (T Eustachia)	St. Eustachia		Sint Eustatius
Saba [I]	Suba		Saba
St. Bartholomey [I] (T St. Bartholomew)	St. Bartholomy		St Barthélemy
St. Martins [I]			St Martin Sint Maarten
Burmudas [I] (Barmudas)		Bermudas	Bermuda
Scilley [Is]		Scilly	Scilly
Lizard [P]		Lizard	Lizard

MS		*Modern*		*MS*
Latitude	*Longitude*	*Latitude*	*Longitude*	*Magnetic Variation*
17.15 N	62.10 W	17.11 N	62.35 W	
T 17.[0]2 N	61.55 W	16.58 N	62.19 W	
(D 17.00 N	61.5[0] W)			
16.50 N	61.47 W	16.45 N	62.14 W	
		15.57–16.03 N	61.10–48 W	
18.15 N	62.50 W	18.14 N	63.05 W	5.15 E
17.36 N	62.40 W	17.33 N	63.00 W	
17.42 N	62.55 W	17.42 N	63.26 W	
17.55 N	62.35 W	17.55 N	62.50 W	
18.10 N	62.50 W	18.05 N	63.05 W	
(T 18.05 N	62.50 W)			
		31.18 N	64.45 W	
49.57 N	3.32 W			
49.54 N		49.56 N	5.13 W	6.40 W

APPENDIX B

Selected Place Names: Halley's Second Voyage

Note: See explanation for Appendix A, p. 349, for criterion for selection, which applies to Appendix B. When very large areas are named, e.g. Brazil, no co-ordinates are given. There is no table at the end of the MS of the Second Voyage, so that the abbreviation T is not used in this case. However, there is a table in Dalrymple's version, hence the inclusion of T in that D category. Additional abbreviations for this appendix: A = Archipelago; B = Bay.

MS	*D*	*Atlantic Chart*	*Modern*
London	London	London	London
Madera [I]	Madeira	Madera	Madeira
Palma [I]	Palma		La Palma
Ferro	Ferro (T Faro)	Ferro	Hierro
Teneriff	Tenneriff		Tenerife
Sall [I]	Sal	Sal	Sal
Bonavista	Bonavista		Boa Vista
St Iago	St. Jago	S Iago	San Iago
La Praya (Praya)	La Praya (Praya)		Praia
May [I]	May	May	Maio
Fernando Loronho	Fernando Loronho	Ferdinando Loronho	Fernando de Noronha
St. Thomas [C]	St. Thomas	S Thomas	Sao Tome
Frio [C]	Frio	Frio	Frio
Abrothos [A]	Abrolhos	Abrolhos	Abrolhos
Rio Janeiro	Rio Janeiro	R Ianuero	Rio de Janeiro
Grande [I]	Grande	Grande	Grande
Good Hope [C] (Bon Esprance)	Good Hope (Bon Esperance)	Bonne Esperance	Good Hope
Tristan da Cunha) (Tristan d'acunha)	Tristan da Cunha) (Tristan d' Acunha)	Tristan da Cunha	Tristan da Cunha
St Helena	St. Helena	S Helena	St Helena
Martin Vaz	Martin Vaz		Martin Vaz
Trinidad [I] (Troindada)	Trinidada	Trinidada	Trinidade
Pernambuc (Pernambue, Pernambouc, Reciff)	Pernambuc (Pernambouc, Reciff)	Pernambuc	Recife

MS		Modern		MS
Latitude	*Longitude*	*Latitude*	*Longitude*	*Magnetic Variation*
		51.30 N	0.10 W	
		32.45 N	W	
28.25–48 N		28.40 N	17.50 W	
27.40–50 N	19.00 W	27.45 N	18.00 W	
	17.00 W	28.15 N	16.35 W	
16.35–55 N	23.00 W	16.36 N	22.25 W	1.55 W
16.00–20 N	23.00 W	16.00 N	23.00 W	
		15.07 N	22.40 W	
14.50 N	23.30 W	14.53 N	22.30 W	0.08
		15.08 N	23.13 W	
		3.50–25 S	35.25 W	
		21.54 S	40.59 W	
22.55 S	43.40 W	22.59 S	42.00 W	
	44.45 W	22.53 S	43.17 W	11.30 E
		23.07 S	46.16 W	
		34.20 S	18.25 E	
37.25 S	18.46–19.20 W	37.15 S	12.30 W	5.36–6.00 E
15.52 S	6.30 W	15.58 S	5.43 W	2.00 W
20.25 S	27.21 W	20.30 S	28.52 W	
20.25–29 S	29.50 W	20.30 S	29.20 W	6.30 E
8.10 S	35.30 W	8.06 S	34.52 W	4.38 E

MS	*D*	*Atlantic Chart*	*Modern*
Brasile	Brasile (Brazil)	Brasile	Brazil
Villa Olinda	Villa Olinda		Olinda
Carribie [Is]	Carribbe	Caribbe	Caribbean
Guiana	Guiana	Guiana	Guiana
Barbadoes [I]	Barbadoes	Barbados	Barbados
Bridge Towne (Bridgetowne)	Bridgetown		Bridgetown
Carlisle [B]	Carlisle		Carlisle
St Christophers [I]	St. Christopher's (St. Christophers)	S Christopher	St Kitts
Antego [I]	Antego	Antego	Antigua
Anguilla [I]	Anguilla	Anguilla	Anguilla
Eustachia [I]	Eustachia		Sint Eustatius
Saba [I]	Saba		Saba
Sambreo [I]	Sembrero (T Sombrero)		Sombrero
Dogg [I]	Dog		Dog
Bermoodas [Is]	Bermudas	Bermudas	Bermuda
St Georges [I]	St George's (St Georges)		St Georges
Nantucket	Nantucket	Nantucket	Nantucket
Newfound Land	Newfoundland	Newfoundland	Newfoundland
Anglois [C]	Anglois		English
S Maries [B]	St. Maries	S Mary	St Mary's
Pine [C]	Pine		Pine
Raze	Raze	Raze	Race
Bulls [B]	Bulls		Bulls
Sphere [I] (Sphear)	Sphere		Spear

MS Latitude	MS Longitude	Modern Latitude	Modern Longitude	MS Magnetic Variation
		8.00 S	34.51 W	
		13.02–21 N	59.00 W	
		13.06 N	59.37 W	
		13.05 N	59.37 W	5.25 E
17.20 N	62.[o] 8 W	17.25 N	62.45 W	
		17.09 N	61.49 W	
		18.14 N	63.05 W	
17.40 N		17.33 N	63.00 W	
		17.42 N	63.26 W	
18.40 N		18.37 N	63.26 W	
		18.18 N	63.17 W	
32.10–20 N		31.38 N	64.45 W	
T, D 32.10–24 N)				
32.24 N	63.45 W	32.24 N	64.42 W	
		47.00 N	53.40 W	
		46.38 N	53.35 W	
		46.38 N	53.10 W	
		47.31 N	52.38 W	

MS	*D*	*Atlantic Chart*	*Modern*
Toads Cove	Toads Cove (T Toad's Cove)		Tors Cove
Broyle [C]	Broyle		Broyle
Scilley [Is – S]	Scilly	Scilly	Scilly
Plymouth	Plymouth	Plymouth	Plymouth
Causon [B]	Causon		Cawsand

MS		Modern		MS
Latitude	*Longitude*	*Latitude*	*Longitude*	*Magnetic Variation*
	54.00 W	47.13 N	52.51 W	
		47.03 N	52.52 W	
49.50 N		49.50	6.10 W	
		48.19 N	4.10 W	
				7.13 W

APPENDIX C

Selected Place Names: Third Voyage

Note: See explanation in Appendix A, p. 349, for criterion for selection. The names below are listed generally in order of first appearance in Halley's journal of the Third Voyage. Usually three spellings are given: according to the journal; according to the Channel Chart; according to a modern source (usually from a Hydrographic Chart of the Royal Navy, Ordnance Survey maps, etc.). In some cases a name appearing in the journal docs not appear on the Channel Chart, and in a few cases there may be uncertainty about the modern equivalent; hence the second and third columns are not complete. Geographical position, i.e. latitude and longitude, and magnetic variation (declination) were less important considerations on the Third than on the First and Second Voyages, and so they are omitted. Additional abbreviation for this appendix: R = Rocks.

Journal	*Channel Chart*	*Modern*
Deptford		Deptford
Gravesend	Gravesend	Gravesend
Redsand	Red Sand	Red Sand
Spanyard	Spaniard	Spaniard
Flatts		The Flats
Downs	Downs	Downs
South Foreland	S. Foreland	South Foreland
Dunginess	Denguness	Dungeness
Calis	Calais	Calais
Riprapps	Ripralps	The Ridge (Le Colbart)
Dover	Dover	Dover
Ambleteuse	Ambleteuse	Ambleteuse
Bullogne	Bologne	Boulogne
Estaples	Estaples	Étaples
Treport	Treporte	Tréport
Dieppe	Dieppe	Dieppe
Caux [C] (Antifer)	de Antifer	d'Antifer
Seyn		Seine
Beachy Head	Beachy Head	Beachy Head
Brightholmston	Brithelmston	Brighton
Selsey Bill	Selsey	Selsey Bill

Journal	*Channel Chart*	*Modern*
Dunnose	Dunnose	Dunnose
Oares (Ourse)	Owers	Owers
St Helens	St. Hellens	St Helens
Spitt Head (Spithead)	Spit Head	Spithead
South Hampton (South-hampton)	Southampton	Southampton
Cows	Cowes	Cowes
Hurst Castle	Hurst Castle	Hurst Castle
Isle of Wight	Isle of Wight	Isle of Wight
Needles	Needles [P]	Needles
Christchurch	Christ-Church	Christchurch
Bunchurch	Bunn Church	Bonchurch
Culver [C]	Culver Cliffs	Culver Cliffs
Barfleur [C]	Barfleur	Barfleur
Cherburg	Cherburg	Cherbourg
Querqueville	Querqueville	Querqueville
Hague [C]	la Hague	Hague
Aldernay [I] (Alderney)	Alderney	Alderney
Noz de Jouberg (Jourbery [C])	Jobernoz	Nez de Jobourg
Sark [I]	Sark	Sark
Jersey [I]	Jersey	Jersey
Swanwick	Swanage	Swanage
Dirouilles [R]	Dirouille	Dirouilles
Ecrehou [R]	Erehou	Ecrehou
Guernsey	Guernsey	Guernsey
Pierres de Leche (Paternosters)	Paternosters	Pierres de Lecq (Paternosters)
St Martins [P]	St Martin	St Martin
Russell		Russel
Casketts	Casquetts	Casquets
Portland	Portland	Portland
Pierre de Bray	Le Bray	Braye [R]
St Albans (Saint Albans)	St Albans	St Albans
Plymouth	Plymouth	Plymouth
Eddistone	Eddistone	Eddystone
Lizard [P]	Lizard	Lizard Hd
Deadman [P]	Dodman	Dodman Pt
Falmouth	Falmouth	Falmouth

Journal	*Channel Chart*	*Modern*
Foy	Fowey	Fowey
Ushant	Ushent	Ushant (d'Ouessant)
Pendennis [P]	Pendennis	Pendennis
Torbay	Tor Bay	Tor Bay
Dartmouth	Dartmouth	Dartmouth
Sept [Is]	Sept	Les Sept
Bretagne	Bretagne	Brittany
Grosnez [P]		Grosnez
St Clements	St Clements	St Clement's
Frehell	Trelrell	Frehel
Heaux	Les Heux	Les Héaux
de Brehat [I]	Brehaut	de Bréhat
Douvre [R] (Doure)	Daure	Douvres
La Horraine (Canyn)	Le Haraine	de la Horaine
Rousie	Rochabell	Roch ar Bel
Start [P]	Start	Start
Treaclepots (Treacle Potts or Triagons)	les Triagnons (Treacle Potts)	des Triagoz
Bass [I]	de Bass	de Bas (Batz)
Minquiers	Mincquires	Minquiers
St Hilary	Hellier	St Helier
St Aubin		St Aubin
Corbiere [R]	Corbiere	La Corbière
Loo (Stream)	Looe	The Looe
Cardinalls Hat		
Swan [C]		
Puller	Puller	Pullar
Barrows		
Eastbarrow		
Gilkicker [P]	Gilkicker	Gilkicker
Gallions [Reach]		Gallions

APPENDIX D

Description to accompany Halley's Atlantic Chart

THE

Description

AND

USES

Of a New and Correct

SEA-CHART

Of the Western and Southern

OCEAN,

Shewing the Variations of the

COMPASS

The projection of this *Chart* is what is commonly called *Mercator's*; but from its particular Use in *Navigation*, ougth rather to be named the *Nautical*; as being the only true and sufficient CHART for the *Sea*. It is supposed, that all such as take Charge of Ships in long Voyages, are so far acquainted with its Use, as not to need any Directions here. I shall only take the Liberty to assure the Reader, that having taken all possible Care, as well from Astronomical Observations, as Journals, to ascertain the Scituation and Form of this *Chart*, as to its principal Parts, and the Dimensions of the several Oceans; he is not to expect that we should descend to all the Particularities necessary for the Coaster, our Scale not permitting it. What is here properly New, is the *Curve-Lines* drawn over the several Seas, to shew the Degrees of the *Variation* of the *Magnetical Needle*, or *Sea Compass*: which are design'd according to what I my self found in the *Western* and *Southern* Oceans, in a Voyage I purposely made at the Publick Charge in the Year of our Lord 1700.

That this may be the better understood, the curious Mariner is desired to observe, that in this *Chart* the Double Line passing near *Bermudas*, the Cape *Verde Isles*, and Saint *Helena* every where divides the *East* and *West Variation* in this *Ocean*, and that on the whole Coast of *Europe* and *Africa* the *Variation* is Westerly, as on the more Northerly Coasts of *America*, but on the more Southerly Parts of *America* 'tis Easterly. The Degrees of *Variation*, or how much the Compass declines from the true North on either Side is reckoned by the Number of the Lines on each side the double Curve, which I call the *Line of No Variation*; on each fifth and tenth is distinguished in its Stroak, and numbered accordingly, so that in what Place soever your Ship is, you find the *Variation* by Inspection.

That this may be the fuller understood, take these Examples. At *Madera* the *Variation* is 3 and ½d. West; at *Barbadoes* 5½d. East; at *Annabon* 7d. West; at Cape *Race* in *Newfoundland* 14d. West; at the Mouth of *Rio de Plata* 18d. East, &c. And this may suffice by way of Description.

As to the Uses of this *Chart*, they will easily be understood, especially by such as are acquainted with the Azimuth Compass, to be, to correct the Course of Ships at Sea: For if the Variation of the Compass be not allowed, all Reckonings must be so far erroneous; And in continued Cloudy Weather, or where the Mariner is not provided to observe this Variation duly, the *Chart* will readily shew him what Allowances he must make for this Default of his Compass, and thereby rectify his Journal.

But this Correction of the Course is in no case so necessary as in runing down on a Parallel *East* or *West* to hit a *Port*: For if being in your Latitude at the Distance of 70 or 80 Leagues, you allow not the Variation, but steer East or West by Compass, you shall fall to the Northwards or Southwards of your Port on each 19 Leagues of Distance, one Mile for each Degree of Variation, which may produce very dangerous Errors, where the Variation is considerable; for Instance, having a good Observation in Latitude 49d. 40m. about 80 Leag. without *Scilly*, and not considering that there is 8 Degrees West Variation, I steer away *East* by Compass for the Channel; but making my way truly E. 8d. *N.* when I come up with *Scilly*, instead of being 3 or 4 Leagues to the South thereof, I shall find my self as much to the Northward: And this Evil will be more or less according to the Distance you sail in the Parallel. The Rule to apply it is, That to keep your Parallel truly, you go so many Degrees to the Southward of the *East*, and Northward of the *West*, as in the *West Variation*; but contrariwise, so many Degrees to the Northwards of the *East*, and Southwards of the *West*, as there is East *Variation.*

A further Use is in many Cases to estimate the Longitude at Sea thereby; for where the *Curves* run nearly *North* and *South*, and are thick together, as about Cape *Bona Esperance*, it gives a very good Indication of the Distance of the Land to Ships come from far; for there the Variation alters a Degree to each two Degrees of Longitude nearly; as may be seen in the *Chart.* But in this Western *Ocean*, between *Europe* and the *North America*, the Curves lying nearly East and West, cannot be Serviceable for this Purpose.

This Chart, as I said, was made by Observation of the Year 1700, but it must be noted, that there is a perpetual tho' slow Change in the *Variation* almost every where, which will make it necessary in time to alter the whole System: at present it may suffice to advertise that about *C. Bona Esperance*, the West Variation encreases at the Rate of about a Degree in 9 Years. In our Channel it encreases a Degree in seven Years, but slower the nearer the Equinoctial Line; as on the *Guinea* Coast a Degree in 11 or 12 Years. On the *American side* the *West Variation* alters but little; and the *East Variation* on the *Southern America* decreases, the more Southerly the faster; the *Line of No Variation* moving gradually towards it.

I shall need to say no more about it, but let it commend it self, and all knowing Mariners are desired to lend their Assistance and Informations, towards the perfecting of this useful Work. And if by undoubted Observations it be found in any Part defective, the Notes of it will be received with all grateful Acknowledgement, and the Chart corrected accordingly.

E. HALLEY.

This CHART is to be sold by *William Mount*, and *Thomas Page* on *Tower-Hill.*

APPENDIX E

Selected List of published Maps arising from Halley's Three Voyages in the *Paramore*

Note: Only those terrestrial maps by Edmond Halley resulting from his voyages of 1698 to 1701, or derived from these, are included in the following list. The list specifically excludes Halley's earlier maps, e.g. his southern hemisphere planisphere or star chart (1680), and his map of the Trade Winds published in the *Philosophical Transactions* (1686), as well as his Draught of the Thames estuary and parts of the coast of Sussex, all made before 1698. It also excludes Halley's later cartographic work, such as his map of the passage of the moon over England (1712).

The listings are not complete but suggest something of the influence of Halley's cartography. Various of his maps were also reproduced in John Seller's *Atlas Terrestris* and, on the continent, in the compilations of F. Halma, R. Ottens, L. Renard, and P. de Pretot. More recently maps by Halley have been used, wholly or in part, as illustrations in a number of books and articles. In the map titles below generally only foreign words are rendered in italics, although on some English versions certain English words are italicized.

The Atlantic Chart and Derivatives

1 A New and Correct Chart shewing the Variations of the Compass in the Western [North Atlantic] & Southern [South Atlantic] Oceans, as observed in ye year 1700 by his Maties Command by Ed. Halley. R. Mount & T. Page, I. Harris, sculpt., London, 1 sheet: 22.5 by 19.5 inches.
(Proof copy without dedication or text, 1701.)

2 Another state, with dedication to 'Gulieme III', King William III, and with margins added containing explanatory text signed: E. Halley, 1701. [See Appendix D.]

3 Another issue, with margins added containing explanatory text signed: E. Halley, in *The English Pilot, The Fourth Book*, 1737.

4 Another edition, without the dedication. The description has been re-written by the publishers after Dr Halley's death (in 1742), 1753.

5 Revised edition, without the dedication and entitled 'A New and Correct Chart of the Western and Southern Oceans Shewing the Variations of the Compass According to the latest and best Observations', W. & J. Mount and T. Page and Son on Tower Hill, London, 1760.

6 Another copy. J. Mount and T. Page, London, 1773.

7 *Carte des variations de l'Aiguille dans l'Ocean Occidental & Meridional Suivant les observations fait en 1700 . . . par E. Hallei*, etc. (*In Loix du magnetisme par M. Le Monnier*) 9.5 by 11.5 inches, 1776.

8 A Chart of the [Atlantic] Ocean between South America and Africa, with the tracks of Dr E. H. in 1700, etc. 1769.

The World Chart and Derivatives

1 *Nova & accuratissima totius Terrarum Orbis tabula nautica, variationum magneticarum. Index juxta observationes Anno 1700 habitas; constructa per Edm. Halley*. A new and correct Sea Chart, of the Whole World shewing the Variations of the Compass as they were found in the year 1700. Sold by R. Mount and T. Page on Great Tower Hill, 1 Sheet 20 by 57 inches (or two sheets).

Note: Pasted on the bottom of some copies (and probably added later) is an explanation similar to that prepared for the Atlantic Chart (See Appendix D) but. with some additions to account for observations in areas not covered by the earlier chart. Apparently the publishers revised the World chart in 1740 when Charles Leadbetter was employed to make changes based on the observations of Robert Douglas. This work was inaccurate; but a few years later, in 1744, William Mountain, F.R.S., made a revision with the assistance of James Dodson, as indicated below; this was revised in 1758.

2 *Indice variationes magneticas dentante ad observationes circiter Annū. 1744 habitas, renovata, Guielmo Montaine, et Jacobo Dodson*. (With *An Account of the Methods used to describe Lines on Dr. Halley's chart, etc.*) *1758*.

3 *Accuratissima Totius Terrarum Orbis Tabula Nautica Celeberrimo Viro Edmd. Halley, LLD Anno 1770 Constructa Indices Variationes Magneticas denetante ad Observationnes Circiter Anno 1756 habitas, renovata Gulielmo Montaine et Jacobe Dodson, R.S. Sociis*, Dedicated by William Montaine, FRS, to the Lords Commissioners for executing the office of Lord High Admiral of Great Britain; 1 sheet, 20 by 47 inches, 1758.

4 Another edition with part of the eastern sheet repeated on the west. (With an account of the methods used to describe lines on Dr Halley's Chart on the Terraqueous Globe . . . by William Montaine and James Dodson), 3 sheets, each 20 by 24 inches, 1758.

5 Another edition, without the English title and dedication and with letterpress in French and Dutch, 3 sheets, 2 sheets of text, 1760.

6 Another edition, showing ocean currents, 1762.

7 A Correct chart of the Terraqueous Globe on which are described lines showing the variation of the magnetic needle. Originally composed in the

year 1700 by the celebrated Dr Edmund Halley. Renewed by William Mountaine and James Dodson, F.R.S., according to observations made about the year 1756. Laurie and Whittle, 1 sheet 20 by 47 inches, London, 1794.

The Channel Chart and its Derivatives

1 A new and correct Chart of the Channel between England and France, with considerable improvements not extant in any Draughts hitherto Publish'd: showing the Sands, Shoals, depths of Water and Anchorages, with ye flowing of the Tydes, are setting of the Current: as observ'd by the Learned Dr Halley. Sold by Mount and Page on Tower Hill, London, 2 Sheets 25 by 19 inches, 1702.

2 Another edition, 1708.

3 Another edition, 1750.

4 Another edition, 1755.

5 A New Chart of the British Channel extending from the North Foreland to Scilly Islands on the English Shore and from Dunkirk to Ushent on the French. Collected from Accurate Surveys where unto are added the Flowing of the Tydes and Setting of the Currents as they were observed by Capt. Edm^d^ Halley, London: W. Mount & T. Page, 1 sheet, 30 by 71 inches, 1776.

The Chart of the Island of Trinidada

1 A Draft of the Island of Trinidada taken by Capt. E. Halley in 1700 (MS).

2 [Another in D 1773, 1775.]

APPENDIX F

Brief Calendar of Halley's Three Voyages in the *Paramore*

Year		*Date*	*Event*
1692/3		11 January	First suggestion of Voyage – Hooke's *Diary*.
		—- March	Proposal to Royal Society concerning Voyage.
1693		12 April	Assistance of Royal Society promised.
		12 July	Queen Mary II encourages the project.
		17 July	Pink ordered to be built by the Navy Board.
1694		1 April	Pink to be launched and named.
1696		4 June	Halley's commission as Master and Commander.
		4 June	Admiralty orders Navy Board to take security.
		15 June	Men to be borne in the usual way.
		15 August	*Paramore* to be laid up in wet dock.
1697/8		16 March	*Paramore* to be rigged for Czar Peter.
1698		23 July	*Paramore* to be girdled to better carry sail.
		9 August	*Paramore* to be sheathed and fitted for voyage.
	First Voyage	15 August	Rigging begins on *Paramore* for Halley.
	First Voyage	19 August	Halley's second commission.
	First Voyage	15 October	Orders and Instructions issued.
	First Voyage	20 October	*Paramore* sails from Deptford.
	First Voyage	29 November	*Paramore* sails from Portsmouth in Benbow's fleet.
1698/9	First Voyage	26 February	*Paramore* at Paraiba.
1699	First Voyage	3 July	Court Martial of Halley's Lieutenant, London.
	First Voyage	20 July	*Paramore* paid off at Broad Street, London.
	Second Voyage	23 August	Halley's third commission.
	Second Voyage	24 August	Rigging begins for Second Voyage.
	Second Voyage	12 September	Orders and Instructions issued.
	Second Voyage	16 September	*Paramore* sails from Deptford.
1699/1700	Second Voyage	1 February	*Paramore* at 52° $24'$ S Halley's farthest south.
1700	Second Voyage	18 September	*Paramore* paid off at Broad Street, London.
1701	Third Voyage	26 April	Halley's fourth commission – rigging begins.
	Third Voyage	12 June	Orders and Instructions issued.
	Third Voyage	14 June	*Paramore* sails from Deptford.
	Third Voyage	16 October	*Paramore* paid off at Broad Street, London.
1702		20 April	Halley paid a special gratuity.
1706		22 August	*Paramore* sold.

BIBLIOGRAPHY

(Institutional abbreviations: B.L. = British Library; N.M.M. = National Maritime Museum; P.R.O. = Public Record Office; R.S. = Royal Society. For charts and maps see Appendix E, pp. 368–70.

A. *Manuscript Sources*

LOGS AND/OR JOURNALS

EDMOND HALLEY, commander: Journal, 20 October 1698 – 11 July 1699. (A copy of the ship's log kept at sea, in another hand but signed by Halley.) B.L. Add. MS 30,368 (1), fol. 1–9.

—— Journal, 16 September 1700 – 9 September 1700. (A copy of the ship's log kept at sea in another hand, but with amendments presumably by Halley.) B.L. Add. MS 30,368 (1), fol. 10–36.

—— Journal, 14 June – 16 October 1701. (Holograph), B.L. Add. MS 30,368 (2), fol. 37–47.

OTHER ORIGINAL RECORDS – OFFICIAL

ROYAL NAVY, Admiralty Orders to the Navy Board, 12 July 1693 – 22 September 1698. P.R.O. ADM/A/1797–1857.

—— Captain's Letter Books, 19 June 1696 – 18 February 1701. P.R.O. ADM. 1, 1831–72.

—— Commission and Warrant Books, 4 June 1696 – 26 April 1701. P.R.O. ADM/6/5–6/6.

—— Deptford Yard Letter Books, Series 1, 13 October 1693 – 11 January 1696. P.R.O. ADM. 106/3291–2.

—— Lords Letter Books, 16 March 1697/8 – 20 April 1702. P.R.O. ADM. 2, 178–82.

—— Navy Board Minutes, 17 July 1693 – 14 March 1701/2. N.N.M. Sergison Papers 37–46.

—— Orders and Instructions, 15 October 1698 – 12 June 1701. P.R.O. ADM. 2, 25–7.

—— Secretary's Letter Books, 7 July 1698 – 17 February 1701/2. P.R.O. ADM. 2, 395–402.

—— Ships Employed on Scientific Missions between 1669 and 1860. P.R.O. ADM. R 3/34.

TREASURY, Treasury Papers, 23 June 1693. P.R.O. T 54, 14.

OTHER RECORDS – NON-OFFICIAL

BRITISH LIBRARY, Sloane MS 4024.

ROYAL SOCIETY, *Collectanea Newtoniana*, March 1693 – 27 January 1701/2. R.S. vol. IV (1837), no. 4, 25–7, folios 28–72.
—— Council Minutes, 6 July 1693 – 8 March 1698/9. R.S. vol. 2.
—— Journal Books, 12 April 1693 – 12 November 1701. R.S. vols. VII–VIII.

B. *Printed Sources*

ARBER, E. (ed.). *The term catalogues*, vol. 3 (1697–1709). London, 1906.
ARMITAGE, A. *Edmond Halley*. London, 1966. (In *British men of science*, gen. ed. Sir G. de Beer.)
Atlas maritimus & commercialis; or, a general view of the world. London, 1728.
AUBREY, J. *Brief lives*, ed. A. Clark. Oxford, 1898.
BAILY, F. *An account of the Rev. John Flamsteed*. London, 1835.
BAUER, L. A. 'Halley's earliest equal variation chart', *Terrestrial Magnetism*, I (1896), 28–31.
BEAGLEHOLE, J. C. *The Life of Captain James Cook*. London & Stanford, 1974.
BERKELEY, G. *The analyst*. London, 1734.
Biographia Britannica, vol. 4. London, 1757. pp. 2494–520 ('Edmond Halley').
BIRCH, T. *The history of the Royal Society*. 4 vols. London, 1756–7.
BISWAS, A. K. 'Edmond Halley F.R.S.: hydrologist extraordinary', Royal Society of London, *Notes and Records*, 25 (1970), 47–57.
BRAY, W. (ed.). *Memoirs, illustrative of the life and writings of John Evelyn, Esq. F.R.S.*, vol. 2. London, 1818.
BRITISH ASTRONOMICAL ASSOCIATION. *Edmond Halley, 1656–1742: a conversazione to celebrate the tercentenary of his birth*. London, 1956.
BRITISH MUSEUM, *Catalogue of additions to the manuscripts in the British Museum in the years 1876–1881*. London. 1882.
BULLARD, Sir E. 'Edmond Halley (1656–1741)', *Endeavour*, 15 (1956), 189–99.
—— 'Edmond Halley, the first geophysicist', *Nature*, 178 (1956), 891–2.
BURKE, Sir J. B. *A genealogical history of the dormant, abeyant, forfeited and extinct peerages of the British Empire*. London, 1883.
BURNEY, J. *A chronological history of north-eastern voyages of discovery*. London, 1819.
—— *A chronological history of the discoveries in the South Sea or Pacific Ocean*, vols. 3 & 4. London, 1813–16.
CARRINGTON, A. H. *Life of Captain Cook*. London, 1939.
CASSINI, J. D. *Éclipses du premier satellite de Jupiter pendant l'année*. Paris, 1692.
CHAPMAN, S. 'Edmond Halley as physical geographer, and the story of his charts', Royal Astronomical Society, *Occasional Notes*, 9 (1941), 122–34.
CHENEY, C. R. (ed.). *Handbook of dates for students of English history*. London, 1945; reprinted with revisions, 1961.

CLOWES, Sir W. L. *The Royal Navy: a history*, vol. 2. London, 1898.
COHEN, I. B. *Introduction to Newton's 'Principia'*. Cambridge, 1971.
COLLEDGE, J. J. *Ships of the Royal Navy*, vol. 1. London, 1969.
COOK, J. *The journals of Captain James Cook on his voyages of discovery*, ed. J. C. Beaglehole. vol. 1, *The voyage of the Endeavour*. London, 1955. (Hakluyt Society Extra Series, no. 34.)
DALRYMPLE, A. *An account of the discoveries made in the South Pacifick Ocean, previous to 1764*. London, 1767.
—— *A catalogue of the extensive and valuable library of books ... late the property of Alex. Dalrymple* ... London, 1809.
—— *A collection of voyages chiefly in the Southern Atlantick Ocean*. London, 1775.
—— *Two voyages made in 1698, 1699 and 1700, by Dr. Edmund Halley*. London, 1773.
DAMPIER, W. *Dampier's voyages*, vol. 1. London, 1711.
—— *A new voyage round the world*. London, 1697.
—— *A voyage to New Holland, &c. in the year, 1699*. London, 1703.
DAMPIER-WHETHAM, W. C. D. 'William Dampier, geographer', *Geographical Journal*, 74 (1929), 478–80.
DEFOE, D. *An essay upon the trade to Africa* ... London, 1711.
Dictionary of national biography, vol. 8 ('Edmund Halley' pp. 988–94). London, 1909.
EVISON, F. F. 'Geophysics and the world of Edmond Halley.' Inaugural address, The Victoria University of Wellington, New Zealand. Wellington, 1968.
FALCONER, W. *A new universal dictionary of the marine*. Modernized and enlarged by W. Burney. London, 1815.
FLAMSTEED, J. *Historiae coelestis ... catalogum stellarum fixarum britannicum*. London, 1712.
FRY, H. T. *Alexander Dalrymple and the expansion of British trade*. London, 1970. (The Royal Commonwealth Society Imperial Studies, no. 29.)
GARDINER, R. A. 'Edmond Halley's isogonic charts', *Geographical Journal*, 137 (1971), 419–20.
GELLIBRAND, H. *A discourse mathematical of the variation of the magneticall needle together with its admirable diminution lately discovered*. London, 1635.
GILL, I. *Six months in Ascension*. London, 1878.
GOULD, R. T. *The marine chronometer*. London, 1923.
GRANT, R. *History of physical astronomy*. London, 1852.
GRAY, I. 'Peter the Great in England', *History Today*, 6 (1956), 225–34.
HALLEY, E. 'An account of the cause of the change of the variation of the magnetical needle; with an hypothesis of the structure of the internal parts of the earth', Royal Society of London, *Philosophical Transactions*, 17 (1692), 563–78.
—— 'Astronomiae cometicae synopsis', Royal Society of London, *Philosophical Transactions*, 24 (1704–5), 1882–99.

HALLEY, E. *Catalogus stellarum Australium, sive supplementum catalogi Tychonici* . . . London, 1679.

—— 'De visibili conjunctione inferiorum planetarum cum sole, dissertatio astronomica', Royal Society of London, *Philosophical Transactions*, 17 (1691), 511–22.

—— 'An historical account of the trade winds, and monsoons, observable in the seas between and near the tropicks, with an attempt to assign the phisical cause of the said winds', Royal Society of London, *Philosophical Transactions*, 16 (1686), 153–68.

—— 'Methodus directa & geometrica, cujus ope investigantur aphelia . . .', Royal Society of London, *Philosophical Transactions*, 11 (1676), 683–6.

—— 'Methodus singularis quâ Solis parallaxis sive distantia à Terra, ope Veneris intra Solem conspiciendae, tuto determinari poterit', Royal Society of London, *Philosophical Transactions*, 29 (1714–6), 454–64.

—— 'Observations made on the eclipse of the moon, on March 15, 1735/6', Royal Society of London, *Philosophical Transactions*, 40 (1737–8), 14.

—— 'Observations of latitude and variation, taken on board the Hartford, in her passage from Java Head to St. Hellena, Anno Dom. 1731/2', Royal Society of London, *Philosophical Transactions*, 37 (1731–2), 331–6.

——'Some remarks on the variations of the magnetical compass', Royal Society of London, *Philosophical Transactions*, 29 (1714–6), 165–8.

——'A theory of the tides at the bar of Tunking', Royal Society of London, *Philosophical Transactions*, 14 (1684), 685–8.

——'A theory of the variation of the magnetical compass', Royal Society of London, *Philosophical Transactions*, 13 (1683), 208–21.

——'The true theory of the tides, extracted from that admired treatise of Mr Isaac Newton, intituled, *Philosophiae naturalis principia mathematica*; being a discourse presented with that book to the late King James', Royal Society of London, *Philosophical Transactions*, 19 (1697), 445–57.

HARRISON, E. *Idea longitudinis: being a brief definition of the best known axioms for finding the longitude*. London, 1696.

HAYDN, J. *The book of dignities*. 3rd ed., ed. H. Ockerby. London, 1894.

HELLMANN, G. *Neudrucke von Schriften und Karten über Meteorologie und Erdmagnetismus*, no. 8. Berlin, 1897.

HEWSON, J. B. *A history of the practice of navigation*. Glasgow, 1951.

HINKS, A. R. 'Edmond Halley as physical geographer', *Geographical Journal*, 98 (1941), 293–6.

HOWSE, D. and SANDERSON, M. *The sea chart: an historical survey based on the collections in the National Maritime Museum*. Newton Abbot, 1973.

HUMBOLDT, A. von. *Cosmos: a sketch of a physical description of the universe*, vol. 1, translated by E. C. Otté. London, 1849.

KIRCHER, A. *Magnes: sive de arte magnetica opus tripartitum*. 2nd ed. Cologne, 1643.

KIRWAN, L. P. *The white road*. London, 1959. Reprinted as *A history of polar exploration*, London, 1962.

KITSON, A. *Captain James Cook, R.N., F.R.S.* London, 1907.
LANEGRAN, H. 'Alexander Dalrymple, hydrographer.' Unpublished Ph.D. dissertation, University of Minnesota, 1970.
The London Gazette, no. 924, September 1694.
LYONS, Sir H. *The Royal Society, 1660–1940: a history of its administration under its charters.* Cambridge, 1944.
MACKY, J. *Memoirs of the secret services of John Macky, Esq.* London, 1733.
MACPIKE, E. F. *Correspondence and papers of Edmond Halley.* Oxford, 1932. (History of Science Society Publications, New Series 2.)
——*Dr. Edmond Halley: a bibliographic guide to his life atranged chronologically.* London, 1939.
——*Hevelius, Flamsteed and Halley: three contemporary astronomers and their mutual relations.* London, 1937.
MAINWARING, Sir H. 'The seaman's dictionary', in *The life and works of Sir Henry Mainwaring,* ed. G. E. Manwaring and W. G. Perrin, vol. II. London, 1922. (Navy Records Society, vol. 56.)
MANNING, T. D. and WALKER, C. F. *British warship names.* London, 1959.
Mariner's Mirror, 52 (1966), 202 and 394. ('Queries and Answers'.)
MASEFIELD, J. (ed.). *Dampier's voyages.* London, 1906.
MAUNDER, E. W. *The Royal Observatory, Greenwich.* London, 1900.
NARBOROUGH, Sir J. *An account of several late voyages and discoveries to the South Seas ...* London, 1694.
Nature, 21 (1880), 303–4. ('On Halley's Mount.')
NEWTON, Sir I. *The correspondence of Isaac Newton,* vol. 2 (1676–87), ed. H. W. Turnbull, and vol. 4 (1694–1709), ed. J. F. Scott. Cambridge, 1960–7.
——*Philosophiae naturalis principia mathematica.* London, 1687.
NORMAN, R. *The newe attractive.* London, 1581.
Notes and Queries, series 11, vol. 4 (1911), 85 and 108. ('Notes on Halley's marriage certificate.')
——series 13, vol. 154 (1928), 152–3, and vol. 155 (1928), 24–5. ('Jottings about Dr. Edmond Halley.')
OLIVER, S. P. 'Proposed monument to Halley', *The Observatory,* 35 (1880), 349.
POOL, B. 'Peter the Great on the Thames', *The Mariner's Mirror,* 59 (1973), 9–12.
PRIVY COUNCIL 3. 'No. 1. Dispute concerning the limits of Nova Scotia or Arcadia, 1750–55.' No. 1430 (1926), 3755–7.
PROUDMAN, J. 'Halley's tidal chart', *Geographical Journal,* 100 (1942), 174–6.
Quarterly Review, 55 (1835–6), 112.
QUILL, H. *John Harrison: the man who found longitude.* London, 1966.
QUINN, D. B. *The Hakluyt handbook.* Cambridge, 1974. (Hakluyt Society, Second Series, no. 144.)
REEVES, E. A. 'Halley's magnetic variation charts', *Geographical Journal,* 51 (1918), 237–40.

RHEEDE, H. van. *Hortus indicus malabaricus* . . . Amsterdam, 1678–83.
ROBINSON, A. H. W. *Marine cartography in Britain*. Leicester, 1962.
ROBINSON, H. W. and ADAMS, W. (ed.). *The diary of Robert Hooke, 1672–1680*. London, 1935.
RONAN, C. A. 'Edmond Halley and early geophysics', *Geophysics: Journal of the Royal Astronomical Society*, 15 (1968), 241–8.
——*Edmond Halley: genius in eclipse*. London & New York, 1969.
ROYAL SOCIETY. *The record of the Royal Society*. 4th ed. London, 1940.
RUDOLPH, A. J. 'Materials for a bibliography of Dr. Edmond Halley', with notes by E. F. MacPike, *Bulletin of Bibliography*, 4 (1904), 54–7.
SELLER, J. *The English pilot*. London, 1677.
SHIPMAN, J. *William Dampier: seaman-scientist*. Lawrence, Kansas, 1962.
SOTHEBY & CO. *Catalogue of valuable autograph letters, 1877*. London, 1877.
STEARNS, R. P. 'The course of Capt. Edmond Halley in the year 1700', *Annals of Science*, 1 (1936), 294–301.
TANNER, J. R. (ed.). *Samuel Pepy's naval minutes*. London, 1926. (Navy Records Society, vol. 60.)
TAYLOR, E. G. R. *The haven-finding art: a history of navigation from Odysseus to Captain Cook*. London, 1956.
——*Late Tudor and early Stuart geography 1583–1650*. London, 1934.
——*The mathematical practitioners of Tudor and Stuart England*. Cambridge, 1954.
THROWER, N. J. W. 'The discovery of the longitude', *Navigation*, 5 (1957–8), 375–81.
——'Edmond Halley and thematic geo-cartography', in *The terraqueous globe*, Los Angeles, William Andrews Clark Memorial Library, 1969.
——'Edmond Halley as a thematic geo-cartographer', *Annals of the Association of American Geographers*, 59 (1969), 652–76.
——*Maps and man: an examination of cartography in relation to culture and civilization*. Englewood Cliffs, New Jersey, 1972.
'*The Times' index-gazetter of the world*. London, 1965.
TOOLEY, R. V. *California as an island*. (Map Collectors' Series, no. 8.) London, 1964.
WALISZEWSKI, K. *Peter the Great*, translated by Lady M. Loyd. London, 1897.
WALLIS, H. M. 'English enterprise in the region of the Strait of Magellan', in *Merchants and scholars*, ed. J. Parker. Minneapolis, 1965.
WALTER, R. (ed.). *Anson's voyage around the world*. Revised by G. S. Laird Clowes. London, 1928.
WATERS, D. W. *The art of navigation in England in Elizabethan and early Stuart times*. London, 1958.
WATT, R. *Bibliotheca Britannica, or a general index to British and foreign literature*. 4 vols. Edinburgh, 1824.
WRIGHT, E. *Certaine errors in navigation*. London, 1599.

INDEX

The numerals in brackets – (1), (2) and (3) – refer to the three voyages of the *Paramore*

(1) 20 October 1698 to 16 September 1699.
(2) 16 September 1699 to 10 September 1700.
(3) 14 June to 16 October 1701.